MARICAS

Engendering Latin America

Maricas

Queer Cultures and State Violence in Argentina and Spain, 1942–1982

JAVIER FERNÁNDEZ-GALEANO

University of Nebraska Press

LINCOLN

Portions of chapter 6 were previously published in Spanish as "Cartas desde Buenos Aires: El movimiento homosexual argentino desde una perspectiva transnacional (1963–1983)." *Latin American Research Review* 54, no. 3 (January 2022): 608–22, doi.org/10.25222/larr .109; and "Una ciudad inventada: Los exiliados homosexuales argentinos en la España de la transición democrática (1973–1983)," in *Redes transatlánticas: Intelectuales y artistas entre América Latina y Europa durante la Guerra Fría*, edited by Verónica Abrego and Thomas Bremer (Madrid: Iberoamericana, 2023).

The University of Nebraska Press is part of a land-grant institution with campuses and programs on the past, present, and future homelands of the Pawnee, Ponca, Otoe-Missouria, Omaha, Dakota, Lakota, Kaw, Cheyenne, and Arapaho Peoples, as well as those of the relocated Ho-Chunk, Sac and Fox, and Iowa Peoples.

∞

Library of Congress Cataloging-in-Publication Data

Names: Fernández-Galeano, Javier, author.
Title: Maricas: queer cultures and state violence in Argentina and Spain, 1942–1982 / Javier Fernández-Galeano.
Description: Lincoln: University of Nebraska Press, [2024] | Series: Engendering Latin America | Includes bibliographical references and index.
Identifiers: LCCN 2023049017
ISBN 9781496234971 (hardback)
ISBN 9781496239556 (paperback)
ISBN 9781496239822 (epub)
ISBN 9781496239839 (pdf)
Subjects: LCSH: Sexual minorities—Argentina—History—20th century. | Sexual minorities—Spain—History—20th century. | Sexual minorities—Legal status, laws, etc.—Argentina—History—20th century. | Sexual minorities—Legal status, laws, etc.—Spain—History—20th century. | Homosexuality—Argentina—History—20th century. | Homosexuality—Spain—History—20th century. | Sexual minority culture—Argentina—History—20th century. | Sexual minority culture—Spain—History—20th century. | BISAC: HISTORY / Latin America / General | SOCIAL SCIENCE / Gender Studies
Classification: LCC HQ73.3.A7 F46 2024 | DDC 306.760982—dc23/eng/20231109
LC record available at https://lccn.loc.gov/2023049017

Set in Minion Pro by Scribe Inc.

To Andy,
to my kin,
to the people I fantasized about getting
to know as I wrote about them,
to those I got to know,
and to those who have departed since

CONTENTS

List of Illustrations   ix

Acknowledgments   xi

Introduction: Marica Politics?   xv

Part 1. Anti-Marica Discourses and Praxis

1. Forensic Sexual Violence:
The "Deviant" Bodies and Minds of Maricas   3

2. The Tacky and the Sublime:
Transatlantic Entendido and Marica Cultures   39

Part 2. The Erotics of Masculinity

3. Exotic Lubrications:
Performing Masculinity in Sex Markets   69

4. "People Don't Know What a Homosexual Is":
Argentine Soldiers' Sexual Culture   98

Part 3. Marica Politics

5. Travesti and Marica Prisoners:
Clothes, Performance, and Resistance   141

6. From Inverse to Converging Paths:
Early Sexual Activism in Argentina and Spain   177

Conclusion:
Marica Archives and Histories of Emancipation   238

Notes   245

Bibliography   281

Index   297

ILLUSTRATIONS

1. A drawing of a marica   xviii

2. Transcript of an interview   31

3. Juan Gil-Albert   48

4. A censorship report   56

5. Atelier Club   64

6. Peter's album   81

7. *Poder de macho*   82

8. The 1978 *International Guild Guide*   106

9. Cárcel Modelo in Barcelona   145

10. *Locas, plumas y maricas*   146

11. Drawing by Luis Troitiño   178

12. Letter to the Mattachine Society   184

13. Armand de Fluvià   207

14. Article in *Triunfo*   223

15. Anonymous note   224

16. *Boquita hambrienta*   235

17. Ricardo Lorenzo and Héctor Anabitarte   236

18. One of Marina's letters   240

ACKNOWLEDGMENTS

"It takes a village" is more than a saying. This book is only in your hands thanks to these people. Archivos Desviados is a vertex in the preservation and sharing of marica archives, to which I owe much of my supporting visual material. My editor, Emily Casillas, has been an advocate for this book since I first emailed her. The peer reviewers offered an insightful and generous reframing of the book's contributions, helping me identify and address multiple methodological issues. After peer review, each chapter was read by scholars whom I consider experts in the content. Counting on their sophisticated feedback has been a privilege: Chiara Beccalossi (chapter 1), Jorge Luís Peralta (chapter 2), Santiago Joaquín Insausti (chapter 3), Moisés Fernández (chapter 4), Lawrence La Fountain-Stokes (chapter 5), and Piro Subrat and Juan Queiroz (chapter 6). I have also been quite fortunate to work with James N. Green, whose work informs the field of LGBTQ+ history in South America. Since my time at The New School, Federico Finchelstein has been an invaluable colleague in the field of twentieth-century Argentine history. Zeb Tortorici and I share our relentless passion for all shapes and forms of queer archiving. I always confide in Jennifer L. Lambe, intellectual and friend extraordinaire. Robert Douglas Cope, who sadly left us in 2019, brightened Brown's History Department with his wisdom, kindness, and candidness. Many years ago, I reached out to Francisco Vázquez García and Geoffroy Huard, major experts in the history of sexuality in Spain, and my admiration for their work has developed into a lasting friendship and collaboration. Wesleyan University was my academic community during the COVID-19 pandemic as I revised this book through stimulating discussions with Natasha Korda and colleagues and students at the Center for the Humanities. At the Universitat de València, Enric Novella and Àlvar Martínez Vidal have supported my historical research at the intersection between medicine, gender, sex, and social danger theory. I am part of the research group MASDIME, where I have had the pleasure to learn from colleagues including Rafael Mérida Jiménez, Geoffroy Huard, José Antonio Ramos Arteaga, Alberto Mira, and Isaias Fanlo.

I acknowledge funding from the Juan de la Cierva postdoctoral program at the Universitat de València, the Andrew W. Mellon Postdoctoral Fellowship at Wesleyan University's Center for the Humanities, the Mellon/ACLS Dissertation Completion Fellowship, the Martin Duberman Fellowship (City University of New York), the Harry Ransom Center (University of Texas at Austin), the Phil Zwickler Memorial Research Grant (Cornell University), the Global Mobility Research Fellowship, the Cogut Center, the Steinhaus/Zisson Grant by the Pembroke Center for Teaching and Research on Women, the Joukowsky Fund, the Peter Green Scholarship, the Skidmore Fund for Latin American History, the William G. Mcloughlin Fund for European History, and the Tinker Grant by the Center for Latin American and Caribbean Studies. As I conducted research for this book, I was fortunate to work with archivists who are deeply committed to preserving and making accessible the materials that they curate. The staff of the Archivo Intermedio and the Museo Penitenciario in Buenos Aires gave me access to fundamental state records. Cristián Oscar Prieto at the Comisión Provincial por la Memoria in La Plata generously showed me the most relevant files from the Dirección de Inteligencia de la Policía de la Provincia de Buenos Aires. Gisela Galassi at the Archivo General de la Provincia de Santa Fe went every day with me to the police station as we searched for cases of maricas arrested by the Rosario police department. In Spain, where my research mostly relied on provincial and judicial archives, I met incredibly dedicated archivists, including Laura Pérez Vega in Sevilla; Enric Nogués Pastor, Alba Blasco, Carlos Tortajada, and Victor Pons in València; and Anna Ollé Rubio, Meritxell Soler Cos, Joaquin Martinez Perearnau, and Francesc Xavier Gayan Felez in Barcelona. Last, but definitely not least, there were the people whom I interviewed and who—by sharing with me their experiences—gave sense to this book: Héctor Anabitarte, Marcelo Benítez, Dante Bertini, Emili Boïls i Coniller, Ramón Cadenas Cornejo, Serafín Fernández Rodríguez, Armand de Fluvià, Rafael Freda, Salvador Guasch, Ricardo Lorenzo, Blas Matamoro, Rubén Mettini Vilas, Tania Navarro Amo, Carlos Oller, Jordi Petit, Sergio Pérez Álvarez, Juan José Sebreli, Manuel Angel Soriano Gil, Pablo Stajnsznajder, Rubén Tosoni, and Sara Torres.

In trying to resist the ethos of academic competition, I have found people who are driven by passion and generosity and with whom I share the day-to-day struggles of research in the fields of queer and trans studies in Latin America and Iberia. Joaquin, your penetrating intellect, lack of filters, and drive to live are a counterbalance I very much appreciate. In Argentina, Natalia Milanesio, Pablo Ben, Cole Rizki, Patricio Simonetto, Mir Yarfitz, Máximo Fernández, and many others have made queer and trans studies a vibrant, enthusing, and politically significant field. Richard Cleminson, Giulia Quaggio, Javier Cuevas, Víctor Ramírez, Gema Pérez, Moisés Fernández, María Rosón, Lucas Platero, Rafael Cáceres, Chema Valcuende, Paco Molina, and many other friends have transformed the field of LGBTQ+ historical studies in Spain.

There are the people I want to keep in my life. Teresa and José Maria raised me, and now I enjoy every single second I can spend with them. Chiqui, Curro, and Pablo, my siblings, are with me in every step I take. Gracia has the magic to heal me. Andrew T. Creamer, Andy, shaped every comma of this manuscript as my informal editor and most passionate reader. Andy's sense of humor, warm embrace, and infinite care keep me afloat.

INTRODUCTION

Marica Politics?

This book argues that queer and trans genealogies ought to incorporate *marica* archives like Hugo's oral history, collected by Archivos Desviados.[1] Hugo (1943–2020) aptly traces how marica cultural codes informed the genesis of the (homo)sexual emancipation movement. Mir Yarfitz and I have argued elsewhere that *marica* historically referred to "subjects assigned male at birth who adopted a feminized persona through sexual practices, embodied and spoken languages, and social interactions, including relationships with masculine men, situational gender switching, and subcultural codes."[2] Hugo's testimony fits this definition, but by that I do not mean to put the burden of representativeness on it. Hugo was born in Caballito, a neighborhood of Buenos Aires. He and his friends alternated between he/him and she/her pronouns (which I will replicate in my writing about them). Since his early childhood, she occasionally dressed like a woman—using sheets for a long dress à la Evita Perón and makeup stolen from his mother. As an altar boy in the parish church, he and one of his peers secretly imitated vedettes in the church gardens, turning leaves into feathers. Sexual abuse by the priests tarnishes these memories. It was only by meeting other maricas when he was an adolescent that she discovered the joy (*alegría*) of togetherness, a "marvelous awakening" (*despertar maravilloso*) despite social scorn and police harassment.

He started to frequent downtown cruising spots, including cinemas, public restrooms, and the Augustus bakery, which she describes as maricas' own cathedral, "a swarm of *locas*."[3] In between sexual encounters, maricas turned Augustus into a sort of "cultural center": they shared information on recent police raids and discussed poetry, art, and movies (like the 1964 Argentine premiere of *Las amistades particulares*, an adaptation of its namesake novel by Roger Peyrefitte). Hugo was "catechized" in marica codes by his new kin. Carnival and its preparations—like sewing dresses—were crucial components of marica sociability, since maricas' cross-dressing became an object of popular celebration during that time of the year. During the day, Hugo worked for an insurance company. When the workday was over, she put on her makeup, met a marica friend, and together they cruised for sex downtown while singing flamenco and praying to the Virgin Mary when young boys (*chongos*) harassed and insulted them. Spanish dancing companies (*las locas españolas*) performed at the Avenida theater, a landmark for Buenos Aires maricas: "We all identified with flamenco, with gypsies' lament, because it was like our marica lament."[4] Anti-marica police harassment was constant. Hugo was once tortured by police officers, who called themselves machos while hitting metal against metal above Hugo's head. Hugo also spent several days in the Devoto Prison in the early 1960s, having a passionate love affair with another prisoner whom she met in the weekly mass and using their hands to communicate without words through the cell bars. When President Juan Domingo Perón died in 1974, his followers flooded Buenos Aires downtown to mourn him, and this became an orgiastic opportunity for maricas like Hugo, who seduced and had sex with plenty of Peronist *chongos*.

In the early 1970s, Hugo and one of her friends founded a camp order of "impure" nuns.[5] They requested and were granted permission to live in the monastery of San Camilo and later the convent of Santa Inés, turning their own dormitories into a marica/queer convent, until they were expelled for bringing *chongos* into the convent and having sex with them at night. In 1973, Hugo ran into a street protest staged by Eros, the section of the Frente de Liberación Homosexual (Homosexual Liberation Front, or FLH) led by Néstor Perlongher, and asked them how she could become part of their movement. Hugo remembers fondly the role that Héctor Anabitarte's political guidance and affection played in his own process of self-empowerment. The formation of the Catholic homosexuals' group within the FLH was Anabitarte's idea. One of the most joyful moments in Hugo's memory is the founding of *Somos* (the FLH's publication). To celebrate the consensus they had reached on the publication's name, they drank and smoked marijuana, danced, and cracked jokes while Hugo sang *cuplés* popularized by Spanish singer Sara Montiel, sharing an "unforgettable feeling of freedom and hope."[6]

However, Hugo also relates how some FLH activists (the group Profesionales) despised maricas and *afeminados* (feminine males) like Hugo because, in their opinion, maricas' scandalous personas and habit of cruising for sex antagonized potential adherents. Hugo counterargues with juxtaposition: there were activists who had lost "the poetry of being a homosexual" for the sake of maintaining hyperintellectualized views, and there were maricas who put their bodies on the line, demanded respect, and did not want to be objects of study. After the parenthesis of the last dictatorship, Hugo reassumed his LGBTQ activism and commitment with the left, being aware of the postdictatorial regimes' flaws—"democracy was heterosexual," he said. Fear of police and his own family repeatedly led him to destroy his own compromising belongings during the last dictatorship, including Anabitarte's papers. In view of this forced erasure of his own archive, Hugo warns that taking care of our "struggle" entails remembering our marica ancestors. Hugo, like many of this book's protagonists, treated marica subjecthood as transcendent while simultaneously parodying transcendence as a camp artifact.

I grew up a sheltered *mariquita*—feminine, sensitive, and familial, even Catholic—in Badajoz, a municipality in the region of Extremadura, which many Spanish people associate with rural culture. My deepest fear was to be called a *maricón*—despised as hypersexual and feminized—and instead I ended up identifying as gay, a comparatively easy-to-pronounce word that often works to deactivate prejudices by referencing mainstream paradigms. The

FIG. 1. A drawing of a marica for the cover of *Somos* no. 6, drawn by Fuad Zahra. Courtesy Archivos Desviados, based in New York City and Buenos Aires.

term "homosexuality" feels unfamiliar to me, too full of fricative sounds, as if pronouncing it entails the intentionality of marking someone as something other than. I only learned to use "queer" as a graduate student—it is not originally a Spanish term—and while I use it in communication with English speakers, it never crosses my mind when I think of maricas' pleasures or experience them. Yet since this book is written in English—which could merit a longer discussion on the international structures of academic knowledge production—I am going to use "queer" as a verb more than as a noun in reference to sociocultural practices that unsettle normative regimes.[7]

Aims, Scope, and Contents

Maricas' daily lives were triangulated among gender playfulness, aesthetic creativity, and the power-knowledge nexus. Throughout the next six chapters, this book juxtaposes two knowledge paradigms: one psychoanalytical and focused on nurture in Argentina, and another biological and focused on nature in Spain. Underlying both paradigms, penal positivism defined maricas' acts and/or condition not as personal liability but as a danger to society related to criminality and marginality.[8] The first chapter examines positivism in Argentina and Spain, a frame according to which forensic doctors decided on the dangerousness (not the liability) of maricas, mariquitas, putos, and other "deviants." I first deal with the Spanish vagrancy courts and then with the Argentine Classification Institute, looking at how both institutional frames legitimated anti-marica violence. While state officials tried to eradicate marica culture, some homosexual men focused on transforming or overcoming it. Moving in concentric circles across the Atlantic, the second chapter traces how *entendidos*—the ones in the know, a term used among middle-class homosexual men—derided maricas' sex and modes of self-expression. Entendidos' disdain barely masked their investment in sexual circuits dominated by maricas. Part and parcel of coded debates on proper queer (in)visibility, the fashion and embodied languages of public figures such as Miguel de Molina and Alfredo Alaria (a Spaniard exiled in Argentina in the 1940s and an Argentine exiled in Spain in the 1960s, respectively) incited their fans to desire and identify with them. Entendidos idealized their own identity, which they perceived as distinctly less perverse, less visibly marked, and more masculine than maricas' performance. Hence the first two chapters together delineate anti-marica discourses.

In the third chapter, masculinity reappears as an artifact of marica pleasure and stereotyped performance in sex markets in the context of developmentalist economic policies in Argentina and Spain, where policymakers encouraged consumer culture but tried to curtail its underlying tenets of individualism and immediate self-gratification. The state rhetoric of workers' incremental access to consumer markets was insufficient to neutralize the appeal of transactional gay sex. Many working-class males mimicked the disgruntled masculinity embodied by James Dean and Marlon Brando, wearing tight jeans and smoking cigarettes to entice homosexuals and maricas. The fourth chapter incorporates Argentine courts-martial records produced between 1966 and 1983 to unveil authorities' and forensic doctors' investment in a sexual culture based on the relations between masculine machos and feminine maricas. These roles were often perceived by participants in same-sex acts as part of their playful strategies of mutual enticement, whereas officers' policing of this culture produced a voyeuristic archive of sexual practices that subverted the passive/active binary. Argentine military officers reacted to the explosion of eroticism in mass culture between the mid-1960s and early 1980s with a pornographic gaze that shed light onto homoerotic pleasures. The third and fourth chapters together place masculinity at the center of maricas' erotic and social lives.

Chapter 5 looks at Argentine and Spanish marica inmates in the 1970s and argues that their sociability, intimacy, and aesthetics had a major role in shifting criminologists' primary concern from latent to manifest homosexuality or from maricas' inability to inhibit themselves to their unwillingness to do so. This chapter is core to my argument that maricas' persistence in being visible and enjoying themselves is inextricable from the logics of formal queer politics emerging in the 1970s. The last chapter discusses formal queer activism, fraught with internal tensions as some activists tried to dissociate homosexuality from marica politics by using labels such as "gay" while others reclaimed vernacular labels. This chapter argues that overall, sexual liberation movements were shaped by and emanated from vernacular marica cultures. To conclude, the last pages trace the life stories of Argentine gay activists who arrived in Spain from 1973 on, becoming fully involved in local sexual politics. For most of these activists, exile was a no-return path. The last two chapters together intimate that marica subjectivities underlie the initial formalization of LGBT activism. The book's arc establishes maricas' continued significance in queer politics, hopefully dispelling any misconceptions that middle-class gay activists with international connections might have fully taken that space.

The book's chronological framework aligns with its analytical interventions. State officials' interest in regulating queer and trans lives heightened globally from the 1940s because of a series of interconnected trends, including the crystallization of the homo/heterosexual binary, an unprecedented increase in public spending, World War II and Cold War militarization programs, queer visibility in urban areas, the new concept of "gender" and gender-affirmation surgeries based on racialized notions of body plasticity, and the cult of medical expertise and technocratic management, among others.[9] The 1980s mark the transition to a new phase in marica politics in Argentina and Spain. LGBT+ activists gradually presented their demands to the public in connection with AIDS campaigns and human rights agendas; the distinction between gender and sexuality gained ground in both mass-media discourses and daily practices; and the end of the Cold War gave place to a new socioeconomic model in which neoliberalism apparently triumphed in public planning. This is not *at all* an end-of-history narrative of progress, which would obfuscate how police violence continued targeting racialized and transgender people, sex workers, HIV patients, and other vulnerable and/or marginalized sectors. The arc of *Maricas* closes in the 1980s not to imply a drastic discontinuity in the relationship among taxonomy, violence, and trans and queer lives but because that relationship shifted in ways that require a specific mode of analysis distinct from my foci in this book, which are the local specificities, temporalities, and political potentialities of different models of marica subjectification.[10]

My interlocutors are friends and colleagues in the fields of queer, trans, and marica studies. The historical connection between Argentina and Spain is well established, is multifaced, and touches on issues of race, colonialism, and globalization, which affect culture, economy, and sex. After the *corralito* economic collapse in December 2001 in Argentina, many citizens of this country moved to Spain. This was just the latest episode in a series of historical events connecting both countries. Whiteness and violence play a major role in this story. In both Argentina and Spain, racism often operates through "color-blindness," the assumption that the population is ethnically homogenous and minoritized subjects' race—Black, Indigenous, and Roma, among others—has a marginal role in national history.[11] Official records constantly and explicitly allude to class, but less so to race. Spaniards colonized Argentina's territory in the early modern period. Argentina's economy boomed in the late nineteenth century and early twentieth centuries, attracting millions of Spanish immigrants, while Argentine elites favored European immigration overall to "whiten" the country. Through these migratory currents, kinship ties and mutual-aid networks extended across the Atlantic, providing a potential escape for citizens of both countries when political regimes turned against sectors of civil society.[12] Just to mention one last example, Natalia Milanesio begins her recent book on "the unparalleled sexualization of Argentine culture and society after 1983" by discussing a poem of utopian overtones by a Spanish sociologist involved in the progressive reform of sexology in Spain in the aftermath of the *franquista* regime. In her reading of the poem, Milanesio suggests that "pleasure, well-being, identity rights, and choice" were key societal tenets in postdictatorial Argentina and Spain, connecting the intellectual sphere and mass media of both countries despite the different chronologies of their democratization processes.[13]

For most of the period studied in this book, *franquismo* was the political regime in Spain. General Franco became the dictator after a civil war and stayed in power for almost four decades (1939–75) with the support of the military as well as fascist, nationalist, Catholic, and technocratic civilian sectors. Franco's regime channeled mass politics within a single-party apparatus that organized mobilizations in support of the dictator.[14] Argentine politics followed a different course. Peronism emerged in the 1940s as a powerful populist movement that improved the living conditions of disenfranchised and working-class sectors while dismissing significant tenets of parliamentarian pluralism. General Perón was ousted by the military in 1955 and forced into exile. Peronism was banned yet remained a central actor in national politics, splitting into a left wing and a right wing while Perón lived in exile in Spain in the 1960s and early 1970s. For a short period (1973–76), Peronism was again in power in Argentina, and its internal splitting escalated into violent conflicts.[15] Franco died in 1975, an event that many Spaniards associated with hopes of democratization, while Argentines suffered the brunt of state terrorism under a regime installed through a military coup in 1976. These political trajectories correlate with the adoption of different scientific paradigms. Psychoanalysis was marginalized in Franco's Spain; the Freudian polymorphous libido was seen as incompatible with the Catholic doctrine that was the law of the land. In Argentina, by contrast, psychoanalysis became in these decades a ubiquitous discipline incorporated into mass culture and everyday social and political debates.

Given these local particularities, and insofar as I initially characterized my project as a transnational history, this book witnesses my failure.[16] Following Jack Halberstam and Saidiya Hartman, there is much to be said about intellectual endeavors that fail. They test the limits of the possible to denounce the violence that shaped historical records and silenced subaltern subjects.[17] Queerness and failure are akin: both deviate from linear narratives, point toward contingency and arbitrariness, and lead to a reconsideration of established parameters.[18] Rather than being the transnational history I intended to write, this book traces how maricas' experiences were archived as a by-product of state violence, which also shaped subjects' exile trajectories and international exchanges. Although I draw inspiration from and converse with the scholarly corpus that examines the role of gender and sexuality in nation-building (and each chapter includes sections on relevant political events), this book expresses foremost a visceral desire to recognize maricas' experiences.[19]

Archives and Ethics

From my first encounter with transcripts of Argentine soldiers narrating their sexual encounters in response to officers' salacious lines of questioning, I have used official documents to trace marica cultures and simultaneously denounce the violence of pathologization and sexual abuse. I treat police files, judicial records, medical reports, novels, fandom letters, clothing items, memoirs, and erotica as integral parts of a "rebel archive," which requires modes of analysis that are attentive to sources' specific nature and their interwovenness.[20] Since this book focuses on a relatively recent historical period, many significant archival repositories have yet to be located or opened to researchers, including the records of the Buenos Aires police department and several Spanish vagrancy courts, which impedes the elaboration of reliable statistics on the impact of state policies on a national scale. My qualitative analysis centers instead on some of the harshest effects of state violence, including social isolation, the stigmatization of victims of sexual assault, and public shaming. While I have occasionally elaborated and used statistics when the full data set is available, my focus is on maricas' lived experiences through their cultural artifacts. I approach these experiences and artifacts being aware of archival voyeurism. Authorities engaged with marica subcultures to establish their scope and cyphered meanings but in doing so also betrayed voyeurism as a principle of policing. Zeb Tortorici argues that archival voyeurism is virtually inescapable when pursuing queerness in the past.[21] Jennifer L. Lambe points out the "danger of historical voyeurism" in reproducing certain sources.[22] Sources that capture authorities' violent intrusion into subjects' intimacy become both precious and thorny. *Maricas* foregrounds authorities' roles in curating and preserving a rich repository of imagery and textual representations of sex and intimacy. Spanish police officers reassembled and taped together torn pieces of amateur photographs of interracial anal and oral sex; Argentine military officers were obsessed with ejaculation. While I cite defendants' explicit testimonies and describe and reproduce their personal erotica, I do so because of their historical significance as embedded in both state violence and subcultural practices.

There are noticeable asymmetries in the production of and access to different kinds of historical records. To give one significant example, the military records I consulted in Argentina were housed in civilian archives because of democratic projects to clarify the military's role and responsibility in crimes against humanity. That is not the case in Spain; my last experience consulting courts-martial records entailed entering a military base with a research topic innocuous enough to the colonel overseeing the archive. Military officials in Argentina were patently fascinated by the intricacies of pleasure and how maricas experienced it. Criminologists and military officers believed that to fight your enemy you must know him well: the more they could get maricas to talk about their pleasures and transcribe their testimonies in detail, the better. Spanish officials preferred to paraphrase depositions, occasionally interjecting vulgar words used by the defendants but overall keeping a comparatively formal tone. Court records in Spain reveal the tensions and overlaps between fascist (aggressive and overtly sexual) and Catholic (restrained and decorous) models of masculinity.[23] Officials seemed to believe that producing overtly explicit records would only add to the affront that maricones posed to national mores. Yet they intriguingly preserved the defendants' erotic photographs and love letters, as if they did not perceive their own agency in these curatorial practices or considered them necessary to contain the danger of homosexuality. To read these sources, one must be aware of how criminalized subjects navigated mechanisms of policing and censorship. As the Spanish author Juan Gil-Albert put it in 1955, "Speaking in a low voice is still speaking, but only to those who have an alert ear."[24] Listening to that low voice, we might encounter veiled messages in holy cards, photographs, films, and even police records and suicide letters.

To protect the privacy of individuals named within archival records, I have substituted their names with pseudonyms and removed other identifiers. I only use actual proper names when referring to authors' published works or to informants who gave me explicit permission to cite them. In terms of the use of gender pronouns, there is evidence that many maricas shifted between male and female pronouns or preferably used female pronouns. I have used the gender pronouns that subjects used for themselves, often inconsistently, according to the available sources. These sources are mediated by violence and by the passing of time, and subjects might have used the grammatical gender that they thought authorities expected them to use. To avoid "retrospective gender assignation," sometimes I use gender-neutral nouns—including defendant, prisoner, and

patient, among others.[25] I also use the term "queer" broadly referring to practices or desires that destabilized heterosexist norms.
This does not entail an attribution of intentionality but rather a
recognition that subjects came to be part of the historical record
in ways that, at least partially or temporarily, excluded them from
normativity. Most of the sources that I analyze in this book are
by-products of the authorities violating individuals' intimacy, so
reading them is a recapitulation of the epistemological violence
entailed in their inception. While researching and writing this
book, I occasionally wondered whether silence would be a better
choice than perpetuating distorted archival representations of subjects' lived experiences. However, through personal experiences,
I have developed a deep investment in historicizing the pathologizing and criminalizing views on queer and trans people to promote the critique of those views. Maricas' experiences are not "of
the past" but rather have ramifications and continuities into the
present that call into question any attempt at precise periodization.

Personal investment entails the danger of overidentification.
There is no denying that throughout this book, I tend to express
more sympathy for the people classified as "deviant" than for the
people classifying them as such. Yet deviance and normativity are
not mutually exclusive categories; the same person can be classified as deviant while trying to transfer that stigma to someone
else. Moreover, while *Maricas* focuses on subjects who, at some
point, were categorized based on their alleged violations of heterosexist norms, this does not imply that those subjects perceived
themselves to be part of a coherent community defined by nonconformity. Archival sources show how different vectors of power
inequality—including gender, class, ideology, race, ethnicity, and
nationality, among others—shaped relations between subjects.
The temptation of overidentification ought to be tempered by
an acknowledgment that ultimately, the historical actors in this
book are grouped together by my analysis in ways that might dif-
fer from their self-identification. That is particularly true for men
who identified with a paradigm of masculinity as defined not as
much by heterosexuality as by power. Many of these men gained

purchasing power, without purportedly relinquishing a dominant position, by objectifying their bodies using a language of sexual availability (cigarettes, tight pants, posture, etc.) to seduce other males who compensated them for sex. These stories do not easily align with a project of queer history focused on identity and community formation, as they pinpoint that a performance of masculinity defined by power and violence was a central ingredient in the erotic economies navigated by maricas.

Transgender, Queer, Gay . . . and Marica History

Through its focus on how interpersonal relations construct and eroticize gender, *Maricas* converses with transgender history but does not squarely fit within it. Recently, a trove of innovative research has situated trans* at the core of the history of gender nonconformity in Argentina and Spain.[26] Now there are comprehensive twentieth-century trans histories for both countries.[27] Maricas subjectivities challenge gay essentialism, the notion that people who engaged in certain sexual practices without embracing a gay identity were alienated, while also problematizing a clear-cut taxonomic distinction between gender and sexuality. In this book, I position myself alongside other scholars who historicize that distinction and refute its universalization and naturalization.[28] Scholars like Cole Rizki have conceptualized *travesti* not just as an identity category but as a "critical mode" that "disavows coherence and is an always already racialized and classed geopolitical identification that gestures towards the inseparability of indigeneity, blackness, material precarity, sex work, HIV status, and uneven relationships to diverse state formations."[29] Although marica and travesti present different chronologies and uses, both are critical lenses to consider issues other than identity, including performance, sociability and mutual-aid mechanisms, sexual pleasure and courtship rituals, state and forensic violence, geographical mobility, and labor niches. As George Chauncey notes, no history of "queer subjectivity and sexual practice" makes sense without putting "gender embodiment and performance" at the forefront. Chauncey prefaces the 2019 reedition of the seminal *Gay New York*, first printed almost two decades ago, with an acknowledgment: "What today we might distinguish as 'homosexuality' and 'transgenderism' were intimately linked; indeed, neither of those terms, simply transposed from our own era, captures the complexity or alterity of that era's categories of experience and identity."[30] Chauncey recognizes that history is written from and responds to political concerns in the present, which is why we will always revisit the past.

Historical records intimate epistemological modes other than current taxonomies, whereas exoticizing the past or treating it merely as an object of antiquarian interest obfuscates how the very notion of the past is constructed through its entanglement with the present (and the future).[31] I embrace the seeming paradox of acknowledging that maricas before the 1970s were neither "gay" nor "trans" and yet their history overlaps and is significant for trans, gay, queer, and other cognate genealogies. Imposing a univocal reading of subjects' essential interiority based on fragmentary and mediated archival records—like judicial, medical, and prison files; press articles; and even personal papers—which capture specific moments in subjects' trajectories, is a fallible attempt to neutralize the uncertainty over what these subjects did and felt the rest of their lives. *Maricas* incorporates uncertainty, as it relates to subjects' ways of refracting taxonomic schemas. At the same time, the semantic root *maric-* combines with different suffixes to create terms that convey gradations of scandal: from the infantilized mariquita to the unassimilable *mariconazo*. These are, to be clear, neither mutually exclusive nor essential categories but rather contingent on context—a person would act and be considered alternatively as mariquita, mariconazo, and many other overlapping yet distinct terms including *bujarrón*, *loca*, *puto*, *sarasa*, *gay*, and *travesti*, among others.[32] As Horacio F. Sívori documented through his ethnographic work in 1990s Argentina, locas/maricas form linguistic communities through embodied performance and the use of labels whose meanings are only familiar to them.[33]

This book traces tensions and overlaps between maricas' lived experiences and an array of taxonomies.[34] State authorities used taxonomies to discipline maricas, but people who identified as gay or homosexual elaborated anti-marica taxonomies as well, as I discuss in chapters 2 and 6.[35] Maricas created their own taxonomies, which I would deem vernacular following Kadji Amin; they focused on "external behaviors that generate identity effects" within "time-and-place-bound subcultures."[36] My approach decenters the liberal nation-state as the normative site for sexual subcultural formation and recasts the relationship between geography and power by incorporating nonelite actors—rural and low-income people, soldiers, prisoners, folk music fans, and defendants' mothers, among others—who expressed themselves through spirituality, fashion, and performance. This book also focuses quite a lot on *ars erotica*, not just because I like to write about randy stuff, but because it's overwhelmingly present in the archives. On the one hand, the proliferation of discourses on sex might seem like a logical result of authorities' interest in *sciencia sexualis*.[37] On the other hand, multiple scholars have placed sex and intimacy at the core of vernacular marica cultures.[38] Masculinity underpinned anti-marica violence and yet was also a device or artifact of maricas' sexual pleasure (this paradox is explored in depth in chapters 3 and 4).

Sex and intimacy mattered significantly for maricas and their own sense of selfhood. To give one specific example, travesti advocate and sexual worker Ivana Tintilay interviewed hairdresser and carnival celebrity Andrés Berón about marica culture in 1980s Jujuy, in the Argentine interior. Promiscuous relationships with machos figure prominently in Berón's very concrete definition of the marica—usually the meaning of this label is more amorphous and open to overlaps with other labels. Berón related finding a marica family for the first time at the hairdressing academy. Marica kin taught Berón body-enhancement techniques and how to laugh at their own "disgraces" to survive. Together, they went into the streets of their remote town dressed femininely and flamboyantly, even at the peak of dictatorial rule. Maricas treated one another as female, but most of their acquaintances and the saloons' clients did not, so they lived "transiting in ambivalence" (*transitando en esa ambivalencia*), which did not bother them that much.[39] They dressed like women for parties and carnivals, but not for their day jobs. Starting in the 1980s, travestis remained close to maricas but gradually abandoned gender switching and made their bodies visibly feminine though breast implants and other modifications. Berón vocally refused to be called either gay or trans. In fact, during the first LGBT+ meeting celebrated in 1996 in Rosario (Argentina), Berón and other self-aware maricas demanded to be included as "M" in the movement's acronymous but were told that they were gay. The next chapters explore the potential of approaching maricas' daily life in a way that pays respect to their self-positioning in the world.

MARICAS

PART 1

Anti-Marica Discourses and Praxis

ONE

Forensic Sexual Violence

The "Deviant" Bodies and Minds of Maricas

Argentine and Spanish medical doctors contemplated their forensic techniques as part of a transnational repertoire of tested knowledge. Among these techniques, Ambroise Tardieu's digital rectal
examination, or DRE (1857), and Ernst Kretschmer's threefold body
typology (1921) were widely used by forensic doctors. Both authors
believed that homosexual males showed measurable physical traits,
which made their work particularly suitable for the collection of
the kinds of "objective" evidence preferred by judges and prison
managers.[1] The DRE was a form of state-enforced sexual violence,
forcing rectal digital examinations on the defendants to establish
the existence of anal dilation and fissures as proof that they had
been penetrated. Furthermore, departing from Tardieu's clinical
descriptions of both participants in anal sex, the use of the DRE
in Argentina and Spain only targeted males suspected of having
performed the receptive sexual role, contributing to the double
stigmatization of the so-called passive homosexual, feminized in
both medical and popular representations.

In addition to these techniques, the highpoint of social Dar-
winism and Anglo-Saxon racial theories at the turn of the twentieth century relegated the Mediterranean and Latin America to
a subordinate position. In response, national elites in these set-
tings embraced a common heritage of Catholicism and Latin languages and culture. Thus, scientific communities became deeply
invested in transatlantic ties that demonstrated their belonging to a
"Latin" world defined by a distinct and more humane treatment of

marginalized populations. This translated into the popularization
of "Latin" authors, among whom Cesare Lombroso (1835–1909),
the Italian authority on criminal anthropology, firmly held that
personal dispositions determining criminal behavior could be sci-
entifically measured.[2] Adherents to this "revolutionary" form of
positivism, of unlimited trust in science's potential to drastically
improve society, saw themselves as advancing a more humane
treatment of disgraceful individuals fated to commit crimes.[3]

After all, if science could unequivocally establish and measure
the hereditary and environmental factors leading a person to vio-
late social and legal norms, then what sense did it make to punish
that person based on an antiquated definition of personal liability? In other words, criminologists and forensic doctors who followed the Italian positivist school considered the Enlightenment
notions of "free will" and liability as relics of previous centuries
that led to unjustified punitive measures.[4] They wanted to break
away from the classical penal tradition, represented by Cesare
Beccaria's *On Crimes and Punishments* (1764), which in their view
overestimated the individual's capacity to decide on his acts, gauge
potential consequences, and rehabilitate himself.[5]

The Italian Enrico Ferri (1856–1929) was one of the authors who
most influenced Argentine and Spanish positivist criminologists.[6]
He proposed indeterminate sentences to be applied through regular examinations of convicts by forensic doctors who would decide
whether or not their release would be harmful to society.[7] Thus,
the scientific discipline of criminology would render the judiciary's role almost obsolete, leading to a model of management
of predisposed criminals that prioritized society's interests over
individual rights. Ferri adhered to a Darwinian interpretation of
socialism that viewed social engineering, the scientific management of antisocial tendencies, as a remedy for liberal individualism.[8] Among the most fervent advocates of the positivist penal
school in Argentina and Spain were prominent socialists such as
the Argentine criminologist José Ingenieros and the Spanish law-
maker Luis Jiménez de Asúa.[9]

These figures contributed to the institutional apparatus through which positivist penal and criminological theories were applied to the management of "antisocial" populations. In Argentina, Ingenieros founded the Institute of Criminology in 1907, later renamed the Classification Institute (Instituto de Clasificación). Through a set of forensic techniques, from biotypes to psychological examinations, the institute's criminologists measured inmates' "dangerousness" and the potential threats they posed to society and made recommendations on their probation and release requests, affecting the nationwide management of the prison population.[10] On an even larger scale, positivism became a full-fledged social engineering system in Spain, as a majority-left congress passed the *Ley de Vagos y Maleantes* (Vagrancy Law) in 1933 during the short-lived Second Republic (1931–39). This law was drafted by progressive jurists Jiménez de Asúa and Mariano Ruíz-Funes and targeted "antisocial" populations: beggars, prostitutes, pimps, and alcoholics, among others.[11] The 1933 Vagrancy Law did *not* define homosexuality as antisocial. On the contrary, the Second Republic eliminated any mention of homosexuality from the Penal Code, decriminalizing it de facto.[12] Soon after, however, the mass political upheavals of the 1930s led Spain and Argentina to take significantly divergent trajectories.

As the Franco regime purged the scientific community of its progressive elements, most of whom were executed or forced into exile, the study of sexuality was left to experts who subscribed to the regime's fascist and Catholic ideologies. Since the regime severed the scientific community's international ties in its attempt to shield Spain from the evils of liberalism, scholarship on homosexuality replicated prewar theories infused with Catholic moral doctrine.[13] The regime also marginalized psychoanalysis.[14] Freud's theories first arrived in Spain in the early decades of the century, when the liberal intelligentsia, led by philosopher José Ortega y Gasset, advocated maintaining sexuality within the realm of morality. Ortega further argued that psychoanalysis usurped the role of Catholic confession in dealing with internal turmoil and sexual guilt.[15] During the Franco regime, Catholic psychiatrists decried psychoanalysis for its "sinful pansexualism," its indulgence toward sexual "perversions."[16] Only a few of the forensic doctors who collaborated with the vagrancy courts incorporated a psychodynamic perspective.[17]

A more common approach to homosexuality was an eclectic blend of biological theories and Catholic doctrines. According to Francisco Molina, the hegemonic school of "national psychiatry" reconciled biological essentialism with Catholic and legal notions of free will and liability by treating homosexuality as a contagious condition and public health issue.[18] This was a departure from earlier debates between Gregorio Marañón, an internationally famed endocrinologist who described homosexuality as a hormonal disorder, and Catholic thinker Antonio San de Velilla, who saw it as a violation of God's laws.[19] Marañón was comparatively sympathetic to homosexual people's issues, since he opposed criminalization on the idea that no one is liable for a biological condition, while still advising homosexual people to sublimate their desires through Catholic devotion.[20] Yet Franco-era medical doctors, such as Valentín Pérez Argilés, turned Marañón's theory around. Pérez Argilés reasoned that predatory homosexual individuals were liable for spreading their biological disease when they lured other people into sex in the same way that patients with tuberculosis were to be held accountable if they intentionally infected other people.[21] Following this reasoning, state agents enhanced the view that homosexual individuals were depraved predators to be stigmatized through the vernacular label maricón. Moreover, judges often enabled sexual assault on homosexual individuals by establishing that the latter had relinquished control over their own bodies by virtue of their same-sex desires.

As the Franco regime rose to power, many Spaniards fled to Argentina between the 1930s and 1940s, including Ángel Garma, the leading Freudian psychoanalyst in Spain, who booked passage for Buenos Aires in 1938, escaping fascism.[22] He maintained that paranoia was often a symptom of inhibited (i.e., sublimated) "passive" homosexuality, thus supporting the view that male sexual receptiveness was not only pathological but also related to other dangerous behaviors.[23] Garma played a leading role in institutionalizing psychoanalysis in Argentina, where it came to be the hegemonic frame for understanding homosexuality. Hence, at the Classification Institute, psychoanalysis intersected with positivist criminology through a focus on prisoners' unconscious sexual drives developed through family dynamics and participation in urban subcultures.

The Argentine middle class pursued psychoanalytical self-exploration to signal their status and cosmopolitanism. In addition, after the fall of Perón in 1955, different governments promoted the incorporation of psychoanalysis into the public health system as part of their modernization projects.[24] As a result of these developments, from the late 1950s psychoanalysis became a "belief system" permeating all kinds of social and political debates.[25] This historical process had significant effects on the categorization of homosexuality. Sigmund Freud, the architect of psychoanalysis, in 1905 described latent homosexual tendencies as virtually universal, leaving open and unaddressed the possibility that biology played a role in their development.[26] He traced how the individual's life trajectory—primarily his parents' gender roles—might lead him to repress these instincts and become "neurotic" or act on them as a "pervert."[27] In other words, perverts and neurotics were the inverse of each other.[28]

Emphasizing the nurturing of homosexual individuals, both state agents and investigated individuals represented a masculine performance as an indication of a recoverable heterosexual libido—namely, of a treatable neurotic disorder. In contrast, the double gender reversal of maricas, actively enticing other men to perform the "passive" sexual role, was taken to indicate an imprinted disdain for ethical norms—diagnosed as a sexual "psychopathy." From the authorities' perspective, this schema incorporated a view on sexual violence between males that put the burden of legal defense on the victim, with anything short of self-endangering resistance being defined as consent. In other words, Argentine criminologists, medical doctors, and psychoanalysts incorporated the sexual subculture of machos and maricas.

In this chapter, I first deal with the Spanish vagrancy courts

(1955–1970), which operated on a positivist frame according to which they adjudicated not the defendants' liability but their dangerousness. These courts enhanced the view that homosexual males were *viciosos* who offended Spain's values with their pursuit of excessive desires. In contrast, the defendants and their allies, mostly their mothers, argued that same-sex desires were a guiltless bodily condition. Concurrently, similar schemes were being implemented in Argentina. The second part of the chapter analyzes Argentine prison records to trace psychoanalytic theories' focus on homosexual males' paranoia and inhibitions to pathologize maricas' vocal attitudes.

The Vagrancy Law

In 1932, the newly emerged Spanish Second Republic eliminated any reference to homosexuality in the Penal Code. Although this government drafted and enacted the *Ley de Vagos y Maleantes* (Law of Vagrants and Miscreants, or Vagrancy Law) in 1933, this law initially paid no attention to homosexuality.[29] Luis Jiménez de Asúa, a reputed jurist and member of the Spanish Socialist Workers' Party, was one of the main proponents of the new law. While concerned about keeping the arbitrary powers of the police in check, he argued, "Every society has the right to defend itself against fearsome subjects, even before they commit any crime."[30] The Vagrancy Law was thus based on the new concept of pre-criminal dangerousness, which was defined as "antisocial, immoral and harmful activity" that revealed an "inclination to crime."[31] The kinds of individuals and conduct typified as dangerous under the new law included vagrants, beggars, pimps, illegal gaming, the sale of alcohol to minors, currency speculation, and habitual drunkenness, among others. In theory, the dangerous individuals were not considered culprits in the usual sense; instead, they were described as unfortunate. Yet in practice, those who fell into that category were imprisoned. Jiménez de Asúa's declared intent was to protect individuals' freedoms and the liberal system by clearly categorizing conduct that the police had been arbitrarily repressing. However, even he recognized that the concept of pre-criminal dangerousness could contribute to abuses of power by the state when the latter did not abide by democratic principles.[32] In fact, the law ended up providing a legal framework for the repression of marginal lifestyles under Franco's regime.

In 1954, the Franco regime revised the Vagrancy Law to include homosexuality, first as actions and a condition and subsequently just as recurrent homosexual acts following a decision by the Special Tribunal of Appeals and Revisions.[33] Alberto Mira argues that the main goal of the 1954 reform was to prevent the spread of homosexuality, perceived by Francoist authorities as a result of the corrupting effect of modernization and the influence of foreign and upper-class homosexuals.[34] Gema Pérez-Sánchez, on the other hand, claims that "Francoism's obsession with criminalizing and containing homosexuality" reveals the anxieties of the regime about the sexual connotations of "fascism's glorification of male camaraderie" and the peripheral position of Spain with respect to other Western powers.[35] The revisions made to the law of 1933 are italicized in the following translation of the first article of the law of 1954:

> First article. The second and eleventh section of the second article and the second section of the sixth article of the Law of Vagrants and Miscreants, of 4 August 1933, are now written in the following way:
>
> Article second. Second section. The *homoxesuals* [*sic*], ruffians and pimps.
>
> Article second. *Eleventh section. Likewise, they can be declared dangerous as antisocial those who, in their activities and propaganda, repeatedly incite the execution of crimes of terrorism or robbery and those who publicly justify those crimes.*
>
> *They can be as well the object of the same declaration those who, in any way, disturb with their conduct or endanger the social peace or the public tranquility.*
>
> Article sixth. Second section. To *homoxesuals* [*sic*], ruffians and pimps, to professional beggars, and to those who live on someone else's begging, exploit minors, the mentally ill or the

disabled, the following measures will be applied so they fulfill them in succession:

a) Confinement to a work camp or Agricultural Colony. *Homoxesuals [sic] subject to this security measure must be interned in special Institutions and, at all cost, with absolute separation from everyone else.*

b) Prohibition from residing in designated places or territories, and obligation to declare their domicile.

c) Submission to the surveillance of Delegates.[36]

The text of the 1954 revision of the law claimed that its aim was "not to punish, but to protect and reform" while preventing "acts that offend the healthy morality of our country because they are an affront to the traditional heritage of good customs, faithfully maintained in Spanish society."[37] The "security measures" applied to those defendants declared a social danger included confinement in an agricultural colony or work camp for a maximum of three years, although in practice the convicts were often sent to common prisons. There were also prohibitions against residing in a particular place, usually the province where the defendant had resided until being arrested, and subjection to surveillance by delegates—state agents who supervised the convicts' behavior after they were released.[38]

Since the law stipulated the prosecution of dangerous individuals even if their criminality could not be "immediately proved,"[39] judges' interpretations of the evidence that was required to condemn the suspects varied greatly. The judicial evidence was collected through the regime's governance structure, which was based on entrenched hierarchical social relations and the control of local communities through centralized state institutions and agencies: the governor, the mayors, the Guardia Civil, and the police. This state apparatus collaborated with local influential figures—mostly the propertied classes, the church, and the educated minority—in order to maintain public order, morality, and obedience to the regime. This context of cooperation is necessary to understand the roles of these state institutions and of certain influential figures in the court proceedings regarding homosexuality. The objective of these court proceedings was not just to decide if the defendants were homosexuals but also to understand their positions in their communities and their overall social behavior. Defense lawyers therefore tried to present their clients as respectable and well-connected members of their communities. In other words, judges decided the defendants' potential future criminality based on their past normalcy.

"Vicioso maricón"

The centuries-old concept of *vicio* (from the Latin term *vitium*) became central in adjudicating liability and people's rights over their own bodies. Vicio entails an excessive (beyond any self-restraint) pursuit of desires that becomes harmful to oneself and others.[40] According to Francisco Vázquez García and Richard Cleminson, medieval sodomites were defined by their vicio, their lack of self-control to avoid the practice of discharging semen into an "erroneous vessel," which included bestiality, same-sex intercourse, and nonreproductive sex in general. Likewise, Vázquez and Cleminson problematize teleological approaches to the history of homosexuality by emphasizing the multiplicity of representations and categories that coexist at any moment, including the persistence of the frame of vicio during the period of "curtailed medicalization" in Spain between 1850 and 1939.[41] In Francoist courts, the adjective *vicioso* appeared hand in hand with the term "maricón," which belongs to the same semantic family as mariquita and yet had quite different connotations. Ethnographer Dieter Haller argues that "maricón" had overtly sexual connotations, and when combined with the concept of vicio, it referred to men who engaged in homosexual acts as an acquired taste (versus the inborn femininity attributed to mariquitas).[42] Being publicly exposed as a maricón could have potentially tragic consequences. In 1969, for instance, a defendant tried to kill himself after the Guardia Civil threatened to parade him through the village so that everyone would know that he was a "maricón."[43]

In its use by witnesses within the Francoist courts, the phrase *vicioso maricón* underemphasized the agency of the man who anally penetrates another man to overemphasize the agency of the man who desires to be penetrated, based on the expectation (shared by state agents) that sexually receptive men were the ones who led their partners to have intercourse. For instance, in 1962 in the court of Barcelona, a man accused an individual nicknamed "the healer" of being a "vicioso maricón" who asked the witness and a third man to "fuck him in the ass" in exchange for hosting them.[44] The witness said, "Que hacía que le dieran los dos por el culo," implying that the defendant had aroused, coerced, or paid them to have sex. Even though individuals like the defendant were labeled "passive," they were expected to actively pursue their desire to be penetrated in a way that complicated the gendered binary between activity/masculinity and passivity/femininity.

In other cases, the defendants tried to transfer liability from themselves to their occasional impulses by using the concept of vicio. Several defendants claimed in Bilbao in 1966—possibly encouraged by the officers interrogating them—that vicio had subjugated them into having sex with other men.[45] In other words, while it was implied that an individual labeled as vicioso identified with his "perverse" sexual agency, an individual who claimed that vicio felt alien to him could use this as his legal defense strategy.

The authorities treated the defendants labeled maricones who reported being the victims of robbery, harassment, or sexual assault as threats to society; therefore, the latter would have no other option than to keep these incidents to themselves to avoid exposure. For instance, an individual staying in a boarding house in Barcelona in 1962 was robbed by another guest, who left him the following note: "I am not going to work to give you the money and still have to fuck you in the ass. Look, I am taking all of this [your belongings], but I warn you that if you go to the police and they catch me I will say that you are a *maricón* and I will prove it, so you will lose as much if not more than I will. The best you can do is shut up and not look for more lovers. Bye."[46] The man who wrote this note was aware that the victim of his robbery was vulnerable on account of his pursuit of being penetrated. Insofar as he had exercised his sexual agency in a way that disturbed gender roles and the conventions of masculinity, police officers were likely to shun him as a maricón.

Gender performance and community reputation became the main criteria to judge whether the defendants were to be treated as sexual predators possessed by their vicio. For instance, in 1959 in an Andalusian village, a middle-aged cook reported that a younger farmhand had coerced him into having sex and robbed him in the middle of the countryside. Months after this incident, the cook ran into the farmhand in a bar and the latter called him a maricón and threatened to slap him if he did not leave. Confronted with this public shaming, the cook reported these events to the Guardia Civil. This led to a trial at the end of which the cook was classified as a danger to society, imprisoned, and exiled, despite the fact that he had been the one reporting to be a victim in the first place.[47] It is noteworthy that the cook did not report the rape and robbery immediately after they happened, but rather he did so after being publicly accused of being a maricón. As a last resort to protect his honor and personal integrity, he had appealed to the state apparatus, which ruled that as a homosexual, the victim was the danger to society. This ruling corroborated that maricones had no other option than suffering sexual assault and harassment in silence, since their exposure could only lead to harsher institutionalized punishments.

An alleged victim of sexual harassment who was labeled a maricón (and thereby questioned in his masculinity) could only expect some protection from the state if the trial did not produce enough evidence about his gender performance reflecting his sexual desires. Even in cases of nonmasculine minors, authorities debated whether their gender performance had incapacitated them to claim the status of victim of sexual assault. This scrutiny was a form of state violence imposing on nonmasculine individuals the burden of proving that they had not brought on the sexual assault. For instance, in 1962, a twenty-one-year-old defendant apparently tried to coerce a fourteen-year-old minor into performing oral sex on him in a bathroom, until the minor's father heard them and intervened. The defendant alleged that the minor had looked for him to have sex.[48] The minor testified that before this episode, the defendant had repeatedly explained to him that, as a maricón, he could not reject the defendant's sexual requests, which he hadn't told his family before because he felt ashamed.[49] In this way, this minor was socialized to believe that he had no sexual rights over his own body because he did not look masculine enough and that this situation ought to be a shame for his family. The Guardia Civil reported that the minor was "effeminate," considering this a significant factor to place in its report.[50] His father, trying to excuse his nonmasculine behavior to counteract the doubts about his sexuality, clarified that his son's "calmer-than-usual character" was due to his asthmatic bronchitis.[51] The judge ruled that the adult defendant was a danger to society, but he did so *against* the recommendation of the public prosecution.[52] Regardless of which version of the events was true, the fact is that the investigating authorities had questioned the minor's version mostly because of his "femininity." In other words, they shared with the alleged abuser the view that maricones, who were visible in their nonmasculine behaviors, relinquished control over their own bodies by virtue of their attraction to men.

Individuals suspected of engaging in homosexual acts often tried to transfer the stigma of the term "maricón" to other defendants. By motivating the defendants to publicly disavow each other in this way, the law's implementation undermined nonnormative relationality. Thus, in 1964 in Huelva, a nineteen-year-old man and a fifty-four-year-old man who lived together were arrested after a third man asked the younger one if he "gave it by the ass" to his older companion.[53] This led to a fight as the older man tried to defend the younger man's honor. Once in the police station, the younger man disavowed the older man by describing him as a maricón with whom he had chosen to live out of economic necessity.[54] By severing nonconforming people's social ties, the authorities aimed at turning the law's definition of homosexuality as "antisocial" into a self-fulfilling prophecy. In this line, masculine men who socialized and had fun with maricones—dancing with them, for instance—were encouraged to use this label to disavow them. In 1961 in Barcelona, a nineteen-year-old industrial worker declared that he had been arrested "for hanging out with *maricones*" with whom he enjoyed singing and dancing.[55] The defendant was affirming his own masculinity by disavowing his nonmasculine acquaintances. However, this strategy backfired, as the judge cited this declaration as proof of his dangerous condition and sentenced him to prison.[56] It was not enough that this defendant disavowed maricones; his acts had demonstrated that he was not repulsed by their sexuality and public presence, so his tolerance by extension turned him into a danger to society in the judge's eyes. On a larger scale, many nonconforming individuals performed a "traditional" femininity, centered on church and home, to carve a delimited space of practical tolerance, which then became a common legal defense strategy.

Forensic Studies

Under the Vagrancy Law, homosexuality belonged to a "border area" between criminology and psychiatry, along with other "antisocial" behaviors and mental disorders such as alcoholism or psychopathy.[57] The fact that the law, in theory at least, was meant not to attribute criminal liability but rather to protect society from those inclined to misconduct created a unique situation in which factors that diminished the defendant's self-control could be considered aggravating instead of exonerating. Thus, a slight difference in doctors' assessments of defendants could situate them in the purview of either criminal law or psychiatry. Therefore, forensic doctors faced pressures from above and below. While state officials leaned toward a criminal approach leading to incarceration, suspected homosexuals and their allies showed their preference for a clinical approach leading to hospitalization or incapacitation. As a strategic defense, many individuals chose to attribute their homosexual acts to any other disorder rather than admitting that they felt attracted to the same sex. In the negotiation of stigma, few labels carried negative connotations comparable to those of homosexuality. However, the rulings of judicial authorities and the writings of scientific experts restricted the definition and application of every medical theory that had proved itself appropriable by defendants.

Domingo Saumench Gimeno, forensic doctor at Barcelona's Vagrancy Court, wrote his 1960 doctoral dissertation on the "Cálculo médico legal de un índice de peligrosidad" (Medico-Legal Calculation of a Dangerousness Index). He theorized—counterintuitively, given that he collaborated with a National-Catholic dictatorship—that a man avowing interests in sex and crime was an indicator of normalcy, while interests in family and religion were indications of dangerousness. The law mandated that forensic doctors such as Saumench evaluated the defendants' mental status, age, previous job performance, and ability to work.[58] This focus on functionality suggests positivism's alignment with the regime's organicist view of society as a body in which every member has a role.[59] In this line, Saumench described "asocial" individuals as "parasites" that hindered the normal functioning of society and thereby ought to be the target of the law even more than "antisocial" individuals who openly opposed social norms. In other words, he was more concerned about nonproductive than about nonconforming individuals. He followed the Nazi leader Joseph Goebbels in thinking that asocial people displayed genetically determined pathological behavior. In a self-contradictory manner, he added that forensic doctors should look at social dangerousness as a phenotypic phenomenon.[60] Forensic doctors played a significant role in pathologizing demographic groups disenfranchised by the Franco regime: the leftist working class, groups who survived through the informal economy, unattached women, the Roma, and homosexual people. According to Saumench, the working class was biologically inclined to criminality because their diet was lacking in nutrients.[61] Similarly, single motherhood was, in his opinion, a sort of Darwinian evolutionary process that excluded the descendants of biologically inferior women from the privileges of legitimacy. Finally, merging psychoanalytic and racial theories, he concluded that Roma communities prevented the proper formation of their members' superegos.[62]

Saumench vehemently pathologized homosexual males' "traditional" interest in family and religion. For his dissertation, he studied one hundred prisoners sentenced as dangers to society by the court of Barcelona. Out of this sample, eleven prisoners were classified as homosexual. The study subjects underwent detailed interviews and projective tests, including the Rorschach. They were also asked about the titles of books that caught their attention, and then these results were compared to two control groups formed by "normal" people (students and social workers) and mental patients. According to this methodology, homosexual men were particularly interested in religion, family, health, celebrities, and social work. The studied subjects might have voiced their interest in family and religion to respond to conservative authorities' expectations. However, prisoners sentenced for other charges did not do the same.[63] Maybe these interests reflect dynamics of social integration that encouraged mariquitas to perform traditional femininity, associated with church and home. Saumench hypothesized that these interests were related to prisoners' neuroses. Given their sexuality, he assumed that their religious feelings were inauthentic and their interest in family related to their Oedipal complex. In contrast, according to Saumench, "sexual life" and "war and crime" were normal interests common to all the studied groups. They demonstrated, in his view, natural instincts of reproduction, self-preservation, and aggression.[64] Ultimately, this forensic taxonomy relied on the fascist-inspired view of reproductive, aggressive masculinity as a national value. Forensic doctors excluded from this definition of manhood those individuals who let other men leave a trace on their bodies through penetration.

Body Measures

Forensic techniques were a form of state violence inflicted upon the defendants' bodies. Clinicians invasively measured their penises and the diameter and dilatation of their anuses. As María Elena Martínez discusses, forensic doctors since the Enlightenment era had been invested in a positivist logic of detached observation in order to elaborate "objective" taxonomies and apply them to the subjects of observation.[65] Forensic doctors claimed to be trained to expose bodies' *legibility*: that their shapes portend character predispositions and the individual's gestures betray his inner gender. Thus, the "evidence" that doctors gathered was subsumed into their personal impressions; if the defendant did not perform masculinity convincingly during their interview, then that would be recorded as scientific proof against him. Doctors occasionally incorporated forensic typologies to enhance their authority, which proved either contradictory or inapplicable. Among others, German psychiatrist Ernst Kretschmer had developed in the 1920s an influential body typology. He argued that there were correlations between three basic constitutional body types (leptosome, athletic, and pyknic) and psychopathologies.[66] He claimed that manic depression had a higher prevalence among those showing a "pyknic" (stocky) body. A slender "leptosomatic," on the other hand, was more likely to suffer from schizophrenia and homosexuality.[67] In the vagrancy courts, this typology proved itself irrelevant, since it did not match the results of anal exams. For instance, in 1964 in Sevilla, the forensic doctor reported "anal stigmas" and abnormal genitals in a "pyknic" defendant but not in a "leptosomatic" defendant.[68] In 1970, the prison population at large was classified within this typology, providing data that did not support Kretschmer's theory.[69]

Physical exams perpetuated the double stigmatization of "passive" homosexual men through their bodies.[70] Forensic doctors assumed that anal intercourse only left traces on them. Following Tardieu's studies, "passive" homosexuality would be evident in a funnel-shaped anus ("infundibuliform") and the "relaxation of the anal sphincter, extreme dilatation of the anus, anal ulcerations and fistulas."[71] Spanish forensic doctors recorded these signs but completely disregarded Tardieu's theory on the deformed penis of "active" homosexual men, assuming on the contrary that anal penetration did not leave traces on them. Forensic reports on suspected homosexuals issued from the mid-1950s to the 1960s are generally very short. They tend to focus on the defendant's anatomy (especially his anus) and gender performance. In the Canary

Islands, for instance, forensic doctors routinely noted an "infundibuliform" anus or a rectum that was easily penetrated during the DRE as "stigmas" of homosexuality. According to one report, a rectum that "easily allowed the introduction . . . of a finger" was more reliable evidence than an infundibuliform anus, but neither was irrefutable.[72] These were flawed techniques according to forensic doctors themselves. Not only were they only applicable to "passive" homosexual men, according to doctors, but these doctors also recognized that many of these men exhibited *no* clinical signs of being penetrated, whereas these same "signs" could appear in nonhomosexual men who suffered from hemorrhoids.[73] Therefore, hemorrhoids became a defense strategy for defendants who were aware of these flaws. Notably among them was an elite man and fascist sympathizer. The forensic doctor and a private physician certified that this man's anal sphincter could be dilatated due to hemorrhoids, so the defendant was acquitted.[74]

Judges relied on forensic evidence of anal intercourse but tried to maintain rules of decorum that prevented the trials from centering on the defendants' erogenous organs. This became the case when a forensic doctor posited that well-endowed men were more likely to leave traces on other men by penetrating them and that the sphincters of penetrated men could be more or less elastic. In 1964, a doctor reported to the Sevilla court that a defendant had "normal sexual characteristics."[75] However, a subsequent report clarified that anal penetration does not leave a trace on all men, since the "penis in erection varies in length and thickness" and individuals who are penetrated show different degrees of sphincter elasticity.[76] This report explicitly feminized penetrated men by describing them as performing a woman's role. The judge sentenced the defendant as a "danger to society" without further digging into these anatomic variables of uncertainty.[77] If the DRE did not match doctors' personal impressions of the defendants' gender performance, then doctors were likely to trust these impressions. Thus, the DRE was discarded in favor of the defendants' gestures and voice, taken to be the main symptoms of their "effeminacy."[78] Sometimes, if the physical exam and forensic doctors' impressions contradicted each other, the reports' wording gave judges leeway to rely on either.[79] Doctors' impressions of the defendants' morality were often the only forensic evidence for "active" homosexual men, who by doctors' definition were not identifiable in the DRE. For instance, in the case of a defendant accused of prostituting himself with other men by exclusively performing the "active" role, the forensic doctor recorded his "impression of [the defendant as] hypercritical, masturbatory, and immoral."[80] Forensic reports were generally used to corroborate the attribution of responsibility and sexual roles in police reports. The state apparatus was traversed by an assumption of masculinity. Public servants, from police officers to doctors and judges, communicated with one another, taking for granted that they shared an embodied masculinity that allowed them to read the essential Otherness of feminized men. However, the defendants and their allies challenged the aims of these essentializing dynamics by using the body as a legal defense.

The Body as Legal Defense

The body was a central site of dispute between authorities and nonconforming individuals because of the widespread notion in Spain at that time that same-sex desires were inscribed in an individual's bodily essence. Therefore, legal debates centered on the defendants' responsibility for acts that supposedly stemmed from a pathological physiological condition. Many defendants preferred medical treatment rather than a common sentence, probably because living conditions were better in hospitals than in common prisons.[81] Therefore, they relied on eclectic theories that traced the etiology of homosexuality to the body and on judges' statements on the law's rehabilitative aims. The range of physical conditions to which homosexuality was attributed included everything from meningitis and brain traumas to thyroid and hip problems. Furthermore, prosecutors and judges decided on the validity of medical certificates based on their moralistic evaluations of the defendants' behaviors before their arrest.

Strategic pathologization, through a medical theory that traced homosexuality to brain traumas, worked in favor of a defendant from a privileged background judged in Málaga in 1961. The reports on him were so contradictory that it was difficult to reconcile all his behaviors into a coherent image.[82] He had two BAs and was awarded a PhD, had published on literature and science, and was once an active member of the fascist party Falange and the students' union.[83] However, after moving to the coast of Málaga, he reportedly began to drink to the point of intoxication and exhibited homosexual behavior. The public defender presented a plea explaining that the contrast between his client's behavior before moving to Málaga and the "creature" that he had become in this province under the effects of alcohol could be the consequence of a personality disorder produced by brain trauma.[84] Not in vain, Dr. Valentín Pérez Argilés had argued in 1959 that encephalitis was among the possible causes of homosexuality.[85] The judge disregarded the lawyer's petition to subject the defendant to psychiatric examination and ordered instead his internment in a rehabilitation center for alcoholism. The sentence did not mention the charges of homosexuality.[86] The defendant's social standing, along with medical debates on brain injuries affecting sexual orientation, led the judge to focus instead on the lighter charge of alcoholism.

In a case similarly related to intoxication, a connection was established from meningitis to sexual psychopathy and attenuated responsibility, so the defendant was forcibly committed to an asylum. Upon his arrest, the eighteen-year-old defendant confessed that an older man had paid him for sex. He alleged that he suffered from headaches as a consequence of the older man performing oral sex on him.[87] Later interrogated in prison, he claimed that alcohol affected him more than other people because he had suffered from "tuberculous meningitis" as a child.[88] His doctor linked this meningitis with a conduct disorder, and subsequently, two other doctors concluded that this disorder consisted "in a sexual psychopathy . . . that makes him indifferent to moral and social issues."[89] Even though the defendant had not essentialized his sexuality, through successive medical exams it was established that his acts reflected a sexual psychopathy caused by a physical pathology. The judge transferred the case to the civilian governor, who committed the defendant to the provincial asylum.[90] In this case, doctors inscribed in the defendant's body history an alleged lack of moral criteria, leading to his involuntary commitment.

Marañón's endocrine theory was the most common way to trace a defendant's sexuality to his body history. However, these cases suggest that most judges did not care as much about essentialized same-sex desires as they did about their fulfillment in acts. For instance, in 1967 in Barcelona, a man went to the police station to file a report. Another man had beaten and robbed the plaintiff while he cleaned the aggressor's penis after performing oral sex on him.[91] The plaintiff was charged with homosexuality, even though he had initially reported these events as the victim. The forensic doctor reported that he was a "congenital" homosexual.[92] The defense lawyer argued that endocrine factors beyond the defendant's will accounted for his homosexuality.[93] However, he was deemed to be a danger to society as a "constitutional sexual invert," proving that essentialization did not prevent punishment.[94] The defendant's sister notified the court that her brother had died before the judge's pronouncement, probably because of neglecting treatment of his hemophilia.[95] Different layers of victimization coalesced over the defendant: first assaulted by a sexual partner, then charged by the police, and finally dead because of medical negligence in prison. Informing the process was the resolution of Judge Sabater Tomás of Barcelona, one of Spain's main legal experts on sexual "danger," to restrict the normalizing implications of essentialism.

However, the functioning of the state apparatus was plagued with incoherencies, as other state agents were unaware of essentialism's potential to normalize nonconforming people and in fact promoted its adoption during the investigation process. The defendants' answers to leading questions reveal the incoherent negotiation between expert categories and lived experiences. Some defendants were allegedly uncertain about whether their sexuality was an inborn condition. Alternatively, others characterized it as such (possibly feeling encouraged to do so and aware that this category had exculpatory connotations) to describe, immediately after, lived experiences of being initiated into or exploring homosexual pleasures in ways that did not fit within that category. One defendant even acknowledged being an inborn invert, only to then contradict himself by claiming that his exclusive heterosexuality was evident in his marriage plans. All these answers were recorded in a case judged in the court of Bilbao in 1957, when officers apparently insisted on asking every defendant if they were "inborn inverts," unevenly inscribing this category in judicial records. Even though officers' questions were not recorded, the fact that every defendant addressed this question proves that it was routinely asked. At the same time, it must be noted that these records are significantly mediated, since the defendants' answers were paraphrased (not transcribed) in the third person by secretaries. The defendants' recorded answers varied broadly: "he is an inborn sexual invert"; "he thinks he is an inborn sexual invert, even though he did not have homosexual relationships until he was twenty years old"; "he thinks he is an inborn invert, because when he was twelve years old . . . he masturbated with other boys . . . he considers himself normal and not inclined to people of his same sex, as proved by the fact that he is going to get married soon"; "he doesn't know if he is an inborn invert, since he did not feel inclined toward other men until approximately a year and a half ago, when he met [two men] with whom, due to their frequent contact [*roce* in Spanish], he started to engage in homosexual practices"; "he thinks is an inborn invert, since when he was thirteen years old . . . [an older man] initiated him in these practices, always consisting in touching, kisses, and masturbations, so he thinks his inclination toward the masculine sex comes from that time."[96] This repertoire of recorded answers suggests that individuals attributed their sexual self-realization to significantly different factors, from biological determination to sexual playfulness.

Like police officers, many forensic doctors were not fully aware of top officials' preference to restrict the category of inborn or congenital homosexuality. In fact, their reports often served the defense's arguments. In 1964 in Sevilla, the court's forensic doctor portrayed the defendant as a "congenital feminoid with homosexual tendency and anal stigmas."[97] The defense lawyer seized upon the term "congenital" to argue that biological determination was incompatible with legal liability.[98] He seemed familiar with Marañón's works, as he argued that homosexuality was a "defective" condition equivalent to that of a "blind or hunchback person, since no one is responsible for his own hormonal configuration." The lawyer normalized inborn homosexuality by comparing it with extramarital sex as "normal" moral failures.[99] He also emphasized that the district attorney had omitted the adjective "congenital" in the charges, with the intention of obscuring the law's internal incoherencies. Nonetheless, Judge Abundancia of Sevilla ruled that the defendant was a danger, since there was forensic evidence of his engagement in homosexual intercourse.[100]

Thus, Judge Abundancia implicitly responded to the lawyer's normalization of congenital homosexuality by treating the defendant as if no mention of his physiology had been made. Abundancia applied the law harshly with the goal of moralizing the population. Given that Abundancia's priority was the isolating punishment of homosexual men, the relationship between "perversion" and mental pathology appeared quite irrelevant to him. This became evident in 1961 when an eighty-year-old widow claimed that her son, a suspected homosexual, could not be a danger to society because his family cared for him in spite of "abnormal reactions" related to his "sickness."[101] She submitted a certificate by a private physician, who traced the defendant's sexuality to hip problems that had prevented him from working since he was a child. This incapacity—the physician vaguely argued—might have caused in the defendant "pathological mental states, which sometimes can be framed within different perversions."[102] Despite the far-fetched medical argument that the defendant's hip problems were related to his homosexuality, Abundancia judged him to be a danger to society.[103] The mother's attempt at exculpating her son clashed with Abundancia's determination to punish and moralize homosexual men.

In Barcelona, since Judge Sabater Tomás had published on the law's rehabilitative aims, his works could be cited to support the advantages of medical treatment. In this way, hospitalization reconciled

Sabater Tomás's statements with the defendants' aspirations to avoid imprisonment. However, the trajectory of these petitions demonstrates Sabater Tomás's arbitrary moralism in deciding who was granted this alternative. First, for these pleas to be effective, the defendants had to cover the costs of hospitalization. Thus, strategic pathologization became another form of class-based discrimination. In fact, the superficial treatment of these defendants when they were committed to the Frenopático (Barcelona's most prestigious private asylum) raises the question of whether psychiatric treatment responded to the patients' need for an alternative to prison or to the law's stated rehabilitative aims. After all, patients paid for their own treatment, not the state. Their clinical histories do not contain much information about their homosexual condition. Instead, they follow the administrative procedures necessary to satisfy the court's demands for information about a patient's progress until his discharge. For instance, in 1964 a defendant claimed that a thyroid removal that he had undergone years before had caused his homosexuality. The court's forensic physician relied on Marañón to confirm that this surgery could have exacerbated the defendant's endocrine disorders leading him to commit homosexual acts.[104] Since endocrine surgery could lead to homosexual acts according to the forensic doctor, the lawyer inverted this logic by submitting a certificate that the defendant was going to undergo another surgery that hopefully would contribute to curing his "disorder," being circumcised this time (he did not elaborate on how circumcision was supposed to cure homosexuality).[105] Nonetheless, the judge found the defendant to be a danger to society, so the lawyer submitted an appeal to allow him to serve his sentence in the Frenopático. The judge conceded, stating that he could not "resist the attraction of correction means that can be more efficient than those that he himself had imposed."[106]

Despite Judge Sabater Tomás's statements that he favored clinical treatments of homosexuality, he decided whether to grant this option following his own moralistic criteria. For instance, a family man and breadwinner who allegedly had failed in controlling occasional sexual impulses deserved, in Sabater Tomás's view, more leniency than a man who had pursued a comfortable lifestyle through a relationship with a well-off male patron, even though both were diagnosed in the exact same way. Thus, Sabater Tomás weighed diagnoses against nonmedical factors when deciding what treatment to impose on these men. The first one was a middle-aged industrial worker and family man who, in 1964, declared to the police that on a couple of occasions, he had met men in public bathrooms to masturbate each other. He submitted a plea and a medical certificate petitioning to be interned in the Frenopático to treat his nervous depression without endangering either his job or his family's reputation. The judge granted this petition.[107] However, the result was very different when, a few months later, a man accused of having a long-term affair with a well-off patron presented a similar plea. The court's forensic doctor reported that the defendant suffered from depression and should be transferred to a medical facility. His lawyer presented a petition so that the defendant could serve his sentence treating his nervous depression at the Frenopático. The judge denied this plea, so the defendant served out his sentence in a labor camp.[108] Still, given Sabater Tomás's stated willingness to accept psychiatric internment as a substitute for the standard security measures, other trials followed a similar course.[109] In Spain, hospitalization was a compromise that allowed defendants to escape prison without having to subject themselves to stringent therapies.[110] These therapies reified the assumption that "passive" homosexuality was particularly pathological, a notion that Ángel Garma articulated in his publications after migrating from Spain to Argentina.

Gendering Paranoia

Spanish émigré Ángel Garma was well received in Buenos Aires when he arrived at this city in 1938 escaping from the rise of General Francisco Franco's fascist regime in Spain. He had received his psychoanalytic training in Berlin in the 1920s and became a central figure in the introduction of the new discipline in Spain in the 1930s. According to Mariano Ben Plotkin, since in 1938 "he was the only person in Argentina who had undergone complete formal psychoanalytic training," his credentials were indisputable.[111] In 1942 Garma would become the first president of the Argentine Psychoanalytic Association (APA), which a year later began publishing the influential *Revista de Psicoanálisis*.[112] At this stage, psychoanalytic scholarship primarily concerned itself with men's "latent" homosexual libido. This libido was implicitly feminized in the idea that men who desired to be penetrated ("passive" homosexuals) often developed paranoid fears of other people questioning their masculinity and, thereby, tended to react violently. This gendered theory assumed that the archetypal male homosexual patient was invested in his manly reputation and could not reckon with his desire to be sexually "submissive."

Garma's work was based on the experiences of Spanish psychiatric patients, as he assumed that the norms and effects of masculinity were commensurable across the Atlantic. Given Garma's major role in institutionalizing psychoanalysis in midcentury Argentina, his 1944 article "Paranoia y Homosexualidad" set the tone for Argentine psychoanalysts' views on homosexuality-related disorders in the 1940s and 1950s. This article embodies transatlantic knowledge production. It is based on a series of case studies of patients who had been committed to Spanish psychiatric hospitals in the early twentieth century because they suffered from persecutory or delirious ideas. One such patient imagined that his co-workers were mocking him and spreading rumors about his homosexuality and that a neighbor was planning to emasculate him by forcing him to have sex. Eventually, the patient was hospitalized when he tried to commit a double murder in his town. A different patient suffered from delirious ideas of a conspiracy to castrate and blind him. This patient had published earlier in life a booklet about his infuriated "virile" reaction to a high school teacher trying to molest him.[113] Garma hypothesized that these patients shared their incapacity to sublimate their "passive" homosexual libido—namely, their desire to be penetrated.[114] By reasoning that these patients suffered from a paranoid dread of emasculation because of their desire to be penetrated, Garma contributed to stigmatizing and feminizing "passive" homosexual males.[115]

Building on Garma's hypothesis, Argentine psychiatrists and psychoanalysts examined how same-sex assault entailed the gendered roles of masculine assaulters and feminized victims. Although psychoanalysts were allegedly treating paranoia and not homosexuality, their premise was that patients' incapacity to sublimate their desire to be sexually submissive induced them into a paranoid and frail performance of masculinity. In 1945, Jorge Thénon and Héctor Villar published an article about a middle-class patient who suffered from delirious ideas and tried to demonstrate his masculinity by antagonizing bus drivers. The patient traced this behavior to an episode that took place when he was a medical intern. A co-worker sexually harassed him, showing him his genitals and a feminine undergarment, which he expected the patient to wear when they eventually had intercourse. Finally, one night his harasser co-worker, assisted by other male employees of the hospital, tried to force the patient into dressing like a woman and wearing fake breasts while his co-worker penetrated him. Although the patient managed to escape to the street and eventually brought his assaulters to trial, all of them denied the charges, so no one was convicted. Because of this episode, the patient was diagnosed as suffering from paranoid delirium, which Thénon and Villar treated with electroshocks. Since this treatment did not work, they speculated that psychoanalysis would reveal that the patient's disorder was rooted in his "passive" homosexual libido and craving for punishment, taking Garma's hypothesis to new extremes by placing the blame of sexual assault on its victim.[116]

These views were shared by the criminologists and forensic doctors working at the Classification Institute, who saw a dominant libido as a sign of a normative masculinity, and vice versa. However, through their interactions with maricas, these criminologists departed from the psychoanalytic theory that a paranoid and frail performance of masculinity was the most common manifestation of a feminized desire to be sexually submissive. Instead, they came to identify homosexual males who were unwilling to inhibit themselves as a "major danger" and their performance of masculinity as a positive sign of lessening danger.

Major Sexual Dangers

The Classification Institute's criminologists, who examined prisoners and produced reports on their parole requests, saw homosexuality as a "criminal-genetic" factor, which indicated an increased potential for a prisoner to become a danger to society. They reinforced an honor-driven sexual culture in which penetration was a marker of masculinity, even though they simultaneously conceptualized this culture as an index of "underclass" dangerousness. In other words, criminological reports betray the examiners' prejudices against nonelite subcultures while also incorporating cross-class definitions of masculine honor in terms of sexual competition and a dominating libido. Criminologists evaluated inmates' parole requests based on psychological traits, social background, and "predispositions" but also on distinguishing between sexual behaviors that in their view posed a "major" or "minor" danger. Since the late nineteenth century, most Argentine criminologists held an environmentalist view of sexual perversion.[117] In the 1940s, they adopted psychoanalytic frames to express their belief that sexual orientation was not an essential trait but rather contingent on upbringing and sexual initiation. Following psychoanalytic theory, they traced the etiology of homosexuality to early traumatic experiences and parents' gender roles, specifically "weak" or absent fathers and overprotective mothers.[118] Homosexuality, in criminologists' view, could become "fixated" through noxious influences (and externalized then in gender "inversion," i.e., males' femininity) or sublimated into heterosexuality by conforming to gender norms (i.e., performing masculinity).

For instance, in a file from 1940, the criminologist argued that the prisoner, called La Lita, had irreversibly developed a female psyche because of exogenous, environmental factors. According to the criminologist's rendering of the prisoner's life trajectory, her parents had tolerated her "fixations" (*manías*) when she started to use makeup and help her mother with household chores at age eight. Then when she was twelve, she met an elderly prostitute who lived in the same tenement. This woman had taught the prisoner to properly use makeup and wear female clothes to entice one of her classmates. The prisoner would succeed in this endeavor, and her classmate would come to "possess" (penetrate) her on repeated occasions in the prostitute's home. According to the report, homosexual intercourse cemented the prisoner's female psyche; since her sexual encounters with a classmate, her life "continued at an identical pace, [she] was a woman, felt like a woman, and acted as such."[119] While she had tried to work with her father in the countryside, she soon realized that she was not made for that life. The following are her own words, allegedly transcribed by the criminologist: "I had the same needs as any other woman does, and you can't do anything in the countryside because people talk. . . . I am a serious 'marica,' and it disgusts me when people point their fingers at me. Therefore, I decided to come to Buenos Aires, where I could get what I sought without calling anyone's attention."[120] In contrast to the criminologist's insistence that a depraved environment had induced the prisoner into perversion, she expressed a yearning to fulfill her sexual needs in the capital without being subjected to public scrutiny.

Instead of presenting a univocal definition of femininity, criminological reports reflect how maricas contested state agents over its cultural meaning. La Lita, probably deploying her keen sense of humor as well, claimed that her actions were not any less decent or "serious" than those of any other woman because she followed strict rules of gender complementarity that defined masculinity as penetrative and femininity as receptive. She clarified that she would get an erection and ejaculate while being penetrated by another man. However, she would never allow her sexual partners to touch her genitals because a man drawn to male genitalia "is not a man." The prisoner described how in the city she would initiate a conversation with a stranger man whom she liked, and if this went well, then she would intimate that she was a marica—and, if he picked up on it and engaged further, then she would ask if he wanted to sleep with her. The prisoner also acknowledged that her self-imposed rules of behavior were quite flexible. For instance, while she emphasized that she had never engaged in transactional

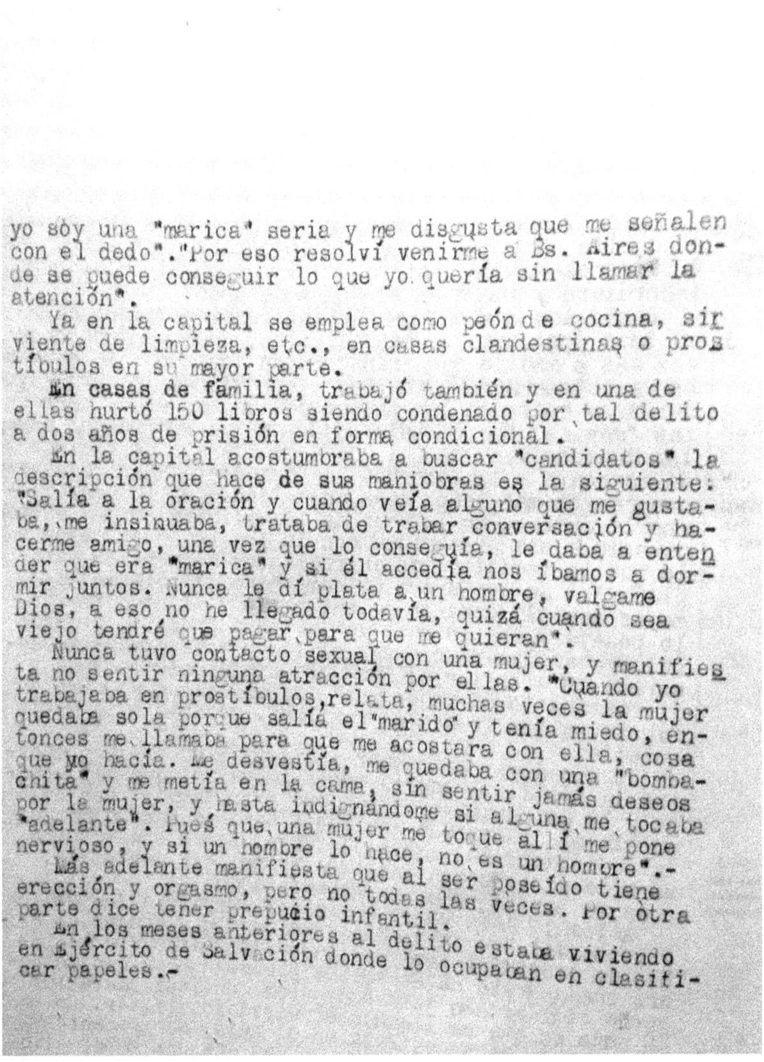

yo soy una "marica" seria y me disgusta que me señalen
con el dedo"."Por eso resolví venirme a Bs. Aires donde se puede conseguir lo que yo querìa sin llamar la
atención".
Ya en la capital se emplea como peón de cocina, sir
viente de limpieza, etc., en casas clandestinas o pros
tíbulos en su mayor parte.
En casas de familia, trabajó también y en una de
ellas hurtó 150 libros siendo condenado por tal delito
a dos años de prisión en forma condicional.
En la capital acostumbraba a buscar "candidatos" la
descripción que hace de sus maniobras es la siguiente:
"Salía a la oración y cuando veía alguno que me gusta-
ba, me insinuaba, trataba de trabar conversación y ha-
cerme amigo, una vez que lo conseguía, le daba a enten
der que era "marica" y si él accedía nos íbamos a dor-
mir juntos. Nunca le dí plata a un hombre, válgame
Dios, a eso no he llegado todavía, quizá cuando sea
viejo tendré que pagar para que me quieran".
Nunca tuvo contacto sexual con una mujer, y manifies
ta no sentir ninguna atracción por ellas. "Cuando yo
trabajaba en prostíbulos, relata, muchas veces la mujer
quedaba sola porque salía el "marido" y tenía miedo, en-
tonces me llamaba para que me acostara con ella, cosa
que yo hacía. Me desvestía, me quedaba con una "bomba-
chita" y me metía en la cama, sin sentir jamás deseos
por la mujer, y hasta indignándome si alguna me tocaba
"adelante". Pues que una mujer me toque allí me pone
nervioso, y si un hombre lo hace, no es un homore".-
Más adelante manifiesta que al ser poseído tiene
erección y orgasmo, pero no todas las veces. Por otra
parte dice tener prepucio infantil.
En los meses anteriores al delito estaba viviendo
en ejército de Salvación donde lo ocupaban en clasifi-
car papeles.-

FIG. 2. The transcript of the interview that contains the expression "I am
a serious 'marica'" (in Spanish, "Yo soy una 'marica' seria"). "Antecedentes
individuales." Instituto de Clasificación, file 2531. Museo Penitenciario Argentino
Antonio Ballvé. Buenos Aires, Argentina.

sex, she admitted that once she aged, she may be willing to pay for sex. After the interview, the criminologist wrote a very negative report on Lita, so she had to serve her full sentence of three years for theft. In fact, the last traces of her in the file refer to her behavior while in prison between 1939 and 1941, including one sanction for hiding a love letter and another one for possessing soap (which prison officers assumed she had obtained as a present from another prisoner, "given [her] condition of passive pederast").[121]

While criminologists saw maricas as a danger because of their sexual femininity, prisoners who challenged the notion that masculinity demanded strict gender complementarity between active and passive participants in same-sex acts were also classified as major dangers. The label *puto garrote* was applied to those men. It was a derivative of puto (literally meaning "male whore"), which had been used as an insult for sexually nonconforming people in the Hispanic world since the early modern period.[122] Puto captured how public shaming, money, and violence mediated relationships of power between masculine and feminine males that also entailed erotic pleasure and intimacy. Masculine men continuously voiced their contempt for feminine putos and physically harassed them.[123] Yet those men were willing to have sex with putos if they could obtain sexual satisfaction or an economic reward from it.[124] The use of grammar in criminological reports suggests that *putos garrote* were considered dangerous because they expressed their sexual agency by being both "submissive" and "dominant." A 1946 report describes an inmate as follows: "[A] homosexual who acts as either a passive or an active pederast. He masturbates [other men] and gets himself masturbated. He intends to practice the 'per anum' coitus and he fancies other men practicing it with him. He gets his virile member [penis] sucked and he sucks other men's, etc. In other words, he is a 'puto garrote' according to the jargon of the criminal underworld."[125] In this excerpt, the person on whom sexual acts are performed is the active subject of the verb (i.e., getting himself penetrated), implying that the direct agent of those acts is merely instrumental to the desires of the recipient. This language appears repeatedly in official reports and depositions to transfer liability to the "passive" participant in homosexual relationships, subjected to a harsher stigma because of his double gender reversal.

Minor Sexual Dangers

Argentine criminologists held that homosexual practices were contingent on exogenous factors—upbringing, sexual initiation, and available sexual outlets. Therefore, they positively evaluated parole requests from prisoners who emphasized exogenous factors in the intertwined development of their (homo)sexuality and criminality and their intentions to rehabilitate themselves. For instance, in 1945, Arturo, a corporal in his early twenties sentenced for having sex with younger conscripts (all of them older than eighteen), was able to persuade a criminologist of his rehabilitation. On the one hand, Arturo's statement provocatively suggested that all males may experience the temptation of finding pleasure by being anally penetrated. On the other hand, he claimed that males ought to resist that temptation by performing masculinity. The criminologist traced Arturo's sexual crime to his upbringing and to external, noxious influences. He recorded Arturo's mother's habit of spoiling him as an "indirect criminal-genetic factor."[126] In addition, a neighbor had repeatedly penetrated Arturo since he was twelve. According to Arturo, at first his neighbor had persuaded him to have sex in this way by promising that they would switch roles afterward, but after a while Arturo lost any interest in switching, having found that being penetrated was quite pleasurable. Continuing this thread, Arturo told the examiner that, while being in the military, he occasionally went to brothels and had sex with women. However, when military life eventually made it impossible for him to have sex with women, he decided to shave himself and use makeup, adopting a feminine appearance to seduce other male soldiers and have sex with them.[127] In other words, Arturo argued that he had performed femininity and pursued male sexual partners because of a circumstantial lack of sexual outlets, implying that in civilian life he might have acted differently.

Arturo crafted a personal narrative that negotiated the meaning

of gender transgression and normativity to persuade criminologists of his rehabilitation. In this line, he stated his liking of soccer (the quintessential masculine sport in Argentina) and disdain
for the "gatherings of active and passive pederasts, their dances,
fictional weddings, and baptisms."[128] Thus, he disavowed the marica subculture that parodied Catholic rites of passage to celebrate
participants' belonging and their sexual and emotional bonds.
This narrative persuaded the criminologist in charge of examining
Arturo, who concluded that there were reassuring signs that Arturo
would be able to reorient his libido. The final report established
that while Arturo's "pederasty" had been a "dissolution factor" in
the army, as a civilian he would not be a danger to society, since
his time in prison had apparently served to mend his behavior.[129]

Similarly, Carlos, a twenty-year-old man convicted of theft,
described in 1951 his sexual imagination as an index of his overall
rehabilitation. He claimed that he was fighting to change his sexual orientation by having fantasies with women, adding that he
was willing to pursue conversion therapy after his release. He also
voiced his disgust at the criminal underworld of "sexual inverts"
into which he had been introduced. Since criminologists saw homosexuality and crime as two intertwined phenomena, the convict's
deposition persuaded them that he was no longer a danger to
society, and they supported his probation request.[130] Criminologists' pervasive belief in the key role of exogenous factors in shaping convicts' criminality and libido led them to favorably evaluate
probation requests that endorsed the rehabilitative aims of prison
sentences and the view of homosexuality as a "criminal-genetic"
factor. In this case, criminologists recorded that Carlos showed
biological homosexual predispositions but considered that these
predispositions were secondary in comparison with exogenous factors. Carlos's parents declared that their son, intelligent and good-
hearted as he was, suffered from a sexual "abnormality." Since he
was an adolescent, they had consulted with medical doctors, who
diagnosed him as suffering from a "physiological deficiency."[131] A
criminologist incorporated this diagnosis into Carlos's psychological exam, tracing his homosexuality both to genetic traits and to

excessive care by his mother. He also argued that exogenous factors played a decisive role in the development of both Carlos's criminal personality and his homosexuality. He posited that Carlos had become a criminal in the same way that he could have become a "couturier" (the choice of this particular profession was not accidental), since his "malleable and docile" personality rendered him vulnerable to domineering individuals. For the criminologist, the shocking side of this was that the person who had dominated Carlos to the point of getting him involved in criminal activities was not an "active homosexual" but a marica.[132] Criminologists assumed that maricas had a feminine psyche and could only be submissive. In this sense, they did not depart much from the sexual culture of machos and maricas that in other instances they analyzed as a symptom of the working class's pathological disdain for sexual norms. However, they still used psychoanalytic concepts to keep a scientific pretense of disavowing "popular" views.

Psychoanalysis and Sexual Abuse

By the early 1950s, criminologists had fully incorporated psychoanalysis to articulate their impressionistic evaluations of prisoners' gender performance, reporting on macho aggressiveness as an index of a heterosexual libido and likely rehabilitation. For instance, a criminologist noted that a prisoner convicted for abusing a male minor exhibited "the combative position that defines the macho." Psychoanalytic theory posited that homosexual individuals were unable to develop their heterosexual libido by resolving their Oedipal complex, their infantile attachment to their mothers. Hence the criminologist admitted that he felt "disappointed" when he found out that this prisoner was not particularly fixated on his mother. Instead, he was attracted to women with whom he had regular sexual intercourse. Therefore, the criminologist concluded that the prisoner was unlikely to relapse, weighing his crime against his masculine demeanor and taking the latter as an index of a heterosexual libido.[133] The prisoner's performance of a legible masculinity by exhibiting macho aggressiveness thus played a decisive role in the resolution of his parole request.[134]

Since masculinity was equated with sexual aggressiveness, judicial authorities considered that sexual abuse compromised the male victim's reputation. In this way, authorities participated in a sexual culture that legitimated a man's use of violence to defend his reputation against the taint of homosexuality. The criminological file of a man convicted of murder includes his 1963 sentence. He had confessed to killing a man who had raped him and then blackmailed him, requesting money to keep the rape a secret. Initially sentenced to fifteen years in prison, the appeal court reduced the time to ten, considering the murder a desperate answer by a "pederast" to protect his "honor" and family life from an "amoral" man.[135] By labeling the victim of rape a "pederast" and the perpetrator as "amoral," the ruling implied that the victim's sexuality was deviant while the perpetrator lacked moral scruples. A psychiatrist working at the Classification Institute concluded that the prisoner had murdered the rapist as an occasional, primitive reaction.[136] This implied that the murder manifested the prisoner's self-preservation instincts. Hence the criminologists recommended his release.[137] The judges and the psychiatrist apparently upheld that the rape of the prisoner had evidenced his homosexuality, to which he reacted instinctively by killing his rapist to restore his "honor." In other words, they only expressed sympathy toward the prisoner because they considered that his "masculine" drive (the murder itself) had redeemed him of his homosexuality.

The sexual culture that equated masculinity with the drive to penetrate led experts to pathologize male victims of abuse. In 1963, an eighteen-year-old man who had been raped in prison acknowledged during his interview at the Classification Institute that his first heterosexual relationship had repulsed him.[138] Criminologists proceeded then to pathologize the prisoner based on those facts: the final report established, within a psychoanalytical logic, that he was stuck in an anal-sadistic phase.[139] According to a psychologist, one of the tests had revealed the prisoner's "covert homosexual tendencies," sadomasochistic elements, and a conflict between his Id and Superego.[140] Combined, these elements suggest that the examiners had inferred that the prisoner was sadistically but unconsciously attracted to other men from the fact that he had been raped, implicitly blaming him for his sexual victimization. Still, the prisoner feeling conflicted about his sexuality played in his favor, since for many criminologists that was a reassuring sign of potential adjustment. His parole request was approved on the recommendation that he seek psychotherapy—a costly course of action that he could pursue thanks to the support of his well-off family.[141] In this as well as in previous cases, criminologists' common ground for negotiating meaning with many prisoners was a sexual culture that established men's self-worth based on their willingness to master other men.

Conclusion

The construction of the "homosexual" as a pathological type is a well-documented historical process for both Argentina and Spain. Social danger theory was from the 1930s the predominant framework for criminologists in Argentina and Spain to conceptualize homosexuality, while the assumed commensurability of masculinity was the unrecognized common ground that enhanced the circulation of positivism across the Atlantic. However, while the elaboration and publication of medical theories have been widely studied, this chapter foregrounds the everyday texture of forensic praxis, including coerced statements, misogynistic prejudices, and the crude empiricism through which medical theories materialized as violence in judicialized contexts. There was a feedback loop between the elaboration of scientific theories and the application of repressive measures, since the data produced and collected because of the trials was used to elaborate the "prototype" of the dangerous subject. The production of scientific knowledge thus reflects the historical context and authorship or agency of specific groups—positioned according to a series of material and cultural coordinates—and overlaps with political discourses on citizenship and morality. As Jennifer Terry points out, since homosexuality became a concept of scientific interest in the nineteenth century, medical doctors used it to set the limits of appropriate identities, body gestures, and social relationships.[142]

In addition to these, Argentine and Spanish forensic doctors and criminologists aimed to regulate feelings (the expectation that homosexuality, pain, and shame must go hand in hand), notions about gender hierarchies in relationships between males (active/passive), and the (in)visibility of alternative sex-affective models in the public space. Another significant particularity of forensic interventions in these countries has to do with the definition of dangerousness according to notions of proper behavior and visibility that punished maricas' sexual agency and femininity. By graduating the dangerousness of subjects according to their gender and eroticism, the state apparatus in Argentina and Spain assumed a moralistic criterion and regulated the boundaries between the private and the public to normalize queer bodies according to ideals of discretion and self-punishment. The next chapter looks at how homosexual men themselves, and *entendidos* in particular, dealt with similar issues of privacy, discretion, and self-control.

TWO

The Tacky and the Sublime

Transatlantic Entendido and Marica Cultures

In 1943, the Spanish singer Miguel de Molina was arrested in Buenos Aires. He was charged with organizing "immoral" parties, but the authorities' real concern was that his shows had become a beacon for the city's homosexuals. According to Molina, a powerful Spanish fascist official bent on destroying him from the foreign affairs bureau played a major role in this arrest.[1] The Molina affair—along with the 1942 "scandal of the cadets," the exposure of private orgies involving recruits and well-off men—led to unprecedented public debates on same-sex desires in Argentina. Philosopher Juan José Sebreli recounts that when he was a child, "the episode was commented on throughout the country, to the point that for the first time, every social sector publicly discussed the phenomenon of homosexuality."[2] Similarly, literary scholar Sylvia Molloy argues that this episode led to the "unexpected outing" of Buenos Aires's "hitherto silenced [homosexual] subculture." Molloy contributes her own childhood memories of 1940s Buenos Aires, where "Spanish dancing, castanets, and things *flamenco* had entered, once and for all, the realm of the *tacky* [italics added]."[3] Argentine elites, in their endless pursuit of cosmopolitan sophistication, rejected any association with flamenco culture, which was all-present in the capital's dancing academies and Mardi Gras festivals and in drag shows throughout Latin America. By the same token, I recall how a historian of Franco's Spain reacted with surprise when I shared with him that I was planning to study Molina's trajectory, since he had always thought of Molina as a "tasteless" folkloric figure. In this chapter, I argue that dismissing certain expressions of sexual and gender nonconformity as "tasteless" contributes to the erasure of maricas' experiences.[4] The following pages investigate these experiences by incorporating judicial transcripts, personal correspondence, literary and oral sources, and folk music and films. The logic of this eclectic combination is not to obscure the differences between fiction and nonfiction but rather to analyze their mutually productive relations through a transatlantic lens. In other words, by putting judicial depositions and novels (among others) into conversation, I explore how shifting cultural ideals and lived experiences informed each other.

This chapter traces—in concentric circles across the Atlantic—the tensions and mutual influences between entendidos' and maricas' ways of expressing themselves. *Entendido* was a label for homosexual men who were acquainted with cultural codes that allowed them to recognize one another. As Jorge Luís Peralta has studied, these codes included references to classical antiquity and the European homophile canon.[5] Entendidos moved in an urban cartography of cross-class sexual encounters by using their economic and cultural capital to seduce other men in a way that inadvertently contributed to the circulation of homophile ideologies. At the same time, entendidos were invested in embodying a modern and respectable identity to counteract authorities' representation of homosexual desires as intrinsically depraved. They disavowed maricas' cultural practices, which they saw as lowbrow and old-fashioned. Entendidos' diatribes against maricas' scandalous femininity do not undermine the latter's agency in the least. If anything, this antagonism is a testament to the hegemony of the marica mode of expressing gender nonconformity among the working class, which will continue informing debates on the possibility of politicizing sexuality in the following decades (as later chapters discuss).

This story begins in the early 1950s with Argentine fans expressing their fascination with the blouses of Molina, who distanced himself from early-twentieth-century drag shows while incorporating their aesthetics in ways that rendered him feminized and "tacky" in the eyes of some observers. The experiences of individuals like those writing passionate letters to Molina informed authors including Juan Gil-Albert and Pedro Badanelli, as they later discussed and disowned the logics of sublimation. The "apologetic" thinking of these authors was disavowed by Renato Pellegrini when he published his novel *Asfalto* (1964). Pellegrini also disparagingly portrayed Buenos Aires's marica/puto subculture, while literary author Carlos Correas called himself a puto and narrated the anonymous sexual encounters that were the core of that subculture. Cross-class relationships between entendidos and working-class "masculine" men subverted the expectation that the latter were not to emotionally engage with and show themselves vulnerable to other men. Entendidos occasionally shared with their working-class lovers the erudite genealogy of homoeroticism, describing creative geniuses like Michelangelo and Shakespeare and the heroes and emperors of classical antiquity as their ancestors. These figures' mythical status provided inspiration for lettered homosexual males before the sexual liberation era but also heightened their disdainful views on maricas who were promiscuous and scandalous. This chapter concludes in a circular way with an examination of Argentine actor and choreographer Alfredo Alaria, who had been a dancer in Molina's company, performing masculinity and modeling himself after James Dean's iconic characters in the 1960s. As young men, such as Catalonian author Terenci Moix, cultivated a cinephile homoeroticism inspired by explicit depictions of athletic male bodies in Hollywood films, they disavowed their entendido predecessors (including Moix's godfather) on the grounds that they had not been able to appreciate the sublime in the tacky.

In this chapter, desire and identification appear not as mutually incompatible—as per Freud, Lacan, and Kristeva—but rather as enhancing each other through what Diana Fuss calls the "homospectatorial look." The "spectatorial subjectivity" that this chapter historicizes inhabits an "ambiguous space where desire and identification appear less opposed than coterminous, where the desire to be the other (identification) draws its very sustenance from the desire to have the other."[6] The coding of homoeroticism in the cinematic performances of figures such as Miguel de Molina and Alfredo

Alaria relied on a delicate balance between their apparent adoption of a heterosexual persona and their use of corporal and fashion signs to invite their fans to both identify with and desire them. These fans fetishized the autographed photographs of Molina and Alaria—photographs that became a form of possession, of physical contact with these performers. At the same time, as the letters written by Molina's fans demonstrate, the desire to possess him through his photographs and blouses was compatible with a desire to impersonate him. Similarly, identification with Alaria only enhanced his fans' desire to possess him through autographed photographs in which he posed exhibiting his muscles and James Dean masculinity. This athletic masculinity was aimed at departing from Molina's androgynous blouses—in much the same way as Molina had earlier aimed at distinguishing his art from drag shows. In other words, the masculine homosexual subject "secures [his] identity by at once disavowing and perpetually calling attention to its abject, interiorized, and ghostly other," the maricas or putos who retain their agency.[7]

Molina

After his first experiences in and expulsion from Argentina, Molina returned in the 1950s under Eva Perón's protection. In this decade, as he became a music and movie star, he received numerous homoerotic letters from his Argentine fans, who among their adulations, shared with him their awe for and fascination with his blouses. These blouses were experienced by fans of all ages as expressions of a yet-to-be-conscious sexual freedom. For instance, Dante Bertini, an Argentine born in 1945 who became a gay activist in the 1970s, remembers, "When I was a kid, I used to see [Molina] in vaudeville shows and on television. He brazenly exhibited the blouses that he claimed with pride to have designed and sewed himself. Being a kid as brave as I was shy, I asked myself how he could be so bold. We were not even aware that he was showing us the real meaning of the word 'freedom' without making an explicit statement, uttering insults, or using protest signs."[8]

Molina himself was aware of the genealogy of this gesture in the drag shows and nightlife of 1930s Madrid (before the Franco era), where flamenco-inspired folk music entered the world of cabarets and music halls. Molina was born in 1908 in Málaga (Spain) into a family of modest means. As an adolescent, he fled from his family to make a living in night shows where aristocratic and popular audiences enjoyed folk music performances. According to Molina, in the 1930s most folk male singers impersonated female stars, but he wanted to demonstrate that it was possible to sing "cuplés" without impersonating a woman. Molina's self-fashioning through extravagant blouses was an ambivalent gesture that both disavowed and nostalgically incorporated drag. While hitherto Molina had been known by a female artistic name (La Miguela), in the 1930s he adopted a male artistic persona while coding femininity through his ornate garments. According to his autobiography, "That is how the blouse was born. It was quite daring and *petardo* [camp] for that era full of prejudices. I made it of Nile-green georgette silk and added some large dark-green velvet circular patches with rhinestones. The sleeves were very wide; I remember almost six feet wide each. Therefore, when I moved them by widely unfolding my arms, they achieved a great theatrical effect. My purpose was not to be dressed as a woman, but [to dress] with a little bit of a feminine air."[9]

Because of Molina's inspiring campiness, the Argentine police targeted his fans. Malva, a marica who was born in Chile and migrated to Buenos Aires in 1943, recalls one night when the police arrested anyone in the audience of Molina's show in the Smart Theater who "had the appearance or smell of a *puto*."[10] Despite police harassment, Molina's fans attended his shows with veneration. The letters they addressed to Molina conveyed as much through silence, omissions, and double or implicit meanings as they did through open acts of naming.[11] The writers resorted to the same ambivalent tone and opacity that characterized Molina's life.[12] Quite uncannily, Molina papers at the Spanish National Library encompass both his correspondence with fans and what seem to be homoerotic drawings and images for Molina's personal use. These are images of men with hyperelongated phalluses that they wrap

around their bodies.[13] In his films, Molina projected a heterosexual persona, while his blouses and personal life allowed maricas
to read him as an idol. Fans' letters often demonstrated an interest
in nationalizing Molina's figure by letting him know that he had
become Argentine by virtue of his prolonged stay in the country.[14]
Molina's fans petitioned him for his worn-out blouses and for the
designs and patterns of those blouses. Men's most common goal
was to wear them as they trained to become Spanish folk performers.[15] Molina's fans appealed to his charity and used his clothing
to frame gender ambiguity in the context of either carnivalesque
cross-dressing or Spanish folk culture.

Most importantly, Molina became an object of desire for many
of his Argentine fans. These men's letters were not salacious. They
relied on a language of double entendre and implicit meanings
instead of openly naming forbidden desires. Sometimes two men
would write and sign their letters to Molina together, and a few of
them even shared an address, implying that they may have formed
a couple.[16] Fans expressed their physical craving for Molina in
terms of anxious desire. One such fan confessed to Molina that
he would anxiously wait for a "divine autographed photograph"
of him, another one asked for a full-body photograph, and others went even further by asking Molina to meet them in person.[17]

The writers of these letters came close to stating homoerotic
feelings through hyperbolic expressions of their fervor and aesthetic fascination, but they never explicitly named their sexuality. One fan related to Molina how he applauded "until my hands
burned like your songs, so suggestive and full of sublime art."[18]
Another one confessed to Molina: "I owe you many moments
full of happiness [because of which] I will never forget you."[19] The
most explicit letters referred to Molina's beauty and to his blouses:
"to request a picture of you to admire not just your artistic qualities but also your personal beauty. Having one of your blouses
would be the aspiration of the moment. I know my request is a little bold."[20] These letters demonstrate fans' unrelenting longing to
establish a connection with Molina. They fetishized photographs of
Molina, stating that these would fulfill their desires. For instance,

a man living in a small village in the interior province of Santa Fe (Argentina) wrote one of the most passionate letters that Molina received: "I admire you from every point of view—as a man, an actor, and a singer. . . . I wish you would send me an autographed photograph. . . . I implore you to satisfy the desire of this faithful admirer."[21] In a later letter, he admitted to Molina: "I adore and praise your voice [and] your virile aspect."[22] These letters expressed a thinly veiled homoeroticism fixated on Molina's manliness. In this line, a fan from Rosario wrote in 1950 about his veneration for Molina, which he expressed in a traditional, family-centered, and Catholic language:

> This letter is to express to you all the appreciation and admiration that I feel for you as an artist and as a man. I will start by stating that God gratified me by giving me the chance to see you performing tonight in the theater "El Círculo." I wanted to thank you for the immensely happy moment my mother and I enjoyed on this unforgettable night, but the theater concierge did not let me. . . . I have to tell you so many things. I am so happy that I don't even know what I am writing, and I am afraid I will tire you with my long letter, but I think you will know how to understand and forgive me. Now Miguel, I want a memento from you beyond the beautiful songs I heard tonight from your sweet and harmonious voice I will never forget: a photograph of you, or otherwise some reply from you to these humble lines where I prove this endearment that I feel for you. Believe me, I swear on my mother, whom I love the most in this world, these lines are full-heartedly the sincerest. . . . Affectionate and tender regards from another mesmerized admirer who from this unforgettable night joins your uncountable list of admirers.[23]

This fan's confession of his feelings stemming from the unforgettable moments that he had enjoyed during Molina's performance played with the conventions of romantic courtship. José E. Muñoz suggests that "campy fascination" with celebrity is "akin to [Ernst Bloch's] sense of astonishment" insofar as "glamour and astonishment [offer] a kind of transport or a reprieve from what Bloch called the 'darkness of the lived instant.' Astonishment helps one surpass the limitations of an alienating present-ness and allows one to see a different time and place."[24] Molina's aesthetics astonished his fans by transporting them into a different time and place—a challenge to contemporary gender norms that was expressed in a Catholic language. In the same vein, a different fan wrote to Molina in 1951, "Something very important and urgent moves me to write these lines to you, which I pray to God will be answered. . . . I beg you in the name of my mother and God, the two beings whom I love the most, that you grant me an interview of a few minutes, and I will eternally thank you."[25] Molina's ambiguous sentimentality, his flamboyant blouses, and the open secrets about his sexuality elicited expressions of affection from Argentine fans that displayed a traditional cultural schema based on sublimating homoerotic desires into Catholic religiosity. Contemporaneously, this same schema became the object of attention for two authors who had migrated from Spain to Argentina.

Theorizing Sublimation

Juan Gil-Albert and Pedro Badanelli presented homosexual men as able to establish meaningful bonds based on self- and mutual respect. They also discussed the productive tensions between Catholic-inspired sublimation and the model of "virile" love that they proposed. Gil-Albert's 1955 essay *Heraclés* could have become part of the homosexual literary canon in Spanish. However, the author did not dare to submit it for revision by the Francoist censors, so the book was only published after Franco's death in 1975. Gil-Albert came from a bourgeois family of València and sympathized with the left. At the end of the Spanish Civil War, he decided to leave Spain for Mexico, where he fell in love with Guillermo, "a handsome waiter of indefinite sexuality." He left Mexico for Buenos Aires in 1944 feeling frustrated by Guillermo's apparent lack of interest in him; but then while in Argentina he received a letter from Guillermo, who confessed his love for Gil-Albert prompting his return to Mexico.[26] In his letters, Guillermo conveyed to Gil-Albert that he had enough "sensibility" to appreciate and honor how extraordinary their "friendship" was.[27] In one of them, he related to Gil-Albert his attendance of a theater play by "our special friend Oscar [Wilde]." At the same time, Guillermo remained attached to popular Catholicism, bidding farewell by figuratively praying to the Virgin of Guadalupe for the well-being of Gil-Albert and his loved ones.[28] The side-by-side allusions to Oscar Wilde and the Virgin of Guadalupe illustrate the singular hybridization between different layers of meaning that allowed these individuals to articulate their experiences.

In the same vein, *Heraclés* captures the ethos of homosexual men whose thinking was infused with the concepts and concerns of Catholic spirituality. Gil-Albert advocated for a "virile love" found in classical antiquity and Walt Whitman's poems.[29] He proposed the term *homo-anímico* (homo-disposed) to redeem homoeroticism of the stigma of depravity. He argued that, while depravity (*vicio*) was rooted in habit, inborn homosexuality was a way of being a man compatible with "correctness, decency, and even chastity."[30] According to Gil-Albert, most Catholic priests exhibited a "refined understanding [of] or, in any case, a dismayed benevolence" for this inborn sin.[31] The author was at once critical of and sympathetic to religious sublimation, which offered commiseration in exchange for not being "belligerent" about homosexuality.[32] Without embracing this cultural schema, Gil-Albert pointed out that homosexual men were able to build a religiosity of their own to deal with their internal conflicts. In his interest in homosexual ethics, Gil-Albert inverted the dominant logic that imbued homosexuality with the negative connotations of pathology, reclaiming instead the ethics of pathology: the potential of the abnormal to illuminate the human condition.[33] In his own words, "Pathology creates ethics."[34] Pathology as a deviation from normalcy encompasses, in Gil-Albert's view, inborn homosexuality and ethics as expressions of extraordinary human capacities for empathy.

The tensions between homosexual ethics and Catholic dogma were also a driving concern for the Spanish-born priest Pedro Badanelli (1899–1985). In 1929, Badanelli had published the novel *Serenata del amor triunfante* (Serenade of triumphant love) about

FIG. 3. A portrait of Juan Gil-Albert in Rio de Janeiro (Brazil) in 1944. Unknown photographer. Biblioteca Valenciana Nicolau Primitiu. Fondo Juan Gil-Albert. Reproduced with permission by the copyright holders of the Gil-Albert Collections.

a sister and a brother who fall for the same man. The publication of *Serenata* provoked a significant scandal that moved Badanelli to leave Spain for Argentina, where he was appointed parish priest of Suardi, a remote village in the Argentine province of Santa Fe.[35] In 1959, Badanelli published in Buenos Aires his book *El derecho penal en la Biblia* (Penal law in the Bible), criticizing the Catholic Church's stance on homosexuality. Similar to Gil-Albert, Badanelli's arguments were infused with the Catholic belief that the spirit elevates the flesh. Homosexuality for Badanelli is not defined by practices but by a "double intercommunication, in body and soul," between same-sex individuals.[36] Through an analysis of Thomas Mann's *Death in Venice*, he argues that homosexual men can be chaste and pure—rejoicing in the contemplation of classical male beauty, longing to admire and protect it—and that this "platonic" passion is actually the most fulfilling.[37] The logic and gratifications of sublimation were a central theme for Badanelli and Gil-Albert, while both suggested that religious sublimation was likely to cede to a physical but spiritualized "virile" love. The eroticism of masculinity, in their view, purified lust insofar as male bonding highlighted the sublime aesthetics and ethics that men shared by virtue of their sex.[38] Ultimately, both authors were trying to reinscribe homoeroticism as a sign of civilization in a way that reinforced the exclusion of people whom they deemed not masculine or respectable enough to belong in this elitist cultural schema. However, at the same time, most entendidos participated in cross-class urban subcultures that facilitated the circulation of the genealogies of "virile" love and creative genius that inspired Badanelli and Gil-Albert.

Entendidos and Their Lovers

Cross-class homosexual subcultures brought together men with different economic and educational backgrounds who shared ideas about romanticism, Catholic spirituality, and the erudite genealogy of homoeroticism. State authorities policed these relationships to trace the "dangerous" circulation of apologetic views on homoeroticism. For instance, in 1955 a group of men were arrested in Bilbao (Northern Spain's major industrial hub), accused of throwing immoral parties. Among the attendees were two wealthy brothers, one of them married to a woman. The single brother had discussed renowned homosexual figures (*personalidades*) during one of their parties to make the argument that homosexual people were completely normal and should be treated as such. This incident was related by other attendees, including a working-class man who shared with the police how this discussion upset his religious sensibilities. This defendant was probably performing naïveté to exculpate himself, since he had accepted a silver lighter from one of the siblings. However, the authorities were particularly concerned about the fact that these cross-class private events had become an opportunity for a debate on the genealogy of homosexuality. When they interrogated the suspected instigator, he claimed that he merely had fostered an "intellectual" conversation on Spanish literature. This statement suggests that he had read some of the homophile classics and then used their ideas to seduce working-class men. Apart from exhibiting his erudition, he and his brother had been willing to give "presents" to the men who caught their interest, including accompanying them on trips to Cairo and Paris. The choice of these cities proved their sophistication and economic prowess but also suggests an emotional attachment to times and places where homoerotic cultural expressions had thrived (from ancient Egypt to the Paris of *Les poètes maudits*). In fact, the brothers enjoyed the company of artistic individuals, including a dancer and a rhapsodist. At their parties, they served alcohol and played records so that men would dance together. Another attendee, a Cuban citizen, admitted that homosexuality did not scandalize him because he was used to the "moral climate" of his homeland, where according to him it went unnoticed. However, he condemned the siblings' ostentation of their "immorality" and wealth to seduce young men. Similarly, a neighbor stated that she screamed out "of terror" when she woke up in the middle of the night and saw through her window a group of young men, all nude, in the home of one of the siblings.[39]

These witnesses stressed their outraged and terrified reactions to the public display of homosexual subcultures to situate themselves on the side of the authorities. The brothers, on the other hand, acknowledged their homosexuality but blamed their acts on being intoxicated. The penalties for the married sibling (the one whose file is available) were quite mild. Given his marital and economic status, he was released from prison after only two months, the time he had served while awaiting his sentence.[40] Although he was forced to move from Bilbao to a different town where he would be surveilled, the report from the probation officer described him as a "great stockholder," indicating that his privileged status mattered a great deal to the authorities.[41] Status differentials also mediated the relations between participants in these subcultures as privileged men capitalized on them to seduce other men. However, these power-mediated erotic liaisons also led to an exchange of ideas, which became concerning for state authorities as it spread positive views on homosexuality based on its distinguished genealogy.

For this and other reasons, in 1959 Argentine authorities seized copies of an edition of a student-published literary magazine that included Carlos Correas's short story "La narración de la historia" (The narration of history) about cross-class sexual encounters between men in public spaces of Buenos Aires. Although Correas was charged with obscenity and the magazine *Centro* did not publish any subsequent issue, it is worth noting that these were a posteriori measures.[42] In other words, authors in Argentina did not have to submit their works to be revised by censors prior to publication as their counterparts in Spain had to do at that time, which gave the former a relative freedom in comparison to the latter. The story by Correas vindicated abjection, breaking with bourgeois morality to embrace cross-class homosexual sociability in anonymous sexual encounters. The narrator of the story is a twenty-something educated man who meets a dark-skinned "lumpen" adolescent (*morochito*) in the Constitution train station, the major hub for the working-class suburbs. They stare at each other until the narrator asks the adolescent to light his cigarette, a common and safe strategy of approach that leads to a casual conversation about their lives. Amid this conversation, the adolescent clarifies that "in sexual relations he is the macho and nothing else," pointing to his sense of masculinity being rooted in the gendered passive/active binary.[43] The narrator confirms that he understands this code by replying that he had already inferred that from the adolescent's "penetrating" look, which "inverts" don't have.[44] In Correas's literary portrayal of this encounter, status differentials produce the mutual attraction between the characters. They participate in a kind of economy of eroticism by which they perform cultural refinement and rugged manliness to entice each other. The narrator fetishizes the adolescent's lumpen masculinity—violent and naïve at the same time—and the latter the narrator's culture, which he exhibits by teaching him some English words and about the myths of classical antiquity.[45]

Thus, the cross-class circulation of the canon of illustrious homosexual figures appears once again as the entendidos' strategy of enticement—a coded knowledge that eroticizes its possessor as well as his relations with other men by tracing them to a genealogy of great men. Correas implies the effectiveness of this strategy, as the characters eventually arrive at a vacant lot by the highway where they caress, kiss, and hug each other and then masturbate until ejaculation.[46] The abjection of the story partially stems from this blend between highbrow culture and lowbrow sexual spaces, between the myths of Roman emperors and rushed orgasms in the shadows. This story centers on how sex and affection between men upset the gendered roles and status differentials that mediate their relations, but at the end, it becomes an impossible story, as those mediating factors impede the full realization of the hinted potential of erotic liaisons. The process of mutual exploration between the characters does not end well. The narrator fears that he may be assaulted and is uncertain about whether the adolescent expects economic compensation. However, the latter eventually admits that he loves the narrator and proposes they "share their lives."[47] Yet the narrator does not show up to their last date. Instead, he opts for a relationship with a middle-class male dancer who works at the Colón theater. This option partakes of the emerging entendidos' ideal of long-term partnerships between men who

are "equal" or like each other in terms of their socioeconomic status and educational background.

As scholar Carlos Surghi has noted, translating Genet's 1949
Journal du voleur (*The Thief's Journal*) deeply impacted Correas.
He came to understand the role of homosexuality in his subjectivity as driving him toward abjection by approaching the "underclass" of Buenos Aires. He broke with his privileged social milieu by
labeling himself a puto who was attracted to lumpen, masculine-
looking *chongos*.[48] Correas's experiences and ideas reflect sexual
subcultures based on the mutual fetishization between men who
were differentiated from one another by gender role and status.[49]
However, in the 1960s entendidos' ideals would shift toward a
model of virile love between equals, which relegated gender-coded
"inverts" to the margins.

Peyrefitte's Readers

The trajectory of French author Roger Peyrefitte's works illumi-
nates how the ideal of love between equals came to be hegemonic
among entendidos in the 1960s. It also points out the state policies and social dynamics shaping the circulation of the homophile
canon in Argentina and Spain. The first Spanish-language edition
of *Les amitiés particulières*, a novel about an intimate relationship
between two male students at a Catholic boarding school, was
published in Buenos Aires in 1956 by the editorial house Tirso,
led by Abelardo Arias and Renato Pellegrini and thoroughly
studied by Jorge Luís Peralta. The government of Buenos Aires
sequestered the book for six months, but this measure did nothing but increase public interest in it. Tirso published two print
runs totaling more than six thousand copies and later a paperback edition. Between 1956 and 1967, they would continue publishing books centered on homoeroticism or written by renowned
homophile authors, such as Roger Peyrefitte, Henry de Monther-
lant, and Julien Green. These authors had explored the relationship between the erotic and the platonic while keeping a strategic
silence about sex. Peralta has noted that these three authors shared
their ties with the French homophile movement and a Catholic

upbringing that led them to reflect on the tension between purity and sensuality as a common experience for homosexual men in coming to terms with their desires. Their works followed certain codes of discretion, elegance, and educated sensibility and did not include explicit sex. Instead, Tirso targeted entendidos through their aesthetic codes, which included the male beauty ideals of the Greco-Roman classical antiquity.[50]

In contrast, Spanish authorities harshly censored Peyrefitte's novels. *Les amitiés particulières* was forbidden in Franco's Spain. (It was not published in Spain until 1978, three years after the dictator's death.) However, in 1963 the publisher A.H.R. had submitted all of Peyrefitte's works to be "revised" by censors at the Spanish Ministry of Information and Tourism. "Readers" (censors) 8, 26, 27, 29, and 31 reported on this submission, all agreeing that Peyrefitte was an excellent writer, cultured, well-traveled, and familiar with the aristocratic and diplomatic circles that he described in his novels. Some of his works were authorized for publication considering that their content was inoffensive, and others were authorized on the condition that negative depictions of the Catholic Church were erased. However, most of Peyrefitte's novels, including *Les amitiés particulières*, were censored because they portrayed homosexual characters.[51]

Censors used tropes of putrefaction to dismiss Peyrefitte's subtlety and sentimentality and convey their visceral disgust for homosexuality. In their view, homosexuality showed the degeneration of the body, never the transcendence of the soul. One censor wrote about *L'exile de Capri* that it had a "marked sensual and immoral character, showing a *putrefied* milieu of homosexuality, which is presented, to be true, not in a pornographic crude way, but as a lifestyle surrounded by poetry, flowers, a literary ambiance, etc."[52] A different censor used the same metaphor to point out that *Les amours singulières* "smells like sodomy too."[53] The protagonists of Peyrefitte's novels were moral beings who had elevated feelings for each other. In contrast, the Franco regime codified homosexual individuals as "dangers to society" who egotistically pursued sexual gratification against the Catholic values of the nation.[54] This view trickled down to lower-tier censors as their supervisors instructed them to be particularly vigilant regarding the taboo against homosexuality. One of these censors reported about *Les amitiés particulières*, "Since this is such a dangerous matter, which the author apparently intends to excuse and even presents as agreeable . . . I consider, following the instructions that were given to us in this office at some point, that its publication should not be authorized."[55] The homophile strategy of introducing sympathetic views on homosexuality by avoiding "pornography" and presenting homosexual characters guided by noble feelings did not overcome the significant institutional challenges created by Franco's regime.

Nevertheless, Peyrefitte's forbidden novels circulated clandestinely in Franco's Spain. In at least one case, the regime's interest in promoting tourism as a source of national revenue inadvertently created the conditions for the introduction of Peyrefitte's novels from Argentina. Ramón Cadenas, a gay man born in 1945, bought several of Peyrefitte's novels in a bookstore that a couple of French communists owned in the tourist coastal town of Torremolinos. They had smuggled them from Argentina and sold them, taking advantage of the Francoist authorities' off-the-record policy of leniency toward the international tourists living in this town.[56] *Fabrizio Lupo*, a homophile novel by Italian author Carlo Cóccioli, was also smuggled from Argentina to Spain. Cóccioli's life trajectory points out once again the central role of transatlantic exiles in the development of the homophile canon. Carlo Cóccioli was an Italo-Mexican author born in Livorno, Italy, in 1920. In World War II, Cóccioli fought as an antifascist *partigiano* and was subsequently recognized with a silver medal for his heroic actions. After the war, the publication of his novel *Fabrizio Lupo* in France escalated into a scandal that forced him to move to Mexico in 1953.[57] The novel centers on a young Catholic man who struggles with his homosexuality and eventually commits suicide. Emili Boïls i Coniller, a gay man born in 1938, read it when one of his friends ordered it from Argentina in the late 1950s. Emili had struggled with similar issues; he entered a monastery when he was only an adolescent, only to be expelled soon after when he confessed that he

INFORME

¿Ataca al Dogma?   Páginas
¿A la moral?   Páginas
¿A la Iglesia o a sus Ministros?   Páginas
¿Al Régimen y a sus instituciones?   Páginas
¿A las personas que colaboran o han colaborado con el
   Régimen?   Páginas
Los pasajes censurables ¿califican el contenido total
   de la obra?

Informe y otras observaciones:
      Roger Peyrefitte, es sin duda de ningún género un gran
escritor, que llega casi a genial. Su estilo literario es for-
midable, su cultura vasta y de sus obras se desprende su gran
conocimiento del gran mundo de la aristocracia, de la diploma-
cia así como una gran erudicción adquirida no solo por el estudio sino por los viajes. Sin embargo estas grandes cualidades,
no bastan para permitir, aun en edición de lujo, algunas desus
obras, que como "L'exilé de Capri", tienen un marcado carácter
sensual, inmoral, de ambiente putrefacto de homosexualismo, pr
sentado, eso sí, no de una manera grosera o pornográfica, pero
sí como un mm estilo de vida al que se le rodea de poesía, de
flores, ambiente literario, etc. etc. Toda la obra está salpi-
cada por el mismo tema, llena de invertidos, aparte de tner
otros defectos de fondo. DEBE DENEGARSE. En cuanto a las otras
obras sometidas a informe, "Les ambassades" PUEDE AUTORIZARSE
con las tachaduras de las pgs. 301 y 303, y "La fin fin des
ambassades", PUEDE AUTORIZARSE con la tachadura de la pg.280.
Esta última obra,es continuación cronológica de la anterior.
Ambas tienen por fondo el "gran" mundo de la aristocracia, el
escándalode la embajada de Francia en Grecia mic.

Madrid, 30 de Abril de 1963

El Lector

FIG. 4. Censorship report on April 30, 1963. The censor reported on multiple
novels by Roger Peyrefitte. File 1680/1963, initiated on March 26, 1963, box
21/14468. Archivo General de la Administración. Alcalá de Henares, Ministerio
de Cultura y Deporte, Spain.

desired other men.[58] Cóccioli's sympathetic portrayal of the internal turmoil of Catholic gay men appealed to Emili and helped him
understand himself. In his own words, "This heartrending work,
along with Whitman, has been as much or more influential for
me than the Bible. It [helped me] clear up my mind, identify, and
normalize myself."[59] Emili blends *Fabrizio Lupo*, Walt Whitman's
poems, and the Bible into a personally idiosyncratic genealogy
that helped him perceive same-sex desires as spiritually elevated.
This illustrates homophile men's creative responses to the homophobic doctrines spread by the Catholic Church.

The tensions between Catholicism and homoeroticism continued informing the circulation of the homophile canon in Spain
into the late 1960s. At the same time, readers of Peyrefitte were
vocal in affirming their identity. In 1968, a nineteen-year-old student was arrested and charged with homosexuality in Barcelona.
Among his belongings was a copy of *Les amitiés particulières*. The
student eventually admitted that he had had a sexual relationship
with another young man, traveling together to different towns on
the coast, until his lover's family had him committed to a psychiatric hospital the day before the student was arrested.[60] The patient's
parents allegedly hospitalized him because he had attempted to
sedate them by leaving on the gas so that he could rob them while
they slept. He was diagnosed with a psychopathic personality disorder, treated with electrotherapy and antipsychotic medications,
and discharged less than a month after his hospitalization. The hospital file of this young man includes two photographs. In one of
them, he wears only his underwear and lies in bed while he lights a
cigarette. In the other, he poses in formal attire at a party, with two
women holding his arms. On the back of the photograph, someone wrote a date and a dedication in Dutch translated into Spanish, "Regards [kisses in the original Dutch] from a Dutch girl of
the Illetas beach."[61] These photographs capture moments of casual
hedonism and the patient exhibiting his own body to the camera.

Yet the file also indicates the tensions between the patient's sexuality, his religious vocation, and his family's moral views. The hospital staff noted in his personal background that he had become

introverted and uninterested in his studies when he was nine or ten years old, isolating himself from his classmates. Then the priests who taught at his school took an interest in him. He developed a religious vocation and tried to study at several theological colleges. He was expelled from all of them despite his "excellent" intelligence. His family noted that he had never hung out with girls and "paid excessive attention to effeminate aspects and homosexual issues."[62] He lived for a while in a hotel with the student who was arrested carrying Peyrefitte's novel. Maybe they identified with the novel's story of two students at a boarding school who are forced to part ways. Life imitates art. The relationship between the young men in Barcelona ended with one of them being forced by his family into a psychiatric hospital and treated with electroshocks and the other one imprisoned and exiled.

During his trial, the student refused to be classified as an "invert" and reclaimed instead the term "homosexual." Through this self-labeling, the student opposed the notion that same-sex desires stem from a natural androgyny of the soul ("inversion"). The transcript of the student's deposition in front of the Court of First Instance reads, "He is not an *invert*, according to his interpretation of the meaning of this term. Instead, he considers himself and acknowledges to be a *homosexual*."[63] The student's disidentification with inverts was related to his familiarity with Peyrefitte's work. One of Peyrefitte's most prominent readers in Argentina reached the same conclusion. While in Spain the a priori Francoist censorship kept this debate circumscribed to the vagrancy courts, in Argentina literature brought it to the court of public opinion.

Renato Pellegrini, Peyrefitte's publisher in Argentina and a literary author himself, also believed that "inversion" ought to be overcome if "homosexuality" was to be fully realized in relationships between virile men who were equal to each other. Pellegrini pursued this argument by contraposing highbrow masculine sentimentality with lowbrow femininized instinct, implying that the latter was a kind of animalistic atavism to be vanquished. Pelligrini's most well-known novel was titled *Asfalto* (Asphalt), a metonymic reference to metropolitan life, and published by Tirso in

1964. It includes a fictional dialogue in which an experienced man, Ricardo, explains to a younger newcomer to Buenos Aires, Eduardo, why the term "homosexual" should be used to counteract the stigma of the term "invert." Ricardo equates inverts with maricas and putos and describes them as recognizable by their appearance (i.e., gender roles and performance) and lack of respect for ethical boundaries in their constant pursuit of sex. Homosexual men, on the contrary, would act on the "purest feelings" and "natural inclinations."[64] The fact that both Pellegrini in Buenos Aires and the unknown student in Barcelona (both readers of Peyrefitte) saw "inversion" as detrimental to their own cause indicates that respectable masculinity was many entendidos' ideal in the 1960s.

Asfalto was temporarily sequestered because of its "obscenity," and Pellegrini spent three months in prison. However, the Supreme Court ruled that the novel should be allowed.[65] According to Peralta, this marked a generational break from homophile pioneers such as Abelardo Arias and Roger Peyrefitte, who had used a discreet and enigmatic tone in their works.[66] *Asfalto*, on the contrary, explicitly discusses a varied repertoire of sexual practices, from oral sex to urolagnia. It is the coming-of-age story of an adolescent, seventeen-year-old Eduardo, who moves to Buenos Aires and is introduced to the intricacies of the homosexual identity. Before moving to the capital, he has a first homosexual encounter when he and another man masturbate until ejaculation, which leaves Eduardo with an "undefined feeling of impurity."[67] This episode suggests that mere sexual release is "impure," although less so in nonmetropolitan areas than in Buenos Aires, where it is the raison d'être of a widespread subculture. Indeed, in the capital, Eduardo encounters the nocturnal predatory males who wander the public spaces of Buenos Aires looking for sex and who are described in animalistic terms as "a special race of the city. . . . A one-night stand is their nourishment."[68] At this moment, Ricardo comes to Eduardo's rescue. Ricardo is a freethinker who questions the existence of a judging Almighty and feels commiseration for the "spiritual poverty, misery, and abject resources" of normal men.[69] At the same time, he censures individuals driven by their low instincts, such as an old man who performs oral sex on other men in a public bathroom.[70] Pellegrini uses this man's fading condition as a metaphor for the fate of inversion, which in his view is to become an anachronism.

The story's tone is representative of entendidos' cult of virility yet also reflects the role of camp in private sociability. During his exploration of the homosexual underworld, Eduardo meets a cultured bookstore owner who invites him to a party. During this gathering, one of the guests performs Spanish folk music in drag and later recites a poem by Rimbaud, which entices another participant to "sink his face in [the performer's] butt." Spanish folk music and French poetry are incorporated into a gender parody that plays with different registers of cultural sophistication. Later, as two of the attendees discuss whether the party is a gathering of putos, one of them argues that this term "degrades the sanctity of our homosexual condition."[71] This "sanctity" stems in the novel from interpersonal bonds that go beyond the sexual. By the end of the novel, Eduardo meets a young man, Marcelo, whose apartment is decorated with statues of classical divinities. Marcelo is the quintessential entendido. He shares with Eduardo his knowledge about Marcel Proust, James Joyce, and Arthur Rimbaud, as he guides Eduardo into a "more authentic, deeper life." Marcelo explains that "violent and fleeting" physical desire is the opposite of love.[72] Hence Eduardo finally understands that being a homosexual, with this term's connotations of elevated feelings and restricted cultural codes, is different from being a promiscuous puto or invert. In the last scene of the novel, Eduardo kills the old puto who wanders public bathrooms looking for men to pay for or coerce into having sex. This act symbolizes the dialectical relation between homosexuality and inversion, by which Eduardo's self-awareness as a homosexual leads him to kill an archetypal invert. Pellegrini's disparaging portrayal of putos as predatory and guided by low instincts was his way of disavowing Buenos Aires's marica culture. He advocated for the entendidos' ideal of dignified friendship between virile men who were equal to each other, unapologetic, and acquainted with a distinguished genealogy of creative genius.

Police records reflect how the ideal of friendship between virile men translated into entendidos' self-affirming attitude when reproached for their sexuality. In 1965, a conflict at a fine arts school in La Plata (the capital of the Buenos Aires province) between a teacher and the chair of the department (whom I will call Gerardo) escalated into the opening of a police file. The police investigation focused on allegations that Gerardo's teaching techniques mirrored his leftist views and that he was a homosexual. During a departmental meeting, the teacher had treated Gerardo "as a socializing element [a reference to Gerardo's leftism], pried into his sexual problem, and judged his acts as the chair." In response, Gerardo called her a "corridor gossiper."[73] The teacher presented a formal complaint, and the headmaster interrogated Gerardo. During this meeting, Gerardo responded that the teacher should read the Simple Verse XXXIX, a poem by the nineteenth-century Cuban revolutionary leader José Martí (1853–95).[74] This is the poem Gerardo referred to:

> I have a white rose to tend
> In July as in January;
> I give it to the true friend
> Who offers his frank hand to me.
> And to the cruel one whose blows
> Break the heart by which I live,
> Thistle nor thorn do I give:
> For him, too, I have a white rose.[75]

Gerardo might have used this poem to code entendidos' view that true friendship between men (homosexuality) was not shameful but a source of self-affirmation to confront homophobia, coded as "cruelty." Gerardo stated that he felt fortunate to belong to another "sector" that was well equipped to navigate many issues. This might have been his way of holding that true male bonding within a restricted group defined by its enlightenment allowed entendidos to rise above a hostile environment. While Gerardo seemingly imbued Martí's white rose with homoerotic symbolism, Martí, according to Sylvia Molloy, had "busied himself with the task of heterosexualizing Whitman."[76] Martí tried to erase homoeroticism from the work of the renowned U.S. poet, whom he admired profoundly. Yet since the late nineteenth century, Whitman's poems inspired authors such as the Spanish poet Federico García Lorca in their interest in dignifying homoeroticism. Lorca's "Ode to Walt Whitman" is embedded with moral hierarchies that distinguish the noble macho Whitman from animalistic maricas.[77] The continuities with Gerardo and Argentine entendidos' self-positioning on a high moral ground point to a Hispanic literary tradition of despising maricas.[78] While entendidos clung to that tradition of idealizing virile same-sex love, by the 1960s Hollywood films were making explicitly erotic images of male bodies available to mass audiences. Silently sitting in cinemas, there were adolescents who cherished the images of Hollywood male actors' well-built bodies, which helped them explore their own forbidden sexuality.

Bodies on the Screen

As 1960s homosexual cultures incorporated pop icons and Hollywood movie stars, entendidos were increasingly seen as passé. Their elitism seemed artificial for a younger generation that came to appreciate the sensuality of mass culture. For instance, Terenci Moix, an author born in Barcelona in 1942, wrote his autobiography using Hollywood films as a major narrative thread. Terenci's godfather was an older, well-off cousin who introduced him to entendidos' circles when he was a kid. However, Moix came to understand his godfather's sophistication as a form of self-apology, citing Pasolini: "They will tell you that Michelangelo, Shakespeare, and Rimbaud were homosexual as well . . . but the *mariquitas* of this century neither paint nor write books; they don't even read them. They enjoy a Marlene Dietrich old movie, a Judy Garland song, [and] Rockettes covered in feathers and sequins."[79] Female movie stars provided a language of self-expression for gay men who identified with their glamour and over-the-top dramatic lives.[80] In hindsight, Moix found that during his childhood in Barcelona, the sublime and the tacky blended into popular culture, as he found immense joy in witnessing older women sharing rumors about the neighborhood.[81] Another way of escaping the difficult reality of Franco's Spain was going to the cinema, especially since censors paradoxically favored the homoerotic deciphering of Hollywood films by discounting it. While these censors forbade the exposure of female bodies, the male torsos of gladiators and Christian martyrs passed the censorship and became homoerotic icons.[82]

Using similar strategies, the Argentine Alfredo Alaria (1930–99), who started his career in 1949 in Buenos Aires as the first dancer of Miguel de Molina's company, came to be a gay erotic icon in 1960s Spain.[83] Molina recalls in his autobiography how, while a member of his dance company, Alaria led the other dancers onto a Uruguayan beach where they were arrested for scandal, probably for being naked.[84] In Molina's account, this episode becomes symbolic of the sexual freedom of a younger generation, which he nostalgically observes from afar. Alaria molded his persona on the beauty ideals of bodybuilding magazines and youth countercultures, especially James Dean's 1955 film *Rebel without a Cause*. In the photographs that he signed for his fans, Alaria wears a loincloth and leather boots and holds up a torch to highlight his oiled muscles or shows his James Dean–disheveled looks, wearing a leather jacket and lighting a cigarette while he stares at the photographer. Alaria's leather clothes and bare chest depart from Molina's androgynous blouses, pointing to the erotic cult of virility in physique magazines and Tom of Finland's works.

Following the inverse path that took Molina to Argentina in the 1940s, Alaria moved to Spain in the 1960s, starring as the protagonist in the 1961 film *Diferente*. While Alaria's decision to leave Argentina for Spain might seem quite unique considering the criminalization of homosexuality under the Franco regime, other figures followed the same trajectory, suggesting that sometimes the key was to start a new life in a place where one's reputation was unknown, regardless of the hostile political and legal circumstances in that new place. Peralta studies how Gustavo Juan Pueyrredón (1925–56), whose elite family was anything but supportive of his homosexual lifestyle, moved in the mid-1950s from Buenos Aires to Barcelona, where he decorated El Atelier, a "club for maricas."[85]

FIG. 5. Atelier Club, Barcelona, 1955. Supposedly, this was a well-known meeting place for the maricas of the city. The photo shows the decoration by Gustavo Juan Pueyrredón (1925–56), an Argentine expatriate. Courtesy Archivos Desviados, based in New York City and Buenos Aires.

Alfredo Alaria's *Diferente* showed male muscular bodies within a homoerotic narrative frame. It centered on Alfredo, a young man with artistic inclinations who is pressured by his relatives to renounce his passion for theater and work in the family construction business. According to Alberto Mira, the film moved between subtlety and boldness "to sublimate the most obvious aspects of the homosexual representation."[86] Yet the code was quite easy to decipher. In one of the scenes, Alfredo visits a construction site and catches sight of a muscled, sweaty worker using a jackhammer. The camera zooms in on Alfredo, who—fixated—tries to look away, but he can't. Instead, he stares at the worker while the camera gets closer, alternatively focusing on Alfredo's eyes, then on the worker's biceps, and then on the thrusting of the jackhammer.[87] The references to anal penetration and the fetishizing of working-class men's physique in this scene were arguably obvious.

The film also coded homoeroticism through the entendidos' literary canon. Alfredo kept in his room books by Marcel Proust, Oscar Wilde, and André Gide, whom Gil-Albert significantly called

his three evangelists.[88] Even though entendidos' sense of refinement was falling out of fashion, their legacies remained. Alaria's
film ends dramatically with the accidental death of the protagonist's father and Alfredo pleading for God's help as he embraces
a tree during a storm.[89] Alejandro Melero argues that this final
scene perpetuates the view that homosexual men lead tragic, lonely
lives.[90] While the film focuses on the tensions between homosexual desires and a conservative environment without providing an
easy way out, it also promotes an identification with the protagonist's dilemmas. What is more, by recreating the protagonist's gaze
at male bodies, the film indicates the explicit mapping of eroticism
onto masculinity that is centered in the next chapter.

Conclusion

Urban cartographies of homosociability and sex are the infrastructure or substratum over which literary and theoretical arguments
on the relationship between homoerotic desires, cultural identity,
and religious and class-specific values of respectability were built.
The inseparability between entendidos' interventions in public
debates and the architecture of their desires—eroticized by gender performance and materialized with *chongos* and maricas in
private parties and dark streets—produced a paradoxical relationship between theory and praxis: on paper, entendidos aimed for a
respectable subjectivity that would separate them from maricas;
in sex and privacy, entendidos were often not that distinct from
maricas, equally invested in an erotic cult of masculinity, the joys
of promiscuity, and a baroque over-the-top sentimentality and aesthetics that external observers interpreted as feminizing. In other
words, the distinction between maricas and entendidos—based
on class, cultural capital, the performance of masculine respectability, and access to elite circles—was significant for entendidos
themselves, but from the perspective of maricas and self-identified
"normal" people, this distinction was not so relevant: the trope and
subjectivity of the marica hegemonized the representation and mate-
rialization of gender and sexual nonconformity, hence entendidos'
underlying tone of frustration. Rather than a model of long-term

egalitarian partnerships between homosexual men, the eroticization of difference, the playfulness of the seduction between machos
and maricas, and the semiotics of anal penetration and hypergen-
dered bodies were the most common ways of experiencing sex
on the margins of familism. While entendidos despised and neglected
the perspective, agency, and interests of maricas and their partners,
the next chapters explore these elements, beginning with the masculine men's participation and performance in libidinal economies
not dominated by them.

PART 2

The Erotics of Masculinity

Exotic Lubrications

Performing Masculinity in Sex Markets

Foreigners—sexual inverts—have been identified who had chosen
young men as the object of their preference, inducing them into
exotic lubrications [a euphemism for homosexual behavior].
These recurring events and the contact between local people and
foreigners have produced a psychological phenomenon: specifically,
the vanishing of the sense of morality.

—POLICE DEPARTMENT FILE, 1960; italics added

In this police report produced in 1960 in Torremolinos, a coastal
town in Spain, "exotic lubrications" communicated the idea that
foreign currency was a powerful social lubricant, one that emas-
culated Spanish young men by lowering their defenses against the
penetration of international visitors' "depraved" morality. The language used in this report, including the verb "inducing" and the
adjective "exotic," explicitly situates homosexuality as a foreign
influence, alien to Spanish customs. Yet the report also reveals
officers' limited trust in Spanish young men's capacity to resist
the temptations of gay sex, especially when it entailed an economic reward. In the late 1950s and early 1960s, media images of
masculinity informed the fantasies of and desires for a Marlon
Brando / James Dean type. Embodying that aesthetic was, in turn,
a profitable entry into circuits of transactional sex with men. Thus,
from the late 1950s, young men wore tight blue jeans and white
T-shirts while rebuffing middle-class respectability. By engaging

in gay transactional sex, these young men obtained the means to participate in consumer culture, which—in its incentivization of hedonism—spawned a generational challenge to state authorities' promotion of a subservient labor force. These experiences reveal the internal incoherence of 1960s economic policies in Argentina and Spain, where policymakers encouraged consumer culture but tried to curtail its underlying tenets of individualism and immediate self-gratification.

In other words, the authorities' promotion of imported consumer habits did not necessarily foster conformity, as they had expected, but rather turned consumer goods such as tight pants into signifiers of social and sexual disconformity. Furthermore, erotica and porn were also among the consumer goods that became increasingly available in urban markets and inserted in global production and distribution networks. In brief, the state rhetoric of workers' incremental access to heteronormative consumer markets did not neutralize the appeal of transactional sex, which relied on filmic images of a generational rebellion that was becoming a tangible reality.[1] This chapter connects aesthetics, tourism, and consumer culture under militarized regimes through a focus on the eroticism of power—the fraught fact that power not only represses the libido but also entices it. Alan Sinfield proposes three reasons why "power differentials are remarkably persistent in gay fantasies." First, fantasy "shows astonishing fixity," no matter how much we would prefer to think of it as a space of freedom and self-expression; second, desires "are embedded in the power structures that organize our social beings," a perspective that informs my reading of the materials in this chapter; and third, hierarchy in relationships is sexy, a complex fact that connects violence and pleasure.[2]

Power's sexiness traverses a multiplicity of contexts and situations that affect the formation of marica cultures. U.S. soldiers stationed in Spain—a client nation in its relationship with the United States—were described as "hot" by local men. Argentine military serving authoritarian governments were internationally known as willing to engage in paid sex. And broadly speaking, men who performed masculinity through domination (and violence) were often looked for by maricas. While tight jeans marked a dominant masculine physique, maricas enticed men by deploying high-value consumer goods, such as cars. These dynamics raise critical questions: Is it possible to disentangle the appeal of consumer goods from that of their owners? In the relationships between individuals who monetized their masculine performance and those who consumed it; who held power over whom? To address these questions, the chapter begins by analyzing media representations and public debates on male sex work in Argentina, setting the background for the treatment of this phenomenon as a criminological issue between the 1950s and 1960s. The second section looks at visual materials from both personal collections in Argentina and institutional archives in Spain and traces maricas' roles in representing their own desires and iconographies of masculinity. The third section proposes that policing transactional gay sex was a fraught issue in Spain, where international tourism was a source of revenue most valued by the authorities. The fourth section maintains the focus on Spain but closes the circle by returning to criminological and semipublic representations of male sex workers in the 1960s and 1970s.

Argentine Criminology and the Fashion Codes of "Virile" Sex Workers

From the late 1950s, there were public debates, albeit incipient and peripheral, on Argentine youngsters who wore tight jeans and rejected the values of middle-class respectability underlying state-promoted consumerism. This was a moment when keeping the youth in line with ideals of long-term upper social mobility had become a pressing political issue. Arturo Frondizi had been elected president that year on a platform that included ending the ban on the Peronist Party—which had been in effect for more than a decade—and improving workers' living conditions. In 1961, Frondizi joined President Kennedy's Alliance for Progress, which embodied the Cold War developmentalism that drove the agenda of his government. The consumer culture driving this agenda was represented in the ownership of valuable goods—a television and an

automobile—and the lifestyle of a new technocratic and mana-
gerial middle class. At the same time, the population of the shantytowns that proliferated in metropolitan areas was manifestly
excluded from this model of economic development. After some
initial concessions to unions, including a wage increase, the Frondizi government implemented orthodox liberal policies responding to a cyclical economic crisis. Overall, this period resulted in the
subordination of the labor force to industrial machinery through
"rationalization" schemes. Moreover, Frondizi could not fulfill his
electoral promise of lifting the ban on Peronism without antagonizing the military, which eventually overthrew him after the Peronist victory in the 1962 provincial elections.[3] The political rhetoric
of the Frondizi era continuously appealed to workers to postpone
their demands in exchange for forward-looking promises.[4]

In this context, certain fashion codes signaled either unwillingness to postpone self-gratification, the sexualization and commodification of virility, or both. Among middle-class students, the James
Dean / Marlon Brando style codified familiarity with avant-garde
intellectual trends and existentialism. In the 1950s, intellectual-to-be
Oscar Masotta wore blue jeans and projected a "desired and desirable image [with] a certain, careless way of wearing his coat, permanently [smoking] a cigarette, and a smile oscillating 'between
pity and nothingness.'" Among those who admired this masculine
performance were Masotta's close friends and homosexual writers
Carlos Correas and Juan José Sebreli.[5] Among other men, the much-
commented tight jeans could be part of their appeal for maricas
who would pay them for sex. Decades later, queer intellectual and
activist Néstor Perlongher preluded his study on male sex work in
Brazil by describing the body language of *michés* (male sex workers): "The first thing one sees is their bodies in blue jeans . . . rustic
fabrics, more opaque than shiny, that adhere viscously to a protu-
berance [penis] they highlight. There is in those overexposed bodies a whole staging of rigidity, toughness, and rudeness. . . . [They
are called] taxiboys in Buenos Aires, chaperos in Madrid, hustlers
in North America, michés in Brasil. . . . This variety of denominations expresses as well non-transferable peculiarities."[6]

Perlongher insightfully identifies a human type that is both recognizable throughout Western metropolitan areas and grounded
in specific local cultures. He describes young men, whose ages
oscillate between fifteen and twenty-five years old, wandering
through "moral regions" where older potential clients seek them
and know what to expect from them. Michés (*taxiboys* or *chaperos*) were attractive to their homosexual clients partly because they
performed heterosexuality. The semantic relationship between
taxiboys and chongos is of significance to understanding how sex
work was conceived as a praxis that created a distinction between
different ways of performing virility. Perlongher interviewed a
"marica" who knew chongos who were factory workers and "exemplary husbands" but had sex with "locas" who seduced and fon-
dled them in crowded public transports. Chongos would request
to be paid for these encounters, which the marica interpreted as
the mechanism that chongos used to avoid recognizing that they
enjoyed sex with males. Michés, on the other hand, made a living
off these encounters and could not pretend that they constituted
just an occasional release. Perlongher concludes that "the virile
prostitute would be a subspecies within a much broader type: the
macho or chongo, a male who, without renouncing the masculine prototype, neither necessarily prostituting himself, has sexual relationships with 'maricas.'"[7] *Chongo* was what maricas called
their sexual partners, not what the latter called themselves. In
other words, sex between masculine men and maricas was quite
extensive and did not entail the former perceiving themselves as
"deviant," a phenomenon that shaped a "virile" prostitution by
youngsters who performed a delicate balance between trying to
look "macho" and having sex with maricas as their main, if not
only, source of income.

Following in the wake of Perlongher's masterful ethnography,
other authors argue that male sex work as a phenomenon distinct
from chongo masculinity emerged in the 1980s in conjunction with
paradigm shifts in gay sex. Perlongher relied on Peter Fry's classical 1982 study of the "competition" between the "hierarchical"
model of sex between chongos and maricas and the "egalitarian"

model of sex between gay men who accepted themselves and each other as such.[8] Authors like Santiago Joaquín Insausti correlate the disaggregation of "masculine prostitution" from generalized paradigms of working-class masculinity with the popularization of this new gay sex model in the 1980s.[9] Before then, Insausti argues that paid sex between males was a "gender technology" that worked to "galvanize hierarchies that, in a certain way, were the precondition for desire and eroticism."[10] Furthermore, for Insausti, these were fluctuating dynamics, as masculine youngsters were often willing to pay maricas for much-needed sexual release, and roles varied depending on the implicated subjects' ages. While Insausti associates taxiboys as a human type with 1980s gay culture, my reading of fashion codes and first-person accounts suggest that "virile" sex workers were recognizable from at least the 1960s. These were men whose socioeconomic background appears imprecisely defined in the sources but who aspired to have access to fashion and consumer items shared with middle-class youth countercultures (the James Dean style) and thus distinguished themselves from the Peronist organized working class to which chongos often belonged. Media, consumer culture, and urban development—as much as if not more than gay sex paradigms—shaped this phenomenon.

In fact, the fashion of "skintight trousers and other body conscious" designs had originated in 1950s London, where they were sold by Bill Green, a gay physique photographer who founded the Vince Man's Shop in Soho. While the shop initially targeted a gay clientele, over time it came to popularize eroticizing male clothes among broader audiences.[11] Following this trajectory, in early 1960s Argentina, this aesthetics became associated with male transactional sex. Historian Valeria Manzano documents this trend by citing the writer David Viñas, who described a "Marlon Brando category" of working-class youngsters "tightening their *bluyíns* [blue jeans] to sell their ass to the best payer."[12] Fashion designer Paco Jamandreu narrates his liaison with a "jóven iracundo," whom he was initially reluctant to meet, fearing that he would be one of those "dirty, starving *chongos*."[13] Jamandreu's friends warned him against "animal-like" youngsters who always returned to their hookups (*yiro*), no matter how much their lovers/patrons cared for them.[14] Instead, he met nice-looking blond Tony, whom he describes as a homosexual who enjoyed playing the "macho," and they fell for each other.[15] Jamandreu explicitly distinguishes "chongos" from "iracundos," a label derived from the term "Angry Young Men," which was initially used in the mid-1950s for a generation of British playwrights and filmmakers who denounced middle-class hypocrisy from the outsider position of "distasteful" working-class men. John Osborne's 1956 theater play *Look Back in Anger* marks the introduction to the public of this group's views on controversial and taboo issues, including sex.[16] Jamandreu's use of the term "iracundo" suggests the possibility that incipient beatnik-era counter-cultures provided a set of self-fashioning codes for young men who aspired to keep their masculinity intact while having regular compensated sex with other males.

These youngsters performed a fetishized rough masculinity to entice their patrons. These dynamics were openly discussed in a scene of the Argentine film *Tiro de Gracia* (1968), which censors cut for that very same reason.[17] A youngster wearing the Marlon Brando fashion of jeans, a white T-shirt, and a leather jacket wanders in Plaza San Martín, a popular site for same-sex transactional sex. Situated between a major military base, the affluent Recoleta neighborhood, and the Retiro train station, this square offered the anonymity of a crowded commuter hub and a convenient location for encounters between young military recruits and well-off men willing to pay for sex.[18] The homosexual character in the movie explains to a third man that he prefers cheap, transactional relationships with "taxiboys" or hooking up with men who understand (*entienden*) codes of mutual recognition by which they meet each other in cinemas, streets, and public restrooms.[19] The appeal of taxiboys as potential sexual partners lay in their masculinity, signified in jeans and leather jackets, but their rebellious attitude made them unlikely candidates for long-term liaisons. These commitment issues were part of the fantasy, since emotional unavailability was central to the masculine performance. In the movie, the youngster stares defiantly at the camera while the voiceover of the homosexual character portrays him as profoundly disgruntled and feeling condemned by society.

Youngsters' feeling that society did not offer them the channels to obtain self-gratification on their own terms—thereby justifying their participation in transactional sex—was perceived as a danger to society. The intertwined ideals of middle-class consumerism and heterosexual familism informing the Argentine government's rhetoric also shaped criminologists' scrutiny of disgruntled youngsters in the early 1960s. As I explained in the first chapter, the Instituto de Clasificación (Classification Institute), part of the prison system, examined prisoners and produced reports for authorities' consideration of their parole requests. The institute's criminologists saw homosexuality as a "criminal-genetic" factor, which indicated an increased potential for an inmate to become a danger to society. Homosexuality, in criminologists' view, could become "fixated" through noxious influences (and then externalized in gender "inversion," i.e., males' "effeminacy") or sublimated into heterosexuality by conforming to gender norms. In the case of masculine youngsters, criminologists focused on whether they were willing to leave behind the immediate gratifications of transactional sex in exchange for uncertain prospects of upper social mobility.

Hence conventional business attire became a prisoner's way of communicating his willingness to sacrifice the rewards of transactional sex. In 1964, an institute psychologist argued that a prisoner had learned how to use his genitals as a kind of "Aladdin's lamp" that allowed him to instantly get anything he wanted—referring to the prisoner's previous involvement in transactional sex with men whom he met in cinemas or in the street. The prisoner was diagnosed as suffering from psychopathy on account of his "hedonistic" and "over-excitable" sexuality, among other factors, but the psychologist noted that he had been attracted to a "cultured" male partner who treated him tenderly.[20] In addition, when asked to draw himself, the prisoner portrayed his ideal self wearing a tie and a hat and carrying a suitcase, in the business attire of a middle-class professional. The trace of the inmate's pencil is as much a direct result of his bodily actions as a drawing of his mental mapping of social conformity. His self-presentation strategy worked—the institute recommended his release.[21] The criminologists apparently considered that the prisoner's aspirations of upward social mobility and appreciation of culture diminished the threats posed by his sexuality.

While criminologists considered that youngsters who aspired to a middle-class lifestyle had been rehabilitated, apathy toward this lifestyle was recorded as an index of dangerousness. Hence when in 1964 a prisoner coherently articulated why the possibility of performing the normative masculine roles of breadwinner and family head did not excite him, the criminologist interviewing him noted that he was unlikely to rehabilitate himself. This young man came from Santiago del Estero and had been convicted of theft.[22] He had been an orphan since age twelve, when he had had his first sexual relationships with a woman and with his male peers at the reformatory school.[23] Despite his above-average intelligence,[24] he refused to pursue the tedious life of a married, hardworking consumer and citizen:

> This young man of intelligent, intense, childish, and somehow feminine facial traits has something about him that sets him apart from the typical criminal and approximates him to the "beatnik." [He] lucidly chose to turn down the life of a peaceful, hard-working citizen, and instead consecrated himself to live outside the norm. . . . His reasoning about this issue gives him the air of a younger brother of Orwell, Miller, and Kerouac, whom most likely he has not read. . . . He refused to work because he despises a life of weekly, deadly boredom just "to go on Sundays to watch a movie with the wife and the son."[25]

According to the criminologist, the prisoner's attitude embodied the "beatnik" generational experience captured by Orwell, Miller, and Kerouac, a deliberate and coherent rejection of normative family life, including its trivial rewards through consumer leisure. He then cited the U.S. sociologist Paul Goodman (whose works, ironically, inspired the 1970s gay liberation fronts) to argue that any effort to adjust nonconformists (*disconformes*) was futile, since they were fully aware of social norms yet had decided not to follow them. This was the key to the generational challenge of youngsters who consciously decided to follow an alternative path to that which society expected them to take. Assuming that the prisoner participated in this trend, the institute recommended in 1967 that his pardon request be denied based on his average-to-significant dangerousness.[26] In October 1969, a prison officer reported that he showed a defiant attitude and had to be constantly watched over given his homosexual tendencies.[27] The treatment of this prisoner indicates that criminology's primary concern was shifting from men unable to men unwilling to rehabilitate themselves, in line with the declining appeal of middle-class familism for a generation coming of age worldwide in these years. The semiotics of masculinity as a sexual commodity became a criminological concern while simultaneously permeating marica visual iconographies in personal and institutional archives.

Visual Archives of Sexualized Masculinities

Archivos Desviados (Deviant Archives)—a grassroots archival project led by Juan Queiroz—hosts a collection of photographs and collages that foregrounds the entanglement between power and sexuality in marica culture. Queiroz found an album of homoerotic collages along with press clippings and an English-language novel titled *A Thirst for Something More* in a secondhand bookstore. María Rosón studies a tradition of photographic albums that produces a narration of the self that challenges hegemonic morality through the imbrication of material and affective practices.[28] Literary scholar Jorge Luís Peralta and I wrote a piece on these found materials for the activist digital platform *Moléculas Malucas*.[29] As we elaborate in that piece, there is not much information on Peter D., the person who created the collages, wrote the novel, and collected the clippings; neither do we know how and why his collection ended up in the bookstore. This lack of detailed provenance information might seem problematic in terms of treating these materials as illustrative of larger sociocultural patterns, but at the same time,

it is symptomatic of deficient institutional support for the preservation of archival materials that pertains to intimate experiences
of homoeroticism. Our working hypothesis is that Peter D. was
born in an English-speaking country but spent most of his life
in Argentina. The images in Peter's collection are assemblages of
male organs, clothing items, and faces cut from mainstream newspapers and magazines. The faces of well-known Argentine actors,
singers, and sportsmen are incorporated into recreations of sexual
acts and postures including oral sex and anal penetration between
multiple participants. A key element in these erotic tableaux is the
phallus that Peter adds to every male figure. Historian Liza Sigel
studies 1940s homoerotic photographs of boxers that were altered
by an anonymous artist who "rendered individuals naked, aroused,
and resplendent." In the postwar United States, anonymous artists
altered images from the popular press "to express queer desire" and
transform "heterosexual images into those of hidden homosexual
longing."[30] Likewise, phalluses emerged from Peter's hands as if he
were a potter molding clay. He added disproportionate penises to
his collages by cutting into phallic shapes print paper with a color
resembling human skin. Peter's alterations became more evident
as years passed, but there is a significant continuity in terms of
the sort of male physicality that called his attention. The clippings
in his albums suggest, because of the paper's qualities and photographed men's aesthetics, that Peter began to gather these materials at some point between the 1950s and 1960s. Peter collected
portraits of young and middle-aged men, many of them athletes
or boxers, with facial hair and muscled bodies.

Peter simultaneously purchased issues of a U.S. bodybuilding
magazine called *Tomorrow's Man* (1952–71), one of them dated February 20, 1959, indicating that Peter started his collecting career in
the 1950s. Peter's erotic imaginary points to the centrality of bodybuilding magazines for the international formation of gay communities. Peter probably subscribed to receive these magazines
by private mail order, as millions of readers interested in homoerotic images did worldwide. For Thomas Waugh, this readership
became the main foundation for the social networks, consumer

habits, aesthetic ideals, and sexual identities of gay men in the 1940s and 1950s.[31] Peter's consumer habits and curatorial practices demonstrate his penchant for a male physicality that denoted strength and domination. According to Peralta, the two key paradigms of homoerotic beauty in contemporary Argentina were the ephebe and the chongo. While the ephebe was androgynous, delicate, and embodied sublime classical beauty, the chongo was rough, hypermasculine, and domineering.[32] Peter's erotic imaginary centers on this second set of traits, while incorporating a predilection for upper- and middle-class fashion codes (suits and ties) that contrast with youngsters' tight blue jeans.[33] The scarce images of ephebes in Peter's collection serve to highlight the eroticism of male figures who dominate the ephebes for the sake of their own pleasure. Peter projected his desire toward domineering men by creating images of phalluses and penetrating male gazes to arouse himself. He established a dialogue between himself and photographed men who looked directly into the camera and into him. Many altered photographs show a "macho" enjoying other men's sexual attentions, incorporating Peter in the scene as a voyeur through the dialogues and the macho's arousing gaze. Sometimes, the macho invites Peter and any other voyeur to enjoy a scene of oral sex (Look at him sucking me! or ¡Miren cómo me va [a] chupar!). In a different image, a man in a suit grabs the penis of a masculine man (brunet, leather jacket over his naked chest, jeans, and hands on his hips) and invites Peter and others to taste it (Do you want to taste it? or ¿Quieren probarlo?) while receiving oral sex himself. Fashion's semiotics eroticize the interclass dynamics that permeated relationships between chongos and maricas. Likewise, military paraphernalia, guns, and cartridges denoted domination in an image titled Poder de macho (macho power), but soldiers also performed feminized sexual roles, as in a collage (Juego de cuatro or foursome) where Peter put a phallus in front of a soldier who had fully opened his mouth, probably to give an order, repositioning military belligerence to signify maricas' sexual receptiveness. As Matt Houlbrook points out, up until the 1960s the "erotic fantasy of masculine physicality" often fixated on soldiers involved in an "institutionalized erotic trade"—namely, "distinguished traditions of exchanging sex for money and consumerist pleasures with older, wealthier men." Like in Peter's collages, British guardsmen's "erotic allure" laid on the "charged gaze" through which they communicated their willingness to sexually engage with other men. The guardsman trope's meaning is unstable; it oscillates between a nationalistic symbol and the coded circulation of the rent boy's iconography.[34]

From his first experiments with black-and-white images, Peter kept playing with mainstream photographs while fixating on the fantasy that machos use other males to please themselves by receiving oral sex and penetrating them. In one of the first scenes of anal sex that Peter created, the written dialogue invokes the presence of a phallus, as one man asks another if he can feel it (¿La sentís?). In these scenes, maricas find pleasure in being sexually dominated, being penetrated, or staring at a penis. In a collage representing a threesome, a man seemingly forces another to perform oral sex on a rugby player—the text says, "Suck it or I will beat the shit out of

FIG. 6. An image of Peter's collection of black-and-white photographs of muscular men. Courtesy Archivos Desviados, based in New York City and Buenos Aires.

FIG. 7. One of Peter's collages, which he titled *Poder de macho*, depicting the
visual codes of masculinity and the exercise of sexual domination. Courtesy
Archivos Desviados, based in New York City and Buenos Aires.

you!"—but simultaneously the threatened man expresses delight at the view of the penis (¡Qué pija divina!). In this sort of image, the potential of physical violence is part of the role-play. Peter materially created images of sexually violent men and positioned himself as a voyeur, playing with masculinity as a device of his own forbidden desires. As Richard Dyer notes, "Gay porn is always in this very ambiguous relationship to male power and privilege, neither fully within it nor fully outside it."[35] The relationship between Peter and the fantasies he materialized on paper embodies a complex positionality versus masculinity, which for maricas could be both an object of desire and the root cause of the daily violence they suffered. Along with the phallus, Peter crafts a male gaze that penetrates him and commands erotic submission, becoming a signifier of the masculinity that maricas themselves created.

In Francoist Spain, photography was also a fundamental technique for cultivating marica desires and commodified masculinities. In 1965, a defendant from Barcelona was accused of having a long-term affair with a well-off man who maintained him.[36] The police confiscated his collection of erotic photographs. This included a drawing of a brunet sailor penetrating a muscular, blond male who only wears a T-shirt, has an erection, and is leaning on a tree, and a foreground photograph of anal sex where the man playing the receptive role grabs the penis of the inserter as if to guide it into him. The faces of the models are out of frame, probably a strategic decision to ensure their anonymity. Amateur visual culture reframed the relationship among desire, power, and gender by eroticizing men who took a leading role in intercourse while exhibiting their receptiveness to penetration. The joy, intimacy, and eroticism in the defendant's personal photographs contrast with the sobriety of mugshots in which he posed in a suit with a contrite expression, anticipating the harshness of the penalties that were imposed on him.

One of the first pieces of evidence in a different file from Barcelona is a chest-up portrait of a handsome young man, confiscated during a raid of a boarding house. Ten male guests and the owner were arrested when the police found out that some of them were sleeping together. The police reported that in one of the rooms, there was a "large taint, apparently of semen," sustaining the impression that the boarding house was a sexually charged space.[37] One of the arrested men claimed that he had known the man in the photograph for four years, and on the night of his arrest, he had handed the photograph over to another of the guests. The photographer skillfully framed and highlighted the contours of the model's athletic body, who posed sideways and looked up. The bottom half of his body is out of frame, leaving it open to the viewer's imagination whether he is fully naked (this could be a preemptive strategy in case the photographs were exposed). The fact that the model and the man who kept the photograph had known each other for a long time and the conventionalisms of the erotic portrait indicate that this image was produced within "a subcultural community [that was] participating in the representation of its own desire," as Waugh has argued for a different set of materials.[38] The model's relationship with the recipient of the photograph suggests that he was in fact an "erotic subject" as much as an object. His sparkling but elusive eyes are extremely eloquent. He is not looking into the camera but slightly up, as if gesturing toward the sublime.

A different file includes a photograph of a nude body in its entirety. The artist took the photograph from the back of the young model, who posed in a grain field. This angle preserved his anonymity while foregrounding his buttocks and back muscles. He separated his legs and extended his arms in a posture that provided a partial glimpse of his penis, and he highlighted his muscles by tensing them. He surrendered himself to the photographer's gaze by leaning his head down. While everything in this photo hints at the model yielding himself to the photographer, the same defendant who kept it also owned a foreground image of an erect penis. In this one, the model (who might even be the same one in the previous photo) has his shirt pushed up and his pants pulled down, revealing his hairy body, and delicately holds his erect phallus with two fingers while keeping his other hand on his hips in a self-exhibiting posture. The way in which the model exhibits his phallus without gesturing to any sexual initiative might be read as a form of self-eroticization to entice the photographer, who might as well perform a sexual act (such as oral sex) on the model. The defendant who owned these photographs, a forty-nine-year-old sailor, apparently confessed that he had bought them in the red-light district and used them to seduce young "inverts."[39] The circulation, exhibition, and touching of queer erotica was entangled with the formation of an urban subculture of individuals who met semi-clandestinely to form bonds of friendship and sex, as well as with the informal sex tourism industry. Spanish authorities faced the challenge of policing transactional sex between males while being aware that (homo)sexual markets played a significant role in the economic development promoted by Francoist policymakers.

Sex Work and Gay Tourism in Spain

Antonio Sabater Tomás was Barcelona's vagrancy judge and a lead-ing proponent of a harsher persecution of homosexuality. His 1965 study of youth criminal cultures paid attention to the transna-tional codes of youngsters who kept photographs of James Dean and wore "tight jeans, highlighting their body shape."[40] He also called attention to the expanding phenomenon of young poor men prostituting themselves with sexual "inverts."[41] In the mid-1960s, the significance of "homosexual trade" for the tourism industry in Southern Europe subverted authoritarian regimes' schema to maintain "a supposedly unchanging conservative time-scape."[42] According to historian Richard Cleminson's study on Salazar's Portugal, the state project of "regressive modernity"—namely, tourism-based economic growth combined with exemplary pun-ishments to maintain the facade of moral rigidity—encountered widespread popular resistance. When police officers humiliated local males known to be homosexuals or involved in transactional sex with well-off international visitors, the public expressed sym-pathy toward those men.[43] The explanation lies in the confluence of two paradigms: the normalization of males' sex work to con-front socioeconomic issues such as unemployment and inequality, and maricas' social integration.[44] In Spain, young men involved in sex work were called *bujarrones*, and most of them had recently immigrated from poorer southern regions to metropolitan areas, such as Barcelona.[45] By the late 1960s, the rituals and expectations of transactional sex between bujarrones and middle-aged men (*carrozas*) appeared quite regulated in specialized bars in Barcelona. A young Andalusian man who worked in one of those bars was arrested in 1968. He declared that waiters worked on a 20 percent commission in exchange for letting patrons flirt with and touch them. These waiters also occasionally arranged paid sex dates with patrons.[46] Wearing tight jeans to work, young men enticed affluent patrons who fetishized their masculinity and paid them for sex. Among these patrons, there were international tourists who played a central role in the Franco regime's economic schema.

To promote economic development, the Francoist authorities adopted a double moral standard, allowing international tourists and national elites greater sexual freedoms than common Spanish citizens. Police officers looked the other way when tourists and wealthy or well-connected Spaniards violated morality codes. The government's 1959 Stabilization Plan facilitated tourism's breakthrough by devaluing the Spanish currency. In this way, a new cabinet of Catholic technocrats put an end to the overvaluing of the *peseta*, which had symbolized the regime's pride in economic autarky. As Sasha D. Pack argues, this policy responded to the expansion of tourism as much as it catalyzed it. Throughout the 1950s, it had become evident that tourism was the only competitive sector that could offset Spain's trade deficit. Therefore, without fully acknowledging it, the authorities decided to promote this sector to finance Spain's industrialization.[47] Since wealthy gay men were among those who brought much-needed foreign currency into the Spanish economy, self-styled Catholic authorities accommodated these visitors' customs.

The earliest gay enclaves to emerge in Franco's Spain were elite spaces, where upper-class Spaniards and international visitors enjoyed exceptional freedom that incidentally exposed the stringent morality imposed on the rest of the Spanish population. Spain's appeal as a gay destination lay in its proximity to the rest of Europe, its beaches and warm weather, its publicized exoticism, and—last but not least—its complacent local men. European and U.S. gay men's purchasing power played a significant yet informal role in their relationships with local men. This situation resembles Italy's sustained popularity as a homosexual destination in the interwar period, while fascism was on the rise. Lorenzo Benadusi suggests that one of the ingredients to this sustained interest was the way in which visitors and locals engaged "in relationships somewhere between prostitution and love" by mingling "financial needs and emotions."[48] However, the political turmoil of the 1930s led first into the Spanish Civil War (1936–39) and then into World War II (1939–45), disturbing the circuits of homosexual tourism that would resurface in the early 1950s.

Gay tourists started then to visit resorts on the southern and eastern coasts of Spain, which at that time preserved their bohemian reputation and fishing towns' bucolic appeal. Sitges had been a vacation resort for Barcelona's bourgeoisie and artists in the early twentieth century, while Torremolinos, on the coast of Málaga, was undeveloped and appealed to elite visitors who shunned mass tourism.[49] The authorities had a hypocritical attitude toward this phenomenon. As Pack shows, the central government delegated the "policing of customs" to local authorities. Since these authorities were deeply invested in tourism revenues, by the early 1960s the consensus in coastal provinces was unofficial tolerance for forbidden practices, including revealing swimsuits, with tacit limits such as not wearing them in city streets.[50] In official reports on gay tourists—such as the one at the beginning of this chapter—police officers showed a strikingly different attitude. State policies are inscribed in historical records in a distorted way; while police officers could be bribed or instructed to not harass affluent tourists, they did not leave written evidence of this practice.[51] Instead, they occasionally arrested some tourists whose violations were particularly visible to maintain the facade of law enforcement. The 1960 report by the Torremolinos police department shows their stated, rather than practical, commitment to prevent the spread of gay tourism. While this report was a significant piece of nationalistic rhetoric through performative moral panic, it did not prevent police officers from looking the other way when it was convenient for the local and national economies.

In terms of the judicial prosecution of homosexuality, although the evidence is still partial and further research must be done on the vagrancy courts, acquittal rates were apparently higher in coastal touristic provinces such as Málaga.[52] Meanwhile, judges Sabater Tomás and Abundancia showcased the law's moralizing goals in Barcelona and Sevilla respectively, both regional capitals of national significance. This policy went unnoted in published memos and legislation, so whether this double judicial standard was ever remarked on is unclear. Did national authorities communicate informally to local authorities and judges? Were judges locally lobbied by tourism's business interests? In practice, those carrying out the law excluded foreign nationals sentenced as dangers to society from some security measures (internment in a prison or work camp and surveillance) that were standard for non-elite Spanish citizens, forcing them instead to leave Spain, a comparatively bearable penalty. Local working-class men benefited from judicial and police leniency toward gay tourism through self-eroticization. For instance, while Ramón worked as a bartender in Torremolinos, he realized that seemingly small physical gestures were rewarded by the gay clientele. As he maneuvered behind the counter, his tight pants revealed his pubic hair to the delight (*morbo*) of the bar's patrons, which Ramón then decided to "exploit." At that point, Ramón's tight pants were not available for mass consumption in Spain. He and other Spanish men had found a gay tailor in Málaga who designed close-fitting clothes for them. Moreover, among Ramón's patrons there were a couple of gay Londoners, owners of a large department store, who always brought clothes to give away when they visited Torremolinos every couple of months. Body-conscious male aesthetics became popular in locations such as Torremolinos through the relations between international visitors and local men (which, in the case of Ramón, entailed casually exhibiting his pubic hair behind the bar counter). As Ramón concluded, "Fashion marked a new era."[53] Tight jeans signaled a public explosion of erotic exhibition, which previously had been

reserved for the elite's private spaces. In the early 1950s, gay aristo-
crats' private parties had anticipated the liberalization of customs
in coastal towns. In 1950, a Spanish nobleman who spent seasons in
Torremolinos and Marbella was sanctioned for an inflammatory
sign (of unknown content) that had appeared at the door of the
civil governor's private residence and for affronting the regime
and the police.[54] This way of challenging Francoist authorities was
beyond the reach of most other defendants. A decade later, he
was accused of homosexuality and brought before the vagrancy
court. Police officers included the aristocrat's attendance at an
"immoral" prehistoric-themed party and his acquaintance with
poor young men as evidence of his homosexuality.[55] However, after
a three-year investigation, he was acquitted in view of his social
standing, evidenced by references to his involvement in international real estate development. Elite international circuits created
spaces of sexual exceptionality insofar as the law's moralizing aims
did not apply equally to individuals from a privileged class status.

Sitges also emerged as an elite gay resort in the 1950s, as demonstrated by the backgrounds of international defendants whose
cases were heard by the Barcelona Vagrancy Court. For instance,
in 1958 an Ivy League graduate and retired vice president of a U.S.
company was charged with homosexuality after he accused a local
man of stealing from him. The accused thief, however, claimed
that the defendant owed him the money for his sexual services.[56]
The retiree's defense lawyer portrayed the defendant as a devout
Catholic (certified by a local priest) whose privileged status allowed
him to travel the world.[57] The "pioneers" of the gay communities
of Torremolinos and Sitges, including this defendant, were elite
men who had the means to travel the world looking for sexual
adventures. In the end, Judge Sabater Tomás ruled the retiree to
be a danger to society because his quarrels with a local man risked
causing a public scandal.[58] However, even though Sabater Tomás
prided himself in his toughness when it came to homosexuality,
the most he could do when judging international tourists' behavior was force them to leave Spain.

Still, vagrancy courts tracked down the circulation of queer erotica and tourism's effects on visual culture. Erotic photographs captured the defendants' self-fashioning, aesthetics, and subculture but also colonial power dynamics and the fetishization of Black people. For instance, a series of photographs confiscated in Málaga in 1963 erased the Black models' individuality by synecdochally foregrounding their genitals. These objectifying images stemmed from a colonial context, as they were kept by a British subject, Harold, who had been deployed in Africa, most likely Nigeria, where he returned after being expelled from Spain. At some indefinite moment after Nigeria gained its independence from the United Kingdom in 1960, Harold had moved to Spain. There, he established a relationship with a Moroccan subject, Abdilla. Given that Spain colonially occupied part of Morocco until 1958 under the guise of a "protectorate," Abdilla's status was inscribed in the postcolonial relationship between Spain and Morocco. His vulnerability to arbitrary policing became evident in December 1963, when he was arrested on a train and his suitcase was confiscated. In his suitcase, police officers found an English gay porn magazine and amateur porn photographs. Abdilla was arrested and charged with homosexuality. When he was placed in a cell, he took the opportunity to rip up the photographs into pieces. Eventually the police officers discovered this, and they had to painstakingly reassemble them. One can imagine them holding up, examining, and trying to fit each piece back together as if they were working on a jigsaw puzzle. The reassembled images were of Black men exhibiting their genitals to the camera, performing oral sex on each other, and penetrating a middle-aged white man whose face is out of frame.[59] State agents' role was not just to erase gay pornography or prevent its circulation but also to reconstruct it to trace the effects of sexual tourism in the country. In this line, they reconstructed these photographs and interrogated Abdilla, who declared that the confiscated materials were not his but rather belonged to Harold.[60] After being taken into custody, Harold denied the accusation and testified that they belonged to Abdilla.[61] Both Harold and Abdilla were eventually declared to be dangers to society and expelled from Spain.

Homosexual practices and pornography were judged against indicators of social status, so international defendants were acquitted on account of their contributions to economic development. For instance, in 1964 on the Canary Islands, nineteen-year-old barman Fernando was accused of robbing two tourists—a German named Hans and a Belgian named Maxime—and admitted that he did commit the crime because he felt disgusted by the acts that he had carried out with them. After meeting the men, he had gone to their apartment and engaged in sex: "While [Fernando] was standing, bending over the bed, Hans introduced his virile member in his anus, while Maxime, lying down in the bed facing up, sucked his penis."[62] On other occasions, Maxime penetrated Hans while the latter penetrated Fernando, and on yet another night they had an orgy with another young man. By describing these scenes in detail, the defendant was appealing to the authorities' stated belief that foreign gay men were corrupting the local youth. Finally, Fernando stole the foreigners' jewelry and a safe in which they kept money, a gun, and photographs of Maxime performing oral sex on Hans and a Black man performing oral sex on Maxime. Although the context in which these photographs were taken is unclear, they reflect the fetishization of Black men. Moreover, the authorities' double standard manifested itself in disparate sentences for the same violation depending on the defendants' nationalities. The judge acquitted both Hans and Maxime, considering that they had a steady income and had not caused any trouble up until then, yet declared Fernando to be a danger to society based on reports by the security forces according to which he had shown bad conduct in general and a tendency to rob in particular.[63]

While authorities often spared defendants from wealthier European countries any penalty on account of their "respectable" status, a citizen of Cuba (colonized by Spain until 1898) was racialized through the assumption that he was naturally prone to physical contact and lacked the prejudices that defined "civilized" nations. In other words, legal arguments deployed in cases of postcolonial subjects significantly differed from those used for Northern

European defendants. The Cuban citizen, Norberto, was arrested in 1965 in Málaga in connection with the arrest of a Spanish citizen named Carlos, who was apprehended while running in the street wearing only a shirt. Carlos claimed that he had been escaping from the indecent advances of Norberto. According to Carlos's statement, Norberto had invited him over for dinner, offered him a few alcoholic drinks, and then suggested that he take a warm bath and lay down on a bed for a massage. Following these activities, Norberto showed him pornographic photographs of women and men, including himself, and then tried to hug him and climb into the bed with him, at which point Carlos jumped up and ran out into the street, seminaked.[64] Throughout his statement, Carlos repeatedly made references to Norberto's blackness, suggesting that it made him feel like potential sexual prey. When Norberto, who was employed by a touring variety show, was arrested, he clarified that he had indeed massaged Carlos with Vicks VapoRub, but only to cure the latter's coughing, and that the photographs that he'd shown were simply of the performance troupe to which he belonged.[65] Norberto's lawyer acknowledged that his hospitality was excessive when measured by Spanish standards. Yet—he argued—it was common in Cuba's latitudes. He also argued that Carlos, who had just left the seminary, misinterpreted Norberto's gestures as a threat to his virtue. In other words, the lawyer suggested that Carlos overreacted on account of the sexual puritanism instilled in him by training to be a Catholic priest.[66] Norberto was acquitted; perhaps the evidence was not strong enough to demonstrate that he had used photographs to seduce Carlos or the latter had misinterpreted the images and the Cuban's hospitality because of his own racial paranoia and sexual prudery. At stake here was the definition of pornography as either absolute or relative to how different cultures define appropriate interpersonal physical boundaries. Based on the second definition, Norberto's lawyer argued (and the judge apparently agreed) that his client was just acting on a "natural" tendency to establish closer physical contact, stemming from environmental factors such as latitude. Othering defendants from former colonies was a way of asserting that Spain's European status was evident in local people's respect for interpersonal physical boundaries.

This brand of reactionary nationalism also informed judges' approach to fashion and its relationship with sex work and consumer culture.

Cigarettes, Jeans, and Cars

In 1972, Sabater published a book mapping youth counterculture as a growing cradle for "antisocial" behavior. In contrast with his previous 1965 treatise on youth criminality, in which he devoted only a couple of pages to homosexuality, his 1972 book included a whole chapter on the issue. This chapter indicates the extent to which homosexuality had become one of the authorities' major concerns. Yet Sabater Tomás's discussion of visual culture in his captions to dozens of photographs has hitherto been overlooked. His 1972 work has the format of a coffee table book, and—given that its multiple photographs capture 1960s and 1970s fashions—its visual material is uncannily reminiscent of Valerie Steele's 2013 *A Queer History of Fashion*. Sabater Tomás asks whether homosexual people suffer from a "*vicio* or sickness" of an "intimate character" that calls for special clinical measures.[67] The photograph next to this caption shows a young man in a leather jacket and tight jeans. He wears no shirt, so his unzipped jacket reveals his hairy bare chest, while he keeps his hands in his pockets in a provocative posture. In other words, Sabater Tomás uses these photographs to provide his own answer to the rhetorical question that he posed verbally. He focuses on the body language and aesthetics (tight jeans, leather jacket, rebellious self-exhibition) that allowed masculine men to participate in transactional sex circuits as a way of implicitly arguing that this was the most common and dangerous modality of homosexual relationship, justifying the state's implementation of punitive measures. Sabater Tomás then illustrates through several photographs the phenomenon of transactional sex. On the next pages, there are five photographed men with their eyes blacked out. All of them are young, long-haired, and wear their pants tight around their hips. Three of them are smoking cigarettes. One of them wears bell-bottom trousers and holds his cigarette down while smiling at the camera. Another one licks his lips. Two others are seated in the street, one of them partially exhibiting his bare chest under his leather jacket. In this way, Sabater Tomás captures the embodied language of transactional sex, the self-assured posturing of sex workers who used eroticizing clothes and the casual gesture of smoking a cigarette to convey that they had spare time and, thus, signal their sexual availability.

Contemporaneously, Spanish filmmakers explored the theme of young athletic men who exhibited their bodies to entice potential clients and, indirectly, to have access to high-value consumer items, vehicles foremost. As Alejandro Melero notes, short films and scripts produced by students at the Escuela Oficial de Cinematografía (Official Cinematography School) were the most explicit and realistic depictions of this subculture, because they were exempt from the Francoist censorship, unlike any other film.[68] In 1963, Pere Balañá i Bonvehí graduated from the school by presenting the short film *Un día más*. These films were projected for students' families and friends, not for the public. In *Un día más*, a young man reminiscent of James Dean—smoking indolently, wearing tight jeans, a white T-shirt, and slicked hair—cruises in Madrid's Parque del Oeste and meets a middle-aged man in a suit. The script reflects Balañá's self-censorship, materialized in crossed-out words, and his interest in the eroticization of male physicality: "His face covered in sweat, his T-shirt almost unbuttoned, over his jeans, his chest moving at the same pace that his out-of-control breathing. . . . The remains of a beautiful body, of a youthfulness prematurely worn out ~~because of the excesses of a certain vice~~ [crossed out in the original]."[69] The juxtaposition between the character's sweaty, beautiful body and the director's initial acknowledgment and later erasure of homosexuality pinpoints what were the limits of cinematographic creativity under Franco's regime. The man in the suit gives the young character money and a ride on his motorbike to the place where he is meeting his girlfriend. Implicitly, this scene foregrounds the main elements of contemporary gay transactional sex: cruising in public spaces, interclass encounters coded in clothing items and body postures, young men's performance of masculinity (encompassing heterosexuality), and vehicles and cigarettes as common exchange items.

Cigarettes and jeans were also among the rewards that Spanish young men could obtain from their relationships with foreigners, in a circular logic by which the reward could then become part of these men's appeal in sexual circuits. The Franco regime's cession of military sovereignty over Spanish territory to the United States also contributed, ironically, to creating exceptional spaces beyond the purview of the Vagrancy Law. U.S. soldiers stationed in Spain engaged in sex with local men with little concern about the potential legal consequences, thus taking advantage of and sexualizing the uneven dynamics between a hegemonic power and its client nation. U.S. soldiers, with access to consumer goods far surpassing the average Spanish citizen's, became a common presence in Madrid and Barcelona and on the coast of Cádiz. Their relationships with local men often showed a complex mingle between sexual attraction and collateral material rewards. Serafín Fernández, a gay man born in Spain in 1944, for instance, used to wait by the road that connects Madrid with a U.S. military base so he could be picked up by U.S. soldiers who passed by in their cars. He would perform oral sex on them, and then they would give him a "present" or invite him for a drink. This is his recollection: "Americans were hot. They were young soldiers who put me in the car, took us outside of Madrid, where we did what we had to do. Then, they gave me a package of *Winstons* [cigarettes], jeans, or whatever, as a present."[70] Since he sought out and enjoyed these encounters, he considered these gifts to be a gesture of generosity. At the same time, the fact that he received jeans and cigarettes illustrates how these kinds of encounters popularized consumer goods associated with a generational rebellion against social conformism. Cars played an important role in these encounters, both as semiprivate spaces for sex and as symbols of personal autonomy through purchasing power, which encouraged masculine men to participate in these circuits.[71]

Conclusion

If young men offered a masculine performance associated with generational rebellion—coded in fashion styles and body postures, signifiers of interest in consumer items like vehicles, and uninterest in normative work ethics—and maricas desired, consumed, and remunerated this performance, who held more power in these exchanges? The fact that this question cannot be answered in a conclusive way indicates how the interplay among sexuality, gender hierarchies, visual languages, and consumer markets led to the commodification of masculine physicality and domineering roles in sex. Criminologists like Antonio Sabater Tomás and the Classification Institute examiners treated youngsters' performances as intrinsically paradoxical. In their reports, they assimilated these young men with generational referents like James Dean and beatnik authors whose nonconformism was impregnated with masculinity while emphasizing that young men's preference for gay sex over a normative work life and their "passiveness" toward the future feminized them. In exploring how this sexual subculture operated, criminologists documented the visual codes through which men seduced one another and traced consumer items (vehicles, cigarettes, jeans, leather jackets) through which males communicated their respective roles in potential sexual/transactional encounters.

The continuity in visual tropes between state archives and private collections like Peter's collages—where maricas had free rein to recreate their own erotic imaginaries—bespeaks the historical specificity of sexual icons. Likewise, maricas' hands resurface on multiple occasions directing the staging of sex: Peter manually created the images of men (including military men) who seduced him with their gaze; the Spanish judicial archives include a photograph of a man guiding with his hand the penis that penetrates him and multiple photographs confiscated from men who posed in ways that highlighted the male physique's eroticism. Soldiers were objects of queer desire and involved in transactional sex with civilians, mediated by cars' fetishistic allure, as Serafín's story and the next chapter trace. Yet soldiers also adhered to a disciplinary structure inserted in the state apparatus that persecuted sexual and gender dissidence. The boundaries between this structure and marica culture were more porous than official statements acknowledged. In fact, the next chapter argues that the Argentine military's judicial processing of alleged homosexuals induced the reification of marica and macho roles and the documentation of the mechanics of their social and sexual encounters.

FOUR

"People Don't Know What a Homosexual Is"

Argentine Soldiers' Sexual Culture

In 1966 in Argentina, a military judge asked a soldier on trial if he felt pleasure and ejaculated when a man anally penetrated him, to which the soldier replied, "Mister Judge, I experience an enormous satisfaction when I am penetrated, and I am able to ejaculate, since at those moments I masturbate at the same time."[1] Soldiers accused of homosexuality and facing courts-martial under the Military Code between the mid-1960s and early 1980s described their sexual acts with a striking level of detail. The deposition transcripts reflect either a self-affirming attitude that openly challenged normative masculinity (as in the deposition above) or recruits' purported unawareness of the Military Code's definition of the violation. Many conscripts claimed to ignore that sex with other males undermined their masculinity. In 1979, a conscript allegedly had sex with a gay man who picked him up in his car. He clarified that he had performed the "man's role" ("haciendo yo de hombre"). He performed unawareness that the authorities' notion of masculinity excluded sex with other males, implying that there was a significant gap between his rural upbringing and the state's definition of sexual deviance:

> INVESTIGATING OFFICER: Why did you commit the acts that you have admitted to?

> DEFENDANT: When we were in the car the man asked me to do it, and since he had been feeling me up, I was excited. He neither promised to give me money nor did I ask him. . . .

OFFICER: Didn't you ever commit these sorts of acts before joining the Army?

DEFENDANT: I didn't know that it was wrong or that it was a crime.

OFFICER: Did you receive any kind of information about this issue in civilian life?

DEFENDANT: Never. I used to spend the week in the country-side chopping wood with my seven brothers. Some Saturdays, we rode to the village on our horses. . . . *There, people don't know what a homosexual is.*[2]

The conscript strategically argued that at no time between chopping wood and visiting the closest village did someone describe to him what a "homosexual" was and looked like or how to avoid becoming one. He supposedly went to a movie theater for the first time in his life when they gave him a free ticket on the naval base. And he did not remember receiving any explanation about homosexuality being shameful or punishable during his military training. Therefore, when a man offered him a ride in his car, felt him up, and offered him sex, he accepted. If this narration was the defendant's way of performing naïveté for the sake of his legal defense, the fact that he thought this could be a credible performance hints at the fact that the sexual regime defined by sexual object choice (the hetero/homo binary) was not fully hegemonic in the late 1970s. In the next pages, I argue that one of the military officers' aims was to socialize soldiers in their definition of and views on "homosexuality." This endeavor had the collateral effect of creating a voyeuristic archive to undermine soldiers' statements that masculinity was compatible with same-sex sexual practices.

Soldiers' narrations and performances reflected a sexual culture organized around binary gender roles, with *machos* on one pole and *maricas*, also called putos or locas, on the other. To punish "offenders," the military questioners incited the testimonies that they so desired. Matt Houlbrook argues that, in Britain, the guardsman is "an object of queer desire" who "rarely speaks for himself," his body becoming the "passive inscriptive surface" onto which fantasies are projected.[3] Argentine military records, on the contrary, foreground conscripts' mediated testimonies and their attempts to interpret officers' expectations and appeal to judges' benevolence. Houlbrook locates the cause of discursive tensions in the "recalcitrant body that persistently refused to play its allotted role within these fantasies of masculinity."[4] Argentine courts-martial more resemble a comedy of errors in which both accused soldiers and those who investigate them are invested in making sex between males intelligible but instead produce a script of sexual excess, playful gender roles, and normalized violence.

The courts-martial of recruits and officers accused of homosexual acts served at once to reinforce a sexual culture based on enticement and domination and to monitor its disruptive effects on military discipline and the reputation of the military institution. Machos were assumed to be "normal" or "real men" who, lacking other sexual outlets, occasionally engaged in sex with other males while always performing an "active" sexual role as the inserter in anal sex and recipient of oral sex. They always had to keep a domineering position that excluded showing vulnerability to other males by developing affection for them or letting themselves be penetrated. Since their libido was theoretically heterosexual, the expectation was that they would play "hard to get" before acceding to sexual entreaties by other males and justify any acquiescence by needing to "get off." Maricas, putos, and locas, by contrast, were all roughly equivalent appellations for a feminized male who, in theory, performed predominantly or exclusively a receptive role ("passive") in anal sex and a giver role in oral sex. Since maricas were assumed to possess a "true" homosexual libido, they were also expected to take the initiative in seducing other males to fulfill their desires.[5] Beyond these expectations, sex and affect often appeared entangled; maricas' active pursuit of sexual pleasure was anything but submissive, and machos found pleasure and comfort—and not just release—in their relationships with other males. For Fernández and Insausti, "these sexual activities between men cannot be categorized as homosexual. On the contrary, the very performance of same-sex sexuality served to shape hetero-sexuality."[6] Masculinity, rather than heterosexuality (a term that soldiers rarely if ever used), best encapsulates the operationaliza-tion of same-sex sexuality for producing linguistic and material systems of power through the semiotics of penetration.

The legal and medical codes that sustained these proceedings in theory did not contemplate a different treatment of defendants depending on whether they had performed a "passive" or an "active" sexual role. During the defendants' depositions, prosecutors and interrogating officers tried to convey to the accused that physi-cal intimacy between males was stigmatized and a violation of the Military Code in every case. In fact, sentences established roughly the same penalties for participants in homosexual inter-course independently of their sexual role. Article 765 of the 1951 Code of Military Justice simply referred to "dishonest acts with a same-sex person inside or outside a military site" and established different penalties depending on rank and the use of coercion.[7] Subsequent rulings clarified that "dishonest" acts encompassed every "activity that leads to sexual pleasure, including prepara-tory acts of approaching, between individuals of the same sex."[8] Thus, the military jurisprudence seemed to establish a clear and encompassing definition of homosexuality as the pursuit of sex-ual pleasure between males.

However, subjacent to this apparently simple formula, the gen-dered sociability between machos and maricas permeated every proceeding of the courts-martial and provided a common ground for all actors implicated in the trials. The judicial proceedings constantly reinforced a gender binary between active and passive participants—penetrator and penetrated—which investigating offi-cers saw as a distinct personal identifier. This binary was so per-vasive that defendants could be reduced to their sexual role, as in a 1978 case in which the person who transcribed the depositions of two soldiers added below the defendants' signatures the sex-ual role that each of them had performed.[9]

While in other national contexts military codes served in the long run to establish the homosexual/heterosexual binary based on sexual object choice, Argentine officers and medical experts were too invested in the sexual culture of male domination to systematically undermine it.[10] To begin with, although the Military Code established harsher penalties for coerced sex, the transcripts of interrogations and the courts' rulings show that many officers were more likely to believe that feminized males seduced other soldiers than to trust them when they reported sexual violence, which was probably a correlate of a view of maricas as libidinous and luring. Likewise, the harsher penalties for officers who had used their rank and different strategies of seduction to be anally penetrated by or perform oral sex on enlisted men were contemplated in the Military Code and served to control the disruptive effects that the feminization of these officers may have had on military discipline and conscripts' masculinity.

The terminology used during the trials also demonstrates that the concept of homosexuality was anything but hegemonic. Well into the 1980s, interrogating officers resorted to common-use terms such as puto or marica during the defendants' depositions. Officers conducting the trials played a double game with the defendants, initially taking advantage of their performed naïveté about the Military Code's definition of homosexuality to extract explicit, quasi-pornographic narrations of their sexual encounters, and then using these narrations to humiliate them as the first step of their resocialization in a proper, self-controlled masculinity. Interrogators' questions reflect their duplicity about the marica/macho model. On the one hand, they instructed the defendants in the idea that every form of same-sex physical intimacy marked the participants as sexual deviants. But on the other hand, their insistence on extracting information about the defendants' seduction strategies, sexual roles, and orgasms points out that they were deeply invested in the notion that an individual's status is determined by his gender and sexual role performance and the "true" orientation of his libido, manifest in desires as much as in acts. Thus, they reproduced the view that putos/maricas had a "true" homosexual libido while "machos" succumbed to the pressure to release sexual tension by any possible means.

Similarly, medical examiners gendered the diagnosis of psychopathy, vaguely defined as an imprinted tendency to dismiss ethical and social norms. They submitted reports that presented soldiers who had performed a "passive" sexual role as psychopaths, since their libidos led them to seduce other men, dismissing ethical norms. In contrast, soldiers who had performed the "active" sexual role were only diagnosed as psychopaths when there was some indication that they had taken advantage of vulnerable homosexual individuals, sexually or economically. Defense lawyers, for their part, generally emphasized the contingent, external factors that accounted for their defendants' sexual behavior but also portrayed their libidos in different terms depending on their sexual and gender roles: as fixated in the case of maricas and recoverable in the case of machos. Peter M. Beattie argues that "conscription allowed states to move sexual 'science' out of medical journals and to apply hygienic and eugenic theory to a large cross section of a nation's male population."[11] However, in the case of courts-martial in Argentina between the 1960s and 1980s, sexual science had little sway in comparison with a sexual culture of gendered roles of domination and seduction that permeated from male sociability in the barracks to depositions, legal defenses, and medical diagnoses.

The bulk of the preserved courts-martial records date from approximately the same years when military interventionism in Argentine political life peaked, from Onganía's coup in 1966 to the end of the "National Reorganization Process" (1976–83). As political tensions and violence between the dictatorial state and opposition groups escalated in Argentina between the late 1960s and early 1970s, many young men showed their reluctance to enlist in the military. In these years, homosexuality became a common strategy to avoid military service used by those who opposed military rule, including "hippies." Miguel Cantillo was part of the countercultural movement of hippies who opposed the military dictatorship and describes how he "met pals who thoroughly studied the drawing and psychological tests by which military psychologists scrutinized the candidates' mental status. Others carefully prepared

a psychopathic performance . . . and [there were] those who pre-
tended to be paranoids, homosexuals."[12] Homosexual recruits were
usually discharged with a red mark on their enrollment card.

Given that admitting to being a homosexual could be a strategy
to avoid military service used by those who opposed military rule,
physicians and psychiatrists often distrusted recruits' statements
about their sexuality and even psychologists' evaluations during
the recruitment's medical examination.[13] For instance, when the
psychologist who interviewed one of my informants during his
recruitment in the late 1960s reported that there was something
out of the ordinary about him, probably his homosexuality, he was
subject to further screening by military psychiatrists who decided
that he was apt for service.[14] Military physicians trusted the digital rectal examination the most to detect and exclude homosexual
recruits, establishing an implicit equation between homosexuality
and the "passive" sexual role. Another informant, who did his
military service in the 1960s, remembers how during the medical exam the recruits were asked to undress and bend over so that
physicians could look at their anuses. When the turn came for a
recruit who was ahead of him in line, the physician looked at his
anus and said, "Some people have passed by here, right?" After
that, this informant never saw the recruit again; he assumes he
was discharged. There is evidence that this part of the exam may
have been expected. In fact, a common refrain among the adolescents of this informant's neighborhood was that the best way to
avoid mandatory military service was to have sex with a particularly well-endowed boy.[15] The medical premise that anal dilation
is a reliable sign of homosexual intercourse filtered into conventional wisdom and people's strategies to resist military recruitment.

This chapter follows the course of courts-martial of soldiers
accused of homosexual acts. The first section focuses on soldiers'
sexual culture and how investigating officers perceived and intervened in this culture. The second section argues that a collateral
effect of these courts-martial was the creation of a voyeuristic
archive of soldiers' sexual desires and pleasures through the interrogations led by investigating officers. The third section reveals

medical examiners' and psychologists' gendering of the diagnosis of psychopathy, incorporating the distinction between machos and maricas. The fourth section deals with the personal narratives presented by the defendants and their lawyers to diminish their responsibility based on the contingent, environmental factors that led to their engagement in "deviant" sexual practices.

Soldiers' Sexual Culture

Argentine recruits' willingness to participate in transactional sex became widely known, to the point of being mentioned as one of the attractions of Buenos Aires for gay travelers in a U.S. travel guide. The 1978 *International Guild Guide* was published in Norfolk, Virginia, by Ronnie Anderson. The edition was based on letters from readers who had visited different places of the world and shared information about gay bars and meeting places. The section on Argentina informed the guide's readers that "military [men] are cooperative and appreciative," a subtle reference to widespread transactional sex between recruits and civilians.[16]

In fact, a year later the intelligence department of the Mar del Plata naval base initiated an investigation into accusations that numerous conscripts had been prostituting themselves with men living in the city. The soldiers would meet these men in recreational spaces such as amusement arcades or would be invited by them to take a ride in their cars, indicating once again the centrality of vehicles in transactional gay sex dynamics. One of the interrogated conscripts admitted to having gone twice to a chalet owned by a man with whom he committed "aberrant acts" in exchange for money. On a different occasion, he went out with three other conscripts and a man who owned a red Fiat 600, who paid each of them for sex. Other conscripts' declarations reflect similar patterns: one of them had sex with a man in a blue Dodge Polara, and another one was picked up in a blue Fiat 128 by a man who took him to his apartment and paid him. A corporal openly admitted that his strategy was to seduce men to rob them, by using a revolver that he was playing with while being interrogated.[17] These interrogations of soldiers accused of homosexual acts revealed the

ALGIERS

(French is the language, free boys
the rule and a warm gracious culture that welcomes you. The hotels
are safe and homosexuality generally goes unnoticed - to the point of
encouraging it.

L'Opere
15 rue Said Bakel

Blue Note
Avenue Claude Debussy

Le Triomphe
27 Rue Zahan Ahmed

Lotus
rue Didouche Mourad

L'Etoile
Avenue Pasteur

La Couple
25 rue de Tripoli

Public Baths
Near Place des Martyrs in the
Casbah.

OC: Grand Poste (YC)
(under the Clock)

Pont Polignac (YC)

Rue Balay,
Rue Mace,
Avenue Zola

ANGOLA

(Our advice still is "Don't go," but
if you must, things have improved
somewhat from last year.)

LUANDA, ANGOLA

Bar Triumfo (GI, C)
Rua Missao De S. Paulo

Cafe Magestic (G)
Rua Missao de South Paulo

Cervejaria (G)
Largo D. Joao IV

Pastelaria Versailles (GI, H)
Largo, D, Joao IV

Restaurante Polo Norte
Rua Duarte Pereira

ANTIGUA

ST. JOHN'S

White Sands
(has cottages and a private beach
with pleasant hotel management.)

Bucket of Blood

ARGENTINA

(Homosexuality is legal over the age
of 22 and like most Latin countries, is widespread from adolescence on. Military are cooperative
and appreciative.

BUENOS AIRES, ARGENTINA

Banos Castelar (Baths)
1148 Av. 25 de Mayo
37-8594

Bar Academia (G, H, M, RT)
(Late — 1:00 to 5:00 a.m.)

Bar (G, WE)
Libertad & Cordoba

La Bola Loca (S, YC, WE)
(8 a.m.to midnight)
850 Maipu St.

Boom Cafe (G)
Corner of Florida and Tucuman

Cafe Augustus (M, Aᐩ
(8 a.m. to midnight)
895 Florida St.
32-8955

124

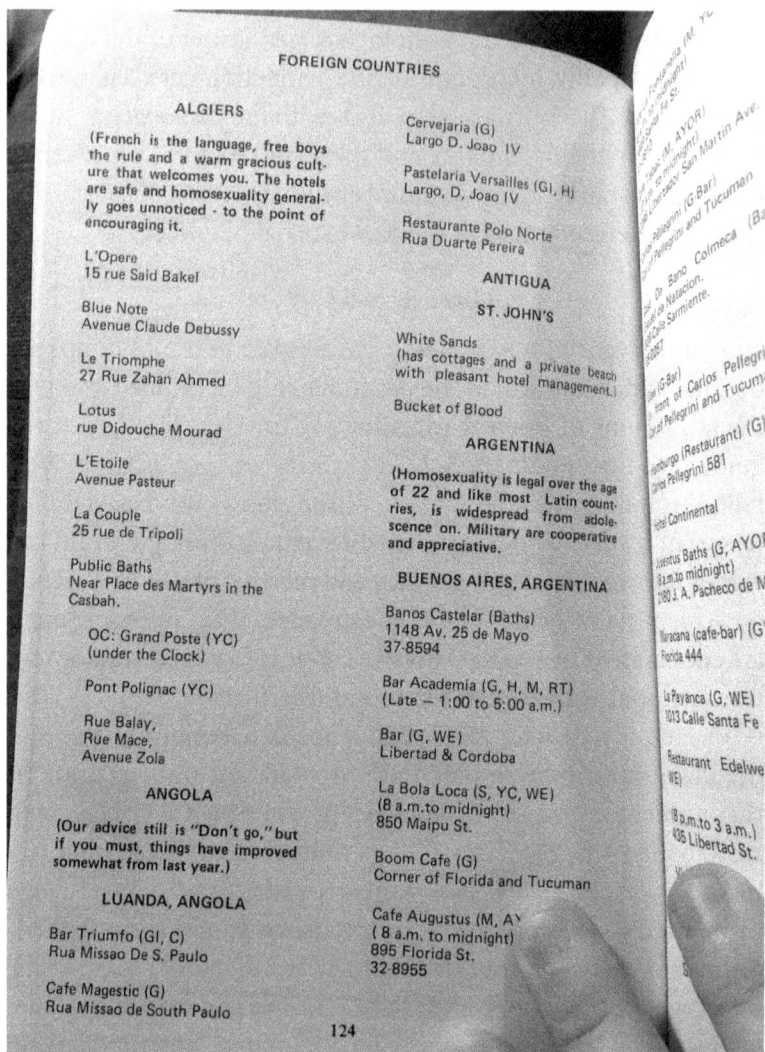

FIG. 8. Characterization of Argentine military men as sexually available, published in the 1978 *International Guild Guide* (includes author's hand holding down the page). Folder: International Guild Guide (65–78), IGIC ephemera, Gay Guides, box 3. New York Public Library Rare Books and Manuscripts Division, New York.

existence of an extended network through which conscripts introduced one another to well-off men, many of them from Buenos
Aires, who paid for their sexual services.

These relationships relied on power differentials materialized in
ownership of valuable consumer goods. Car and home ownership
was associated with a middle- or upper-class lifestyle and afforded
these homosexual men a significant degree of personal autonomy
and protection from public scrutiny. According to conscripts' declarations, they usually had oral sex in their patrons' cars and anal
sex in their homes. Conscripts remembered quite well the model
and color of these cars, even though they were apparently unable
to recollect the names and addresses of the men whom they had
met (maybe they were trying to protect their anonymity). Since
the 1960s, as Adriana Premat points out, "the middle-class thirst
for knowledge, progress, and a good quality of life" and embrace
of the "outward signs of modernity" expressed itself in an "obsession" with acquiring a television and a car.[18] By offering a ride to
the conscripts, maricas showed that they had access to valuable
consumer goods in a context in which mass media connected
those goods to aspirations of upper social mobility. They impressed
on the conscripts that having sex with them was a way of getting
access to consumer culture. Houlbrook criticizes the interpretative paradigm that reduces these encounters to soldiers' commercial motivations or "a contingent response to social inequality and
low wages." Homosex was, beyond an "instrumental response to
poverty," a normalized process in the formation of masculinity.[19]
In Mar del Plata, insofar as conscripts desired maricas who gave
them access to their cars and chalets, the latter could demand a
performance of masculinity that pleased their taste. Violence was
the basic mechanism to restore gendered hierarchies, like in the
case of the officer who exhibited the revolver that he had used to
rob maricas.

There are different reasons why soldiers' engagement in homosexual acts came to light in the first place, but most often some
degree of "publicity and violence" preceded the initial investigations, as Margot Canaday points out for the U.S. military.[20] Sexual

violence was a common occurrence in military barracks, a way of asserting one's masculinity by dominating other males. A particularity of the military's judicial treatment of these kinds of cases was officers' reluctance to acknowledge same-sex sexual assault, battery, rape, and coercion. By dismissing accusations of sexual abuse, the military's judicial system protected the perpetrators and stigmatized the victims. Officers' biases regarding sexual-role and gender binaries shaped the perceived credibility of the accusers' and defendants' narratives. For instance, after two recruits testified that a corporal who previously had been a boxer coerced them into letting him perform oral sex on them, the charges against the corporal were dropped.[21] In the investigating officers' frame of mind, receiving oral sex was not seen as an act one was coerced into. Furthermore, the corporal's masculine persona did not fit with the image of the marica, the feminized homosexual male who enjoyed giving oral sex and receiving anal sex.

Sexual violence shaped maricas' experiences both before recruitment and during their military service. One soldier related in the early 1980s the recurring episodes of sexual harassment that he had suffered since he was a teenager. An adult neighbor, a brother, a schoolmate, and a gang of young males had all, at different times, tried to force him into sex, assuming that his feminine persona revealed his sexual availability. The soldier sadly admitted, "I thought that here [in the military] I would find the comradeship that I could not have in civilian life, but it was all different [from what I expected]."[22] Rumors about his sexuality spread in the barracks. Eventually one soldier approached him and pressured him to have sex, after which he only felt increasing contempt from other soldiers. Maricas were expected to be sexually available and enticing and despised for this same reason. In judicial terms, this translated into officers' tendency to see maricas as "instigators" and therefore unlikely to be victims of coercion.

In 1976, a corporal involved in an investigation of homosexual acts described how another corporal had forced him into having sex in a bathroom: "[He] took me by my hair and threw me against the wall. There, he forced my pants down, and introduced his penis

in my anus until he finished."[23] A third corporal forced him to
perform oral sex on him. However, the interrogator showed his
distrust of this version of the events, asking the deposing corporal at which moments he forcefully resisted. The corporal replied,
"At the beginning, but once they introduced their penises in me,
I stayed calm. The only thing that I wanted was for them to finish
so I could leave."[24] Given that the burden was put on rape victims
to prove that they resisted to the point of endangering themselves,
the chances were that the alleged perpetrators' versions would be
believed over the victims'. In this case, the other two defendants
denied that there had been any rape, claiming that the victim was
a willing participant. The tribunal believed the suspected perpetrators' version of events and found all three of them liable.[25] The military courts willfully ignored sexual violence between soldiers and
held alleged perpetrators' versions of events in higher regard than
those of the alleged victims. In this way, their sentences perpetuated
officers' prejudices about maricas' tendency to entice other men.

According to soldiers' depositions, penetrating another male
was often a source of pride in the conversations that they had in
the barracks. The view that a man's masculinity was reinforced
when he dominated another man through anal penetration provided a social space for soldiers performing an active sexual role
to openly share their participation in homosexual acts. Soldiers
could even aggrandize themselves or improve their reputation by
these means. In 1964, for instance, three conscripts involved in an
investigation of homosexual acts related how a corporal had told
them about his "adventures," including boasting of an occasion in
which he had had sex with a "tender, divine" soldier. The corporal
had gone to the infirmary where the soldier served, laid down on
a stretcher, put Vaseline on his penis, and convinced the soldier
to have sex. The corporal also bragged that the soldier conveyed to
him how much he had enjoyed it.[26] The penetrated soldier's pleasure, however, appeared in the corporal's narration not necessarily
as an aim that he had sought to achieve but simply as an outcome
of the corporal's sexual prowess. The fact that the corporal openly
bragged about his capacity to give sexual pleasure to other males

by penetrating them illustrates the extent to which this was seen as a sign of masculinity.

Conversely, for a soldier whose masculine reputation was questioned, penetrating another man could be a mechanism to restore his honor. In the late 1960s, the case of a subofficer came to trial after he had tried to penetrate a soldier to prove his manliness to other people. According to the subofficer's deposition, he had been subjected to multiple humiliations "for his feminine manners and reactions" since he was a child. Later in life, he married and had a son, but his tribulations continued. He found out that one of his son's classmates had taunted him about his father's feminine nickname. The subofficer developed an obsession to prove his manliness and was "desperate" to do so by penetrating another soldier.[27] However, the soldier with whom he was trying to have sex reported him.

As military men of different ranks interacted with one another trying to assert their own masculinity by dominating and emasculating their sexual partners, the roles that some men had performed as civilians were reversed in the context of the barracks. In the early 1970s, a defendant admitted that before being recruited he used to participate in transactional sex performing the penetrating role. However, after enlisting in the navy, he met a corporal who began to tease him about his "tender" and "delicate" personality and feminine perfume. This escalated into the corporal showing him his erect penis, which the soldier touched for reasons that he was not able to explain.[28] Thus, their interactions had gone from the corporal feminizing the soldier by referring to his "delicacy" to the corporal erotically exhibiting his erect penis to signify his masculinity.

In other cases, the relationships between machos and maricas followed a complex dynamic that subverted the expectations of a dominating masculinity and a submissive femininity. During a 1977 court-martial, the defendant (whom I will call Mario) described himself as a "normal" man. He proceeded to give a detailed narration of the seduction events involving himself and another soldier (whom I will call Samuel). Mario recurrently described Samuel as a "puto." The following is a conversation between Mario and Samuel as the former remembered and reproduced it during the initial investigation. For the sake of clarity, I transcribed it and translated it into English, adding Mario and Samuel's names to their respective lines and including in square brackets Mario's occasional comments to set the stage for the investigating officer.

MARIO: I am going to ask you something, but don't get mad. Why are you so interested in me?

SAMUEL: Because I like you and you are a quiet, good guy.

MARIO: Look, in the company there are guys who are prettier than me and can be as good as I am.

SAMUEL: But I fell in love with you on the first day that I saw you. . . .

MARIO: Why do you want to have a relationship with me?

SAMUEL: I already told you: because I love you and I desire you.

MARIO: If they catch us, we will go to prison.

SAMUEL: For love, that would be nice.

MARIO: It would be for you. I don't like the idea at all.

SAMUEL: Don't get mad at me. [At that moment he touched my cock.] Soon this will be mine only.

MARIO: I don't know about that. I have to think about it first.

SAMUEL: Don't you want to be my boyfriend?

MARIO: I don't know [I said, playing hard to get]. I have to ask my parents [then I laughed out loud].

SAMUEL: Don't laugh. I am talking seriously.

MARIO: Me too.

SAMUEL: Aren't there maricas who marry *machos*?

MARIO: I know there are, but those are insane, and I am not insane enough to become your husband.[29]

Mario seemed to believe that he enjoyed some kind of complicity with the interrogating officer. He expected the latter to agree that by "playing hard to get" and laughing at a marica's entreaties and affection for him he had preserved his masculinity, even though he had repeatedly penetrated another male. Masculinity, in Mario's view, was incompatible with showing oneself vulnerable to another male, either by expressing affection for him or by being anally penetrated. Therefore, insofar as he had received the affection and penetrated another male, his conduct was only mildly reprehensible.

The sort of marriage between maricas and machos that Mario and Samuel referenced was a common element of the social landscape of Buenos Aires in the late 1970s. First-person accounts confirm that in the working-class suburbs of Buenos Aires, there were maricas who performed "feminine" domestic roles in semipublic relationships with "real men." Some neighbors, especially women, apparently accepted these maricas' feminine personae and their marital status.[30] Yet Mario's deposition highlights that machos and maricas who married each other were tolerated as "deviants." Their binary domestic and sexual lives were socially recognized without subverting the view of heterosexuality as the normative ideal. In contrast with his awareness that entering into a stable relationship with another male would impinge on his masculine status, Mario described their sexual acts quite openly, almost proudly:

SAMUEL: I was waiting for you honey.

MARIO: What were you waiting for?

SAMUEL: To be by your side. [He started touching my cock, so I got a boner. I couldn't take it anymore, so I said, "Go to the bathroom." Before I had finished telling him, he was already there. I went to the bathroom, where he was waiting for me.]

SAMUEL: Finally, we are alone, and I have you all for myself.

MARIO: You didn't make me come here just to tell me that. Did you?

SAMUEL: No. [Samuel pulled his pants down while I pulled my underwear down. . . .]

SAMUEL: Come here silly, I know how to make it come back to life. In my hole, I would make a dead man's cock hard.

MARIO: Stop it, asshole, I am not dead.

SAMUEL: I know honey. [We spent fifteen minutes like that. He touched me, but nothing happened. Finally, I got a boner, and he turned around. . . .]

SAMUEL: You are being silly, put spit on it so it gets in easy.

MARIO: Stay still.

SAMUEL: It's okay daddy, don't get mad at me. [I was nervous because if they caught me, I was screwed. I put spit on my cock, and I pushed it in slowly.]

SAMUEL: Slowly daddy, it hurts. . . .

MARIO: Why did you come looking for me if you can't take it? . . .

SAMUEL: Come on daddy, I am about to come.

MARIO: Hold it a bit, let's come together [and then I came just like that].[31]

Mario represented his own libido with the intention of projecting a masculine persona. First, by emphasizing that Samuel had to sexually stimulate him for a long period of time, Mario made it clear that his body was responding to external stimuli rather than to internal desires. In other words, he claimed that his body had responded mechanically instead of being driven by sexual attraction toward other men. Second, his version of events implied that he did not care whether or not Samuel was sexually gratified. As a "real man," Mario focused on his own pleasure and treated the feminized marica as an instrument. Third, he framed Samuel as the seducer and attributed the expertise and initiative to have anal sex to Samuel, who knew how to produce an erection and about saliva's lubricant qualities. And fourth, Mario seized every opportunity in his deposition to convey how well-endowed he was; the size of his penis apparently was, in his view, another sign of his masculinity.

The sexual acts and displays of affection between Mario and Samuel took place in private, whereas in public Mario kept a visible distance between himself and "putos." When Mario and Samuel were on leave, they traveled by train to Buenos Aires. Upon arriving at the station, Samuel tried to hug Mario, who stopped him by saying, "The last thing that I would want is that my friends saw me hugging a puto."[32] Mario let Samuel manually stimulate him and kiss him in the bathrooms of the military base (and justified this relation because of his sexual release needs), but in his own neighborhood he avoided any public display of affection. The last part of the deposition centers this contrast:

> SAMUEL: Good evening sweetheart. How did you enjoy your leave?
>
> MARIO: I had a great time. My brother and I fucked a pair of locas.
>
> SAMUEL: I am sure that I am only getting the leftovers then.
>
> MARIO: I don't think so. I have nothing left. [I went to bed to lay down, and Samuel came to me.]
>
> SAMUEL: Why are you mad at me?
>
> MARIO: For no reason. [Then he started touching my cock.]
>
> SAMUEL: You know what? I love you more every day.
>
> MARIO: I love you too, as a friend, and I appreciate you a lot, but the odds are against you.
>
> SAMUEL: Let's go to the bathroom.
>
> MARIO: Okay, but this is going to be the last time. Otherwise, everyone is going to know that you are a puto, and I don't want that. [I stood up, went to the bathroom, and fucked him again. When I was leaving the bathroom, he called to me.]
>
> SAMUEL: You are a very kind, good guy. [He started crying then. I was going to stay, but I went to my bed instead. Nothing else happened after that night.][33]

Throughout his deposition, Mario made it clear that he had treated Samuel as a sexual object. In fact, by referring to he and his brother having sex with "a pair of *locas*" while he was on leave, Mario implied that sex with feminized males, a normalized practice

among working-class men in Buenos Aires, did not entail a particular attachment to any of them.[34] Yet in the last conversation
that Mario had with Samuel, he apparently acknowledged his
"friendly" affection for him and showed concern that he might
be exposed as a puto.[35] Why did Mario reference displays of affection and concern for Samuel that went against the performance of
masculinity that he had depicted before? Either he implied that
these displays were part of his way of playing with Samuel's feelings, or he had developed some sort of affection for Samuel despite
his efforts to demonstrate the opposite. While the answers do not
appear clear in the deposition, the conversations and encounters
that Mario remembered in quite remarkable detail suggest that
he had enjoyed being intimate with Samuel as well as the attention that he had received from him. This relationship between a
macho and a marica reinscribed the hierarchy of power between
masculinity and femininity but was also traversed by sexual and
affective liaisons that question the expectation that "normal" men
would treat putos or maricas with derision. Houlbrook notes that
for military males involved in homosex, "intimacy, sex, black-
mail, theft, and assault constituted a continuum within the same
cultural terrain, all underpinned by dominant understandings of
masculinity."[36] Yet maricas also served in the military and articulated a subjectivity underpinned by receptiveness, playfulness,
femininity, and self-affirmation.

Affection between men filtered into military records as some
defendants openly expressed their attachment to each other while
state agents tried surreptitiously to capture this emotional investment as a measure of culpability. In a 1970 case, a twenty-five-year-
old defendant had apparently convinced a twenty-one-year-old
defendant to maintain a sexual relationship, mostly consisting of
the former performing oral sex on the latter. The younger soldier
eventually reported these acts, apparently advised by his father
and with the intention of correcting his behavior before getting
married. In his confession, the younger defendant declared that
the older defendant had tried to persuade him that prejudices
against homosexuality were "invented by men [and that] no one

can judge what is good and evil."[37] It seemed then that the older defendant was critical of moralistic views on same-sex sexuality. In the resulting investigation, the older defendant admitted to the acts and that he had shared his personal problems with the younger defendant looking for his support. The investigating officers offered the two soldiers the opportunity to hold a private conversation so that they could agree on their version of the events. The officers' invitation was a ruse for the purposes of entrapment. The investigators secretly recorded the men's conversation, an intrusion into the soldiers' intimacy that exposed these men's personal vulnerabilities and used them as judicial evidence. According to the audio evidence introduced at trial, the older soldier had tried to persuade the younger to deny the accusations. Yet he had also showed his concern about the future of their relationship, placing his fate in the hands of the younger soldier: "I learned everything from you. This I also learned from you, that's why I put [the decision] in your hands."[38] In a subsequent deposition, the older defendant eventually admitted how invested he was in this relationship with the younger soldier: "I needed him a lot, because he is a very special person for me. . . . He listened to me when I told him my problems and advised me. . . . When he disappears from my life, I won't look for anyone to replace him, because he is unique. No one else can give me what he gives me."[39] The fact that the defendant was in love, his defense lawyer argued, differentiated him from the promiscuous, predatory homosexual individuals who wandered the streets, although the lawyer suggested that his defendant could become one of them if he did not receive some help.[40] Despite the lawyer's efforts, the jury dismissed the idea that affection was an exonerating circumstance and sentenced both defendants to prison and discharge, with a slightly harsher penalty for the older soldier based on the accusation that he had corrupted the morality of the younger soldier.[41]

As in the last case, a recurrent pattern in the military court files was for an older officer to entice and pursue a younger recruit until the latter would relent and penetrate him. Military rank and age-differential sexual relationships of this kind both relied on and subverted military discipline and hierarchy, which is probably the reason why, if exposed, they were often prosecuted. On the one hand, by being vocal about their desire to be anally penetrated by another man of lesser rank, older officers undermined their position of authority. On the other hand, their position of authority allowed them the privilege and access to seduce recruits. In 1970, a twenty-six-year-old corporal, on different occasions, ordered at least twelve adolescent soldiers to come to his room, where he asked them about their physical shape and then tried to engage them in a sexual act. The transition from an apparently routine activity, a physical condition check by an officer, to an erotic situation happened quite suddenly for the recruits: "He asked me if I played soccer and how my physical condition was. I answered affirmatively and that my physical condition was good. The corporal said that he wanted to check this by himself and ordered me to take my pants down to see. . . . He began to touch my genital organs, ordering me to get my penis erect. I asked why, and he answered: to see the size. I replied that I wouldn't do such a thing and put my underwear and pants back on."[42]

When the corporal confessed to this sexual battery, he related that he generally tried this approach with the aim of having sex with men, adopting either the passive or the active role. He chose the youngest recruits assuming that they were less experienced and more likely to accept his entreaties, but this strategy backfired as they reported him instead. In many other cases, however, recruits reported officers' entreaties after having sex with them. By feminizing themselves, the officers who seduced recruits tried to reassure the latter that their masculinity would not be undermined by having sex with them. Showing erotic images of women to the recruits served this purpose; the strategy consisted in arousing these "real" men's libido to increase the chances of them being willing to participate in same-sex intercourse.[43] In 1979, a forty-three-year-old subofficer ordered a conscript to come to his quarters. According to the conscript's subsequent complaint, the subofficer showed him his collection of pornographic magazines. Then the subofficer

took off his pajama pants, put his penis between his legs, and lay-
ing back on the bed, he asked the conscript, "Do you like this?
Don't I look like a woman?"[44] The conscript left the room without
saying a word, but the subofficer invited him over to his quarters
again. Then the subofficer began touching the conscript, applied
lotion on his own anus, and "sat" on top of the conscript's penis
until the latter ejaculated. Their meeting ended with the subofficer masturbating to orgasm in the bathroom and paying some
money to the conscript. The subofficer relied on the power of his
military rank to order the conscript to come to his private quarters but then feminized himself to seduce him, thus subverting
the gendering of military command hierarchies.

Not all relationships between military men of different rank
explicitly relied on this difference. In 1974, a corporal and a soldier established a close friendship. At night, they put their beds
together, so they could talk to one another. On one of these occasions, they looked at a pornographic magazine, which led to the
corporal touching the soldier's genitals.[45] An officer would have
had more possibilities to acquire these materials and conceal their
presence in military facilities. By showing these materials to conscripts and rank-and-file soldiers, officers undermined the military
hierarchies between them as a first step to changing the character of their relationship. At the same time, it was precisely their
military rank that allowed these officers to put enlisted men in a
position in which they did not know if they could refuse to look
at these pornographic publications. Relationships of this kind in
the context of military facilities both depended on and undermined military hierarchies.

Voyeuristic Archives

The military officers' investigation of soldiers whose homosexual practices had become exposed or too disruptive aimed to
bring these soldiers in line with the view that sexual intimacy
with another man was incompatible with masculinity, regardless of whether the implicated actors had recreated gender binaries through their social and sexual performance. To convey this

notion, military officers conducted the interrogations extracting as much information as possible from the defendants about their sexual practices and their ways of navigating the stigma attached to homoeroticism as the first step to then dismantling soldiers' "erroneous" ideas. Thus, the high level of detail in soldiers' depositions and descriptions of their sexual acts served several purposes: (1) to establish different degrees of culpability depending on the soldiers' roles in initiating homosexual behavior and in intercourse; (2) to improve the officers' knowledge and understanding of homosexuality; and (3) to socialize the defendants in the military's views on appropriate masculine roles by humiliating them for their "deviant" practices. As Margot Canaday has argued with respect to the interrogations of women accused of lesbianism in the U.S. military, "military authorities seemed to take pornographic pleasure in such work," while for the women under investigation, "the interrogation itself was a humiliating experience that could approximate psychological rape."[46] The military investigators' demands for detailed descriptions of homosexual acts were not arbitrary. They constructed the image of a "deviant" sexuality both for military officers in charge of the investigations and for the investigated soldiers themselves, who through this shaming process were to become aware of their own "deviance."

The officers investigating these cases desired exhaustive accounts of carnal acts between males. Their cross-examinations of the defendants sought evidence of ejaculation and traced both the trail and final recipient of the arrested individuals' semen, producing a voyeuristic archive. In other words, military records contain detailed descriptions of same-sex encounters that at the time would have been considered too obscene to be printed in any other context. Prosecutors led interrogations to produce transcriptions that reflected as closely as possible the sexually charged interactions between soldiers, including the original vocabulary that they used. When one soldier hesitated with unease about reproducing a sexually explicit conversation that he had with another soldier, the prosecutor prodded him to do so using the original terms:

DEFENDANT: He came to me and asked me, "*negro*,[47] do you
know what I have?" I don't know what I should say now.

PROSECUTOR: Use the same terms.

DEFENDANT: He told me: "you know *negro* what I have . . .
I have a boner."[48]

Furthermore, prosecutors also explicitly coaxed soldiers during their depositions about the level of detail that they expected.
In a trial in 1977, when the soldier began to describe how a corporal touched his testicles, the prosecutor interrupted him: "Please,
I want every little detail about this part."[49] This same prosecutor
could not hide his frustration when another of the interrogated
defendants repeatedly failed to provide him with a satisfactory,
detailed enough description of his sexual encounter with a corporal:

PROSECUTOR (P): What did you do while he touched you?

DEFENDANT (D): I tried to push him and then I came.

P: Did he only touch you with his hand?

D: Yes, just with his hand and he put his face beside my dick
when I came.

P: Did he put something on you, his mouth for instance?

D: Yes, the mouth?

P: Come on, you are the one who has to tell me every little
detail. Tell me again.

D: He sits down on the bed, holds me with his left hand, and
with the right one he "jerks me off" and I come.

P: And where did [it] go? [In the Spanish original this question may have referred to a person.]

D: He went to the bathroom.

P: No, no, what you came.

D: I think he swallowed it, in his mouth.[50]

Ejaculation was a major focus of interest for the investigating
officers, who persistently asked soldiers accused of homosexuality

what events and practices led them to orgasm and where their semen ended up. Interrogators left any formalism aside to clearly establish whether soldiers ejaculated, as in the case of a prosecutor who repeatedly asked the defendant "Did you come?" (¿Acabó usted?).[51] Due to military officers' systematic and deep interest in ejaculation, there exists a comprehensive archive detailing soldiers' specific ways of reaching orgasm. In a trial in 1970, the soldier who had performed the inserter role while having anal sex with another soldier clarified that he had pulled out his penis from the rectum of the other soldier before ejaculation for fear of diseases.[52] And in another case in 1973, in which a corporal seduced several soldiers and performed the receptive role during anal sex with them, we find a varied repertoire: one of the soldiers ejaculated while trying to penetrate the corporal; another soldier ejaculated penetrating the corporal while the latter "used his hands to keep his buttocks open"; a third soldier introduced his finger in the corporal's anus while the latter manually stimulated him until he ejaculated; and a fourth soldier ejaculated on the corporal's buttocks after failing to penetrate him.[53]

Military officers mostly looked for evidence of an "active" participant anally penetrating a "passive" participant until one or both ejaculated, but instead, they found a very diverse range of sexual practices. In other words, the sexually explicit content of the files was a result of the contradiction between authorities' expectation that sex limited itself to penetration to release sexual tension and a much more complex reality. Interrogations were privy to the defendants' vivid descriptions of diverse sexual practices between them and other men, including group sex. In transcripts, the investigators mapped the erogenous zones (anus, penis, mouth) of each of the participants and when and how they were in contact with each other, as well as the journeys and destinations of their semen. In his initial deposition, a navy sailor described his sexual relationships with two corporals, one of whom preferred to play the "passive" role and the other who preferred the "active" role. One night the three individuals met. The first corporal started to perform oral sex on the second corporal until he ejaculated in his mouth, while the soldier watched them. Next, the corporal who preferred to play the inserter role penetrated the soldier, while the other corporal watched them, and then the latter separated them so that he could be penetrated while the soldier watched. In a subsequent deposition, the corporal who preferred the receptive role confessed that he had performed oral sex on several other soldiers, which usually ended in these soldiers ejaculating in his mouth, as the latter confirmed in their depositions.[54]

Apart from extracting information about soldiers' orgasms, during their depositions the military officers had to translate official categories such as "homosexual" into vernacular ones such as "puto." In this way, the defendants could begin to grasp the contrast between the definition of sexual deviance according to the military's legal codes and the definition according to the sexual culture that predominated in the barracks and the soldiers' worlds off the base. "Puto" conveyed much more clearly the stigma of sexual deviance than the term "homosexual" when the judges and defendants were trying to confirm that they were referring to the same human type. In a 1968 interrogation of a fifteen-year-old navy soldier, a judge wanted to make sure that the defendant understood his offense:

JUDGE: Are you a homosexual?

SOLDIER: No, mister Judge.

JUDGE: Do you know what a homosexual is?

SOLDIER: Yes, sir. In general terms, it means being a puto.

[The soldier describes how he and a corporal gave each other hickeys, tickled each other, and hugged each other, most of the time while the corporal had an erection.]

JUDGE: Did you realize that with those hand games, kisses, and "hickeys" you could become a puto?

SOLDIER: I am realizing right now. Not before, sir. And I am fully convinced that this won't happen to me ever again . . .

JUDGE: Didn't any conscript or sailor call you "puto de mierda" [shitty faggot] or "mujercita" [little woman], or something similar that warned you that your behavior with the corporal was inconvenient or prejudicial for you?[55]

This was the kind of negotiation of meaning between sexual categories that the implementation of the Military Code and other state policies required. The official and neutral-sounding term "homosexual" was translated into the derogatory, vernacular term "puto." Once the military judge decided to use this last category for the sake of mutual understanding, his goal was to make sure that the soldier internalized that hickeys, kisses, and other forms of physical intimacy between two males, which he might have normalized as part of military comradeship, could in fact turn him into a puto. The judge seemed almost frustrated that other soldiers had not done this job already by insulting and denigrating the interrogated soldier. For the judge, an early humiliation by male peers or during the court-martial could save the adolescent defendant from a future of sexual deviance and stigma, and "puto" was a much more effective term and deterrent in this respect than "homosexual." Moreover, the judge's explicit reference to the possibility of becoming a puto indicates that he saw sexuality as contingent on external factors and personal trajectories, a view that informed the interrogations as well as the defendants' depositions and their legal defenses.

Military investigators used the term "puto" being fully aware that it referred to the receptive sexual role, even relying on it in depositions to clarify a soldier's role in intercourse when they were not sure that these soldiers understood their inquiries using the active/passive binary. In a court-martial in 1969, two soldiers disagreed about who had played the inserter and who the receptive role, which led an officer of the court to use the term "puto" for the sake of clarity:

COURT'S OFFICER (C): How was it? He was the passive one and you the active one?

NAVY SOLDIER (S): Yes.

C: You say he was certainly a puto. How do you know it?

S: Well, if after what he did with me, two other men got caught, that means he wasn't a saint.

C: Do you know what a puto is?

S: What that is understood to be, yes. Well, it's the guy who makes himself be penetrated ["el tipo que se hace dar"]

C: Did you give it [your penis] to him?

S: I didn't fuck him.

C: Then how did you know that he was a puto?[56]

The interrogated soldier clarified that he had rubbed his penis between the legs and the buttocks of the soldier whom he considered a puto, and since the latter performed the receptive role in this form of nonpenetrative sex, he might do so in penetrative sex too. Both the officer of the court and the soldier focused on sexual roles to define the meaning of "puto," and both agreed that the puto was the receptive partner, whether in penetrative or nonpenetrative sex. However, the soldier also added to this definition that the puto usually made "himself be penetrated," meaning that it was socially expected that he would take the initiative leading to homosexual acts. Thus, the sexual culture of machos and maricas resurfaced in this as in most interrogations.

Psychopathy and Seduction Games

The psychologists and psychiatrists who examined soldiers accused of homosexuality claimed, and probably believed, that they were diagnosing psychopathy according to prescribed criminological and medical criteria that designated an imprinted pathological inclination to dismiss social and ethical norms. They repeatedly affirmed that the diagnosis of homosexuality did not vary depending on sexual role. Yet at the same time, their reports incorporated a sexual culture that established that "passive" homosexuals (maricas or putos) had to entice "normal" men. The latter could either fall victim to this seduction or take advantage of "passive" homosexuals. Psychopathy marked, then, the agent of the malicious effects of perversion, defined according to nonmedical criteria either as the luring passive homosexual or, in fewer instances, as the "normal" man who took advantage of maricas sexually or economically. According to this binary model, the "passive" role marked the "true" homosexual whose sexual instincts were imprinted, while men who occasionally indulged in same-sex intercourse to relieve their urges would perform the "active" role.

At the same time, a diagnosis of psychopathy did not necessarily absolve a defendant from his responsibility; if the court found that the accusations were proven true, then soldiers were convicted regardless of their diagnoses. Only a diagnosis establishing the defendant's lack of understanding of his actions' criminal implications was exonerating. In 1966 two soldiers were court-martialed after the "passive" soldier allegedly drugged the "active" soldier with an aphrodisiac pill in his water so that the latter would penetrate him. The "passive" soldier was diagnosed with "schizoid psychopathic personality with elements of instinctive perversion and great impulsivity" and "transitory alteration of his [own] consciousness" and acquitted.[57] The soldier who had penetrated him was also acquitted given the unconfirmed possibility that the aphrodisiac had affected his conduct.[58]

Psychological reports included in military files reveal the tension between medical experts' attempts to single out abnormal soldiers, the understanding of homosexual relationships in terms of gender binaries, and the psychoanalytical premise that "latent homosexuality is present in everyone."[59] This last statement was made in 1970 by a medical lieutenant in front of a military court that demanded clarification on the report that he had submitted. According to the report, one defendant was not homosexual according to the psychological tests that he took but could have had occasional homosexual behaviors attributable to universal latent homosexuality, which problematized strict classifications and taxonomies.

Among the instances in which only the "passive" homosexual was diagnosed as suffering from psychopathy was a 1976 case involving two soldiers who anally penetrated a third soldier. The latter maintained that he had been raped by the two other soldiers, who claimed that the alleged victim seduced them. According to the forensic reports, the "passive" soldier had an "infundibuliform" anus and relaxed sphincters (taken to be signs of him being anally penetrated in the past) and the psychological tests demonstrated that he had a "compulsive psychopathic personality."[60] In contrast, the reports about the two other soldiers did not identify anything abnormal in the physical or in the psychological exams.[61] Through these diagnoses, the forensic report implicitly gave validity to the "active" soldiers' version of events—that the initiative to engage in anal sex had come from the "passive" soldier, driven by his pathological sexuality. Similarly, in 1979 on the military base in Ushuaia, a middle-aged noncommissioned officer allegedly seduced a young conscript who eventually penetrated him. The officer was diagnosed with hysterical and psychopathic personality traits, and his co-participant with traits of "emotional immaturity" that did not amount to a pathological condition.[62]

These reports represented the desires of "passive" homosexual males as fixated and those of the "active" participants as indiscriminate. Following this pattern, in 1977 Samuel and Mario (whose deposition I analyzed before) were diagnosed with "psychopathic personalities" after having sex on multiple occasions. The logic of these diagnoses was that Samuel, the "passive" homosexual, had seduced Mario, and the latter had mockingly participated in this seduction game just to have some sex, which he openly acknowledged at his initial deposition. Significantly, the report on Samuel noted a "compulsion to reiterated passive homosexual relationships," while the report on Mario noted undifferentiated "sexual compulsions."[63] The implication was clearly that "passive" partners' sexual drives were fixated on other men, while "active" partners' sexuality was undifferentiated and pragmatic.

Examiners diagnosed soldiers who had performed the "active" role as psychopaths when judging that they had demonstrated their imprinted opposition to social norms by taking advantage of vulnerable "passive" homosexuals, like in Mario's case. In another case, the psychologist attributed the "passive" soldier's homosexual acts to alcohol intoxication and an earlier traumatic experience of being gang raped. Thus, the forensic report established that he was not responsible for his own actions. By contrast, according to the psychologist, the soldier who had performed the "active" role was repressing a "great aggressiveness" and was constantly looking for "immediate personal and social gratification."[64] He was diagnosed with a psychopathic personality being responsible for his actions. The two diagnoses operated in tandem: insofar as the "passive" partner was a victim of traumatic experiences, the "active" partner appeared as an aggressor who took advantage of him to satisfy his sexual urges. Similarly, a soldier who blackmailed another soldier whom he had penetrated, threatening to expose him as a homosexual to his family, was diagnosed as a psychopath in correlation with the diagnosis of "liminal oligophrenia" (mental disability) of the penetrated soldier.[65] This was a paradigmatic case of diagnosing "active" homosexual males as psychopaths based on evidence of them taking advantage of vulnerable "passive" homosexual males.

Psychologists often detected signs of psychopathic personalities and homosexuality through the thematic apperception test (TAT), even when every other aspect of the examination was normal. Harvard psychologist Henry A. Murray and his lover Christina Morgan created the TAT in the 1930s. The test, inspired by Jungian psychoanalysis, was meant to reveal the patient's deepest unconscious. During the test, the examiner shows the subject cards with different images and the latter must make up stories that explain those images. Nineteenth-century German Romanticism, which advanced the idea that a literary text opens a window into the narrator's deepest self, inspired Murray's vision of the test. The role of the psychologist would be, then, to decipher the meaning of the subject's narrative.[66] Signs of homosexuality could be recognized by specific content in the stories: "stories in which men kill women" (any card), or "stories in which the hero has been attacked from the rear or pulled to the rear" (card 18). Furthermore, if the subject showed a "high degree of feminine identification," a "derogatory attitude toward marriage and the opposite sex," or included in the story any sexual or genital reference, then these would all be considered signs of homosexuality.[67] This hermeneutical logic assumed an association between male homosexuality and violent impulses, a fixation on sex and genitals, a feminine and yet misogynist attitude, and disdain for heteronormative marriage. While in previous chapters I traced deciphering as one of maricas' techniques to communicate forbidden messages, in this instance deciphering was a technique of psychoanalytic reading that—with no evidentiary basis beyond common prejudices—adjudicated homosexuality on the grounds of "antisocial" behaviors faultily assumed to be correlated with it. Given that the TAT entirely relies on psychologists' interpretations of the stories that subjects elaborate in response to the cards, this test gave examiners significant leeway to establish their diagnoses based on their particular readings of subjects' personae.[68]

In the 1977 case of a soldier diagnosed as having a psychopathic personality, his performances on the Rorschach test, the implicit association test, and the test of the couple did not indicate anything anomalous. He had normal intellectual and working aptitudes. During his interview the examiner noted that he seemed "adjusted to reality," his appearance was "correct and kind," and he was interested in the process. However, the examiner detected "hidden homosexual features" through the TAT, which along with conflicts in the "affective area" resulting from the defendant's judicial situation, led to the diagnosis of being psychopathic.[69] Another soldier diagnosed as having a "psychopathic personality" also had, according to the exam, normal judgment, reasoning, attention, perception, and memory capacities. His answers during the Rorschach test and the association test were normal, and no "lesions of passive homosexuality" were found in his physical exam.[70] Yet the TAT allegedly revealed his repressed aggressiveness, a cyclical-type personality, unresolved Oedipal problems, hidden homosexual elements, and his tendency to lie.[71] Thus, psychologists claimed that through the hermeneutics of the TAT, they could uncover veiled homosexual elements rooted in Oedipal conflicts and issue a diagnosis of psychopathic personality even when lacking any other evidence of anomalous psychological reactions.

Moreover, when none of the tests showed anything notewor-thy, psychologists often took the accusation of homosexuality itself as evidence of ethical flaws that they used to support the diagno-sis of a psychopathic personality, even though these psychologi-cal exams were part of judicial processes to establish whether the defendants were culpable for those accusations. Thus, a soldier was diagnosed as having a psychopathic personality of the homosexual type based on his significant ethical flaws and his "compulsion to the reiteration of passive homosexual relationships" even though his performance on the tests did not indicate anything anoma-lous.[72] Likewise, another soldier was diagnosed as having a com-pulsive psychopathic personality based not on the results of the tests but on an "affective anesthesia with sexual compulsions that determine a loss of ethical norms."[73] The circle was closed insofar as accusations of homosexuality were taken to prove soldiers' sex-ual compulsions and lack of ethics, which became the same diag-noses that were then used to support the charges against them.

Contingent Sexualities

Both defense attorneys and soldiers generally presented a narrative according to which homosexual acts and tendencies were contin-gent on the defendants' personal trajectories more than an essential component of their being. Soldiers' legal defenses focused on the extent to which environmental or contingent factors were exoner-ating. While it is not possible to establish whether this coincidence was due to the defendants' intention to adjust their depositions to authorities' expectations, it points out that the view of sexuality as an essence was not the organizing principle of these judicial pro-cesses. The contingent circumstances to which the defendants attrib-uted their homosexual practices include everything from unreleased sexual tension to phimosis and even paranormal powers. In most cases, soldiers would identify a turning point before which their sex-uality was "normal" as well as an unfortunate or noxious external factor that caused their sexuality to divert from its previous course.

In this way, soldiers implicitly claimed that their masculinity and heterosexual libido were recoverable. For instance, in the late

1960s, one soldier declared that he had had his first homosexual relationship after the death of a girl whom he was dating. He took a train trip with friends during which they were drinking, which led to a friend penetrating him in the bathroom.[74] Another soldier related that in his adolescence he had lived with an aunt in Salta, a province in the interior of Argentina. According to the soldier, a small group of homosexual individuals lived on a neighboring farm and often invited men over to have remunerated sex with them.[75] Whether or not it was true that there was something resembling a homosexual commune in Salta in the early 1960s, the defendant was trying to trace his "deviance" to the corrupting effect of homosexual individuals' willingness to pay for sex as a way of exculpating himself.

Other defendants attributed their homosexual tendencies to paranormal powers to exculpate themselves. In a trial initiated in 1966, the defendant explained that he had started to like men at age seventeen after breaking up with a girlfriend because of pressures from his family. Troubled by this late discovery of homoeroticism, he visited a healer, who supposedly informed him that he had been cursed by his ex-girlfriend.[76] Similarly, in the late 1970s, a soldier claimed that another defendant had used his powers as a medium of the demon Zurbas to scare him into having sex.[77] The alleged medium, for his part, explained that his troubles originated when he was raped at age ten by a gang of adolescents and were recently made worse when another soldier replaced his "good" spirit with an "evil" one during a session of spiritism.[78] In this case, demons and spirits were intermingled with sexual foreplay and seduction. The alleged medium supposedly wanted to be penetrated and approached the other soldier with this goal. The widespread expectation that the feminized "passive" partner was to seduce the "active" partner led to the demonization of the former as a legal defense strategy, investing him with paranormal powers to attain his perverse goals.

The demonization of the "passive" partner to exculpate the "active" partner drew from a sexual culture that assumed that men had to release their sexual tension through penetration leading to ejaculation, engaging in homosexual acts if necessary. Military officers serving as defense lawyers appealed to the court's awareness that among the "uneducated" working classes, penetration of another man was seen more as a sign of masculinity than as a deviant practice. However, defendants who had found pleasure and ejaculated while being penetrated or who had enjoyed performing oral sex on other men could not count on an equivalent legal defense. In other words, while the sexuality of both "active" and "passive" soldiers was represented as contingent on personal trajectories and the sentences were roughly the same, the implicated actors generally attributed the role of instigator and a fixated desire to "passive" homosexuals, in contrast with the malleable libido of "active" homosexuals. For instance, in 1977 the military lawyer of a navy soldier attributed his homosexual practices to "his sexual education [which] is totally incomplete and deficient, as illustrated by the fact that my defendant [only] labels homosexual the one performing the passive role, and refuses to acknowledge the active homosexual as such."[79] In the case of Mario, the defense plea contrasted the "deficient upbringing," which had led Mario to penetrate Samuel, with the latter's demonic character: "The routines of military life put an extremely skillful, sick man in my defendant's way. [This man's] disease deprives him of any scruple or morality. Forgetting what a healthy friendship is, using his demonic tricks, and taking advantage of my defendant's deficient upbringing, he dismissed the consequences to carry out such a repulsive act. This is why, [after] being the prey of a relentless hunt, my defendant is sitting today at the defendants' table. . . . He could not clearly distinguish the differences that exist between an active homosexual and normal manly [sexual] activity."[80]

Without referring to paranormal powers, the lawyer also participated in the demonization of the "passive" homosexual, investing Samuel with the animalistic traits of a sexual predator, as well as with extraordinary skills and malice. The lawyer described the alleged process of seduction in a grandiloquent rhetoric as the "constant fight between good and evil" to which Mario, "a poor guy with mental problems," finally gave in.[81] Both soldiers declared that effectively Samuel (who identified as a puto) had enticed Mario, and the former acknowledged that he had also seduced other soldiers as well as several "machos" when he was a civilian.[82] The social expectation that putos/maricas would seduce machos was translated into legal arguments that favored the latter based on the former's double role reversal: first by letting themselves be penetrated, and second by proactively enticing other men against expectations of marica passivity.

Paradoxically, active sexual drives were seen as both the defining trait of masculinity and a threat to military discipline when they were not properly channeled, rendering soldiers vulnerable to "passive" homosexual males' predatory strategies. Mario's lawyer described the symptoms of sexual deprivation with the terminology of a scientific manual and the tragic tone of a realistic novel: "His pituitary gland still functions, the ratio of androgens in his blood has not gone down. The accumulation of sexual secretions periodically puts him in situations that require a special relief. What should he do in this regard?"[83] The lawyer, then, described military masculinity as a process resembling the "microphysics of power" or the "political technology of the body" theorized by Michel Foucault: "dispositions, tactics, techniques and operations" to bring one's body under control.[84] Among these, the lawyer enumerated a series of steps that typically appeared consecutively: first, caring letters from soldiers' mothers and girlfriends; second, compulsive eating and smoking to appease an "oral anxiety of replacement"; third, sexual fantasies and wet dreams leading to masturbation, at which point it was officers' role to comfort recruits; and finally, transactional sex with women or, alternatively and most regretfully, giving in to other soldiers' sexual advances.[85] In other words, in the case of soldiers who had performed an "active" role, their lawyers appealed to the court's sympathy for men who had lost an internal battle to control their sexual urges.

In innumerable cases, defense lawyers excused the code violations of soldiers who had performed the "active" role on the combination of their unsatisfied sexual needs and educational and social backgrounds.[86] The more distant defendants were from the urban middle class to which military officers belonged, the less aware they were assumed to be that penetrating other males was not appropriate, so rural laborers were assumed to epitomize working-class men's unrestrained yet naïve sexual drives.[87] According to this stereotyped narrative, drunkenness and lack of sufficient sexual opportunities with women were the triggering factors leading some soldiers to penetrate others or let them perform oral sex on them.[88] However, this legal defense did not usually affect the verdict, unless the court considered it proved that the defendant had not been properly instructed on the content of the Military Code during his training.[89] If anything, adolescent recruits who had allegedly been enticed into performing the "active" role were often sentenced to a lighter penalty than their co-participants if these were adult officers who apparently had taken advantage of their rank in order to perform the "passive" role.[90]

The defense strategies of soldiers who had performed a "passive" role describe not a sexuality gone astray because of a lack of sexual outlets but rather a series of contingent pathological circumstances beyond the defendants' control, which had led them to develop a taste for performing a feminized role. This taste would appear more or less fixated in lawyers' accounts depending on the extent to which the defendants' social behavior matched their feminized sexual role. In other words, a male who had occasionally performed a "passive" role but maintained a masculine public persona seemed more recoverable for military lawyers than an individual who had adopted a feminized public persona. Among the first type of case, there was a corporal who, according to his file, came from a normal home, was well behaved and educated, and had a manly sexual life until the incidents that led to his trial in 1970. However, according to his lawyer, he developed a neurosis because of his ugliness and a phimosis (unretractable foreskin), which made sex with women ever more painful for him. Neurosis was a psychoanalytic diagnosis that in Argentine criminological contexts implied a certain optimism about an individual's potential for adjustment based on internal conflicts with his homosexuality. The lawyer poetically expressed this optimism, describing his defendant as "a cocoon that already should have opened itself to the sun's light."[91] In contrast, according to the records of this trial, before he was arrested the defendant had been quite proactive in looking for sex and had seemingly enjoyed it. He had enticed a soldier by letting him know that he longed to have sex feeling like a woman, so the latter penetrated him until both ejaculated, with the defendant masturbating while the other soldier watched him. On a different occasion, he enticed the same soldier by showing him an image of a naked woman, and they had sex again.[92] The judgment of this defendant's code violation contrasted his normative masculine behavior before the incident with his adoption of a feminized persona and sexual role while serving in the military. Despite the lawyer's argument that the defendant's neurosis signaled his recoverability, he was sentenced to a harsher penalty than his co-participant because of his higher rank, older age, and performance as instigator.

In contrast, if the defendant had visibly adopted a feminine persona, lawyers put little emphasis on their potential to adjust to the expectations of masculinity. They argued instead that these defendants did not belong in the military in the first place because of their femininity, and therefore they should not be judged by its codes. In 1967, a defendant confessed to having remunerated sex with men in brothels in Uruguay and Buenos Aires before being recruited. The police department reported that the defendant had adopted a woman's name and had exhibited immoral behavior.[93] According to the file of the court-martial, she had enticed another soldier by manually and orally stimulating him and then instructed him on how to proceed during anal penetration by saying, "Push, just push harder."[94] When asked if she had actually shouted "Turn off that light and let me fuck in peace" at the group of conscripts who caught them having sex, she replied that she might have done so, given a temporary "state of excitation."[95]

This defendant had expressed her femininity as a civilian, vocally expressed desires to be penetrated, was willing to stimulate a co-participant in order to do so, and openly confronted those who dared to interrupt them while having sex. This behavior corresponds with contemporary depictions of Buenos Aires' locas or maricas who performed a sexualized femininity, enticed masculine men, and were quite open about their desires.[96] Therefore, the lawyer did not try to blame his defendant's behavior on unreleased sexual tension or argue that she regretted these acts. Instead, he highlighted that the defendant's "abnormal condition" had been "fueled by degenerate, infected environments," probably referring to the brothels where she had made a living. Given these contingent factors for which the defendant was not responsible, and that she felt like a woman, the lawyer held that liability could not be judged according to the standards applied to men.[97]

While "active" soldiers were excused on account of their unreleased sexual tension, "passive" soldiers were denied the full status of manhood, which in this context was considered a precondition for juridical personhood. Therefore, their lawyers tried to exempt them from the disciplinary codes of an institution defined as exclusively masculine. In fact, in these kinds of cases, some military lawyers were clearly more concerned about distancing themselves from the defendants to reassert their own masculinity than about presenting a convincing legal defense. Such was the case in 1978 when a defense lawyer characterized homosexuality as one of "the human miseries that society has had to bear" since the biblical time when Jehovah destroyed Sodom and Gomorrah. He acknowledged that he shared the court's "indignation and disgust" in the face of a human type that he compared with "lepers." After establishing his moral condemnation of the defendant, the lawyer argued that the latter should have been discarded at the recruitment medical exam, since his sexuality was intrinsically incompatible with military discipline. Finally, he claimed that the defendant's "homosexual natural germ" had been activated by "an active subject," at once partially naturalizing his sexuality and transferring liability to someone else.[98] The concept of "germ" implied potentiality, but the focus remained on the environmental factors that transformed this potential into sexual practices. The defendant himself had acknowledged that he felt "a natural inclination toward men awaken since the first years of his adolescence by causes that he can't explain to himself."[99] The defendant essentialized his sexuality. However, this was a personal narrative that did not resonate as much with officers' expectations as the focus on environmental factors did. Officers' view of sexuality as contingent, along with medical experts' theories and diagnosing practices, contributed to a differential treatment of the defendants, which established a correlation between their gender and sexual performance and their recoverability.

Moreover, military authorities' increasing concern about androgynous fashions that questioned the tenets of masculinity could be used by offenders to displace liability and exculpate themselves. For instance, during a court-martial in the late 1970s, the defendant described a transactional relationship he had had with a man "of effeminate manners, long hair, 20 or 25 years old": "He tried to feel me up, but I didn't let him. I told him to pull his pants down and masturbated a little bit to get an erection."[100] Although he got paid for penetrating this man, the soldier emphasized that he neither felt any desire for him nor let him have any other kind of physical intimacy. In other words, his legal defense strategy consisted of presenting his libido as purely heterosexual but corrupted by a man of dubious appearance. Furthermore, by portraying this man as effeminate and long-haired (implying that he had adopted hippies' fashion), the defendant appealed to officers' contempt for the youth countercultures of the 1970s. This strategy apparently worked, as the defendant was sentenced to a mild prison penalty that he had already served while awaiting the verdict. In contrast, the next chapter traces how androgynous fashions contemporaneously became the target of state policing as a vehicle for nonconforming individuals' self-expression.

Conclusion

In my initial reading of courts-martial, I overtly trusted soldiers' words and their performances of naïveté. I did not take sufficiently into account the fact that performances are defined by the audience they target and archival records by different layers of mediation that reflect power asymmetries between those historical actors implicated in producing them. Masculinity and femininity, as performed in military courts, both overlapped and diverged from the sexual cultures of the barracks in which gender operated as a fundamental element of seduction and enticement. In her study of diasporic Mexican masculinities, Nicole M. Guidotti-Hernández argues that "men's intimacies also made up their lives as political subjects" and "were made flexible by migration."[101] Similarly, while military service in Argentina was meant to socialize men in their proper obligations to the nation (political subjectivity), it also introduced them into a male-only sexual culture that demanded participants to perform gender roles that sometimes were, and sometimes were not, an extension of their masculine identities in civilian life (flexible masculinity). Some soldiers claimed that they acted as maricas and machos when having sex with each other because those were their identities before being recruited, while other soldiers argued that military life had introduced them to uncharted sexual intimacies in which they performed gender roles different from those they had known before.

These depositions imply that military discipline produced homosexuality. The officers' voyeurism during the defendants' interrogations could be interpreted as a response to this disturbing implication. They forced soldiers to provide explicit details about their sexual encounters, and those details could be read as evidence that maricas' unwarranted infiltration into the military ranks (which should have been prevented by medical screenings) was the primary cause of their relationships with other soldiers. In other words, by reifying the macho/marica binary, military officers could pretend that this sexual culture, rather than military discipline, accounted for widespread homosexuality among soldiers. The practical implications of foregrounding marica and macho identities must be taken as a cautionary note when reading official sources that revolve obsessively around these identities. Official sources, at the same time, obscure how officers in charge of investigations performed masculinity in ways that convinced some defendants (those who felt like machos) that they would be treated leniently and others (those who identified as maricas) that they did not have another option than admitting to their own role as seducers. The archive positions the historian in front of a stage on which soldiers perform legible roles in a stereotyped gendered script. As Pilar Espitia argues, "Modesty and obscenity are defined through interpretative acts, namely, through the intentions of those who witness an act, the textual production and framing of the act, and the readers of the act, including us contemporary readers."[102] Taking this theatrical metaphor even further, officers in charge of maintaining that legibility (fixating on desire, penetration, and semen) become the equivalent of stage managers, always orchestrating narratives through their questions and expectations yet invisible to the audience in terms of their own experience of participation in military sexual cultures.

PART 3

Marica Politics

FIVE

Travesti and Marica Prisoners

Clothes, Performance, and Resistance

In the late 1970s, a former Argentine soldier joined a hippie community and was arbitrarily arrested and tortured because of his "androgynous" appearance. He had decided to desert after participating in the atrocities committed at the Navy Petty-Officers School (Escuela Superior de Mecánica de la Armada or ESMA), which became an infamous clandestine detention and torture center during the so-called National Reorganization Process (1976–83). Soon after, the police arrested him and one of his friends because they "wore sandals and had long hair." Their hippie look rendered them into a sexual threat. They were forced to sign a statement, probably admitting to a violation of clause 2H of the police code, which was used to charge gay men and transgender women with prohibited sexual solicitation. An officer called them "putos" and threatened "to beat the crap out of them" and charge them with contempt if they refused to admit to their homosexuality. Police violence was aimed, in this case, at forcibly imposing a pejorative label for homosexual males (puto) on subjects who did not identify with it. After being coerced into signing their statement, they were transferred to a detention center. Upon their arrival, a guard read aloud a report denouncing them as homosexuals and grabbed a high-powered hose and violently sprayed them with it. While these arbitrary arrests were a common occurrence during the dictatorship, this former soldier felt immunized to the punishments inflicted on him by police officers because these were mild in comparison to the tortures that he himself had inflicted on the ESMA inmates: "After what we did in there, you know, there were things that did not shock us too much."[1] In this way, he recognized the irony of military perpetrators, such as himself, being targeted by the state policing of sexuality on account of their gendered aesthetics. Malva, a well-known marica, remembers how in the early 1970s, security forces carried out a "hunt for *maricones*" that targeted "long-haired men, hippies, and girls in miniskirts." Maricones were arrested and hippies had their long hair and bell-bottom pants cut.[2] Malva's testimony's value lies not in its factual aspects—she does not specify either the extent or the perpetrators of this campaign—but in her awareness that police officers targeted maricas based on their appearance, as they did with other groups who adopted fashion codes that questioned traditional gender roles.

From the late 1960s, the popularization of androgynous hippie fashions questioned traditional representations of masculinity and opened new opportunities for maricas to express themselves. In this period, forensic doctors' and criminologists' concerns shifted from latent to manifest homosexuality—in their terminology—or from subjects who were unable to inhibit themselves to those who were unwilling to do it. One of the denominations that police officers in Spain used for males accused of homosexuality was *esteta* (aesthete), which by itself reveals how aesthetic and sexual "excess" appeared intertwined in authorities' criminological frameworks. Maricas held "the power inscribed in the domain of the 'aesthetic,' the 'ephemeral,' and the 'superfluous'" (borrowing from Fabio Cleto's studies on camp).[3] Lawrence La Fountain-Stokes foregrounds "the politics of transformation" in "engaging with abjection as much as glamour" through the sort of acts on which this chapter focuses: "when we don a wig, makeup, breast forms, hip and buttock pads, feminine clothes, jewelry, and high heels, or when we transform our bodies and have gender reassignment surgeries or other cosmetic procedures that change our appearance and bring forth new identities."[4] La Fountain-Stokes uses the neologism "translocas" to trace Puerto Rican drag and trans performance by "disreputable, cross-dressing, effeminate, and transgender" people.[5]

This chapter is a study of maricas' and locas' performance and aesthetics in Argentina and Spain. A such, it relies mostly on archival sources from the 1960s and 1970s in which the distinction between cisgender and transgender subjectivities does not appear articulated as such. There are first-person accounts of maricas' lives in this period, and they diverge in their ways of relating to the term "marica" and its derivatives. Tania Navarro Amo, in *La infancia de una transexual en la dictadura* (2021), conveys how much she dislikes the term "maricón" but adds that this appellative and later the term "travesti" were the ones that Spanish "transexual" women like herself used to identify themselves until at least the early 1980s.[6] Malva was a marica born in Chile who crossed the Andes into Argentina in the 1940s and lived in Buenos Aires for the rest of her life. Her memoir *Mi recordatorio: Autobiografía de Malva* was published in 2011, reactivating cultural frameworks that, up until the 1980s, assumed that maricas' femininity and their sexual desires were intertwined.[7] The Library of Congress catalogs Malva's memoir within the subject headings of Argentine "gay men" and "cross-dressers."[8] This contrasts with Malva expressing that she considers maricas to be very much different from gay men: "Everything has changed in terms of the homosexual modality. I must accept that my condition as such does not match the ways of feeling and acting today."[9] Among other things, maricas had sex with men, not with other maricas, according to Malva.[10] Rather than taking a taxonomic approach to archival records produced as a result of state surveillance, focusing on how maricas who lived in the 1960s and 1970s fit into contemporary "subject headings," this chapter shows how maricas incorporated aesthetics and performance into their individual and collective strategies of survival.

These strategies were—borrowing James C. Scott's phrase—the "weapons of the weak" of maricas.[11] Malva emphasizes that cross-dressers in carnival associations in Buenos Aires's working-class suburbs (*murgas del conurbano*) were offered certain protections by venues and other participants in the festivals. These *murgas* only performed in venues like the clubs Nuevo Chicago and Comunicaciones, which prevented the "hunting of *putos*" by providing private transportation.[12] Hence Malva contrasts maricas' persistence in finding spaces where their performance would be well received and the violence that marked their daily lives. Similarly, Tania Navarro remembers how maricas in Francoist prisons used plaster, aluminum foil, moisturizing lotion, and matches to create a whole makeup set, from mascara to powder, which otherwise were forbidden for convicts classified as "male" by state officials.[13] When she was a child, Tania found a wedding dress in an abandoned house that she put on to dance folk music in a public square, while the neighbors clapped so that she would have background music.[14] In these instances, clothing and makeup were at the core of daily forms of resistance through visibility and gender expression that questioned state surveillance mechanisms and put marica embodiments at the forefront.[15] *Sexilio* was another of these strategies of resistance, a term in Spanish that denotes the centrality of gendered violence and police harassment in queer and trans people's decisions to migrate from one place to another.[16] There were many international sexilios in the 1970s. Argentine maricas perceived Brazil as a more sexually open society to which they could escape when political violence and state homophobia escalated (Malva describes this dynamic in her memoirs).[17] Marce Butierrez and Patricio Simonetto indicate that many Argentine travestis migrated to Europe seeking an alternative to situations of extreme vulnerability, while travestis from the provinces often migrated to Buenos Aires, and in both cases, it was fundamental to count on the support of other travesti friends already installed in the place of destination.[18] Huard argues that, in Spain, the trajectories of sexilio were driven by the opportunities for employment in cabarets, drag shows, and sex work concentrated in metropolitan and touristic areas.[19] Theaters, cabarets, and carnival festivals were the first spaces where maricas could make their feminine performance visible, both in Argentina and in Spain.[20] During carnival, mariconas could freely express their femininity using breast and hip implants.[21]

Police raids and imprisonment were the main mechanisms through which state authorities tried to curtail this visibility, but

FIG. 9. The interior of the Cárcel Modelo in Barcelona. Photo by the author. The photo shows the distribution of the space according to the paradigm of the panopticon. While in theory this architecture subjected prisoners to constant surveillance, in reality, as Tania Navarro remembers, prison guards looked away when marica prisoners were sexually assaulted.

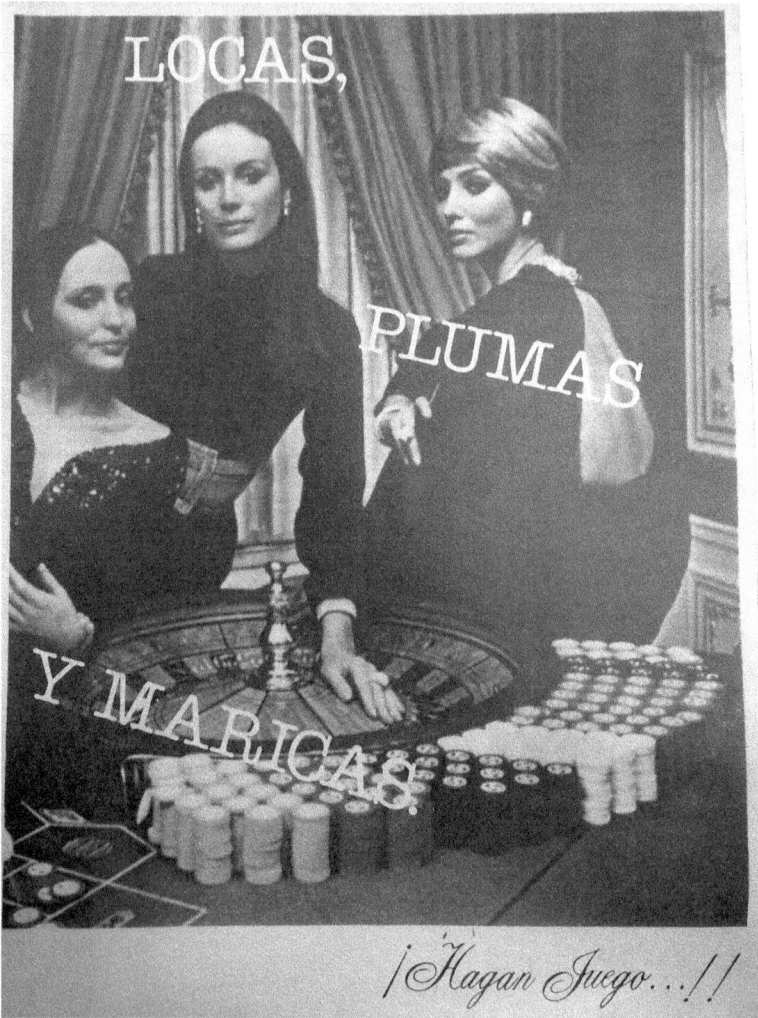

FIG. 10. *Locas, plumas y maricas*, a photomontage of glamorous women that visualize marica femininity. From an article signed by an activist of the Col·lectiu de Maricons Autònoms (Collective of Autonomous Faggots). The article, as a stand-alone piece with no publication date, is included in a dossier on press and society in the Centre de Documentació Armand de Fluvià. Courtesy Centre de Documentació Armand de Fluvià del Casal Lambda.

maricas were also able to transform prisons into spaces of queer sociability. Soledad Cutuli and Santiago Joaquín Insausti note that in Argentina, "prisons were the spaces where [maricas] had enough time and calm to exchange anecdotes and news. Locas ran into each other in the prison cell, they gossiped about other friends whom they hadn't seen in some time, they told each other anecdotes about their hookups and shared strategies."[22] Furthermore, as Tania remembers, sex workers, maricas, and travestis in Barcelona collected common funds to pay the fines imposed on them for exercising their profession in public areas.[23] The use of the term "travesti" was ever more common in these decades and referred to the use of body transformation techniques connected to employment in show business and sex work. There were significant overlaps between this new term and maricas' experiences. In fact, travestis in Argentina often refer to themselves as maricas in intimate conversations.[24] The popularization of the term "travesti" in the 1960s was related to the media visibility that certain celebrities—like the French artist Coccinelle—had in both Argentina and Spain after undergoing gender-affirming surgery and starring in multiple movies and cabaret shows.[25] Travestis built kinship ties with female sex workers, through which they shared knowledge and resources.[26] In brief, the carceral system shaped and reinforced travestis' and maricas' sociability and mutual-aid culture rather than dismantling it, which is why this chapter pays particular attention to maricas' experiences while imprisoned.[27]

This chapter first discusses the memoirs that Argentine fashion designer Paco Jamandreu published in 1975, because they are particularly explicit in discussing the connections between sexual subjectivity and aesthetics. The end of Jamandreu's memoirs coincides with the emergence of hippie fashions in Argentina, which offered maricas a language to express their nonmasculine identities and erotic desires. Through prison files, the second section argues that Argentine criminologists conceptualized aesthetics and fashion as a form of escapism—or, one might argue, a way of imagining alternative realities. Spiritual exploration also figured prominently in the narratives of Argentine prisoners who

foremost expressed their desire to be left alone by the authorities. The next section will explore Spanish criminologists' studies of marica subjectivities and countercultural fashions, which
they considered to be the cause of an increasingly visible youth
rebellion that implied a significant threat to society. This section
also exposes the logics and absurdity of the policing of fashion
in Franco's Spain, where dyed hair or striped sweaters became
enough evidence to target the citizens who dared to wear them.
Travestis' visibility also became one of the targets of police officers, who documented an extensive culture of solidarity among
maricas, travestis, and other sex workers as well as the centrality
of sexilio as a survival strategy. Finally, the fourth section argues
that Spanish mariconas were quite vocal in challenging these policies in prison and in the streets, exhibiting their femininity while
they denounced the regime's cruelty and classism and built alternative communities.

Ephemeral Fashion

Paco Jamandreu's 1975 memoir is the impossible synthesis among
entendido ideals of respectability and self-mastery, maricas' aesthetics and eclectic religiosity, and machista rules of aggressive
behavior. In other words, Jamandreu crafted and performed a
persona that challenged the definition of labels—marica, entendido, and macho—in contraposition to each other. Fashion had
impressed him since he was a child, including his sexual awakening to a "pimp-looking" (*cafisho*) man who wore striped pants
and worked at a circus that visited his rural hometown.[28] As an
adolescent, he moved to Buenos Aires and discovered the cabarets
with drag shows inspired by Spanish folk music.[29] Then he found
tranquility and "purity" through self-definition in his first sexual
experience with another man, very much in line with entendido
ideals.[30] Jamandreu did not think of purity and self-definition as
excluding promiscuity and frivolity. He had sex with "anyone"
and enjoyed the company of people who invested life with a necessary dose of "frivolity, charm, [and] color."[31] Yet he shared with
entendidos their despising, misogynistic view of maricones, a label

that for him epitomized the "degradation," exhibitionism, and lack of self-control that he perceived in males who felt and dressed like women.[32] In the 1940s, he became the personal couturier of Eva Perón, whom he describes in the most flattering terms as a woman deeply committed to improving the fate of the poor and open-minded regarding the homosexuality of several members of her entourage.[33] Jamandreu enjoyed those prosperous years by going to exclusive clubs, traveling to Europe, having multiple lovers, and forming his own entourage exclusively of flamboyant homosexuals who revered him.[34] Still, he hoped his memoir's main contribution to be the distinction that he established between "maricones" and "normal, respectable" homosexual men.[35] Not in vain, his erotic icons were based on the same cult of rugged masculinity that informed Alaria's *Diferente*, as he fantasized about bare-chested construction workers and strong men wearing jeans.[36] In Jamandreu's own admission, Peyrefitte's work influenced him the most in theorizing this cult of masculinity. As any other entendido, Jamandreu traced virile love to the Greek gods of Olympus and argued that it had inspired the creative genius of figures such as García Lorca, Michelangelo, Whitman, and Gide, among others. Jamandreu also agreed with entendidos that feelings were more important than sexual acts and that men ought to be attracted to one another's spirits and not only to their bodies.[37]

Yet Jamandreu developed through fashion an appreciation of ephemerality and "tasteless" expressions of personal autonomy that differentiates him from entendidos. In his view, fashion's changeability inspired self-improvement while still leaving a trace in the clothing of all kinds of women, from society ladies to the *barrio* girls.[38] Jamandreu's appreciation of the ephemeral was quite articulate, as he argued that in order to preserve what one loves the most, one must fade along with it.[39] Therefore, instead of concerning himself with supposedly timeless taste, Jamandreu displayed aesthetics that remind us of Molina's shows: "feathers, rhinestones, velvet, sequins . . . fur comforters (leopard is better) [and] white carpets."[40] Furthermore, while he embraced respectability on his own terms, he also appreciated the freedom of the underworld:

"Between spending four hours looking at *La Gioconda* or spend-ing that time in a brothel in Cali [Colombia], I would not hesi-tate."[41] He added that he would choose to be a "whore" rather than the wife of a businessman, because then he would not have to read "boring books" just because culture is an ingredient of status.[42] Jamandreu's sense of personal autonomy was beyond any con-cern for taste, status, and self-contradiction. Thus, he argued that love must be "intimate and secret" while simultaneously stating his aspiration to "love in public."[43]

Jamandreu also showed his fierce personal autonomy in his eclectic spirituality. He picked and chose those icons that con-soled and inspired him, praying to God on his knees as well as to Marilyn Monroe and Eva Perón.[44] While this eclecticism may at first strike the reader as just bizarre, Jamandreu discusses his beliefs as self-conscious choices within the available repertoire of life-counseling professionals. Thus, he explains that he often went to see fortune-tellers "in the same way that other people go to the psychoanalyst," not because he really believed in them but because they amuse and console him.[45] Since the late 1950s, Jamandreu's life went in the opposite direction from the collective ethos of the time.[46] While he became less frivolous and more aware of the pass-ing of time, the generation coming of age between 1950 and 1962 embraced hedonism through fashion.[47] Meanwhile, Jamandreu spent approximately one week in prison because of an "atavistic impulse" that drove him to beat two people who had affronted his mother. Adding to the pride that he took in this primitive "macho" reaction, in prison he had sex with multiple "nice-looking guys" and after being released he presented on TV a fashion collection inspired by his prison experience.[48] Through this narration, Jaman-dreu arguably targets the notion that machos and maricas are complementary opposites by presenting himself as both aggres-sive and licentious.

In the mid-1960s, Jamandreu incorporated psychedelic light-ing, music, and visual materials in his fashion shows.[49] Later, he launched his career in the United States through the "gaucho" look, which aligned with the vogue and cultural appropriation of

aboriginal and non-Western clothing in the early 1970s.[50] However, the end of his memoir intimates that by the mid-1970s he
had embraced personal decay (in the sense of aging). After his
dearest and most lasting lover leaves him for a woman, Jamandreu
moves to the countryside to study and take care of his plants.[51] In
the last scene of his memoirs, he goes to a bar and meets a long-
haired youngster who offers him sex in exchange for some drinks.
Instead, Jamandreu remembers his deteriorated reflection in a
mirror and decides to spend that night with his "loneliness and
ghosts" but keeping the same love and thrill that he had as an adolescent.[52] Through this scene, Jamandreu suggests that his retreat
into a contented fading condition coincided with the generational
experience of the long-haired hippies.

Unisex Fashion and Spirituality

In the late 1960s, while the Argentine state shifted from Cold War
reformism to authoritarianism, fashion provided maricas with
a new vehicle of gender expression. Although wearing androgynous, tight clothes was read as a sign of hedonism, prisoners
suspected of sexual and gender deviance for wearing that type
of clothing also explored spirituality and aesthetics in their own
ways, according to their criminological files. Fashion scholar Valerie Steele emphasizes that "the hippy countercultural movement
further blurred the lines between gay and straight people. Colorful, decorative clothes (and long hair) were increasingly sported
by men of all sexual persuasions, while both men and women
dressed androgynously in blue jeans and tee-shirts."[53] Androgynous youth fashions were among the concerns of the reactionary
sectors that, through a military coup led by president-to-be General Juan Carlos Onganía, took over the Argentine government
in 1966. Valeria Manzano argues that until the mid-1960s, progressive psychologists and sociologists had been overall confident
in a politically moderate and sexually prudent youth prepared to
bear the democratic values of secular modernity.[54] However, by the
end of that decade, the political radicalization of students and
the popularization of alternative models of masculinity through

rock 'n' roll culture moved experts and authorities alike to adopt an authoritarian approach.[55]

Homophobia drove many people to censure long-haired rockers and hippies as a sexual threat. For instance, Manzano cites fifty-two letters from readers of the magazine *Siete Días*, who discussed whether rockers and hippies were majority-homosexual groups, which in most readers' view would have endangered Argentine national values. Through the "iconoclastic framework" of rock and hippie cultures, young people expressed hedonistic and antidisciplinarian values, which exacerbated their generational rebellion.[56] While many rockers were invested in asserting their masculinity, androgynous fashions became a vehicle of expression for gender nonconformism when combined with a "flamboyant aesthetic" developed since the early 1960s (including silk foulards and other ostentatious clothes).[57] For this reason, during this decade fashion increasingly became a focus of interest for clinical experts on homosexuality. Already in 1963, José A. Opizzo, head of the Sexology Department at the Cosme Argerich Hospital in Buenos Aires, had identified unisex clothing as a vector of gender ambiguity. In his view, "clothing that highlights physical characteristics that are common to both sexes, and most ironically, the popularization of 'anatomic' clothes that hide the only possible externalization of sex" contributed to homosexual males' tendency toward feminization. He also posited that homosexual couturiers might design women's clothes in such a way as to "saturate" heterosexual men with erotic stimulation so that they would lose interest in the female body.[58]

In line with the view that designers used fashion to undermine gender norms, one prisoner who had worked in the fashion industry was described in the most pejorative terms by the Classification Institute's criminologists in 1966. However, while criminologists presented this prisoner's involvement in fashion and design as a sign of his femininity and unlikely rehabilitation, the prisoner discussed his sexuality in terms of sublimation. The prisoner, who came from a middle-class Catholic family, had been convicted of "corruption" of minors. He had allegedly invited several youngsters over (all of them older than or about to be eighteen years old), performed oral sex on them, and let them penetrate him.[59] Among the family-related factors that according to the criminologists nurtured the prisoner's criminality ("factores familiares criminógenos"), they noted that when he was a child he learned "markedly feminine habits" from his female relatives and that an older male cousin had initiated him in mutual masturbation.[60] From then, the prisoner grew obsessed with a dream in which his cousin penetrated ("possessed") him on a lake.[61] To give further credibility to their hypothesis that the prisoner's feminine socialization was related to his sexual conduct, the criminologists noted his occupations in fashion and design: he had worked in a "fashion house" at age sixteen, then he was an employee at different companies, and finally, he became an interior decorator and stage designer.[62] He was, according to the tests, exceptionally intelligent. However, criminologists used his body type (he was a "leptosomatic" in Kretschmer's typology) and gender performance as evidence of his "congenital" homosexuality: "He came to the interview with a passive attitude . . . with markedly homosexual manners, very neatly dressed [*prolijo en sus ropas*] and extremely clean; very shy and inhibited."[63]

The fact that the prisoner expressed himself through an extreme care for his appearance was recorded as evidence of his homosexuality, along with a feminized "passive" attitude. In this case, the prisoner's homosexuality was attributed to both nature and nurture, as the reports implied that his "instinctive perversion" was fostered by his feminine socialization.[64] In March 1966, the institute recommended his release request be denied, arguing that his lack of sexual self-control posed a major danger.[65] The prisoner argued instead in a letter that he was learning to contain his inclination toward homosexual "natural relationships" by sublimating his desires into his work and ascetic life. Obviously, this letter could have been part of the prisoner's strategy to obtain his release. However, it is worth analyzing at length, since it discusses sexual acts, sublimation, gratifying erotic fantasies, and mysticism as interconnected alternatives to channel the libido. The prisoner claimed that his sexual acts had been a sort of "pause" from life-long self-containment. Acknowledging that these acts were illicit, he stressed that he could not see them as such at that moment because, through sexual self-restraint, he had become unable to "intuit a human shape without this sensuality."[66] In other words, he linked sublimation with the fixing of homosexual desires. The prisoner failed to convince criminologists of his rehabilitation, probably due to the pervasive feminization of certain manifestations of creativity and self-fashioning that informed psychiatric reports in these years. For instance, on November 4, 1969, a military recruit accused of homosexuality was subjected to a medical exam during his court-martial, during which the medical examiners identified "signs of effeminacy" in his "narcissistic interests," including his use of clothing to sexually entice other men. They added that the recruit was adopting "artistic behaviors," relating these to his "emotional isolation" and "failure to perceive reality."[67] Medical doctors apparently held that the recruit's body-fitting fashion responded to a sort of schizophrenic creativity, which had disconnected him from his masculinity.

The feminization of certain forms of creativity provided a common ground between criminologists and homophobic social environments, as in the case of an interior decorator examined at the institute in the early 1970s. He came from a middle-class family, and according to the criminologists, the behavior of his father (a womanizer) and an overprotective mother partially accounted for his homosexuality.[68] According to his sentence, issued in November 1970, police officers had gone to his apartment to investigate reports that strange men often visited the prisoner and found him in the company of two naked men, one of them an adolescent. The prisoner tried then to commit suicide by jumping from a balcony, but a police officer grabbed his leg.[69] Once in prison, the Classification Institute's criminologists initiated an investigation into his social behavior, and one of his relatives (a female second cousin) gave her opinion that the prisoner was "effeminate," paid "exaggerated" attention to fashion and aesthetics by using perfume and "very tight" clothes, and prepared his table with much care when he had guests over.[70] The prisoner's former employers agreed that he paid too much attention to fashion and decoration, adding that he showed signs of homosexuality and "hysteria."[71] In other words, the prisoner's acquaintances considered that his interest in self-fashioning and aesthetics feminized him and was excessive or plainly pathological. Criminologists shared this opinion and diagnosed the prisoner as suffering from a "schizoid psychopathic personality," describing his persona as a sort of escapist fantasy.[72] The belief underlying these reports is that aesthetics and self-fashioning provided maricas with a much-appreciated way out of reality, which in criminologists' view ought to be pathologized as a danger to society because it allowed those subjects to build a meaningful alternative to conventional masculinity.

Fashion and spirituality coexisted as prisoners' vehicles for self-expression. A prisoner examined in the 1970s only admitted to heterosexual relationships, but the criminologist trusted instead his own impressions of the prisoner's gender performance. Below the prisoner's typed statement, the criminologist handwrote and underlined that the prisoner was a homosexual, so the formality of the interview was contraposed to and undermined by the informality of gendered body readings.[73] The prisoner's acquaintances similarly focused on his sexualized femininity. A former employer claimed that the prisoner once visited him "wearing makeup and very tight clothes."[74] The prisoner's body-conscious fashion and "effeminate speech" did not prevent some neighbors from caring for his well-being and supporting him. However, another former employer focused on the prisoner's eccentric spirituality, describing how when he was younger he had built in his room a "grotto where he placed many religious images."[75] This prisoner—much like Jamandreu and other maricas—had built a space, both physical and metaphorical, to cultivate an autonomous spirituality that did not require institutional approval. Thus, according to the same employer, beyond his spirituality the prisoner also exhibited the "rebellion toward normal people" that characterized youth cultures in the late 1960s.[76] The prisoner's performance on psychological tests also suggests that he had developed a strong sense of independence from society. One of the projective tests consisted of asking inmates to complete short sentences. The inmate's responses reveal his strategies for negotiating criminologists' expectations of social conformity with his own longing for privacy. In this line, for instance, there are responses that pinpoint the prisoner's apparent conformity:

> I need . . . some help;
> Marriage . . . is the most important and sacred thing;
> My only concern . . . is coming back to society;
> Most girls . . . are cute.

In other answers, the prisoner showed himself unwilling to share his intimacy:

> The best thing . . . I never say;
> What hurts me . . . I don't show;
> In secret . . . nothing.

Other answers suggest a self-asserted attitude:

> My mind . . . works well;
> I want to . . . be happy in life.

And most of the answers expressed the prisoner's longing for privacy:

> When I come back home . . . I want to be at peace;
> What bothers me . . . is company;
> People . . . talk too much.[77]

None of these responses really amounted to the inmate stating his intention to mend his ways by adopting a heterosexual behavior. For instance, to say that "most girls . . . are cute" (la mayor parte de las chicas . . . son lindas) does not mean that one wants to have sex exclusively with women. If anything, he uttered ambivalent phrases that were open to multiple interpretations. This strategy worked toward its goal of leading to a positive report. The psychologist administering these tests concluded that the prisoner was willing to repress his instincts in order to be socially adjusted.[78]

Since criminologists judged the prisoner's homosexuality as playing a significant role in his criminality, and the prisoner had convinced them that he intended to inhibit himself sexually, he was classified as "adaptable" and posing a "medium social danger."[79] Still, the prisoner was not released, probably because he had homosexual relationships and challenged officers while in prison. In any case, the report on him demonstrates that by the early 1970s queer individuals expressed that they wanted to be left alone by the authorities even while their androgynous and body-fitting clothing made them increasingly visible. This desire became the focus of experts' attention when they theorized the role of fashion in "homosexual" subjectivities.

Judging by medical and judicial reports, maricas were quite vocal in the 1960s and 1970s. Juan Carlos Romi treated maricas since the late 1960s while working as a forensic psychiatrist and sexologist at the San Jorge general clinic, the Moyano and Borda psychiatric hospitals, the police department, and the Centro de Estudios Sexológicos (Sexology Studies Center), all of them in Buenos Aires. Most of his patients were forced into therapy, including adolescents who were brought to him by their parents. Romi experimented with different treatments, including conductive therapy. For instance, he recollects advising a gay patient to look at girls on the subway. However, according to Romi, what caught the patient's attention was women's fashion, their aesthetic instead of their erotic appeal. Similarly, Romi realized that testosterone injections increased patients' homosexual drives.[80] He also prescribed anxiolytics to patients whom he considered "sexually disturbed" (including "neurotic" gay men) before psychoanalyzing them.[81] Based on this clinical experience, Romi established his credentials as one of the foremost Argentine experts in sexual "disorders," publishing multiple articles in international journals and defending his PhD dissertation in 1980. Later, he became a vocal critic of treating homosexuality as a pathology. In 2008, he published an article criticizing the classification of "sexual disorders" as mental pathologies in the fourth edition of the *Diagnostic and Statistical Manual* (DSM), used by most psychiatrists internationally.[82] Interviewing Romi in 2017 was a disconcerting experience for me because of the dissonance between Romi's role in pathologizing homosexuality and transgender identities and his self-presentation as a progressive "ally" who expected me to recognize and treat him as such. The fact that I interviewed him at his office in the court where he still worked as a forensic made the experience even more uncanny.

In the 1970s, Romi argued that self-asserting maricas ought to be one of psychiatrists' primary concerns among those patients suffering from sexual disorders. In a 1975 article based on fifty-seven case studies (forty-five of them men), Romi classified "homosexual" individuals into categories supposedly extracted from their own subculture. According to Romi, maricas exhibited a "histrionic" style and exquisite taste and were prone to professions such as fashion, decoration, hairdressing, homecare, dancing, and art in general. Romi defined "maricas" according to the "prison lexicon" as constitutionally "passive" homosexual males who "never consult with a medical doctor because they do not think they have any problems."[83] He also described "chongos" as masculine-looking men who prostituted themselves by performing the "active" sexual role. This taxonomy incorporated maricas' self-acceptance as a negative symptom. In Romi's words, there was a growing "group that could be considered 'untreatable' given that they didn't accept the possibility that their homosexuality was pathological."[84] Since the 1970s psychopathy came to be the diagnosis that Argentine doctors used to convey that individuals who identified with their "homosexuality" ("ego-syntonic") showed a pathological disregard for ethical and social norms and were therefore less treatable than neurotic patients.[85] In his dissertation, Romi described the patients whom he diagnosed as psychopathic "genuine" homosexuals, including an interior designer and "loca" who had a promiscuous sexual life.[86] In contrast, Romi believed that psychotherapy was most effective with patients who occasionally engaged in sex with other men, exhibited bisexual behaviors, and showed signs of anguish or neurosis ("ego-dystonic"). These "patients" had a comparative advantage when arrested by the police. According to Romi, who worked as a forensic doctor for the Buenos Aires police department, when police officers arrested masculine men who had allegedly engaged in sex with other men because of intoxication or another transitory condition, they were released soon after their arrest.[87] In other words, authorities and experts were less concerned about males who had sex with other males than about maricas who used their bodies, sex, and aesthetics to express and enjoy themselves.

Spanish Maricas' Files: Sex and Aesthetics

At some point between 1967 and 1969, a prisoner rhymed in Spanish, "Si no tengo lomo, tocino como" (If there is no steak, I eat bacon), trying to explain to clinical psychologist Fernando Chamorro why he was sexually versatile and not fitting into the passive/active binary that Chamorro insisted upon.[88] The prisoner was not denying his preference for certain sexual roles ("steak"). Rather, he was pointing out that sex is a process of mutual exploration and adjustment between two (or more) individuals. Thereby, he was willing to "eat bacon," temporarily renouncing his own preferences to satisfy a potential sexual partner. This statement may be read as a candid, inoffensive acknowledgment of sexual playfulness, but it became a full-fledged subversion of the institutional edifice supporting the regime's sexual taxonomies. These taxonomies informed public policies, including prison infrastructure projects aimed at isolating "passive" and "active" homosexuals in different prisons as a prophylactic measure to prevent them from having sex with each other. The first step in this direction was the publication of the 1966 General Directorate of Prisons' guidelines for wardens to classify convicts based on the examination of their personality so they could be transferred to prisons specializing in the treatment of psychopaths, mentally disabled individuals, and homosexuals, among other groups. These guidelines aimed at putting in practice "the projected classification of the convict population based on scientific methods of observation and treatment." One year later, a "Special Department of Homosexuals" was created in the Penitentiary Hospital of Madrid, staffed by an endocrinologist, a psychiatrist, and a clinical psychologist.[89] Based on this department's reports, prisoners would be transferred to two prisons located in provincial capitals of the less densely populated Spanish Southwest.

Thus, the prisons of Huelva and Badajoz became specialized respectively in "active" and "passive" gay prisoners.[90] In 1971, Fernando Chamorro published the results of a survey study of two hundred homosexual prisoners, expressing his frustration at the subjects' resistance to these taxonomic schemas, as most of them (131, or 65.5 percent) seemed to be sexually versatile.[91] The question of etiology seems secondary for Chamorro, who states, "All [homosexuals] are congenital and acquired at the same time."[92] His sampling methods are quite questionable; the two hundred subjects included prisoners convicted as homosexuals along with those who were caught having sex in prison but also subjects selected on the basis of their "not very masculine manners."[93] Thus, an impressionistic reading of prisoners' gender performance became one of the scientific criteria used to classify them as homosexual.

Through interviews, psychological projective tests, and physical exams of their genitals and rectums, the department divided these prisoners into four main categories: (1) "Congenital passive" individuals were those who had acted "woman-like" since their earliest childhood and who only had sex with men. Four individuals (2 percent of the sample) were included in this category based on an analysis of their primary and secondary sexual characteristics and their hormone levels.[94] This reliance on endocrinology indicates Gregorio Marañón's long shadow, while the fact that only a small percentage of individuals were classified as "congenital" suggests that—at the most centralized level—medical doctors restricted the use of this category because of its exonerating connotations. (2) "Occasional" homosexual men were those who engaged in same-sex acts when they were isolated from women in prisons and similar male-only institutions. (3) "Acquired habitual" homosexual individuals—the majority group, according to the study—had developed their homosexuality by having sex with other men. The subjects included in this group were classified by the department's doctors depending on their sexual role—"active," "passive," or "mixed" (versatile). (4) A last category was formed by men who prostituted themselves. In line with misogynistic readings of prisoners' personae, Chamorro characterized "passive" homosexual individuals as particularly hostile insofar as they tended to feel comfortable with their sexuality and did not seek any medical treatment. In contrast, according to Chamorro, men who preferred an "active" penetrating role had been likely traumatized by a threatening event or figure in their early childhood. Therefore—Chamorro argued—these men were often troubled by their sexuality and seeking medical help, so they had better chances of being rehabilitated.[95] Medical doctors such as Chamorro suggested that, in fact, those subjects who most openly challenged stereotyped views on masculinity by performing stigmatized roles and femininity were in fact the least likely to submit to authorities' interventions. Other experts opined that fashion was the core element in this dissident trend.

In judge Antonio Sabater Tomás's 1972 book on social dangers, his curatorial practices—selecting images from other Western countries and captioning them—indicate that he saw transnational visual culture and fashion as fundamental factors in the dissolution of traditional mores. Sabater Tomás used images of supposedly homosexual individuals wearing the countercultural fashions of the late 1960s and early 1970s: dotted scarfs, Afro hair, white tight jeans, sunglasses, and hats with feathers, among others. He made the claim that the "institution of homosexual marriage only exists in Australia," displacing the yet-to-come social normalization of same-sex partnerships onto Spain's geographic antipodes and figurative opposite. Along with this caption, two photographs show supposedly married same-sex couples. In the first photograph, two men are walking side by side in a metropolitan area (there are people rushing through and a theater and a bar in the background). The photo was taken from their backs. One of them wears Afro hair and a fur coat, and the other one a long buttoned jacket, like the ones that the Beatles wore. The other photograph shows two people holding hands, both long-haired. Sabater Tomás's selection of these photographs to illustrate same-sex

marriage only makes sense by considering that he was alerting his
readers about a yet-to-be phenomenon, as no state had regulated
same-sex marriage by 1972. Yet for Sabater Tomás, transnational
countercultural fashion illustrated that upsetting possibility. The
photographs in subsequent chapters continue this thread. They
show recreational drug users as part of a psychedelic revolution
against consumer society, illustrated with photographs of hippies with Afro hair holding flowers. In the last instance, Sabater
Tomás attributes all societal maladies to young people's "increasing tendency toward collectively antisocial conduct . . . [wearing]
out-of-the-ordinary clothes as an explicit manifestation of their
repudiation of social norms."[96] He complemented this statement
with a photograph of a young man and a woman holding hands
as they walk in a street. They wear almost the same single-piece
striped dress. Sabater Tomás's choice of unisex fashion as an indicator of young people's dangerous rebellion against inherited social
norms is not coincidental. The sequence of photographs following this one depicts dismayed fans of pop music, motorbike rid-
ers, student protesters, Hare Krishna groups, and—sort of out of
nowhere—what seems to be a guerrilla fighter holding a machine
gun. Hence the visual materials on these pages establish a sort of
narrational, causal connection from unisex fashion to guerrillas.
In subsequent chapters, Sabater Tomás continues to discuss different sorts of fashions—through photographs and captions—from
beatniks to hippies who "advocate for homosexuality, pornography, abortion, nudism, and group marriage."[97] High hats, long hair,
and bare chests recurrently illustrate these arguments.

The belief of top state authorities, such as Judge Sabater Tomás,
that fashion was a central element of youth rebellion, encompassing
sexual liberalization translated into a harsh policing of clothing
and hairstyles that occasionally reached absurd extremes. Even
police training incorporated "hippie" fashion to mark the sector
of the population that the officers were being trained to target.
In a show organized for the minister of governance in December
1969 at the police academy of Madrid, the officers-in-training were
divided into two groups performing the roles of antiriot squads

and "hippie" protesters. The latter wore "sweaters, wigs, and flowered shirts" and carried banners in favor of peace and equality and
against racism and police officers themselves. The performance, as
one would expect, ended with the antiriot squads dissolving the
protest and arresting the participants.[98] The police's performance
of political dissidence by wearing wigs and flowered shirts had a
counterpart in their practice of arresting individuals who wore
flamboyant hairstyles or clothes. Among these, the judicial file of
a man arrested in 1968 revolves almost entirely around his hair.
The initial police report pointed out that he was suspected of having "an irregular lifestyle"; he denied being a homosexual but had
"effeminate" manners and had dyed his hair.[99] To further clarify the
case, a second police report explained that even though there was
no evidence that the defendant had a relationship with his roommate, the latter had admitted his homosexuality to the police officers, which along with the defendant's hair color had given place
to the charges.[100] The defendant argued that he had changed his
hair color to perform in a theater play.[101] To corroborate this argument, he submitted to the court a letter that he had addressed to
his fiancée the year prior: "Nothing disgusts me more than having to wear long hair and dye it. I have little hair and with the dye
it falls out a lot."[102] Whether this letter was authentic or fabricated
during the trial, the fact is that the defendant considered it necessary to justify his hair color in order to prove his heterosexuality.[103] The defense lawyer continued this thread, presenting the
defendant as a Catholic aspiring novelist who had been engaged
to a woman for four years to counteract the charges of homosexuality based on his dyed hair and the fact that he had an allegedly homosexual roommate.[104] All this was to no avail; the judge
declared the defendant to be a danger, and the latter had to serve
a total of six years between prison, exile, and probation.[105]

In 1967, a similar case focused on a horizontal-striped sweater
that a defendant wore. He was a hairdresser, first arrested because
his neighbors complained that they could see him naked while he
showered.[106] Different witnesses declared in his favor and justified the fashion style on which his criminal records focused. One

of them explained that the defendant could not be considered a homosexual; he only went to nightclubs to keep track of the trendiest hairstyles, and the reason why he was arrested when leaving one of them was "his modernist-styled clothing."[107] The defense lawyer provided more details about this clothing and the defendant's criminal records. In 1964, he had been arrested on the street at 3:30 a.m. (probably because police officers suspected that he was in a cruising area), and the second time in 1967 because he was wearing a so-called *Yé-yé* sweater with horizontal stripes and hanging out with two "ladies" who wore miniskirts ("very short dresses"). The lawyer claimed that the defendant's family had made sure this violation would never happen again, advising him to destroy the sweater before it could cause any more harm. Moreover, the police intervention had targeted the women's miniskirts rather than the defendant's striped sweater, according to the lawyer.[108] The *Yé-yé* subculture originated in pop music and involved a clothing style inspired by the Beatles and other bands but adapted to Mediterranean societies, such as France and Spain. Sontag described the *Yé-yé* phenomenon as an illustration of camp's apolitical artificiality, of style over content.[109] Yet when women and maricas showed this style in Franco's Spain, it signified sexual liberalization—like in the image of a unisex dress with horizontal stripes that Sabater Tomás used as an epitome of young people's nonconformism. Likewise, the singer Manolo Escobar dedicated a music video to the miniskirt in 1971. In the video, Escobar forbids his girlfriend to go to the bullfighting ring—Could there be a more traditionally Spanish space?—wearing a miniskirt that brought the lewd gaze of male attendants over her. A Black man wearing a futurist pop jacket rejoiced looking at the woman wearing a miniskirt, further implying that licentiousness was alien to Spaniards. Local district attorneys, in their annual reports, further advanced the hypothesis that there was a correlation among tourism, transactional sex, and contemporary fashion trends. For instance, in 1968 the district attorney of València shared his concern about young men prostituting themselves to access a consumer culture centered on fashion trends, describing "jumbled gatherings of long-haired Yé-yé, hippie, and beatnik [individuals] wearing all kinds of extravagant clothing, in oppressively narrow alleyways."[110] Given the many layers of gender paranoia overdetermining the meaning of *Yé-yé* fashion, it is perhaps unsurprising that the hairdresser was arrested, although in this case the judge followed the prosecutor's advice and released the defendant, since there was not a single piece of credible evidence of his alleged homosexuality.[111] Yet the fact that a sweater led to an arrest and criminal record suggests *Yé-yé* aesthetics' "dangerous" implications from the authorities' perspective.

As a counterpoint to the blurring of boundaries between fashion and "homosexuality," some lawyers claimed that the subcultural practices that provided maricas with opportunities to embody femininity were simply part of the generational "hippie" trend or indistinguishable from mainstream androgynous fashion. A sixteen-year-old defendant who used the female name Soraya was arrested in València (Spain) in 1975, accused of carrying out "antinatural acts" with men, escaping from her parents' home, and working in a bar while wearing women's clothes and makeup.[112] The defense lawyer argued that the accusation of wearing women's clothes was irrelevant because androgynous clothing had become mainstream, and many women wore "clothing more proper for men than for their femininity." The lawyer compared Soraya with Oscar Wilde, both living their sexuality "alternatively as a burden and a privilege, wound and blazon, pain and voluptuosity, source of shame and pride." He also described the one sexual encounter that Soraya had confessed as a "carnal act out of love . . . over the bed of València's orchard and under the ceiling of a sky full of stars."[113] Whether or not the lawyer's literary airs served any purpose is unclear; Soraya was acquitted by a judge who found that there was not enough evidence of her engaging in recurrent homosexuality.[114]

In another court case that also took place in València in 1975, several "inverts" were accused of celebrating a party in a bar, during which they dressed like women to imitate Sara Montiel while other attendees applauded and laughed in an ambience of complicity and community that was interrupted by the police raid. The movie star Sara Montiel was particularly popular among maricas since the beginning of her career. Gay activist Serafín Fernández recalls a queer fascination with her role in *El último cuplé* (1957): "She had a very sticky beauty, very much proper of a diva, and we *mariquitas* like that. We were all in love with her."[115] There is even a file initiated in 1967 in Barcelona against a twenty-one-year-old "esthete" who—according to police reports—was nicknamed Sarita Montiel or la Sara and was arrested as a sex worker who cruised for clients "dressed like a woman, with makeup as such and carrying a purse."[116] Female celebrities' fabulousness was reenacted by maricas who took over the streets to earn a living and make themselves visible. In his research, David Halperin studies how "feminine figures incarnating different combinations of strength and suffering, glamour and abjection, power and vulnerability" became queer icons.[117] Sara Montiel embodies this synthesis with her haughty eyebrows and tight lips, barely hiding her emotional intensity under the glamour of feathers, red lipstick, and diamond jewelry. One of the individuals arrested in 1975 for participating in the drag show party honoring Sara Montiel admitted to having sex with other males and with women. His lawyer claimed that on the night when the defendant was arrested, he was indeed in a party where attendees impersonated celebrities, but "he did not wear any clothes that were unproper to his sex, since he was dressed as a hippie, without female makeup."[118] In addition, the lawyer presented affidavits by the defendant's employer and his parish priest, all of which supported the impression that he was a hardworking citizen who economically supported his family without causing any "scandal" in his neighborhood. He was acquitted on these grounds by a judge who decided to interpret the ambivalent boundary between maricas' cross-dressing and hippie fashion in favor of the social functionality of a citizen who had kept his sexuality private and discreet.

The degree to which the Dangerousness Law facilitated systematic judicial arbitrariness—pardon the oxymoron—becomes evident in a similar case with an opposite outcome. In 1972, multiple men were arrested in Castellón (Spain), accused of organizing private parties in an upholstery business, during which they dressed like women with wigs and "hippie blouses" (*blusones de hippie*), drank liquor and Coke, danced, and had sex with one another. A long-haired Belgian young man reported these parties after being arrested himself for stealing money and a book on sexology from one of the "maricas" who paid him for sex. The forensic report on one of the defendants, a pharmaceutical sales representative, followed a pattern that I have already discussed: the examiner's solidarity toward his own class became manifest in his focus on the defendant's socioeconomic status and refined manners, through which he reached the conclusion that there was no evidence of the defendant's homosexuality. As I noted before, forensic doctors treated "refinement" as a set of class-specific personality traits that working-class maricones could not claim. Despite counting on enough evidence to exculpate the defendant based on his class background and social functionality (as other judges did in similar cases), the judge of Castellón sent the defendant to the prison of Huelva. There, the wardens reiterated that the prisoner's discretion and family background diminished the threat posed by his sexuality.[119] From the late 1960s, maricas incorporated ambiguous hippie clothing into their private and semipublic drag shows and camouflaged their gender transgressions as part of that fashion trend when caught by the authorities. Whether or not this strategy was successful depended on how drag intersected with employment, class background, and public reputation—classified as vectors of social (dis)functionality—and with a judge's discretionary powers. Resistance to this arbitrariness was articulated through maricas' and travestis' embodied languages.

Vocal Mariconas and Travestis

Francoist authorities recorded their own perception that maricas were ever more vocal in expressing their desires, building alternative communities, escaping family controls, and appropriating colloquial terms that carried the stigma of gender "deviance." In 1972, a group of experts on prison rehabilitation examined an inmate in Barcelona, an orphan who had found an alternative family and "certain happiness" in prison, according to the experts' report.[120] He frequented "discreet" people within the "Department of Inverts" and showed himself well groomed and well behaved when interacting with the guards.[121] However, since the prisoner showed no intention or wish to abandon his kin of "inverts," the examiners concluded that he should not be released. Prison wardens and criminologists treated solidarity between maricas as a danger to society but simultaneously recorded how significant this solidarity was for prisoners. In 1968, the Guardia Civil arrested a seventeen-year-old subject who walked on a road looking markedly "feminine." The latter declared that he had escaped from his parents' home because he did not want to be a farmer. Moreover, his parents had tried to intern him, first in a psychiatric hospital and then in a convent, resorting alternatively to medical and religious mechanisms of control.[122] Nevertheless, he was able to escape to Barcelona and prostitute himself with "machos," sometimes dressing as a woman. In this way, he was able to pay back another "maricona" who had lent him money.[123] This defendant's language prefigured the politicization of the label "maricona" in the 1970s. The self-labeling of "mariconas" was a threefold subversive gesture. First, they embraced a label (maricón) that connoted an excessive pursuit of desire by male subjects who dismissed social norms. Second, by shifting this label's gender from the masculine to the feminine (-ona instead of -ón), they brazenly displayed their femininity regardless of social scorn. And third, along with their use of this label, they built communities of mutual support (by lending money to one another when needed, for instance). Conversely, the term "maricón" could be used to shame "discreet" homosexuals for acting as if they did not belong to the same disenfranchised group. In a case initiated in 1961 in Barcelona, the defendant was apparently a homosexual bar owner who wanted to keep "flamboyant" individuals away from his bar, so he overcharged them for their drinks. According to his deposition, one of those patrons had called him "maricón, son of the great bitch" and reported him to the police, so he ended up in prison as a homosexual himself.[124]

These conflicts suggest that the boundaries between maricas' public and private exposure shifted over the course of the 1960s. Private parties, especially those hosted by elite subjects, had been a semiprotected space for gender transgressions and drag for decades. These parties often led to sex between attendees: maricas and working-class men who enjoyed the luxury of these parties and were compensated for their performances of masculinity (these individuals were called "trade" in Anglophone contexts).[125] One such individual declared to the police of an Andalusian city in 1965 that he had been invited to a party hosted by a young local aristocrat. The attendees wore makeup and high heels and changed their dresses multiple times to impersonate different female figures. As the party went on, attendees retreated to private rooms to have sex. However, on a different occasion, the host, wearing a white silk tunic, prevented the defendant and his friends from coming in, explaining to them that the attendees were all high-born ("de alto copete") and not all of them "maricones." Disgruntled by this gesture, the defendant and his friends waited until the party was over and then trespassed into the apartment and stole a record player and other objects.[126] This led into the police investigation. The twenty-three-year-old aristocrat host declared that he dedicated himself to studying music and painting and described his parties: "[We wore] Arabic tunics, sang, and talked about different topics. In effect, we occasionally applied makeup to our lips and eyes . . . with the goal of impersonating a singer, but that did not entail an intention to have sex between men . . . although most attendees were inverts."[127] This social circle had incorporated both the (homo)eroticized Orientalism of the region's Islamic history and the cult to and impersonation of female celebrities. In this case, the young aristocrat was acquitted. His elite status and his investment in keeping a facade of respectable privacy in front of his high-born guests played in his favor.

However, in the late 1960s maricas went from performing drag in private parties and nightclub performances to doing it

publicly in city streets and bars. In 1968 in Catalonia, a night
guard reported that he had entered a bar and found five naked men
dancing with other patrons. The bar owner declared that they had
entered the bar dressed like women, which he had allowed because
this happened during carnival. Then he also allowed them to dance
naked, alleging that he was inexperienced in this kind of situation. According to the police records, one of the arrested individuals wore a bridal dress and the other ones Charleston dresses.[128]
That same year, a forty-four-year-old defendant who worked as a
performer in a nightclub was sentenced as a homosexual. Previously, the Guardia Civil had arrested him once "on a public street,
as he passed by dressed like a woman, fully covered in makeup and
wearing a wig and eyelashes."[129] However, he was brought to trial
for a different reason; according to the eighteen-year-old Jesuit
novice who denounced him, the defendant had tried to penetrate
him. One night, the plaintiff met a group of "inverts" with whom
he went to several nightclubs and, at the end of the night, to the
defendant's apartment. There, he laid in bed, while the defendant
tried to convince the plaintiff with "sweet words" (*palabras melo-
sas*) to have sex by letting the defendant penetrate him. Moreover,
when brought to the police station, the defendant declared that
he was "an inborn homosexual" with "*no reason to hide it*" (no
teniendo porque ocultarlo).[130] The defendant confounded authorities' binary hierarchies (traced in previous chapters) by both showing a feminine gender expression and trying to penetrate a man,
and he verbalized his refusal to conceal himself.[131]

Vocal attitudes translated into political acts as prisoners
denounced authorities' continued harassment of disenfranchised
maricas. In 1965, a seventeen-year-old individual testified during
a case in which large orgies, of fifty to sixty participants, implicated both "bujarrones" and homosexual men in a police investigation. These were supposedly hosted by an affluent middle-aged
man who was sentenced as a danger to society.[132] The adolescent
defendant testified that he had penetrated a soccer player and
was also declared to be a danger to society.[133] Years later, in 1972,
this individual, now a prisoner, confronted the guards and the

warden by refusing to follow their orders. The warden reported that the prisoner had been sanctioned for exchanging love letters and having sex with other prisoners, among other violations, and had stated in front of him that "he did not owe obedience to any civil servant."[134] Afterward, he allegedly refused to adopt the mandatory position during a routine inspection, telling the guard, "Leave me alone. I am fed up with persecutions and with you all" (Déjame en paz, que ya estoy harto de persecuciones y de todos Vds.).[135] Although it is of course possible that authorities were misreporting on these events with the intention of justifying a harsher treatment of the prisoner, it is equally possible that he had in fact denounced authorities' persecution.

Other prisoners similarly denounced the state apparatus's class biases. In 1972, a poor young man from Andalucía convicted at different points of homosexuality and theft (he admitted to prostituting himself with other men but not to stealing) was interrogated by a judge while serving his sentence in the Balearic Islands. He seized the opportunity to publicly denounce the "unfair" application of the law, which exclusively targeted "poor inverts," like himself, while high-born "maricas" were spared the standard penalties. He also argued that homosexuality, as an inborn condition, could not entail liability.[136] This case indicates that some disenfranchised maricas had developed an antiregime political consciousness that stemmed from the authorities' disproportionate targeting of poor people. The lawyers' role became, in this context, the articulation of the defendants' grievances within a language of civilization that might appeal to judges, which also anticipates the strategies of some activists in the 1970s. Thus, in 1968 a defendant addressed a letter to the court of Barcelona, arguing that persecuting people with a "congenital defect" (referring to homosexuality) was a "monstrous" practice and "inconceivable" in a "civilized country," which exposed flaws in the law and in the people applying it.[137] Supporting the hypothesis that this language may stem from the lawyer's intervention, when this individual was arrested again in 1971 supposedly for wearing a wig and makeup in the bar where he worked, his mother addressed a similar letter to the court. She denounced the persecution of her son, an inborn "effeminate," as reminiscent of the Inquisition's times.[138] Through arguments like this, lawyers tempered maricas' expressed grievances by formulating them in terms of a "civilized" treatment of pathology.

Within the pathologizing framework, forensic doctors in Spain (like their Argentine counterparts) implicitly included the tendency to escape or dismiss the restrains of reality into the symptomatology of "homosexuality." In 1965, the reputed psychiatrist Juan José López Ibor examined a defendant accused of homosexuality in Madrid and diagnosed him with a "psychopathic personality with the obsession of escaping." According to López Ibor's report, the defendant was unable to explain the reasons why he chose specific destinations; his apparent "obsession was to leave on a train, without a logical foundation to aim for the place where he was later found."[139] Sexilio, as a major strategy of survival and resistance for maricas who grew up in hostile environments, was inseparable from the power of marica aesthetics to challenge societal norms. In 1976, a sixteen-year-old teenager who worked in a discotheque was arrested in Elche (region of València, Spain) and accused of being a homosexual in constant rebellion against paternal authority. Since the court file discusses her life as a trans woman, I incorporate feminine pronouns into the translations of court records that in Spanish include neutral possessive pronouns such as *su*, which can refer to both the feminine and masculine genders.

Being sixteen, she had already escaped her parents' home several times, at least on one occasion with an older lover who took her to Madrid. For the police, "This way of living and dressing constitutes a latent danger for the education and morality of children."[140] When she was interrogated, she supposedly explained her tendency to escape from her parent, "because she disagrees with their ideas and they restrain her freedoms," and her reluctance to have a stable job, "because her character does not go with it and she likes to be constantly traveling."[141] Philosopher Paul Preciado argues that "aesthetic inappropriateness, the search for social advancement, and geographic dislocation" are three fundamental axes in *cursilería*, a Spanish term for a flamboyant and excessive taste (related, but not identical, to kitsch and camp). In Preciado's analysis, *lo cursi* is politically disturbing when queer and trans people embody it to undermine social hierarchies and geographically and symbolically escape the apparatuses that aim at making them legible.[142] The young people who embraced a countercultural ethos in 1970s Spain shared a series of strategies to live on their own terms: nomadism versus the social mandate of rootedness, identification with public figures characterized by their extravagant style and excessive sentimentality (like Sara Montiel), and the refusal to accept the regime's classist foundations. In other words, individual judicial cases provide a fragmented image of the widespread crisis of the regime's organicist view on citizens' residential, socioeconomic, and sexual status.

The defendant also narrated her first sexual encounter at twelve years old with a French circus performer who penetrated her: "As a consequence of that experience, she felt inclined to those practices, carrying out most of them in Benidorm with numerous individuals of whom she can't give names or addresses since they were many. . . . She carries out these acts because she feels pleasure doing so."[143] The police of Elche argued that the defendant's openness about the homosexual relationships she had for the sake of her own pleasure made her parents uncomfortable as well as "her way of dressing, dying her hair, using makeup, wiggling her hips when walking, etc.," and the police described her as "a constant provocation and challenge to society."[144] This statement was as explicit as possible on maricas' use of aesthetic and embodied language to communicate their nonconformism. In fact, the defense lawyer herself suggested that the defendant's acts could be due to an "adolescent explosion of that rebellion," citing fragments of the declaration that demonstrated the defendant's "independent character, unlikely to yield."[145] The forensic doctor reported that the defendant showed "normal" male genitalia and suggested that an exhaustive endocrine study could help determine the causes and treatment of her homosexuality.[146] The judge sentenced the defendant as a threat to society in April 1977, but the court was unable to impose upon her the penalties of internment and surveillance because she vanished into thin air, properly closing the circle in an investigation aimed at curtailing her sexual nomadism.[147] However, barely one year later the defendant was arrested in Madrid as a sexual worker who "in the María de Molina street completely dressed like a woman in a brazen, ostensible, and provocative way insinuated herself to passersby." What police officers considered to be maricas' exhibitionism of criminal femininity was in fact part of maricas' survival strategy through sex work. The defendant declared to "feel like a woman"—she was taking hormone injections to develop her breasts and was saving to pay for her gender-affirming surgery in Brussels. She was also training to be an *artista travesti*, working in Madrid's gay cabarets and in Ramón Tejela's theater company, with which she performed in two theater plays authored by Alfonso Paso.[148]

In the 1970s, travesti was as much a subjectivity derived from gender roles and performances as a form of employment in the entertainment business and (foremost) in sex work and related to migratory status. A defendant arrested in 1975 in Barcelona used the artistic name Dolly. When the police asked her whether she had injected herself with hormones, she answered that she did so "for reasons related to her job, and because she likes to have breasts."[149] Personal choices aligned with the expectations of travesti show businesses, which in addition provided performers with the income they needed for gender reassignment surgeries—Dolly declared that she was trying to save the two hundred thousand pesetas she needed to undergo this surgery in Casablanca, Morocco—and with official employment documentation (Dolly even had a permit from the Francoist Ministry of Tourism to work in show business).[150] Similarly, twenty-four-year-old Juani was originally from Huelva, Andalucía, but she moved to Barcelona, where the police arrested her in 1975 with the charge of "making his condition of invert publicly ostensible." Juani's life trajectory, as partially captured in her files, indicates how complex and multifaceted travestis' experiences and personal ties were. Interrogated by the police, Juani explained that she "wore makeup on the street because that way she feels more feminine."[151] She reiterated this point to the judge, adding that she "played the woman's role" (actuaba de mujer) in sex with men, although she was married to a woman with whom she never had sex.[152] This was a marriage of convenience—Juani confessed in 1977—with a pregnant female "prostitute" so that her child could take Juani's last name and be raised by Juani's parents.[153] Solidarity between travestis and female sex workers is threaded into the fabric of their social life and resistance to state-imposed family norms.

Arrested once again in 1976, Juani told the police that "travesti" activity (actividad de "travesti") was one of her sources of income, which in this context most likely entails an explicit equation between travestis and sex work (she was arrested for exercising this activity on the streets).[154] She was arrested once again in 1977, this time in Bilbao; her constant transience fits within travestis' strategy of geographical mobility to avoid police harassment. She related that in between arrests she had lived in the "women's neighborhood" (barrio de mujeres) of Santander, referring to the city's red-light district as the one neighborhood where women predominated. She had been employed as an interpreter in Germany and as a painter, singer, and metallurgic factory worker in Huelva. In Bilbao, Juani lived with a single mother (señorita) of five children, probably a sex worker, who hosted and fed Juani in exchange for her services as the children's caretaker. The solidarity between travestis and women at the margins of gender normativity is a constant in these files. The police arrested Juani in Bilbao along with a friend whom she had met in the prison for homosexuals of Huelva and on the pilgrimage to the sanctuary of the Virgin of Rocío (romería del Rocío). The networks of sociability between travesti former convicts extended from the prison into territories and rituals of queer religiosity, such as the subculture centered on the Rocío.[155] In brief, the intricate plots in Pedro Almodóvar's movies about travestis pale in comparison with the real lives of people like Juani, who navigated family, religion, geography, employment, sex, and gender embodiments in ways that were hardly legible to state officers.

Conclusion

The links among fashion codes, gender performance, and political contestation do not fit into causal narratives based on measurable factors. Instead, personal memoirs and police files provide us with a series of recurrent references to retrace how maricas defied state and social controls by appropriating spaces, transforming their bodies, using gendered clothing and communicative styles, and creating solidarity mechanisms and affective ties that traversed prisons' walls.[156] The authorities perceived these strategies as a threat to the existing social order, and maricas/locas/mariconas refused to conform to the official rhetoric of shame and "rehabilitation" that informed police surveillance and prison management. Travestis' and maricas' aesthetics and performances constituted a repertoire of interventions in the public sphere, which made them targets of state violence, and therefore, these interventions could be read as political.[157] For Iñaki Estella, travestis evoke Michael Warner's notion of the counterpublic because they intervene in a "public sphere that cannot be assimilated into the space of the street or open political manifestation in urban space."[158] However, arrest records show that travestis and maricas were also visible and vocal in the streets, adopting attitudes that would cement their significant role in anti-authoritarian political protests. La Fountain-Stokes argues that in the representation of translocas, the "paradoxical tension between irrelevance and danger leads to simultaneous dismissal and over-investment: swept aside because of our supposed frivolity yet simultaneously demonized as horrendous threats."[159] This tension is at the core of maricas' experiences as captured in memoirs, psychological testing results, police reports, and other archives. Their facade of frivolity might seem accessory to the behaviors legally codified as criminal or dangerous (recurrent homosexual acts and sex work, among others). Yet it was precisely frivolity—and its cognates of joy, humor, and playfulness—that called authorities' attention and nourished maricas' expressiveness and their capacity to carry on in adverse circumstances.

SIX

From Inverse to Converging Paths

Early Sexual Activism in Argentina and Spain

In the late 1950s, two homosexual postal employees, Héctor Anabi-tarte and Luis Troitiño, met in Buenos Aires. They were engaged in the postal employees' trade union.[1] Anabitarte was also a member of the Communist Party. At that time, it was common among Marx-ist parties to maintain the view that homosexuality was a "bour-geois" vice proper to capitalist societies. Anabitarte addressed a letter to the leadership of the Communist Youth to raise the issue of his homosexuality, which led the party to refer him to a psy-chiatrist. The latter eventually decided to commit Anabitarte to a mental hospital, where he was treated with electroshocks. Despite this experience, Anabitarte persevered in his union activism and found other individuals who were similarly interested in address-ing social biases against homosexuals. In 1967, Anabitarte and Troitiño convened their marica friends to a meeting in Troitiño's room in a tenant house (*inquilinato*) in Lomas de Zamora, a town in Buenos Aires's metropolitan area. In that room, they formed what seems to be the first self-consciously political homosexual group in Latin America, Homosexuales de Buenos Aires (Buenos Aires's homosexuals).[2] This small group issued a communiqué to the Argentine press demanding the release of homosexual peo-ple arrested and held by the police and published a bulletin called *Nuestro Mundo* (Our World).[3]

In parallel, Emili Boïls i Coniller and Antonio José Mora y Mora, two Spanish homosexual men, went on a spiritual "pilgrimage" in 1966—a walk of 250 miles between Madrid and the caves of Guadix

FIG. 11. Image of the inquilinato drawn in August 2021 by Luis Troitiño. The inquilinato, where Homosexuales de Buenos Aires met for the first time in 1967, does not exist anymore, but the address can be visited by those interested in the history of the FLH. Courtesy Archivos Desviados, based in New York City and Buenos Aires.

in Granada. On this path of self-exploration, they were looking for some answers, for their own way to reconcile their religious vocation and their homosexual desires. Emili had been expelled from a monastery in 1956 because of his homosexuality. The two men believed that through adherence to their faith, they could invest themselves with the "moral authority" to counteract the view of homosexual individuals as depraved sexual predators. To do so, they dedicated themselves to serving the Roma community living in the caves of Guadix by helping take care of their domestic animals, preventing communal conflicts, and providing schooling for their children. Their pilgrimage was the embryo of the Fraternidades Cristianas de la Amistad (Christian Fraternities of Friendship), a Christian-inspired support network for homosexual people and other socially marginalized groups that operated discreetly throughout the last years of the Franco regime. Among other things, their work included a shelter home that Emili personally opened in 1968 and managed in a small town in the region of València.[4]

The paths that led these individuals to form support networks to address discrimination were interwoven with the local conditions in which they developed an interest in overall social justice. This chapter argues that the sexual liberation movements of the late 1960s and early 1970s were shaped by and emanated from vernacular marica cultures. By suspending the use of the categories of center and periphery and the geographical, temporal, and causal frames underlying the narratives on the spread of the gay identity model to national contexts outside of the United States, I will show that early queer activism emerged out of local tensions between different subjectivities. This does not entail dismissing either the ties with international allied groups or the influence of theoretical and literary works published elsewhere. Taking these factors into account, I argue that in Argentina and Spain, sexual activism politicized subjectivities performed along the axes of social class and gender expression and in contraposition to each other.

In Argentina, a heated debate confronted middle-class intellectuals with politicized students, both groups integrated in the Frente de Liberación Homosexual (Homosexual Liberation Front or FLH) but holding different views on marica femininity and on the convenience of collaborating with the militant left. Argentine activists were familiar with several conflicting frameworks to conceptualize sexuality, from the homophile canon of the entendidos to Freudo-Marxism and the vernacular trope of the marica, defined by a provocative and luring femininity. The group Eros, formed by Trotskyist radicalized maricas, became hegemonic within the FLH. They thought that maricas, revolutionary subjects par excellence, had a crucial role to play in subverting the intertwined structures of patriarchal and capitalist domination. However, the FLH had little success in enlisting the militant left's support. The earliest homosexual activism in Spain emerged in a society where Catholicism was mandated by law. Maricas and gay activists in Spain had to negotiate cultural frameworks that normalized the sublimation of same-sex desires and the folklorization of mariquitas. As the leaders of gay activism embraced Freudo-Marxism and liberationism in the 1970s, they dismissed mariquitas as the epitome of alienation.

In these years there were also drastic shifts in the political scenarios of both countries that deeply affected activists' possibilities to publicly advocate for themselves. Between 1969 and 1973
Argentine activists seemed to face more positive prospects than
their Spanish counterparts. The "people's spring," the expansion
of revolutionary popular movements in Argentina between the
Cordobazo (a series of riots by students and workers in the city
of Córdoba against the Onganía dictatorship), and the return of
Perón seemed to provide a promising milieu for sexual liberation
politics. However, the escalation of political violence from 1973
and the systematic program of state terror implemented after the
1976 coup foreclosed on the FLH's strategy. In Spain, by contrast,
the enactment of the Social Dangerousness Law in 1970 strength-
ened the legal framework for the state policing of homosexuality, but the death of General Franco in 1975 released the forces
of opposition to the dictatorship. These inverse political trajectories reveal that the expansion of activism was not necessarily
a story of international linear progress. On the contrary, it went
through periods of development and regression as the expansion
and contraction of democratic opportunities followed different
chronologies in the Southern Cone and Mediterranean Europe.
As a result of these inverse trajectories, Argentine activists went
into exile in Spain and participated in the exhilarating movements of change that spread between the mid-1970s and early
1980s. This chapter first traces the debates about the marica and
potential collaborations with the militant left in the Argentine
FLH. Then it explores the debate about the mariquita in the Movimiento Español de Liberación Homosexual (Spanish Movement
of Homosexual Liberation or MELH).

Glocal Revolutions

The 1960s were a convulsive time for politics in Argentina, cul-
minating in the state's imposition of authoritarian policies. Mass
media projected ideals of upper social mobility and represented
aspirational technological progress through the advertising of consumer household goods such as fridges and televisions. A higher

percentage of the population, and of women in particular, had access to secondary and higher education. Premarital sex was more openly discussed, and young people's participation in the rock 'n' roll and hippie cultures challenged traditional gender roles through an adoption of androgynous fashion and appearance and overall opposition to social conventions. However, this decade of utopian projects and hope for change also witnessed a deterioration of socioeconomic conditions for a large segment of the population. The increasing concentration of the population in large cities, and especially in the Buenos Aires metropolitan area, contributed to a lack of affordable housing and a rise in the number of shantytowns. Economic instability and inflation made it difficult for the working class, but also for the middle class, to access basic consumer goods, further generating a sense of vulnerability and social unrest.[5] Left-leaning students and industrial workers were at the vanguard of opposition to state policies, based on an array of ideologies from Peronism and Third Worldism to Trotskyism and Maoism.[6]

At the same time, reactionary sectors perceived the questioning of traditional gender and family mores and the mobilization of the left-leaning youth as a combined threat. In 1966, a military coup led by General Juan Carlos Onganía installed a dictatorial regime, self-styling it as the "Argentine Revolution" (1966–73). The coup led to Onganía's de facto presidency (1966–70), which implemented "an authoritarian modernization project."[7] The government banned political parties, restrained academic freedoms, and imposed various stabilization and rationalization schemas aimed at enhancing the most efficient sectors of the economy at the cost of employees' bargaining powers and working conditions. These policies were grounded in—and legitimated by—the regime's anticommunism and defense of traditional morality, embodied in its harsh policing and censorship of youth cultures "from the miniskirt to long hair," historian Alberto Romero notes.[8] The intensification of state authoritarianism contributed to the radicalization of opposition sectors led by students and industrial workers. This was the context and catalyst for the formation in 1967 of Homosexuales de Buenos Aires, which comprised less than ten regular members. Héctor Anabitarte took on a leadership role in the group and, along with Juan José Hernández, acted as the liaison with other groups that integrated into the FLH in 1971. Homosexuales usually met in Luis Troitiño's kitchen. During one of these meetings, a neighbor who had noticed their regular assembly denounced them to the police for illicit gambling, but they were released soon after their arrest.[9] *Nuestro Mundo*, the group's bulletin, relied on the legitimacy of empirical studies to present homosexuality as an imprinted condition worthy of sympathy, a strategy for increasing social tolerance that did not question the primacy of heterosexuality. Pablo Ben and Joaquín Insausti argue that the members were working-class homosexual individuals able to draw on their previous militant experiences in trade unions to politicize their sexuality against an authoritarian background (versus the assumption that the emergence of gay movements depends on democratization processes).[10] This analysis focuses primarily on Anabitarte's role and testimonies.

Based on the testimony of the group's co-founder Luis Troitiño (also a postal service employee), Juan Queiroz and myself put forward a slightly different argument: Homosexuales de Buenos Aires was the outcome of a "confluence between Left-leaning trade unionists and maricas who recognized each other and had shared experiences in their workplaces and in the *barrios* at the south of Buenos Aires."[11] There is no doubt that Anabitarte's know-how, based on his experiences in the Communist Youth, provided structure and a sense of political militancy to the group, but at the same time maricas' frivolity and self-indulgence figure in Troitiño's testimony as the glue that kept the group together and motivated. According to Troitiño, "The postal service was infected with maricas, many of whom were provocative and scandalous," especially when they were cruising for sex (*levante*). Maricas circulated the Homosexuales' newsletter among one another, starting with Troitiño passing it to co-workers in the postal service, which he called maricas' "great nest." Within Homosexuales, Jorge Pitana (an employee of the city government) acted as a "sort of great mother" in charge of bringing food to the meetings and socializing other members in maricas' cultural norms, including the use of *carrilche*. This was, according to trans scholar Marlene Wayar, a jargon inspired by *lunfardo* (a slang originating in Buenos Aires's criminal circles) that maricas developed in the mid-1940s to communicate with one another.[12] In brief, the symbiosis between maricas' culture and social networks and the left's militant strategies was the breeding ground for the first politized homosexual group in Latin America, which was almost negligible in numerical terms but inaugurates a new chapter in marica history.

One year later, in October 1968, Santiago, a real estate developer from Buenos Aires, wrote to the Washington DC Mattachine Society. He had first corresponded with them in 1963, requesting to be put in contact with Mattachine members living in or visiting Buenos Aires. The content of this first letter was not political but rather amounted to a personal ad in which he described his physical aspect and upper-class hobbies, including traveling abroad. Santiago labeled himself an "informal delegate" in Argentina of homophile groups Der Kreis (Switzerland) and Arcadie (France), whose leader André Baudry was willing to provide references. Santiago offered to perform this same role for the Mattachine Society and finished his letter asking his addressee to use a discreet envelope when replying, maintaining the discretion that characterized entendidos.[13] This letter pinpoints the coordinates for homophile/entendido sociability. First, upper-class gay men had the means and cultural background to travel internationally. Second, the organizational structure of the European and North American homophile groups and the networks between them were solid enough that they could formalize members' affiliations and exchange information. And third, the motivations for joining this network included both changing the public discourse about homosexuality and a personal interest in meeting potential sexual partners. In September 1963, Franklin E. Kameny, president of the Mattachine Society of Washington DC, let Santiago know that they could not satisfy his request, betraying the group's lack of interest in this potential collaboration with Argentine homophiles.[14]

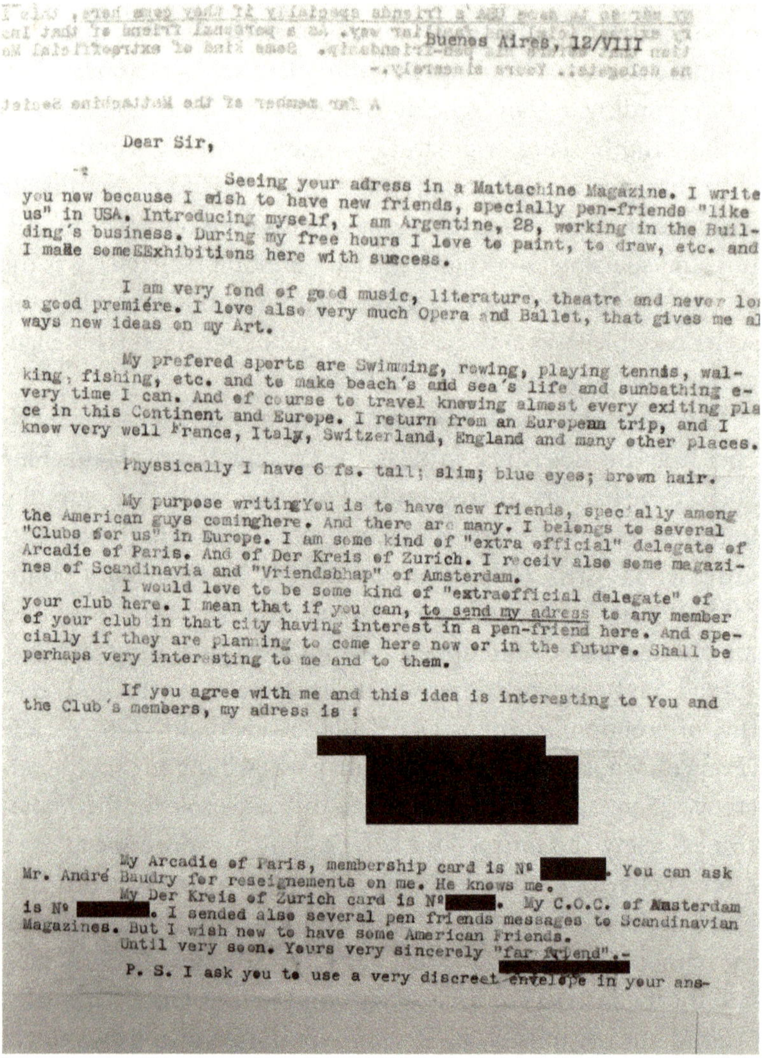

FIG. 12. Letter from Santiago to the Mattachine Society in 1963. Kameny Papers, folder 7, box 82. Courtesy Library of Congress, Washington DC.

Santiago signed his 1968 letter as "Yack" and introduced himself as the unofficial delegate of Arcadie in Buenos Aires but also as the representative of an Argentine homophile group. This group did not seem to have any relationship with the working-class maricas who formed Homosexuales de Buenos Aires, unlikely to cross paths with Santiago. Most likely, the latter was referring to a small social circle of middle-to-upper-class homosexual men who knew about the activities of the European and U.S. homophile groups. In other words, this would be a group of entendidos, well-off individuals who were interested in resignifying homosexuality as a respectable behavior without forsaking either the exclusivity of their social circle or the protections provided by their elite status in the face of police repression.[15]

A few months later, in May 1969, the Cordobazo—an uprising and protest staged by students and workers in the city of Córdoba, the center of the Argentine automotive industry—initiated a cycle of social mobilizations and popular protests against the dictatorship that lasted until 1973. The demonstrations were led by class-conscious workers' unions and university students. Together they took control of the city streets at the end of May 1969, demonstrating the regime's inability to maintain public order. The military's grasp over political life in Argentina continued loosening from then on; industrial and rural workers, students, sectors of the informal economy, and neighbors all shared their frustration with deteriorating living standards and censorship of free speech. This widespread mobilization—the "people's spring" of 1969–73—participated in the era's global cycle of antiauthoritarian protests and was inspired by several different Latin American models, from the liberation theology of Third-World Catholic priests who advocated for the unprivileged populations of the continent's urban shantytowns, to the Cuban socialist revolution and Che Guevara's guerrilla campaigns. In the late 1960s, some guerrilla groups also formed in Argentina, which would go on to carry out high-profile actions in the 1970s, including kidnappings, assassinations, and guerrilla warfare in peripheral regions of the country. The Trotskyist Ejercito Revolucionario del Pueblo (Revolutionary People's Army or ERP) and the Peronist Montoneros were the two main groups with such factions. One unique phenomenon of this period was the ideological split within Peronism—propitiated by Perón's intentionally ambivalent messages from his exile in Spain—between an anticommunist reactionary wing, well represented in the unions'

bureaucracy, and a revolutionary wing organized around the Peronist Youth.[16]

In parallel with the events of Argentina's people's spring, on
June 28, 1969, a group of trans and gay people spontaneously stood
their ground and confronted police officers in a raid at the Stonewall Inn in New York City. This event and those that followed,
known as the Stonewall riots or simply "Stonewall," would come
in later decades in the United States to represent a shift in activists' attitudes and tactics in regard to confronting state repression
and social homophobia, another expression of the rebellious and
militant cultures of the generations that came of age between the
late 1960s and early 1970s.[17] However, in Argentina, the awareness
and influences of events such as Stonewall and other international
homosexual liberation organizations figure unevenly in the historical narratives of the founders of the FLH. The latter's approach to
the transnational sexual liberation movement reflected their positions regarding two pressing debates among homosexual activists
in early 1970s Buenos Aires: the alliance with the militant left and
the potential politicization of marica subjectivities.

In March 1971, the magazine *Confirmado* published an extensive research article based on interviews with subjects who cruised
for sex in public areas of Buenos Aires. These maricas enjoyed
cruising with a sense of self-indulgence (while being aware of the
dangers that this practice entailed), explained the subtle norms
and rituals for seducing chongos, and shared with the interviewer
their experiences with and views on fleeting passion, loneliness,
police harassment, misogyny, "sex change" treatments, and sexual politics. Maricas who met one another in cruising areas and
other social venues were at least partially aware of the structural
discriminations that shaped their daily lives.[18] This was the breeding ground for the formation of the FLH, and yet this group was
never able to fully mobilize maricas' discontent within its politicization schema. Historians and activists generally agree that the
FLH was founded in 1971 as a result of the encounter between
the publishers of *Nuestro Mundo* and middle-class intellectuals,
including Juan José Sebreli and Blas Matamoro, who formed the

group Profesionales. Later, Eros, a group of politicized students led by Néstor Perlongher, joined the FLH and infused the movement with a new militant energy.

Sebreli and Matamoro, both established philosophers by the early 1970s, were connected with the generation of entendidos who had contributed to the popularization of the homophile canon in Argentina, such as Juan José Hernández and Pepe Bianco. The latter translated into Spanish the document *The Women's Liberation and Gay Liberation Movements* (1970) by Black Panther leader Huey P. Newton, which called for an alliance between different emancipatory movements and deeply influenced the FLH. Bianco's disciple, Juan José Hernández, was from Tucumán, like multiple members of the group led by Anabitarte, and connected them with the intellectuals of Profesionales.[19] Marica politics were a controversial and divisive issue from the first meeting of the FLH in August 1971 in Matamoro's apartment. One of the attendees, Teddy Paz, remembers, "In that meeting we discussed how the homosexual's worst enemies were the cartoonish homosexuals. At that time, no one took the marica seriously."[20] Even though people with very disparate backgrounds—from Communist trade unionists to Buenos Aires's intellectual elite—collaborated with the FLH, they all focused on the marica as the figure that animated imaginaries, desires, and fears of homosexual scandal.

Activists' positioning in the homosexual sociability networks and ideological conflicts of the 1970s become manifest in their historical narratives about the relationship between transnational influences such as Stonewall and the formation of the FLH. Sebreli describes how in August 1971 Rubén Massera returned from New York City, where he had worked as a translator for the United Nations, and called him to share his enthusiasm about the activities of the U.S. Gay Power and propose the formation of a similar organization in Argentina.[21] According to Sebreli, after that phone call, he and Matamoro organized a meeting attended by six people: the two of them, Massera, Manuel Puig, Juan José Hernández, and Héctor Anabitarte. In that meeting, Sebreli allegedly proposed the name "Frente de Liberación Homosexual" inspired by the

U.S. Gay Liberation Front (GLF).[22] In this narrative, the FLH was founded partly because of a first-person contact with the experience of gay activism outside of Argentina and the enthusiasm and determination of a small group of intellectuals.

In contrast, Blas Matamoro and Héctor Anabitarte, who also attended the first meeting of the FLH, have a different perspective on the influence of the GLF on the Argentine movement. In my interview of Matamoro, in whose home the meeting was held, he answered my questions about the influence, if any, of Stonewall, affirming that he did not know the term, but remembered the significance of the Mattachine Society.[23] This view of the Mattachine as the main organization of reference for the FLH within the United States neglects the liberationist movements of the late 1960s and early 1970s and may be related to Matamoro's disagreement with the radical politics adopted by the FLH after the incorporation of the politicized students of Eros, led by Perlongher. For Anabitarte and other members of Homosexuales, Stonewall and the formation of the GLF were not foundational events but rather contributed to their awareness of the transnational nature of their activism. According to Anabitarte, they heard the news about Stonewall and "started to understand that there was a gay movement in the United States" through Juan José Hernández, who had visited the United States and brought back a pamphlet about "that first demonstration in New York."[24] Moreover, Anabitarte points out that Arcadie had more influence on them as a theoretical reference. Argentine intellectuals' traditional admiration for French culture and Latin American left-wing activists' antagonism toward the United States' Cold War politics are probably among the factors that explain this preference.[25] Feminist activist Sara Torres similarly emphasizes that members of the FLH translated documents from the United States, but these presented an agenda that did not fit with the logic of sexual activism in Argentina.[26]

There are noticeable divergences among the testimonies by Sebreli, Matamoro, and Anabitarte. Sebreli represents the U.S. Gay Power as playing an influential role, while Matamoro ignores the meaning of Stonewall and instead acknowledges the Mattachine

Society. Anabitarte situates the formation of Homosexuales prior to Stonewall and emphasizes that its relationship with or influences from any North American movement was untenable due to ideological factors and the distinct context in which it arose. Events like Stonewall, as well as other symbolic artifacts of the transnational sexual liberation movements of the 1960s and 1970s, did not have the same relevance for all the Argentine activists of that period, whose heterogeneous positions in this respect reflect their diverse ideologies and class backgrounds. In other words, the interpretation of Stonewall as a foundational moment does not appear reflected in the recollections of activists who situate the effects of this event within a disputed local history.

Maricas in Revolution

The cross-class collaboration and ideological heterogeneity that characterized the activities of the FLH also produced some conflicts between the integrationist politics of respectability and the revolutionary politics of liberation. This tension became most manifest in the debate about maricas/locas. In schematic terms, there was a certain continuity between the homophile vindication of a discreetly masculine homosexual identity and the position of established intellectuals such as Juan José Sebreli and Blas Matamoro. The latter were part of the FLH but wanted to distance themselves from feminized and hypersexual maricas.[27] An article published in 1973 by the group Profesionales in the FLH's bulletin *Homosexuales* ignited this controversy.[28] The authors of the article argued that rigid binary sexual roles (active and passive) and maricas' exhibitionist femininity as well as their "feminine" professions (dancing, fashion design, hairdressing, home decoration, etc.) demonstrated their alienation and served to reinforce the core myths of machismo. The article discussed a social construction of masculinity that defined a man's phallus as the basis of his position as subject and owner in relationships with women, seen as objects and property.

Maricas, according to the authors, renounced their positions as subjects to become sexual objects: "Machismo projects its

ideological codes over a conventional and schematic figure of
the homosexual: the male that has the status of a woman, the
marica, the loca . . . the machista sexual fantasy is the penalizing
aggression against the 'marica' . . . hurting him, penetrating him,
raping him, possessing him as a despicable thing, making him suffer while soothing his anal anxiety."[29] According to the authors,
maricas' vocal attitude versus homophobic environments—their
"exhibitionist and masochist image"—was nothing else but an
"unhealthy acceptance of repression," which contributed to the
machista notion that "maricas" wanted to be punished.[30] Furthermore, the authors described maricas' strategic use of their femininity to arouse their sexual partners as an "aberration." In the last
instance, the authors argued, the "myth of the marica" was func-
tional for machismo, allowing other men to ignore their latent
homosexual tendencies. As an alternative, they proposed egalitarian "authentic homosexual relationships" between individuals
whose sexual practices were flexible and did not fit into the passive/
active binary. The authors acknowledged that maricas were bold
and desirable but denied them any potential agency in their own
emancipation because they defined femininity (encompassing an
exclusively "passive" sexual role) in simplistic terms, as submissive and objectified.

In contrast, politicized students and activists integrated into the
group Eros, including Néstor Perlongher and Marcelo Benítez, considered the marica to be the revolutionary subject par excellence. In
their view, maricas undermined the patriarchal bases of the capitalist system of oppression by maximizing their sexual pleasure and
refusing to conform to the expectations of manliness.[31] The young
activists of Eros wanted to appeal not only to middle-class educated
homosexual men but mostly to maricas who challenged the structures of political and sexual domination with their way of conducting themselves daily. However, the theoretical ground of the FLH
activists' publications and actions prevented them from forming a broader militant platform, according to Perlongher's later
assessment.[32] Marcelo Benítez, who was a young Trotskyist student in those years, epitomizes the position of the group led by

Perlongher: "We fought like bitches, because some of them said 'being a homosexual doesn't mean one can't be a man.' And they said that wearing their pearl necklaces. . . . People like Perlongher and myself were in favor of the marica and treated her as a heroine . . . like the worker for the Marxists, let's say . . . the revolutionary subject."[33] Benítez highlights the revolutionary potential of marica femininity while criticizing, in a mocking tone, the position of those activists who vindicated their identity as homosexual men. Blas Matamoro, who possibly was one of the latter, describes this heated debate in very different terms: "You had to be a uniformed homosexual, dress like a homosexual, so everyone could know it, because otherwise [your conduct] was shamefaced. The homosexual who assimilated himself to his environment was shamefaced."[34] From Matamoro's perspective, the vindication of the marica led some FLH activists to impose a moralistic imperative on homosexual men to externalize their condition through gender performance. This was the opposite of the model of subjectification promoted by the homophile literature.

The two conflicting positions about the marica within the FLH had a certain correlation with activists' positions with respect to the collaboration with Marxist organizations and left-wing Peronists. Matamoro and Sebreli, who rejected the view of the marica as a revolutionary subject, defended at the same time a form of activism focused on intellectual production, using studies and surveys to promote homosexual individuals' self-awareness. According to Sebreli, although they identified with the intellectual left, this was a very undefined, vague identification, which did not lead this group of established intellectuals to adopt militant strategies.[35] On the other hand, Perlongher, Benítez, and other members of the FLH saw the collaboration with the Peronist left and/or Trotskyism as the logical and necessary path to creating a platform based on the alliance among different revolutionary causes.[36] The internal debates among FLH activists were highly sophisticated, as each group formed its own corpus of theoretical works to support its positions. When I asked different FLH activists to identify the theoretical framework of the movement, their answers showed significant variance. Sebreli listed the reports published in 1948 by U.S. sexologist Alfred Kinsey, Simone de Beauvoir's *The Second Sex* (1949), Donald Webster Cory's *The Homosexual in America* (1951), and the novels of renowned French authors Marcel Proust and André Gide.[37] For Sebreli, the FLH was inspired by different postwar humanistic currents such as existentialism, scientific positivism, and literary cosmopolitism. Eros activists, on the contrary, built a theoretical framework that accounted for the capitalist system imposing its bourgeois ideology through internalized shame. Benítez recounts that they had read the works of Austrian Marxist psychoanalyst Wilhelm Reich (1897–1957). When they realized that Reich upheld pathologizing views on homosexuality, they started to read Jacques Lacan and Gilles Deleuze instead.[38] David Cooper's *The Death of the Family*, published in Spanish in Argentina in 1971, also had a significant influence on these activists' critique of the family and its role in capitalist oppression.[39] Eventually, Eros became hegemonic within the FLH due to the group's capacity to mobilize activists willing to engage in public actions.[40] Their goal was not to redraw the boundaries of acceptability but rather to precipitate a sexual and social revolution that they perceived as imminent. They felt inspired by guerrillas' strategies and aesthetics and used feminine noms de guerre (Perlongher's was "Rosa Luxemburgo"). Eros rejected Profesionales' proposal to adopt a structure based on a central committee and subcommittees (like traditional leftist parties), and instead, the FLH maintained the principle of organizational autonomy.[41]

In 1971, a new military de facto president, Alejandro Agustín Lanusse, initiated negotiations with the leaders of Argentine political parties and with Perón to restore the mechanisms of democracy. The negotiations culminated with the open elections of March 1973, won by left-wing Peronist candidate Héctor Cámpora.[42] In June 1973, several members of the FLH displayed their support for Peronism by publicly rallying under their own banner at the airport of Ezeiza to receive Juan Domingo Perón upon his return from his Spanish exile. This strategy did not produce the expected results. In the context of increasing political polarization and violence between 1973 and 1976, the extreme right used the visibility of the FLH to discredit leftist organizations, which responded by distancing themselves from homosexual activism.[43] Leftist activists even created a chant to differentiate themselves from putos during their demonstrations: "We are not putos, we are not drug users [faloperos], we are soldiers of the F.A.R. and Montoneros [Peronist guerrillas]."[44]

While the FLH was trying with little success to establish an alliance with left-wing organizations, the cadres of the latter directed their homosexual members to subject themselves to psychotherapy to develop a heterosexual libido. These cadres maintained that homosexuality was a bourgeois vice, one that would disappear along with capitalist structures of oppression.[45] In the mid-1970s, for instance, Rubén Tosoni was a member of an anarchist group. He perceived dissonance inside the organization between the cadres, who characterized homosexuality as a defect of the dominant classes, and the rest of his comrades, who did not see it as an issue at all. The group's leadership forced Rubén to visit a psychologist, who diagnosed him as manifesting a "will to change." On the contrary, Rubén remembers vividly that he was expressing his "will to be accepted."[46] The premise that individual willpower can overcome sexual predispositions allowed political cadres to view conversion therapy as aligned with revolutionary ideology. As Martin Duberman recounted regarding his decision to pursue conversation psychotherapy in the 1960s, "In order to protest injustice, one must always assume that only will (and never biology or the divinity or the power of history) prevents us from remaking society in the more egalitarian image we wish."[47] However, this principle did not produce the expected results when applied to homosexual patients.[48]

Daniel Molina, member of a Trotskyist guerrilla group, followed the leadership's advice and visited a psychologist to treat his homosexuality. After four or five sessions, he had already decided that conversion therapy was pointless and left it.[49] In November 1974, while serving in the Argentine military, Daniel was abducted by the military police and repeatedly tortured with sleep deprivation and an electric prod until his release in 1983. He felt that being gay "entailed a double punishment. By the military, who used it sometimes to torture [him] even further, but also by [his] comrades."[50] Homosexual people targeted by state violence in those years because of their left-wing activism in turn had to deal with the homophobic attitudes of some of their comrades.

Crisis and Dissolution

Between the last presidency of Perón and the military coup of 1976, the FLH faced a political context of intense polarization. Perón won over 60 percent of the votes in the elections of September 1973, holding the presidency until his natural death in July 1974. Then he was succeeded by his wife and vice president, Isabel Martínez de Perón, until the coup of March 24, 1976. Perón's program was intended to promote sociopolitical stability. He tried to end the internal conflict within the Peronist movement and form a Social Pact between employers and labor to bring down inflation and expand the internal market. However, the 1973 oil crisis led instead to an international economic contraction. Moreover, tensions between the left and right wings of Peronism escalated as the former was increasingly marginalized from positions of state power. The Peronist Youth and Montoneros tried unsuccessfully to appeal to Perón himself. On May 1, 1974, Perón publicly disavowed them during a rally in the square in front of the presidential palace. Montoneros responded by leaving the square to symbolize their rupture with their mythical leader. As the sociopolitical situation deteriorated, terrorist and paramilitary groups became more active, and civilian authorities increasingly called on the military to restore order. From February 1974, the army clashed with the Trotskyist ERP guerrillas in the Tucumán mountains. In parallel, the *Alianza Anticomunista Argentina* (Anti-Communist Argentine Alliance, known as Triple A), a paramilitary group integrated by fascists and right-wing Peronists, launched a terrorist campaign against leftist guerrillas but also against politicized sectors of civil society, including students, intellectuals, and workers.[51]

In February 1975, *El Caudillo*, the official publication of the extreme-right Peronists led by José López Rega, called on readers to exterminate homosexuals who corrupted the Argentine nation as part of foreign communists' strategy. The piece warned that maricones frequented bathrooms looking for sex, corrupted minors, made their effeminacy public by wearing tight clothes, and had even formed a political organization, the FLH, trying to collaborate with the Peronist left. The solutions proposed to eradicate this threat strikingly resemble the policies put in place in Franco's Spain: homosexual people should be shamed and publicly ostracized for didactic purposes, which is what Spanish fascists did with singer Miguel de Molina and others; homosexual people should be isolated in reeducation camps; and movies, TV shows, and theater plays that "spread this perversion to the people" should be forbidden.[52] Simultaneously, since the mid-1970s, men who wore androgynous clothes became a police target. A pamphlet by the FLH (reproduced in their newsletter *Somos*) denounced "'police efforts to reimpose a Cary Grant image' by cutting young men's hair and obligating them to exchange shoes and colored clothes for more sober and 'manly' items."[53] Men's long hair and colorful clothes became politically charged issues because authorities implemented public policies that targeted androgynous youth cultures as a cradle for both homosexuality and subversion. However, under left-leaning Peronist leaders, the police still targeted androgynous-looking men. According to Malva, under Buenos Aires governor Oscar Bidegain (1973–74), who identified with the Peronist left, the police forcibly cut hippie men's long hair and bell-bottom pants, fined women who wore miniskirts, and arrested maricones.[54] The latter were seen as infectious agents of disease, subversion, and gender nonconformity, informing security forces' campaigns to clean the streets of undesirable elements.

In this context, the correspondence with activists from other countries came to operate as a decentralized network with different nodes, each channeling resources, contacts, and information.[55] For instance, the New York-based lawyer and gay activist Robert A. Roth assumed in the 1970s the task of maintaining a fluid correspondence with Latin American homosexual groups on behalf of several U.S. organizations. He was a graduate of Cornell Law School, where he co-founded the Student Homophile League. In New York his legal practice specialized in defending tenant rights. He died in 1990 at age forty from HIV-related conditions. Roth kept a personal archive of his correspondence with Spanish-speaking activists, which provides valuable information on the synergies between transnational networks and personal contacts at the harshest moments of the so-called Dirty War. In March 1974 the FLH sent a letter to the U.S. National Gay Task Force to ask them to use their address in *Somos* so they could still communicate with their readers without endangering themselves.[56] Likewise, the FLH also requested the support of their U.S. allies, in solidarity with the homosexual detainees in the prison of Devoto, to cover some of their expenses, including pencils, cigarettes, toilet paper, and other basic products.[57] In February 1976 Héctor Anabitarte sent Robert Roth a letter thanking him for the economic assistance for covering some of these expenses.[58] Anabitarte and Roth were nodal actors in a transnational solidarity network against a backdrop of authoritarianism, performing roles of "structural integration and cultural negotiation" among different groups.[59]

Argentines who were not politically active also sent letters abroad trying to forge personal connections to mitigate situations of isolation imposed by their political context. In September 1975 a university student sent a letter to the Mattachine Society, whose address he had found in an issue of the magazine *Gay Times*: "My name is Carlos Oller, I'm 18 and I live in Argentina. I'm studying philosophy at the University of Buenos Aires, but above all I'm gay."[60] When I interviewed Oller, he speculated that he had probably ordered the *Gay Times* by mail, although he did not remember the details.[61] The term "gay" in Latin America to encapsulate a new identitarian paradigm based on the flexibility of sexual and gender roles was very incipient in the 1970s and only started to gain ground unevenly in the 1980s.[62] Oller speculated that he was familiar with the term through several English-language publications that he read when he was an adolescent, including the magazines

Time and *Mad* and the local newspaper *The Buenos Aires Herald*. He added, "In that period the term 'gay' in its current meaning was unknown in Argentina. Neither was it of common use among homosexuals. . . . However, it seemed to me like a convenient term that avoided both the clinical tone of 'homosexual' as well as the affected overtone of 'entendido.'"[63] Entendidos' affectation and discretion did not appeal to Oller, an adolescent who intended to express "a sort of innate affinity that connected [him], since [he] was a kid, with persons who were distant from [him] in time and space, an identity that [he] couldn't find in the market of identities of that time."[64] In these early stages of the introduction of the "gay" paradigm, later associated with the politics of visibility and normalization, Oller strategically used this term to express both his sense of belonging to a transnational affective community and his repudiation of entendidos. In his letter to the Mattachine, Oller referred to the FLH as a group that had disappeared, but Roth put him in contact with Anabitarte.[65] Oller remembers that *Somos* was sold in several press kiosks of the city, including one on Corrientes Avenue, where he was able to buy some issues when he was a teenager.[66] However, the deterioration of the political situation preceding the 1976 military coup led the FLH to discontinue the distribution of *Somos*.

The escalation of state violence culminated in the military coup of March 24, 1976, which inaugurated a dictatorship that endangered members of the FLH. The military junta appointed General Jorge Rafael Videla president. The policies implemented during the next seven years were unprecedented in the way they subordinated everything, including economic growth, to the disciplining of society. The state's systematic terrorist schemes were two-sided. On the one hand, state authorities publicly stated that they were combating guerrillas in accordance with the law. On the other hand, the state also covertly "disappeared" tens of thousands of people, with official estimates placing the number of Argentines murdered as high as thirty thousand people. Paramilitary groups were incorporated into the state terror apparatus. The "disappearances" were carried out by the so-called task groups, formed by military and police officers as well as civilians. The victims were usually abducted at night in their homes, taken to one of the hundreds of clandestine detention centers, subjected to systematic mental and physical torture—including electrocution and sexual abuse—and finally executed. The victims' bodies were hidden in collective graves or flown out and cast into the sea. They were called the "disappeared" because there was no evidence of their death. In this way, the state denied its orchestration and direct involvement in the terrorist operations while achieving its goal of spreading a "culture of fear" and physically exterminating sectors of civil society that had exhibited critical thinking.[67]

On the same day when the coup took place, the FLH sent a letter to Roth trying to convey hopefulness despite adverse circumstances: "Today, a coup d'état took place. The military took over the government. Repression will continue. This is a new stage of the Argentine crisis. The homosexual movement today is organized and strong. We will resist. We are growing."[68] The next letter to Roth, from April 1976, already revealed an increasing concern about state violence: "Things are difficult here, but we can keep working. Please, write to us. It is very important for us."[69] The shift in tone between these two letters, from posed optimism to urgent appeals for international solidarity, reflects the lived experiences of the FLH activists in those months. Along with the April letter, the FLH sent a *Boletín de emergencia* that they had published in March, after the coup. The document presented a sophisticated theoretical critique of the rationale for the persecution of homosexuality. It argued that people who release their sexual drives and create alternative forms and spaces of encounter challenge the heterosexual norm that is a fundamental mechanism of class domination.[70] For the FLH activists led by Perlongher, the organization should operate as a revolutionary vanguard, illuminating the way for the liberation of the libido in order to unmask the family's oppressive role.[71] The movement strove to project this activist approach—both inside and outside of Argentina—even up until a few months before its dissolution in the face of state terrorism. Although the FLH as an organization was not a specific target of the military dictatorship, after the coup it became increasingly difficult for the organization to operate in a context of systematic political repression and violence.[72] The FLH dissolved in 1976. Many of its members were also members of other left-wing organizations or had publicly written about their views. Therefore, they had to either go into an internal exile or emigrate abroad, predominantly to Spain.

Transcendent Sexualities

The institutionalized hegemony of Catholicism as a system of thought in Franco's Spain shaped the emergence and activities of its earliest homosexual groups. While censorship and repression did not prevent the politicization of young people and the liberalization of social customs, questioning the regime and its views on morality was prosecuted as a violation of law.[73] In this context, members of the clergy were among the first ones to covertly create a support network to address homosexual people's issues related to their social marginalization as well as to publicly come out as homosexuals themselves. As I discussed before, Catholicism offered mariquitas certain mechanisms of social acceptability at the cost of sublimation. Between the last years of the Franco regime and the early stages of the democratic transition, as some priests acknowledged their homosexual desires and advocated compassion for homosexual people, the Catholic hierarchy attempted to thwart this softening of its condemnatory stance on homosexuality by hospitalizing, excommunicating, expelling, and disavowing these early dissidents.

In the mid-to-late 1960s, a group of Catholic priests and laymen formed the Fraternidades Cristianas de la Amistad (Christian Friendship Fraternities or FCA) to address issues of social marginalization, and first and foremost among its aims was its ministry to homosexual people. Emili Boïls i Coniller was one of its proponents. In 1954, as a seventeen-year-old, he had entered a Claretian monastery in the Pyrenees as a novitiate. However, in 1956, after he confessed his homosexual desires to his superiors, they forced him to abandon his vocation. In the middle of the night, they woke him, and they expelled him from the monastery, leaving him dressed in lay attire in a freezing train station, feeling "sick, defeated, and sad."[74] In the next years, Emili completed his mandatory military service, had his first adult relationship with another man, wrote several books, and opened and managed his own bookstore in València. Then in the mid-1960s, someone entered the bookstore and invited him to attend a meeting of the Hermandad Obrera de Acción Católica (the Workers' Brotherhood of Catholic Action or HOAC). He attended, and the experience drastically changed Emili's perspective on religiosity. The HOAC appealed to workers to fight for social justice and rejected any representation of Jesus Christ that obscured his message of fraternity with ornate rituals. This model of activism inspired Emili to apply a similar approach to homosexual people's issues. In 1966, he met the Andalusian homosexual priest Antonio José Mora y Mora in Barcelona, and together they planned their pilgrimage to the caves of Guadix, which would result in the foundation of the FCA.[75] According to Pau López Clavel, during the last years of the Franco regime, the FCA had a small presence in the cities of Sevilla, València, and Granada, but there are no available membership estimates for this early period.[76] Many people were able to "come out" in a supportive environment in the shelter home that Emili operated from 1968 to 1994, where he developed his own cult of the Virgin Mary as "the mother of worldwide homophiles."[77]

The FCA organized its doctrine around the homophile concept of friendship to counteract the regime's institutionalized view of maricas as dangerous sexual predators with no capacity to control their instincts and establish meaningful relationships. The FCA stayed active in the next decades. By the late 1970s, they too were in contact with Robert Roth. They shared their manifesto with him and were included in Roth's published list of international gay organizations. The members met regularly and counted on the spiritual guidance of a priest, although they were independent of the Catholic Church. Among their goals, they intended to "erase the dirty and viscous image of homosexuality that society has created, publicizing and promoting its human values."[78] In order to do so, they instructed their members to be models of "personal integrity." Standing on a high moral ground was, in their view, the best defense against a "sick" and hostile society.[79]

Catalyzing Events

As gay liberation movements developed in other national contexts, in Spain the Franco regime enacted in 1970 the Social Danger and Rehabilitation Law. As Ben Cowan has noted, the policing of sexuality shifted internationally during the Cold War period.[80] Adding to the classist moral policing (previously codified in the Vagrancy Law), the Social Danger Law reflected the regime's concerns about the decaying morals of a large sector of young people attracted to countercultural movements, psychedelia, and sexual experimentation. The enactment of the Social Danger Law codified the application of "scientific" methods to assess and prevent social behaviors that deviated from the regime authorities' moral views. Paradoxically, the enactment of this law catalyzed the formation of the first homosexual group aimed at confronting the Franco regime's policies.[81] Before its enactment, a draft of the law was to be debated by the Cortes, a nondemocratic legislative body formed by representatives of the core base of support of the regime, which included Catholic bishops, the military, the Francoist trade unions, local authorities, and male "family heads."[82] Two Catalonian gay men, Armand de Fluvià and Francesc Francino, decided on a plan to lobby Catholic bishops to prevent the codifying of homosexuality as a criminal condition in the law (in contrast to homosexual *acts*).[83] Fluvià eventually would become a leading figure in the homosexual movement based in Barcelona. He came from a Catalonian *haute bourgeoisie* family, was raised in a Catholic school, and until the 1970s held moderate political views and was a supporter of Juan de Borbón, son and heir of the last dethroned monarch of Spain.

Fluvià's background allowed him to travel to cosmopolitan capitals such as London, New York, and Paris. In Amsterdam, he accidentally ran into a group of male acquaintances from Barcelona. The encounter led him to join the social events organized by this group. Fluvià was also an avid reader of *Arcadie* and well aware

of events abroad, including the Stonewall riots.[84] Similar to Buenos Aires's entendidos, Fluvià's familiarity with the homophile
agenda was intricately tied to his participation in an urban social
network of well-off homosexual men, who had the means and
motivation to travel abroad to enjoy the broader sexual opportunities of European and North American capitals. However, in contrast to the trajectory of Argentine entendidos, starting with his
campaign against the Social Danger Law, Fluvià initiated a process of politicization and sexual activism to confront the Franco
regime's policies that led him to abandon conservative monar-
chism for Marxism.

Fluvià and Francino's 1970 strategy to intervene in the debate
on the Social Danger Law relied a great deal on *Arcadie*'s readership network. As Geoffrey Huard has studied, they had asked
André Baudry for the contact information of *Arcadie*'s correspondent in Spain. Rafael Rosillo y Herrero, a well-connected aristocrat from Madrid, wrote for *Arcadie* using the pseudonym of Juan
García.[85] He contributed his financial support and political contacts to the campaigns against the Francoist antihomosexual policies.[86] Baudry coordinated international pressures from Paris,
consisting of publications in *Arcadie* and letters from its sympa-
thizers to the Francoist Cortes, protesting the regime's inhumane
treatment of homosexual people.[87] Simultaneously, Fluvià and
Francino sent anonymous letters to the Spanish Catholic bishops
to convince them that homosexuality, as a condition, could not be
codified in the law, even if homosexual acts were.[88] Spanish homophiles' argument focused on a legal paradox: while homosexuality as a personal condition doesn't necessarily have any victims,
the prosecution of homosexuals under the law would victimize
them by isolating and marginalizing them.[89]

Spanish homophiles' strategic decision to appeal to the Catholic
hierarchy to advocate on their behalf has puzzled historians and
activists alike, given that the Catholic Church, as an institution, has
been among the most vocal opponents of LGBT rights in Spain in
recent decades. Armand de Fluvià, whose testimony shapes many
historiographic works on this period, highlights the "naïveté" of

homophiles, including himself, who thought that bishops would intervene in their favor.[90] As contemporary sources demonstrate, until the 1970s the sublimation of homoerotic desires into Catholic religiosity and family networks was one of the few available alternatives that afforded maricas and mariquitas limited compassion from their environments.[91] The letter that the Spanish homophiles sent to the bishops in 1970 relied on a conservative regime of desire that merged homophile politics and Catholicism. They clarified that some of them were Catholic believers and asked the bishops to demonstrate their Christian compassion by interceding on behalf of inborn homosexual individuals who were able to conduct their lives respectably and productively. Homophiles, according to the authors of the letter, were like everyone else and often performed valuable jobs. Yet they were forced to live a double life, full of dissimulation, shame, and guilt. In addition, the new law equated them with "pimps, thugs, drug dealers, vagrants, beggars, prostitutes, etc."[92] By publicly exposing homosexual people, the law would potentially ruin the lives of hardworking, honest individuals. However, they trusted that bishops would use their "moral authority" to prevent this scenario. The "civilized world" was showing its empathy toward homophiles; science had discredited the view of "homophilia" as an antinatural depravity; and in many countries, "respect for human dignity" had led to the decriminalization of homosexuality. The codification of the homosexual condition as a danger to society—the letter argued—would be a departure from the trends that characterized compassionate and civilized Christian societies.[93]

This letter's authors deployed a conservative approach to the politics of inclusion and exclusion in order to appeal to Catholic bishops. The authors' intention was for homophiles to be granted the status of respectable citizens on account of their efforts to contribute to society and keep their sexuality private, while at the same time they vehemently distanced themselves from other marginalized sectors. Moreover, they defended a homosexual condition defined by same-sex desires, but they did not openly oppose the codification of repeated homosexual acts as a danger to society.

This strategy, along with international pressures, achieved partial success. Some Francoist legislators objected to the initial wording of the law. Fernando Herrero Tejedor argued that individuals whose homosexuality was due to biological factors but who abstained from engaging in homosexual acts were not a danger to society. Therefore, they should be spared from the law, which should target instead dangerous, corrupted individuals who performed antinatural sexual acts.[94] The Social Danger Law that was finally enacted in August 1970 incorporated this argument: it only referred to individuals who "carry out *acts* of homosexuality."[95] In a way, Herrero Tejedor had formulated in legal-medical terms the traditional trope of the mariquita—namely, the view that a feminized subject whose "deviation" was inborn could sublimate his desires, usually through religiosity, to avoid stigmatization and criminalization. Articles 82 and 85 of the new law's regulations further expanded this idea by stipulating that the judicial proceedings should establish whether the defendant's homosexuality was due to biology, pathological processes, or other circumstances.[96] Thereafter, forensic doctors had to fill out a standardized form with a section on homosexuals, which read, "It is convenient to distinguish between homosexualities caused by pathological processes or different kinds of circumstances, and those motivated by disorders in the subject's biology. If possible, check the existence of chromosomal abnormalities if there are clinical signs of such."[97] Thus, a system for collecting detailed information on homosexuality's biological etiology was put in place.

However, the Special Court of Social Danger and Rehabilitation of Madrid established that "the acts that the Law encompasses are every lecherous touching between people of the same sex . . . without taking into account if they are carried out by congenital or occasional sexual inverts."[98] It seems illogical that so much attention was paid to the identification of congenital homosexuals when this categorization did not necessarily affect their judicial treatment. Yet this policy allowed the judicial apparatus of the regime to claim that they were applying the law following the imperatives of Catholic compassion and rigorous scientific taxonomies.

At the same time, in practice, the law's main goal remained the moralizing punishment of homosexual and "effeminate" individuals, isolating them to prevent their corrupting effect on society.[99]

While homosexual acts were prosecuted under the Social Danger Law, the homosexual movement shifted from Catholic essentialism and the homophile politics of respectability to revolutionary politics aimed at establishing a coalition with other marginalized sectors prosecuted under the same law. This shift accompanied the efforts of the initial homophile nucleus formed by Fluvià, Francino, and Rosillo to reach beyond their elite social circles to create a broader activist platform. Through the mediation of Baudry, they contacted the Spanish readers of *Arcadie* to share with them their intention to publish their own bulletin.[100] Among those who answered this call were a Jesuit priest living in Barcelona and a teacher living in Madrid.[101] In 1970, they joined the initial nucleus forming the Agrupamiento Homófilo para la Integración Social (Homophile Group for Social Integration, AGHOIS), immediately renamed the Movimiento Español de Liberación Homosexual (Spanish Movement of Homosexual Liberation, MELH).[102] This sudden change of denominations reflects by itself the efforts of Spanish activists to keep pace with the international sexual liberation movement of the 1970s despite the cultural exceptionalism of the Franco regime. The shift from the homophile agenda of social integration to an ethos of sexual liberation—which in most Western European countries traverses the decades from the 1940s to the 1970s—took place in Barcelona, at least in terms of self-denomination, in the span of a year.

The MELH published its first bulletin in January 1972, named *AGHOIS* after the initial denomination of their group. They smuggled the issues out of Barcelona and across the border to France, so Arcadie could then distribute them back to Spanish homophiles as a supplement to their own bulletin. In this way, the activities and authorship of the MELH activists would remain obscured in the case that the bulletin was intercepted by the Francoist authorities.[103] The views espoused in the MELH bulletin show how the group adopted an increasingly confrontational stance regarding homophobic state policies and social attitudes. Simultaneously, MELH activists adopted pseudonyms and a clandestine cell system as mechanisms of protection against state policing. From a leading nucleus (group A), the organization would then expand through the formation of small semi-independent "cells" (groups B, C, D, and so on) that would meet separately.[104] The first meeting of group A on July 10, 1972, was attended by eight men; by the third meeting at the end of that month, ten people attended and discussed the possibility of addressing a dossier to the Catholic bishops. Then in the fourth meeting on August 16, two lesbian women joined the group, contributing to its eventual ideological shift.[105]

One of these women used Amanda Klein as her pseudonym. She militated in the Maoist clandestine Movimiento Comunista de España (Communist Movement of Spain), and she brought a new Marxist perspective to the group.[106] She argued that the MELH should abandon its focus on Spanish homosexual people's traditional mechanisms of social integration—family, work, and the Catholic Church—and focus instead on undermining the "dominant ideology" that negatively shaped their lives. This ideology, shared among capitalist and socialist societies, was defined by several core elements: sexism, the binary between men and women; machismo, the attribution of different gendered roles; and heterosexism, the view of heterosexuality as normative and homosexuality as marginal. Gradually, the MELH activists integrated into their theoretical framework the critique of this dominant ideology.[107]

At the same time, the MELH reached out to other European and U.S. gay groups to denounce internationally the Franco regime's antihomosexual policies. In 1974 Armand de Fluvià, along with two other MELH activists, traveled to the United Kingdom to attend and present at the First International Gay Rights Congress in Edinburgh, where they were received as heroes on account of the personal risks they were taking by appearing.[108] Spanish activists had to take constant precautions to ensure that their communication with international organizations did not expose them to the Francoist authorities and prosecution under the Social Danger Law. For instance, when Robert Roth published Armand de Fluvià's contact information in one of his lists of international gay groups, Fluvià sent him an alarmed letter asking him to erase his real name and replace it with his pseudonym. He explained to Roth that while U.S. activists could be critical of the gay "ghetto," Spanish activists still lived in the "catacombs" with no possibility to advocate for themselves in public. Therefore, they limited themselves to consciousness raising with the hope that a better future may someday come. In the meantime, their correspondence with international groups made them feel less "loneliness and discouragement."[109]

Debates on Marica Femininity

A contentious issue marked the MELH's transition from reformist to revolutionary politics in the early 1970s. Like their counterparts in the Argentine FLH, Spanish activists disagreed about what the group's stance should be on maricas becoming increasingly visible in Barcelona. After Franco's death and during the democratic transition, the failure to settle this issue would lead

FIG. 13. Armand de Fluvià holds a banner with the text "MELH (1971) ESPAÑA PRESENTE. Gay Pride 75" while standing next to Puerto Rican gay activist Rafael Cruet at the 1975 Pride Protest in New York City. Photo courtesy Armand de Fluvià.

to a split between the FAGC (Front d'Alliberament Gai de Catalunya, or Gay Liberation Front of Catalonia) and the CCAG (Coordinadora de Col·lectius per l'Alliberament Gai, or Coalition of Gay
Liberation Groups), which, like Eros, saw maricas and travestis as
a radical rupture with normative social expectations.[110] The development of this debate in Barcelona can be traced through the
translation of different manifestos on this issue—from English to
Spanish but also from Argentine Spanish to Iberian Spanish. In
1971, Armand de Fluvià translated the *Gay Liberation Front Manifesto* published in London. The document implied that feminine
gay males damaged the liberation cause when they performed a
submissive role. It clarified that gay men's femininity or masculinity was not a problem per se. Instead the "compulsive subjection
to roles" was: "the butch seeking to expand his ego by dominating
his/her partner's life and freedom, and the femme seeking protection by submitting to the butch."[111] The manifesto concluded
by establishing consciousness raising among "femmes" as a main
goal of the liberation movement so that they could overcome their
internalized oppression. Looking for vernacular terms from the
sexual cultures of Spain that resembled those of English-speaking
countries, Fluvià translated "butch" into *macho* and "femme" into
mariquita. This last term probably seemed more fitting than maricón and its connotations of a public and bold sexuality. The translation of "femme" into mariquita, then marked as a hindrance to
liberation, marked a departure from the strategies of maricas who,
in previous decades, had resisted the Vagrancy Law by performing a decorous femininity when that gave them the best chance
of escaping a prison sentence.

  While gay activists developed an almost consensual view of
the mariquita as an anachronistic symbol of internalized oppression, they disagreed on whether the boldly sexual femininity of
locas or mariconas should be embraced by the movement. For
instance, an article titled "Las mariconas se rebelan" and published in issue 17 of *AGHOIS* (September–October 1973) reclaimed
the terms "maricón" and *maricona* for the movement while con-
demning the docility and submissiveness of the mariquita. The

article was published in a political context in which the dictator-ship's control over public opinion was rapidly eroding as its tra-ditional base of support, including many members of the clergy, demanded an opening of the political space.

> Priests' unrest was more or less predictable, precisely because of priests' unpredictability . . . but [not] the *maricas*! They have always been so docile, so submissive, so cowardly, so afraid of the master *macho*, so neurotic. . . . What is there to do now for the hundreds of psychiatrists who have "scientifically" backed notions of abnormality, perversion, sickness . . . while filling their offices with trembling *maricones* who believed to be abnormal, per-verse, sick . . . and charging them one thousand pesetas per hour? . . . If *mariconas* get contentious and serious, they will end up asking for too much. They will want to know the expla-nation for uncountable issues that undermine their essence . . . as free human beings.[112]

The gender shift in the text between "trembling *maricones*" (masculine noun) and contentious mariconas (feminine noun) highlighted the revolutionary potential of embracing feminin-ity as well as scandalous sexuality. By the early 1970s, mariconas were, the article claimed, challenging both medical treatments of homosexuality as a pathology and established social expecta-tions of submissiveness. At the same time, the reintroduction of psychoanalysis in the progressive and activist circles of Barcelona by the end of the Francoist period was leading to the conceptual-ization of internalized social expectations of docility as a neurosis. The article's argument was that same-sex desires were not patho-logical, but the socialization of homosexual people in submissive roles and self-degradation was. The same article included a ficti-tious dialogue between a marica and an authoritarian voice that personified the collaboration between the Franco regime and part of the medical community: "—I am not a baby! —Yes, you are, and, even more, a *mariquita* baby."[113]

The voice of authority labeled the rebel homosexual a mariquita as a way of reestablishing the power dynamics that infantilized and deprived queer and trans people of their personal autonomy and forced them into submissiveness. This article evidences the reversal of the self-protection strategies deployed in the vagrancy courts by many defendants in the preceding decades. The activists who participated in the countercultural ethos of the 1960s and 1970s disparaged the mariquita's subjectivity and embraced instead mariconas' sexual and gender subversiveness.

Yet not all members of the MELH agreed with this view. Some of them argued that locas, provocatively feminine homosexual individuals, were excluded from their notion of the "typical healthy homosexual."[114] In January 1974, a group of MELH activists organized a clandestine roundtable in Barcelona to elaborate a "typology of the Spanish homophile."[115] The participants' interventions were transcribed using their pseudonyms instead of their real names to protect them from the regime in the case of exposure. The transcript shows that for the participants, socializing in gay bars was becoming key to a self-accepted homosexual identity. However, according to some of them, there were two types of homosexuals who did not contribute to the cause of liberation: locas/maricas and those homosexuals who did not feel comfortable frequenting gay bars. Most hustlers (*chulos*) would belong to this second type, their performances of hypermasculinity being just a facade to conceal their real sexual desires from themselves and others.[116] A participant named Gorria argued about homosexual men who frequented bars: "[They are] the bulk of homosexual men, let's say, healthy. In the sense that they fully accept themselves. . . . This is an average type, a bank clerk for example, who doesn't have any issues with 'his' homosexuality, because he lives in a large city that affords him a certain level of anonymity. . . . I would not hesitate to describe him as the typical healthy homosexual. Other types are the 'loca' and the hustler; I think we should focus on these three types."[117]

This statement captures the dynamics of inclusion and exclusion at the core of the definition of the "liberated" homosexual. As Regina Kunzel argues with regard to the United States' early homophile and gay movements, in order to counteract a long history of pathologization, many activists tried to sanitize the image of their movement, disavowing the psychological and emotional scars left on queer and trans people by their environments.[118] Resilience distinguished the "healthy" homosexual, who was able to overcome internalized homophobia, accept himself, and become visible in public spaces such as bars. Furthermore, according to Gorria, this average "healthy" type most often came from the urban middle class. Urban anonymity and visibility—two sides of the same coin—were key to the expansion of the sexual liberation movement in Gorria's view. Mir, another participant in the roundtable, contraposed the visibility of a minority of "liberated" homosexuals with an immense majority of "repressed people who [were] only able to have anonymous sex in a bathroom or a cinema."[119] Activists who defined liberation in terms of visibility often saw anonymous sex as an atavism, a symptom of anachronistic repression.

The participants in this roundtable also distinguished between different forms of visibility. When a different participant, Hugo, called attention to the issue of the loca/marica, who was visible and frequented bars but did not fit with their image of the average "healthy" homosexual, Gorria's response implied that locas were a kind of absolute Other. He proposed excluding locas from the subject of the roundtable discussion, so someone "more capacitated" could study them.[120] Hugo proposed instead that the loca's effeminate and "promiscuous" persona did not make her essentially different: "The loca definitely does not have a unique essence," Hugo concluded.[121] The participants in this roundtable were not particularly sympathetic to locas/maricas and their hypersexual femininity. They were defining liberation as an ideal to strive for through self-acceptance and visibility but also as a set of normative expectations that excluded the hypervisible femininity of the loca as much as the "shamefaced" conduct of hustlers and closeted gay people.

The debate about locas/maricas continued throughout the 1970s, connecting the legacies of the Argentine FLH with liberationist politics in Spain. After the 1976 coup d'état in Argentina, some members of the FLH went into exile in Spain, which was initiating a democratic transition after the death of the dictator Francisco Franco. In May 1979, the Barcelona-based countercultural magazine *Ajoblanco* republished the 1973 article that had led to the debate about the marica within the FLH, edited and submitted by two former members of the FLH who were now living in exile in Madrid. The *Ajoblanco* 1979 version enhanced the textual critique of maricas through the visual eroticization of masculine bodies: the text was framed by photographs of masculine-looking men exhibiting their genitals to the camera in self-confident postures.

In the 1979 version, the FLH activists exiled in Spain had changed the original labels in the 1973 version. The passage about machista sexual fantasies in the 1973 version referred to the victimization of maricas. In the 1979 version, it referred instead to the victimization of locas and mariquitas.[122] By the late 1970s, the paradigm of the mariquita's decent femininity was losing ground. As ever more individuals refused to sublimate their sexuality and participated instead in the expanding, visible queer life of larger Spanish cities, "mariquita" came to denote either a "folkloric" performance of femininity in entertainment shows or an infantile, innocent label for feminized males.[123]

The negative representation of maricas in the FLH article republished in *Ajoblanco*, including their characterization as "scapegoats" and decorative objects, might have influenced the arguments of critics of the mariquita in Spain. In December 1979, the poet and novelist Eduardo Haro Ibars published a piece in the Madrid-based magazine *Triunfo* that declared the mariquita a defunct figure.

> Mariquitas are like those old table lamps supported by gilded dolphins. . . . Our grandmothers liked mariquitas and lamps a lot. . . . They took some space, provoked numerous comments, amused, and shed a discreet light over the audience—even concealing some of their wrinkles. Mariquitas were sexless monsters. They had sex, of course, like lamps have bulbs, but it was not visible. . . . "They are sensitive and feminine"—our grandmothers said about them—denigrating them even though they thought they were defending them. . . . The reality of the Hispanic

mariquita . . . has a lot of glitter and a lot of hidden suffering [but] few suicides, which would be a violent reaction against an oppressive environment, and many neuroses [instead]. The Hispanic mariquita fights against his repression, his marginalization, precisely by becoming a mariquita. His neurosis protects him to a certain extent from suicide. Rather, it is a slow and pre-recorded suicide, an attempted murder of the human being in favor of the monster he is forced to be and to feed with his blood. The mariquita—carrying his folkloric burden and being a scapegoat for a certain sexuality—has been forced to wear a flesh corset.[124]

Haro Ibars had qualms about mariquitas precisely because the latter had historically embodied a decorous, inoffensive femininity by sublimating their sexuality in public, relying on matronly figures for their social integration and participating in folkloric entertainment. Mariquitas' strategies to protect themselves from social stigma and the Franco regime's legal apparatus were interpreted by countercultural thinkers in the late 1970s as symptoms of the mariquitas' neuroses, of their internalized repression and self-denial. Mariquitas wore "flesh corsets"; their bodily performances showed their internalization of social expectations. Haro Ibars used the past voice in his analysis, assuming that the times of the mariquita were over. After Franco's death, mariquitas appeared to him as haunting "monsters" of the past. Brice Chamouleau has argued that the Spanish democratic transition had its own "queer ghosts"; despite its facade of inclusiveness, it consolidated the sociopolitical hegemony of the middle class and the erasure of queer subjectivities associated with the countercultural underground of metropolitan cities such as Barcelona.[125] Mariquitas' historical subjectivity was similarly erased and reduced to a symbol of an uncanny past as the homosexual movement's attention shifted toward the fight against HIV.

Oral Histories of Gay Exiles:
Argentines in the Spanish Transition (1973–83)

By the mid-1980s, Anabitarte was going from one gay bar to another in Madrid, sticking on their walls a phone number for an HIV information office. He had to stand by the stickers until the glue dried so the bar owners could not peel them off.[126] As he recollects, many activists were reluctant to acknowledge that the spread of the new disease required an organized response from the gay movement. Just when the consolidation of democracy in Spain indicated that the times were ripe for the sexual liberation long postponed by the dictatorship, news about the first reported cases of HIV infection was interpreted by some activists in the community as a conservative campaign to curtail their freedoms.[127] However, Anabitarte knew Argentine exiles living in Spain who were infected and soon became the leader of grassroots AIDS activism in Madrid. In 1984, he formed along with some friends the Comité Anti-Sida de Madrid (Madrid's Anti-AIDS Committee). By 1990, Anabitarte was the president of the Comité Ciudadano Anti-Sida de Madrid (Madrid Citizens' AIDS Committee), which convened the Fourth International Conference on AIDS, attended by patients from forty different countries and the Spanish minister of health.[128] Except for Sergio Pérez Álvarez, most of the Argentine exiles whom I interviewed developed professional careers, activist networks, and affective attachments in the 1970s and 1980s that led them to permanently settle in Spain. While becoming gradually grounded in Spain, they also maintained their attachment to Argentina, where they would periodically return during and after the period of the military junta.[129]

Argentine gay exiles—especially those who arrived in Spain before Franco's death—emphasize that contingent exogenous factors led them toward this destination, including the possibility of living in a Spanish-speaking country and support networks formed by local gay activists and Argentine exiles. Starting in 1976, the streets of Barcelona became the stage for anarchist-inspired experiments in political and cultural emancipation, including the first demonstrations of a vibrant sexual liberation movement. Argentine activists became fully involved in the sexual politics of the Spanish democratic transition rather than experiencing their exile as a period of expectation that suspended the regular flow of life.[130] In fact, they have a certain sense of authorship regarding the events that took

place in Spain in those years. In the words of Rubén Mettini, former member of the Argentine FLH, "We were forming the country [Spain]."[131] FLH activists also learned from the experiences of
Spaniards who arrived in Argentina decades before escaping the
Franco regime. They saw the events in Spain as a framework of
opportunities to effect concrete changes through the tools at their
disposal, including their activist and intellectual backgrounds, psychoanalysis, teaching, publications in mainstream and gay media,
and soft porn, among others. Oral histories suggest that this framework of opportunities was the result of a significant gap between
Spain and its neighboring countries and between Spaniards' fantasies of modernization and Europeanization and the legacies that
four decades of dictatorship had left in daily life and cultural production.[132] Activists like Anabitarte contributed to strengthening
the ties between Spanish homosexual groups and transnational
networks, mobilizing connections that they had established in
the early 1970s.

The daily occurrence of abductions and political assassinations
was the primary reason why members of the FLH decided to leave
Argentina for Europe. They closely witnessed or were affected
by military and paramilitary groups' activities due to their civic
engagement as intellectuals and union activists or simply threatened
because of their visibility. State violence affected not just guerrilla
fighters but every sector of Argentine society (journalists, students, trade unionists, etc.) that dissented from the regime. Dante
Bertini, one of the cartoonists for the FLH's publication *Somos*,
recalls the many times when he was walking home in San Telmo
with his partner while the Triple A paramilitary squads would be
patrolling the streets in their cars. The patrolmen would yell out
"puto" and "maricón" and verbal threats to Dante and his partner
in attempts to intimidate them. In addition, one day while Dante
was leaving a café on Calle Florida, the main commercial artery,
two plainclothes men stopped him and asked him for his documents. After they reviewed his press credentials, they informed
him that they were placing him under arrest. Afraid that he was
about to be abducted, Dante darted into a nearby bar, shouting

for help, and had someone inside call *La Opinión*, the newspaper where he also worked as a cartoonist. The paper sent over their lawyer to rescue him.[133]

La Opinión, a liberal newspaper created by Jacobo Timerman, published editorials and notes criticizing the human rights violations of the military dictatorship, including the disappearances of political opponents. Thereby, its journalists became targets. Jacobo Timerman and Enrique Raab, both journalists, were among the highest-profile Jewish victims of the dictatorship. In 1977, Timerman was abducted in his own home by "20 armed men" and spent more than a year in clandestine confinement, subjected to tortures including "electric shocks to his genitals."[134] Raab, born to a Jewish family in Vienna in 1932, was—apart from working as a correspondent for *La Opinión*—a member of the Trotskyist Workers' Revolutionary Party and a gay man who lived with his partner. In April 1977, he was abducted and disappeared, leaving behind only a trace of gun shots and blood in his apartment.[135] Considering this climate, Blas Matamoro, a founding member of the FLH who worked at *La Opinión* as well, was also driven to exile in Spain. The military authorities had proscribed the publication and circulation of his book *Olimpo*.[136] Most importantly, his partner, Martín Bartolomé, had been abducted and tortured. Bartolomé had long hair and a beard and worked at the Museum of Fine Arts in Córdoba. As Alejandro Modarelli points out, since the military authorities saw countercultural practices as a cradle of subversion, Bartolomé's hairstyle and occupation (along with a minor error in his ID) were enough to get him arrested. Through the intervention of the renowned conservative novelist Manuel Mujica Láinez, who personally knew Matamoro and Bartolomé, the latter was released on the streets of Córdoba a month after his arrest, covered in his own body excrement.[137] Matamoro described to me how this experience traumatized Bartolomé: "They held him blindfolded for a week in a place where there were seven other people and each day one disappeared and never returned. . . . They electroshocked people. . . . He had to sweep that place blindfolded. One day he dropped the mop, and they forced him to stand nude for an entire night in a courtyard in winter. After [he was released], for years he could not pass by a place where they were grilling meat, because that smell reminded him of the burned flesh of people who were electroshocked."[138]

After this episode, in September 1976 Matamoro accepted an appointment as *La Opinión*'s correspondent in Madrid and joined the many Argentines living in exile in Spain. By reporting on the incipient Spanish democratic transition and criticizing the legacies of the Franco dictatorship, Matamoro implicitly drew parallelisms with the Argentine regime that similarly defined its mission as the defense of Western Christian civilization.[139] Matamoro and other FLH activists sought refuge in Spain despite its unfavorable political climate in the early-to-mid-1970s. Sergio Pérez Álvarez fled Argentina for Madrid in 1973 after receiving multiple death threats by phone. The calls started when a co-worker found some FLH materials in the kindergarten that he directed after the group had held one of their meetings there. One day, Sergio's father answered the phone and heard the threats. Afterward, he convinced Sergio that his best option was to migrate to Madrid, since Sergio had a Spanish passport because both his parents had been born in Spain.[140] In other words, the cultural, legal, and family ties that had been established decades earlier as the result of the massive immigration of Spaniards to Argentina were significant factors leading these gay activists toward Madrid and Barcelona. In the same line, Dante considers that he "didn't choose anything" regarding his destination. He fled to Spain because he found an opportunity through a touristic program sponsored by a Galician-Argentine association, and he initially had no intention of permanently settling in Europe. After leaving behind blue-skied Buenos Aires in summer, Dante's flight landed in Madrid in December 1975. He arrived in a "harsh" city that, amid winter, was still recovering from Franco's funeral in November.[141]

Spain often was not always the first destination for Argentine gay exiles. Rubén Mettini (1948–), for example, decided in 1974 to leave Buenos Aires for Naples in view of the deteriorating political climate under the presidency of Isabel Perón. Mettini was a

member of Eros, the group headed by Perlongher, but that was not
the reason he felt in danger. As a student of economics at Universidad del Salvador, Rubén was in daily contact with left-wing academic circles targeted by the extreme right. He even remembers
that, while he was in exile, his father ended up burning many of
his textbooks, including Marx's *Das Kapital*.[142] Mettini traces the
role of European high culture in the socialization of Buenos Aires
entendidos. When he was in his twenties, Mettini began to spend
less time in Avellaneda, the working-class suburb (*barrio*) where he
had grown up, and more time among city-dwelling entendidos.
He set distance between himself and mariquitas or putos from his
barrio, who were tacitly accepted by neighbors and always available for young men (*chonguitos*) looking for sexual release. Putos/
maricas were also a spectacular presence during carnival, when
they could unleash a "fabulous" personal style by wearing tight
clothes, bright necklaces, and feathers, dancing provocatively to
emulate the vedettes and movie stars of the 1950s.[143] Entendidos,
on the contrary, gravitated toward Teatro Colón, Buenos Aires's
opera house, which Mettini calls "our second home." They organized parties to honor opera divas and private balls for men. They
also frequented cinema theaters specialized in European avant-
garde directors like Bergman, Truffaut, Godard, Fellini, Pasolini,
and Bertolucci. Mettini spent many evenings in his lover's attic,
where they read and discussed the classics of French existentialism and Argentine literature (Cortázar, Borges, Sartre, Camus . . .)
listening to Brahms in the background.[144] In other words, European high culture was one of the main vehicles of socialization
within a homosexual subculture that was implicitly defined by
its geographic and symbolic distance with respect to the putos of
the barrios.

According to Mettini, Spain was not part of the imagined cartography of cultural referents that marked entendidos' sophistication:
"We dreamed of going to Paris, London, or Rome. Spain, plunged
into 40 years of darkness, did not call our attention at all."[145] Mettini spent the period between 1974 and 1977 touring those locations
in Europe that he associated with avant-garde filmmakers. During

that period, he also played a central role in the formation of the Neapolitan branch of the Italian homosexual group Fronte Unitario Omosessuale Rivoluzionario Italiano (FUORI). A job opportunity at Banco de Bilbao eventually led Rubén to move to Spain in 1977. Later, he settled in Barcelona, where another exile (Pablo Stajnsznajder) welcomed him into his apartment, while Armand de Fluvià got him a job as a translator for *Spartacus*, the guide for international gay travelers.[146]

These exiles settled and spent most of their lives in Spain because of a series of contingent practical considerations, job opportunities, and support networks organized through the collaboration between Anabitarte and Fluvià. Pablo Stajnsznajder's testimony confirms this assessment. Pablo was born into a liberal Jewish family and began to participate in leftist activism while a teenager, motivated by the critical thinking that circulated among his classmates at the Colegio Nacional de Buenos Aires, a prestigious and highly politicized public high school. In his own words, "The difficult thing [at that moment] was to not be militant at the age of thirteen."[147] After joining the FLH while studying medicine, the 1976 military coup led Pablo to desperately look for a way out of Argentina, contacting (through Anabitarte) gay groups in Israel, Canada, and Spain. Among these, the movement based in Barcelona was the only one that offered him resources and a support network to help him go into exile. Through Fluvià's mediation, Pablo was assured that in Barcelona he would have an apartment to live in, provided by a gay activist. In addition, Pablo had heard through a family friend that Barcelona was the "new Amsterdam. . . . There were many people who lived in communes and who pursued an alternative way of life, and there was a very powerful anarchist tradition."[148] Pablo struggled with the complicated family legacies of Holocaust survivors. Pablo's father, a Polish Jew, was studying engineering in Lyon (France) at the outset of World War II, but he managed to escape to Argentina after passing through Barcelona and Lisbon. Therefore, when he fled the Argentine dictatorship by moving to Spain, Pablo felt that he was "escaping and returning" at once, traveling his father's path but in the opposite direction. While Pablo saw Barcelona as a warm and welcoming city, Paris felt to him like a threatening, cold, and harsh place, closely associated with the memory of World War II's events, which were forbidden as a topic of conversation in his family, and with the melancholy of the "mythological past" of his disappeared lineage. For Pablo, Paris was the center of "cultural colonialism," of European civilization and barbarism.[149] He felt that he could establish a closer and more intimate relationship with Spain.

Rubén Tosoni followed a similar path. In 1973, the high-profile assassination of the Peronist union leader José Ignacio Rucci persuaded Rubén that going into exile was his best option. He tried to settle in Paris, inspired by Argentine intellectuals like Cortázar, but by 1974 he had decided to move to Barcelona, a more affordable city where he would be able to speak in Spanish. In his own words, since Barcelona "had suffered a lot during the civil war, in some way [people] understood quite easily anyone who was in a situation of helplessness or lacking support."[150] Barcelona was a stronghold of anarchism and Catalonian nationalism. At the outset of the Spanish Civil War, anarchists took over control of the city, one of the few experiments in anarchist governance ever.[151] The city only fell to the fascists in January 1939, foreshadowing the soon-to-come total defeat of the republic in April. Francoist authorities harshly repressed and policed the city's population, creating a suffocating atmosphere.[152] However, underneath Barcelona's "grey, defeated" appearance, the city's rebellious spirit subsisted.[153]

On November 20, 1975, Barcelona exploded in celebrations upon news of Franco's death. Armand de Fluvià recalls how people made toasts with champagne and went to Las Ramblas, the main downtown avenue, to share their joy in a sort of collective catharsis. Fluvià describes the years between 1975 and 1980 as the best of his life, when suddenly everything seemed possible.[154] In the cabarets of the city, travesti performers staged a provocative femininity that drew massive audiences. The Argentine Ángel Pavlovsky starred in his own travesti shows without even wearing female clothes, just by using his witty sense of humor, voice, and bodily performance, which catapulted him into nationwide fame and TV stardom.[155] Pavlovsky offered his solidarity to other Argentine émigrés—when Dante Bertini and his partner arrived in Spain in 1975, they went to the Gay Club in Madrid to meet Pavlovsky, whom they had met before in Buenos Aires, and he offered Dante's partner a job so they would be able to support themselves.[156]

Gay activists who left Argentina in or after 1977 felt attracted by the countercultural ethos of radical experimentation that took hold of Barcelona by the end of that decade. Nazario and Ocaña, both queer artists born in Andalucía, embodied in their street performances the antiauthoritarian spirit of those years. They wandered around the main avenues of Barcelona dressed in the traditional attire of Andalusian women, sang coplas and flamenco, or staged a Holy Week procession singing *saetas* (religious hymns) from a balcony to the image of the Virgin Mary. Rafael Mérida points out that by parodying traditional femininity and Catholic iconographies, Nazario and Ocaña treated them as theatrical masks superimposed on the body. While wearing traditional female attire (a *mantón de Manila* over the shoulders, a carnation on one ear, necklaces, makeup around the eyes, and a loose, long Andalusian skirt), Ocaña would lift his skirt to provocatively show his genitals to tourists and passersby, or completely undress. He refused any identity label but participated in the gay liberation demonstration that took place in Barcelona in June 1977.[157] This demonstration, attended by thousands of people and headed by travestis, was the first public show of strength of the Front d'Alliberament Gai de Catalunya (FAGC) to pressure the state into decriminalizing homosexuality, releasing inmates convicted for this charge, and abolishing the Social Dangerousness Law.[158]

Travesti and marica visibility became, since the 1977 demonstration, one of the most charged, controversial, and transformative issues for the Barcelona queer movement. Historian Piro Subrat has traced this debate through interviews with leaders and participants. There were approximately five thousand people marching on that day. One of their slogans was "We want to be left alone" (*Queremos que nos dejen en paz*), politicizing in explicit terms the strategies of subjects criminalized in previous decades (see chapters

1 and 5). When police officers resorted to violence to dissolve the protest, travestis and maricas, along with a small group of anarchists, belligerently confronted them.[159] U.S. gay activist Cleve Jones, witness to these events, emphasizes that protesters were moved by the "combination of fury and camp effeminate humor" (*combinación de furia y humor amanerado*) characteristic of maricas.[160] Photographs of Tania Navarro and her friends on that day have become nothing short of the main symbol of the LGBTQ+ movement's origins in Spain. According to Tania, travestis' leading role resulted from their willingness to expose themselves and face the police who harassed them daily. She adds another reason why she appears to pose for the photographs documenting this protest: every time she was imprisoned, they shaved her head, but in June 1977 she had been out of prison for months and she felt particularly beautiful. She wore a leather jacket and jeans that highlighted her slender body, and in the photos she either looks directly into the camera or smiles and shouts as she marches along with her friends. In her recollections, that day she went from one gay bar to another shouting, "Let's protest, faggots" (*Venga maricones, vamos a manifestarnos*) in a quasi-festive tone that convinced many people to join.[161]

Most travestis were low-income sex workers who lived and worked in the red district (*barrio chino*). The press, as Subrat documents, was not particularly sympathetic to their plight: mainstream newspapers referred to travestis' "ineffable clothing" and their "parodying homosexual love."[162] Some gay activists too criticized travesti visibility and associated it with machismo, folklore, press sensationalism, frivolity, and lack of freedom in Spain.[163] For that reason, among others, in the aftermath of the demonstration, the Coordinadora de Col·lectius per l'Alliberament Gai split from the FAGC and adopted a radically pro-travesti and pro-marica stance, part and parcel of their uncompromising desire to contest the status quo (similar to Eros in Argentina). They refused to settle for mainstream toleration—which they saw as a subtle form of violence—and vindicated anal revolutionary politics and *la pluma* (literally feather, a vernacular term in Spanish for maricas' brazen femininity).[164]

FIG. 14. The article that *Triunfo* dedicated to the protest in June 1977, highlighting the visibility of travestis. Photo courtesy Centre de Documentació Armand de Fluvià del Casal Lambda.

In July 1978, while Nazario and Ocaña were performing in front of a café in Las Ramblas, the police arrested them for cross-dressing and public scandal. This led to a spontaneous protest, first as the people who had been sitting in the café began to shout and throw objects at police officers, and then as their numbers swelled into a

demonstration of hundreds of people who gathered in Las Ramblas. This showed Barcelona citizens' boldness in their daily confrontations with police officers.[165] Soon after the ratification of the
democratic constitution, the government passed a law on December 26, 1978, removing "homosexual acts" from the Dangerousness Law. However, as Chamouleau argues, the articles of the law
that referred to prostitution and the violation of the norms of
"social coexistence" (*convivencia social*) remained in force and were
applied to prosecute and normalize sex workers, trans people, and
people participating in Barcelona's countercultural movement.[166]

Argentine exile R.A. (who prefers to remain anonymous)
describes late-1970s Barcelona as a city infused with solidarity, joy,
and anarchism. R.A. and his partner had decided to leave Buenos
Aires after some of their friends were "disappeared." Most of them
were gay psychoanalysts who had treated "subversives." R.A. and

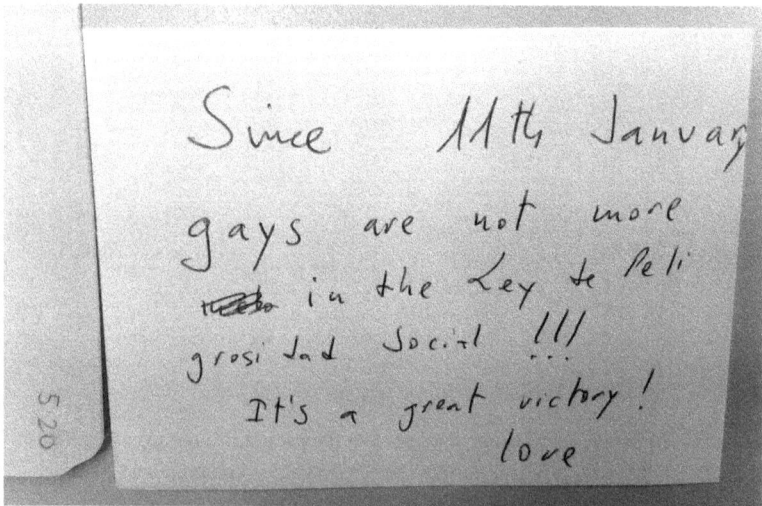

FIG. 15. Anonymous note in the Robert Roth Collections. The unknown
author, probably one of Roth's interlocutors in Spain, celebrates the removal of
"homosexual acts" from the Dangerousness Law. Although the law's change was
approved in December 1978, the note probably refers to its publication in 1979,
which made it legally effective. Note that the author uses the term "gays" to refer
to the people affected by this legal reform, assuming that this category was the
main identity marker for the populations previously targeted by the law. Courtesy
Cornell University Library.

his partner, an FLH activist, felt their lives were in danger, as they knew that the military confiscated their victims' lists of contacts and realized the risks of their names being in the address books of their "disappeared" friends. Fleeing from this suffocating environment, from the institutionalization of fear as a control mechanism, in Barcelona they found a radically different scenario. R.A. compares the "spirit of the [Spanish] transition" to that of May 1968. As if the Franco regime had only temporarily prevented the release of the liberating energies of the 1960s, the late 1970s were, in R.A.'s words, a "moment of promise, of adolescence," when collective transgressions were staged in the streets and parks of Barcelona. For R.A., the Jornadas Libertarias, an anarchist festival celebrated in the Parque Güell in 1977 without any official support or approval, best represents this period.[167] During the Jornadas, Nazario and Ocaña went onto a stage, and the audience reached a sort of "delirious orgasm," as one attending journalist put it, when the performers stripped themselves. While the audience cheered them on, Ocaña intoned a *pasodoble*, a folk dance that emulates bullfighting. Then he shouted to the audience, "I am not a pure *gitana* [Roma woman], I am an anarchist *gitana*. Therefore, I request amnesty for all the *mariquitas!*"—while he urinated on the stage and the audience exploded in applause. This performance triggered a celebration of free love, as members of their audience moved into the surrounding forest to have sex. According to the journalist, the Northern Europeans attending the Jornadas were shocked and unable to grasp the blend of humor and libertarian (il)logics characteristic of Iberian surrealism. The journalist declared the Jornadas a feat of "spontaneity, imagination, creation, and anti-authoritarianism, criticizing power in a raunchy way."[168]

R.A.'s memories point to a common pattern in Argentine exiles' oral testimonies: the identification of a cultural gap between Argentina and Spain due to more than three decades of censorship under Francoism. In the 1970s, many Spaniards were sort of fixated on "catching up," freeing themselves from the chains of authoritarianism and absorbing the changes that had occurred internationally while Franco was in power, including sexual liberation. When R.A. and his partner opened a psychological clinic in Barcelona, the main challenges that they faced were Spaniards' lack of familiarity with psychoanalysis and the suspicion that gay people felt toward any type of therapeutic treatment, given their experiences with state-sponsored "rehabilitation" therapies during the Franco regime.[169] At this moment of hope and suspicion, Héctor Anabitarte and Ricardo Lorenzo contributed their background to radical sexual politics in Spain.

Madrid and Buenos Aires: Two Neighborhoods of an Invented City

The title of this section is a quote by Ricardo Lorenzo, inspired by Italo Calvino's *Invisible Cities*, which epitomizes how exile becomes a path of no return, blurring the boundaries between national identities and replacing them with an affective cartography that constitutes, in Ricardo's words, an "invented city . . . made of scraps," where nostalgia hurts less, as it fades between endless conversations in Buenos Aires's cafés and Madrid's bars. Héctor and Ricardo arrived in Barcelona more than four decades ago, not knowing then that Spain would become their permanent residence. After the restoration of democracy in Argentina, they returned to Buenos Aires for the first time in 1983. However, in Héctor's words, "The idea of living in Argentina seemed impossible. . . . I believe that there is no return, exiles in general have no possibility of really returning."[170] Héctor explains that both the country of origin and the person living in exile are transformed during the period of separation, while affective bonds and professional commitments develop in the host country. As Pablo Stajnsznajder puts it, "There came a time when I found out that I had more friends in Barcelona than in Buenos Aires."[171] Both Pablo and Rubén Mettini visited Buenos Aires while the military was in power, experiencing such a shock that they gave up on the idea of returning permanently. Pablo came back to Buenos Aires in 1979 to complete his medical degree and stayed until 1983. He describes this period as a "return to the abyss" marked by the feeling of living in a "kindergarten"—a metaphor coined by María Elena Walsh to describe how Argentine citizens had lost their autonomy and were infantilized through fear by the dictatorship. To illustrate this environment, Pablo narrates that once he was not allowed to enter a movie theater because he was wearing clogs.[172] Likewise, Mettini's disinterest in returning to Buenos Aires ("I no longer had any desire to return") was accentuated during a visit of a few weeks, when he was arrested on Santa Fe Avenue and spent the night in the police station for being in the company of other young people and wearing an unconventional outfit, consisting of clogs, a shirtless jumpsuit, and flared pants.[173] The lack of freedom in everyday aspects such as clothing, the use of public spaces, or teaching made it difficult for gay activists to embrace the possibility of returning. Argentine activists' involvement in sexual politics, which defines Héctor and Ricardo's trajectory since they arrived in Spain, also contributed to making their exile irreversible.

In 1977 Ricardo and Héctor boarded an Italian ship and sailed into the port of Barcelona. Their friend Beba Eguía, a well-known writer and cultural critic who had hosted FLH meetings back in Buenos Aires, was there to receive them.[174] Ricardo and Héctor soon got involved in the accelerated sociopolitical and cultural changes that were happening in Spain. Simultaneously, they kept the FLH alive during their exile by channeling the institutional correspondence of the group.[175] During their first months living in exile, they stayed in a boarding house. Eguía found them jobs writing biographies of well-known historical figures by editorial request with very short deadlines that often forced them to stay up through the night. In February 1977, they sent a personal letter to Armand de Fluvià and Pablo Stajnsznajder, sharing their observations that "the *Destape* [a term used for the sexual liberalization of 1970s Spain] is apparently real and profound, and Madrid cannot escape it." Yet they were still considering the possibility of moving to Barcelona, as this was the "center of the changes that were happening throughout Spain." They were determined to join social movements in their host country, even while occasionally feeling uprooted: "Not like those Spaniards who came to Argentina in

1939 and spent the next 40 years just talking about Franco."[176] In other words, Argentine gay exiles learned from the experiences of Spanish anti-Francoist exiles, who had crossed the Atlantic in the inverse direction three decades earlier, that obsessing over day-to-day Argentine politics was not going to accelerate their return. According to their letter, the alternative that Ricardo and Héctor had embraced was following the Aristotelian premise of *Realpolitik*, "reality is the only truth." While this would seem to indicate that Ricardo and Héctor considered their commitment to sexual liberation politics in Spain to be a realistic strategy to acclimate to the given circumstances, their correspondence also suggests that participating in gay activists' transnational networks in the 1970s required a certain dosage of utopianism.[177] Likewise, while living in exile, Héctor and Ricardo used the official FLH stamp in their correspondence with other activists to convey that the group was still operational and, hopefully, transform that fiction into a reality. In January 1978, they resumed (on behalf of the FLH in exile) the epistolary exchange with Robert Roth, their former contact with U.S. gay groups. In 1978, Héctor and Ricardo proposed to Roth to organize a conference in New York City in collaboration with groups of gay Latinos, to denounce homophobic repression by the Argentine dictatorship and lobby international organizations, including the United Nations. Their letter also described the situation in Spain, where the homosexual movement was expanding clandestinely. Héctor and Ricardo also volunteered to facilitate the collaboration between U.S. activists and the Madrid-based groups Mercurio, Movimiento Democrático de los Homosexuales, and Frente Homosexual de Acción Revolucionaria.[178] Anabitarte and Lorenzo contributed to strengthening the ties between gay groups in their host country and the transnational networks in which they had participated before their exile. In other words, they activated a sexual militancy that merged the local and the global.

While living in exile, Héctor and Ricardo also tried to recreate the networks of the FLH by collecting press clippings and sending letters to their counterparts in other latitudes. In May 1978, Héctor sent Roth an inquiry about an anonymous exile. A member of the

FLH exiled in New York had sent Héctor the most recent issue of *GaysWeek*, which had republished an interview that the Swedish gay magazine *Revolt* had conducted with an anonymous FLH activist who at that time was living in exile in Paris.[179] The transmission of information through exile networks began with the interview in Paris (how the Swedes met the anonymous exile is a mystery); from there, it progressed to the publication in Sweden, was republished in the United States, and was read by the Argentine activist exiled in New York; through postal mail, the news arrived at the Escorial in Spain; and from there it made its way back to the United States. Each of these steps, by which the interview circulated around the globe, would seem to indicate the fragility of networks that relied on fortuitous readings and personal bonds. Alternatively, this episode could also be read as illustrating the investment of time and resources by participants who kept these networks alive, reading the community press, writing letters, going to the post office, organizing events and publications, and so on.

The provenance of the Paris interview that originated this chain of events is not verifiable, even though the original article in *Revolt* includes photographs of the exiled activist during his interview. However, there is no response from Roth confirming the identity of the anonymous exile, and Héctor and Ricardo do not remember identifying him.[180] The *Revolt* article identifies neither the interviewer nor the interviewee, and the person who translated it into English was Michael Holm, who passed away in 2013. The anonymous exile mentioned that there was a homosexual group that still operated in Buenos Aires but did not explain in detail what his role in the FLH had been. Perhaps he was a sympathizer of the FLH who had peripheral knowledge of the group's activities without having formally joined it, which would explain why other FLH exiles could not recognize him. However, since it is not possible to trace the source's provenance, there is also the possibility that it was an act of fiction. As a political device, it would be aimed at raising awareness and mobilizing readers through the narrative of an archetypal exile that would catalyze the expectations, literary tropes, and national stereotypes shaping European and U.S. gay readers' perceptions of the Argentine "homosexual tragedy." The anonymous exile narrated his upper-middle-class family background, his studies at the French Institute of Buenos Aires, and his leftist activism while in college, which originated both in his witnessing the effects of extreme poverty and in his self-awareness as an oppressed gay person: "At that time I did not realize the connection, but now afterwards I know, that my gayness was the main reason for me to work politically. In the sexual area, I felt oppression myself."[181] This story resonated with the Western literary canon, which foregrounded the experiences of privileged homosexual men who—through interclass sexual relationships with other males—became deeply aware of the pernicious effects that multiple systems of oppression had over themselves and others.[182]

The anonymous exile narrated that he had spent around a year of extrajudicial internment in the Trelew concentration camp in the Argentine Patagonia, subjected to physical tortures that included bone fractures and starvation, until some influential relatives managed to get him released. To conclude, he appealed to readers in Northern Europe to focus their solidarity efforts on Spain and Portugal, where democratic transition processes had opened new opportunities for gay people, in the hope that the situation in Argentina would improve in the future. Beyond questions about the provenance of the interview, this final appeal epitomizes what the internationalist mindset of 1970s sexual liberation movements entailed. According to this mindset, one group's struggle was shared by all; the movement's achievements in Madrid and Barcelona opened the way back to freedom for Argentines living under a dictatorship; and the solidarity that was built through personal correspondence and gay publications was the best way to denounce state power abuses everywhere. In other words, for Latin American gay exiles, the mobilizations that were taking place in Southern Europe were neither alien to them nor a finalized model to be implemented in their own countries but integral to a struggle that crossed national borders and that deeply concerned them.[183]

In this line, Anabitarte and Lorenzo contributed significantly—through press articles, their correspondence, and monographic books—to the debates on sexual politics that were taking place, publicly for the first time, in transitional Spain. These contributions are connected to a radical critique of the co-optation of nonnormative sexualities by the state and consumer markets. Already in February 1976, Armand de Fluvià debated by letter with Héctor Anabitarte about the potential risk that the much-heralded sexual liberation could end up becoming a new class privilege. At that point in the destape, nude scenes (not including genitals) began to appear in films and magazines, expanding the market of erotic consumption for middle- and upper-class heterosexual men, but this tacit tolerance did not have a correlate in legal changes, nor did it include homoeroticism.[184] At the same time, since the early 1970s, magazines such as *Triunfo* and *Cuadernos para el dialogo*, read predominantly by the progressive intelligentsia, had used the subterfuge of covering international events to publish articles on taboo topics, including "sex change."[185] Between the late 1970s and early 1980s, Anabitarte and Lorenzo intervened in the sexual politics of the transition in two disparate ways: in highly theoretical discussions on the nexus between sexuality, oppression, and liberation and in the production of soft porn for popular consumption. Regarding the first facet, their 1979 monograph *Homosexualidad: El asunto está caliente* (*Homosexuality: A Hot Issue*) stands out as a genealogy of homosexual behavior from classical mythology to contemporary social movements. This monograph epitomized the liberationist paradigm, according to which identity categories (homosexual and heterosexual) were incompatible with basic human freedom, insofar as they served to regulate an inherently pansexual libido—whether through gender roles, sexual practices that adjusted to the active/passive binary, or the fixation of the sexual object. Following this argument, sexual liberation would be a touchstone in the abolition of a classist society built on a heteropatriarchal order.[186] Despite the provocative tone of the text, the censor in charge of reading it did not object to its publication, given that the government had initiated a process of liberalization in the publishing sector.[187]

However, this liberalization had its own limits, as Ricardo and Héctor discussed in May 1980 in an article on the censorship of *El libro rojo del cole* (*The Little Red Schoolbook*), first published in Denmark in 1968. A district board of the Madrid city council had distributed this book among a few school principals. The publisher was arrested and charged with an "attack on public morals" and "public scandal" on the premise that the book invited schoolchildren to experiment with drugs, eroded the traditional family, and called authority into question. Sex education thus constituted a new battleground in the fight against censorship and authoritarianism. In the early 1980s in Spain, initiatives to discuss in school "a rewarding sexuality, free of anguish," became an upsetting issue for the government and conservative media. Gay groups such as EHGAM (Euskal Herriko Gay-Les Askapen Mugimendua) traced a parallelism between the arguments used by the government to deny their request for legalization and those that were circulated to denigrate sex education by assimilating it with the "corruption of minors." To undermine governmental censorship, EHGAM released a statement quoting the pages that *El libro rojo* devoted to homosexuality: "Homosexuals caress and make love in the same way as other people do. . . . Their love and feelings are as true as those of others. . . . There are other cultures and moral systems for which homosexuality is as normal and valuable as any other form of sexuality."[188] Educating children on the idea that homosexuality is as valid as heterosexuality—while the book avoided defining these categories as ontologically stable—was then the new frontier for sexual radicalism. In their article, Héctor and Ricardo intervened in this debate by arguing that the ultraconservative reaction to the circulation of the book demonstrated that there was a significant gap between Spain and neighboring countries, since the book circulated freely in the rest of Europe. In this way, Héctor and Ricardo played with the fears and complexes of many Spaniards, who were aware that the sociocultural heritage of four decades of dictatorship played against their aspirations of democratization and integration into the European Union. According to Héctor and Ricardo, the idea of a fluid and recreational sexuality had inevitably

ignited a contrary reaction among some sectors: "First homosexuality escaped from the asylums, now it would escape from homosexuals themselves. . . . The matter becomes uncontainable. . . . It's
as if a cartridge of dynamite was inserted into everyone's ass."[189] In
the early 1980s, gay activists directly confronted state policies that
sought to consolidate the traditional family's moral monopoly by
silencing those who questioned it. In this context, erotic materials offered a strategy to expand the formal boundaries of activism, using provocation to challenge normative social frameworks.

During their exile in Spain, Héctor and Ricardo obtained part
of their income by writing erotic novels. Héctor describes them
as adults-only "soft porn." Among other titles, they authored *La
farmacia de la pasión* (Pharmacy of Passion), *La muchacha de las
sábanas negras* (Girl with Black Sheets), and *Boquita hambrienta*
(Hungry little mouth). According to Héctor, "The press' instructions indicated that there had to be at least one intercourse per
chapter, and at the end sinners should be punished. They were not,
they triumphed, and the director of the collection allowed it."[190]
Héctor and Ricardo used softcore porn as an act of resistance by
avoiding the tragic and moralistic outcome of the novels that was
used as an alibi for their explicit content. On the other hand, while
Héctor and Ricardo challenged this conventionalism, Ceres, their
publishing house, allowed them to do it, suggesting that there was
a sort of tacit agreement between the publishing industry and writers to test the limits of permissiveness by the post-Franco regime.
Héctor and Ricardo used Gian Kisser as their pen name, and their
erotic novels are cataloged in the Spanish National Library. In a
letter that Héctor sent to Armand de Fluvià and Jordi Petit on
June 1, 1980, he suggested that gay activists could use softcore to
build a progressive discourse on sexuality that would be accessible
to a majority audience: "We have already written 10 erotic novels.
It occurs to us novels could be written in the same style, but being
gay and *progre*, more progressive (they almost do not censor us in
Ceres). Could people at *Party* [a popular gay magazine] be interested? Could the FAGC be unofficially interested? For two reasons:
to spread awareness of homosexuality among people who 'do not

read' and, additionally, it could become a source of revenue. . . . I
think that [gay] movements should encompass both the edition of
'non-political' publications and the so-called places of *ambiente*."[191]

In this letter, Héctor advocates for a model of sexual activism
that moves away from intellectual elitism and tries to approach,
through erotic publications, people who frequented the *ambiente*
(gay bars and other spaces of sociability and entertainment) but
did not have a clear political awareness. On the other hand, Carlos Santos, a renowned transition-era journalist, points out that
Argentine political exiles played in general a significant role in
providing the erotic publications that grew exponentially in late-
1970s Spain with an air of sophistication and intellectualism. According to Santos, Spaniards' extreme yearning for sexual freedom
aligned with the high profit margins that erotic magazines produced for companies such as the Zeta group, which edited *Inter-
viú*, *Penthouse*, and other magazines where sex was no longer
represented as sinful. Regarding Argentine exiles' contributions,
Santos concludes, "There had never been, nor will be, a porn magazine written in perfect Spanish like those published by the Zeta
group in those years."[192]

Similarly, Herbert Daniel, a Brazilian gay guerrilla who lived in
exile in Portugal in the 1970s, found a job in the magazine *Modas e
Bordados* (Fashion and embroidery) that allowed him unexpect-
edly to disseminate the tenets of feminism. As Herbert put it with
a fine sense of humor, "What better end could there be in the life
of a retired terrorist than to become a writer for *Modas e Bordados*?"[193] James N. Green points out that, while living in exile, Herbert became open about his homosexuality for the first time. He
also became closer to the feminist movement and published on
disparate issues, from the World Conference on Women, held in
Mexico in 1975, to his precious gay icon, Marilyn Monroe, whom
he described as a tragic object of fantasy.[194] Herbert's feminist publications in an embroidery magazine and Héctor and Ricardo's
belief that softcore could be political suggest that radical activists
revised their former strategies while living in exile to reach people as widely as possible.[195]

Boquita hambrienta

Pase Javier: GIAN KISSER

"Contrabando ideológico"
un Abraze
Héctor y Ricardo

Colección SEXY STAR n.º 73
Publicación semanal

EDICIONES CERES, S. A.
AGRAMUNT, 8 - BARCELONA (6)

FIG. 16. Héctor and Ricardo dedicate one of their erotic novelettes to the author. The title is *Boquita hambrienta* (Hungry little mouth), and their pen name was Gian Kisser. The novelette was part of a weekly serial called Sexy Star, published by Ceres in Barcelona. The authors describe the novelette as "ideological contraband." Courtesy of the author.

FIG. 17. Ricardo Lorenzo and Héctor Anabitarte (*standing*). Photograph by Adelaida Gigli in Barcelona, 1981. Courtesy Héctor Anabitarte, Ricardo Lorenzo, and Archivos Desviados.

Conclusion

Suspending the analytical model built on the terminology of "center" and "periphery" and the geographical, temporal, and causal frames underlying the narratives on the spread of the LGBT paradigm to contexts outside of the Global North, this chapter shifts the focus onto maricas and travestis. Hookups, parties, and the use of subcultural codes were essential elements of marica and travesti life in the 1960s and 1970s and impacted early gay and trans political activists, who heatedly discussed the role of marica and travesti scandal in their own agendas of social change. In tracing these debates, I question the assumption that vernacular categories in Latin America and the Mediterranean were incompatible with LGBT activism. Scholars who subscribe to this assumption argue that activism in these regions originated in the diffusion of identity paradigms from Global North to Global South.[196] Instead, this chapter builds on Spanish-language scholarship that has interrogated whether shifting views on gender and sexuality expanded or contracted the horizons of lived experience. For some scholars, LGBT politics have brought about normalization by marginalizing the exhilarating experience of covert sexual and social encounters in an urban cartography of public bathrooms and other semisecluded spaces.[197] Other authors emphasize the psychological and social costs of state and medical violence.[198] Finally, other scholars address LGBT activist groups' achievements in recent years. Both Argentina and Spain have passed laws protecting sexual and gender minorities' rights, ranging from the legalization of same-sex marriage to the recognition of trans and nonbinary identities.[199] While building on this scholarly corpus, this chapter moves beyond its primary focus on LGBT identities by tracing the role of vernacular categories and cultures. In fact, this chapter suggests that local tensions between different vernacular subjectivities shaped early queer activism.

Conclusion

Marica Archives and Histories of Emancipation

The history of the following letter captures how the tension between pleasure and violence is at the genesis of marica archives.[1] Marina (pseudonymous) committed suicide in Barcelona in 1966. She was bisexual, was pregnant, and had a venereal disease. Along with her dead body, the authorities found the letters—including her farewell missive before overdosing herself with pills—that she had exchanged with her closest friends, four maricas who lived in Andalucía. These maricas playfully referred to themselves with female nicknames like *Francisca, la hija del sol viviente* (daughter of the living sun) and felt emboldened in the same facets of marica life that authorities most despised. They enjoyed flamenco, jazz, and Hollywood movies. They called themselves *vicioso* or *puta* (whore), talked about their "pussy" and insatiable sexual appetites, had sex for money in the touristic town of Torremolinos, cruised in cinemas, and seduced other men, including a monk who joined their social circle. They mocked Catholicism—the collage included with the letter was, according to its author, an image of herself attending the Holy Week processions as a devout lady to see a Jesus Christ impersonator ridiculing himself riding a donkey—and turned to their own autonomous spiritual rituals, allegedly celebrating spiritism sessions that the authorities underlined in the letters as evidence of a sort of heretical cult. The letters also contain drawings, photographs, and collages through which the authors materialized camp aesthetics, discussing their dresses, erotic icons, and fashion trends (they loved anything *Yé-yé* and were less fond of men's long hair). They saw one another as kin and shared the most troubling events of their daily lives. They fought with other maricas, treated bars and discotheques as the scenarios of these battles, and criticized and gossiped about one another. They celebrated their own pleasure and freedom and understood the repressive environment they had to navigate together to survive. In the letters, they openly discussed abortion and suicide as valid options that they could assess together. They mocked parents and authorities. Unfortunately, the police eventually seized this correspondence and used it to prosecute the marica authors as a group of existentialist *viciosos* corrupted by Marina and set in defying authority, morality, and religion.[2] Marica politics, ethics, and aesthetics are core to this story, and to this book overall.

Agents of the state, judiciary, and medical community employed social danger theory to measure individuals' latent criminality, conflating maricas with legal transgression. Maricas rejected this mode of external categorization and elaborated alternative models of community identification that remediated state repression and sexual violence through the pursuit of the sublime, be it erotic, religious, or cultural. In this pursuit, they occasionally drew ideological and iconographic material from the very same institutions that were most antagonistic to their visibility—the Catholic Church, the military, and reactionary mass media. The lexicon of stigma and queer self-affirmation in Spanish (puto, mariquita, marica, maricón) was disputed by historical actors in different positions of power—including self-identifying maricas, their relatives and neighbors, police officers, forensic doctors, judges, homophile intellectuals, and gay activists. The previous scholarship on sexual roles in Latin America and the Mediterranean has assumed that males who are feminized in penetration are perceived as sexual objects.[3] Based on fieldwork in Nicaragua, Roger N. Lancaster argues that sex signifies and constitutes power relations between feminized anal-receptive males (*cochones*) and masculine-looking men (*hombre-hombre*) whose dominant status is embodied in penile insertion. Through his focus on machista lexicon, Lancaster implies that cochones derive their status from

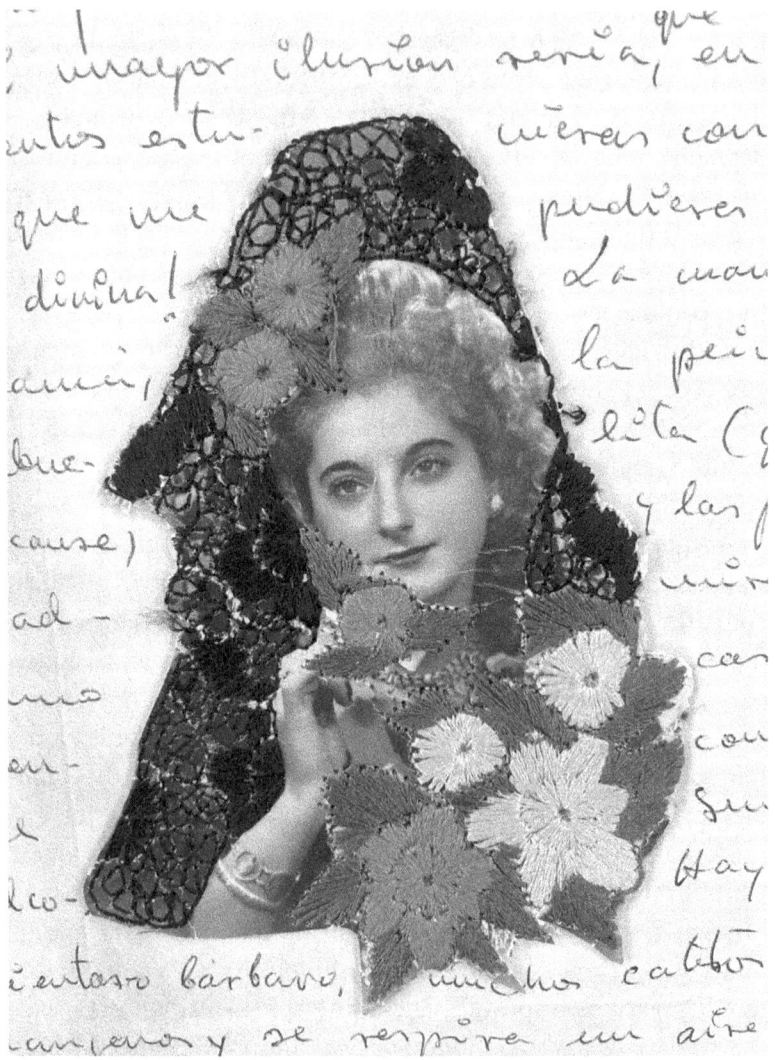

FIG. 18. One of the letters exchanged between Marina and her marica friends. Juzgado Especial de Vagos y Maleantes de Granada, file 44/1966, signatura 11793, Archivo Histórico Provincial de Málaga, Málaga, Spain. Courtesy Archivo Histórico Provincial de Málaga.

being sexually used.⁴ Despite their apparent social integration, they remain objectified.⁵

Abuse undoubtedly shaped maricas' daily experiences. However, objectification was not a static grammar but a contested policy enforced and instrumentalized by state agents. Maricas did not relinquish their desires through sexual receptiveness. Official reports betray a consistent apprehension that maricas showed themselves increasingly self-accepting and vocal. As I explored throughout—and particularly in chapters 1 and 4—sexual violence was a mechanism to restore the gendered order in the view of abusers and state agents alike. State authorities treated males who had been raped or sexually abused harshly. Males who reported having been raped were subjected to harsh scrutiny, required to demonstrate their active resistance, and even treated as complicit just by virtue of not appearing masculine enough. The testimonies and depositions of these trials were many times an extension of the sexual violence inflicted on these individuals. While same-sex sexual violence did not seem to alarm state agents, who informally participated in it and formally questioned victims' testimonies, maricas' affective ties and subculture did elicit authorities' intervention. As Michel Foucault intimated, authorities were more concerned about relationality than about perverse acts.⁶ The main targets were marica communities and bonds that defied the logics of familism that mediated subjects' relationship with the political realm.

Legal debates seemed more inclined to attribute sexual orientation to nature in Spain and to nurture in Argentina. From mariquitas' pretenses of chastity to mariconas and locas' bold promiscuity, clinical diagnoses were not elaborated in a sociocultural vacuum but instead dialogued asymmetrically with vernacular taxonomies.⁷ In Spain, Francoist authorities were met with a trend of popular Catholicism—articulated by defendants, their mothers, neighbors, defense lawyers, and even parish priests—which described mariquitas as suffering from an inborn condition. Defendants and their communities counteracted the judicial treatment of homosexuals as led by excessive predatory desires (*viciosos* in

Spanish). Mariquitas were expected to be feminine, family oriented, devout, and involved in folk culture.[8] Ironically, while the
Catholic hierarchy supported Franco's regime, mariquitas often
found in Catholic religiosity a means of self-expression that—in
contrast to fascism—did not compel them to perform a belligerent masculinity. By being active members of the parish community, supporting their families, and remaining silent about their
sexuality, those individuals carved out spaces of conditional toleration. This vernacular taxonomy had legal significance not only
through the notion of inborn inversion but mostly because it
emphasized community mechanisms to socialize mariquitas into
sublimating their desires.

Scholars have pointed out the effectiveness of strategic essentialism, of naturalizing sexual and gender nonconformity to counteract their criminal treatment as perversion and voluntary offense.[9]
This analysis presumes legal debates based on the classical penal
tradition and individual liability. The positivist penal frame, dominant in many contexts of Latin America and Southern Europe
during extended periods of the twentieth century, goes in a different direction. Standard legal penalties for charges of homosexuality against male citizens were harsher in Spain than in Argentina;
years of imprisonment, exile, and probation under the Vagrancy
and Social Dangerousness Laws, compared to standard penalties of weeks in prison under the police's edicts in Argentina that
referred to publicly scandalous behavior, applied without any
constitutional sanction.[10] In both countries, state policies were
flagrantly classist: middle- and upper-class subjects were often
spared the harshest penalties, and officials constantly expressed
their qualms about the moral standards of people who lived in
poverty.[11] Through a close reading of forensic reports, *Maricas*
reveals the core paradox of state policies that treated vernacular taxonomies as an index of the underclasses' dangerousness
while selectively incorporating them into operational diagnoses to foster anti-marica violence. Class also played a major role
in authorities' decisions about whether arrested males should be
subjected to medical or criminal treatments. Criminological and

forensic reports betray experts' belief that the middle and upper classes were better equipped to exercise self-control to sublimate or reorient the libido through medical treatments. Authorities' and forensic doctors' taxonomies reflect how they perceived different degrees of fixation of the libido based on the legibility imposed on bodies and performance. Forensic doctors treated what they read as femininity, encompassing receptiveness to penetration, as an indication of fixated homosexual desires. These were either interpreted as congenital homosexuality (per Spanish endocrinologist Gregorio Marañón) or as sexual psychopathy (per psychoanalytic theory). Both frames acknowledge that sexual orientation can shift through pleasure. Forensic doctors confronted the fact that masculine men also found pleasure in having sex with other males. If these were occasional acts or there had not been other available sexual outlets, diagnostic reports commonly would reflect forensic doctors' optimistic assessment of the subject's potential rehabilitation. However, if a masculine man had developed a penchant for repeatedly having sex with other males or showed affection for a male sexual partner, then his homosexual desires made him a danger to society in the view of authorities and forensic doctors.

Moreover, according to officials' and medical experts' assessments, the policies implemented in these decades did not prevent maricas from expressing themselves and forming social ties. Camp, spirituality, flamboyant aesthetics, feminized promiscuity, and other understudied inflections of marica language were often conceptualized as alienation in the vocabulary of 1970s gay activism based on the assumption that marica life entailed submissiveness and depoliticization. Quite the opposite, this book argues that there is no understanding queer and trans politics without marica genealogies. This assessment complicates the grand narrative of evolutionary progress from Stonewall in the United States to LGBTQ+ rights elsewhere, which obfuscates how maricas contested state taxonomic projects and police harassment and how they energized early sexual liberation movements by putting their bodies on the line.

NOTES

Introduction

1. Juan Queiroz describes Hugo's testimony as "a staging [*puesta en escena*] of tragic episodes, police arrests, parties, *plumas* [marica femininity], and hookups, constantly transpiring Hugo's fierce militant commitment." Queiroz, "Memorias del desvío." Translations from Spanish to English are mine.

2. Fernández-Galeano and Yarfitz, "Serious Maricas."

3. Similarly, males who had sex with other males in Franco-era Madrid, taking advantage of the anonymity and darkness of the Carretas cinema, labeled this space the Cathedral, since every gay male was baptized there. Olmeda, *El Látigo*, 138–43.

4. Queiroz, "Memorias del desvío."

5. This story connects with Melissa M. Wilcox's concept of "serious parody" as "a form of cultural protest in which a disempowered group parodies an oppressive cultural institution while simultaneously claiming for itself what it believes to be an equally good or superior enactment of one or more culturally respected aspects of that same institution." Wilcox, *Queer Nuns*, 70. The context for this parody is a unique iconographic blend, the result of living hundreds of years "in the convent" and some decades with Hollywood, like Martin F. Manalansan IV puts it regarding contemporary Filipino queer culture. Manalansan, "Diasporic Deviants/Divas," 192.

6. Queiroz, "Memorias del desvío."

7. On *queering* archival evidence, see Muñoz, *Cruising Utopia*, 65; and Marshall and Tortorici, "Introduction," 15–16.

8. Gabriel Giorgi traces a prevalent cultural trope that attributes homosexual people's social "death" to their non-reproductivity so that they are fated to be isolated and unable to have meaningful lives. Giorgi, *Sueños de exterminio*. Similarly, Ricardo Llamas notes that cultural representations of homosexuality have reinforced the notion that "the (supposed) incapacity to procreate or produce life generates disdain for life itself: either someone else's life (explaining murderous or criminal tendencies), but also and above all their own life." Llamas, *Teoría Torcida*, 152.

9. On the racial history of body plasticity, see Gill-Peterson, *Histories of the Transgender Child*; on the relationship between public policies and the homo/heterosexual binary, see Canaday, *Straight State*; and on the structural economic trends that contributed to catalyze gay identities in this period, see D' Emilio, "Capitalism and Gay Identity," 467–76.

10. Lawrence La Fountain-Stokes points out that understanding "local specificities in a global context" is at the core of queer and trans studies. La Fountain-Stokes, *Translocas*, 3.

11. Alberto and Elena, "Introduction," 2–9. Maite Zubiaurre analyzes how, in the early twentieth century, Spanish intellectuals such as Gregorio Marañón and José Ortega y Gasset portrayed Castilians and Basques as representatives of a "pure" Spanish masculinity based on austerity and self-control, in contrast to Andalusians' ambiguous gender and to the largest cities that were the centers of the corrupting influence of modernization. Zubiaurre, *Cultures of the Erotic*, 74–75, 91–92.

12. Historians have long discussed Argentina and Spain's *sonderweg*, or relative exceptionality within the regional trajectories of Latin America and Europe respectively, including the massive influx of European immigrants to Argentina and fascism's lasting reign in Spain. While Argentina was a Spanish colony in the dawn of the nineteenth century, by the early twentieth century it was not only a sovereign nation but economically ahead of its former metropolis and attracting migrants from it. As José Moya has studied, Argentina became a globally significant agricultural exporter while Spain lost its empire and economically lagged its industrialized neighbors. Millions of Spaniards crossed the Atlantic looking for economic opportunities in Argentina, to the point that in this period "the net immigration surpassed that of all the conquistadors and settlers who came to Spanish America during the entire colonial period" (even though many Spaniards eventually returned to Spain). Argentina and Spain became interwoven through these back-and-forth migration flows. Moya, *Cousins and Strangers*, 1. On fascism as a transnational creature and its intellectual sphere in Argentina, Italy, and (tangentially) Spain, see Finchelstein, *Transatlantic Fascism*. In the postwar period, Argentine president Juan Domingo Perón broke with other international leaders and sent food aid to Spain, contributing to the survival of Franco's regime. Rein, *Entre el abismo*, 72–99. Micol Siegel identifies a series of obvious (but, in her view, misleading) factors that justify juxtaposing two national cases: postcolonial relationships, a common language, large-scale migration flows, commensurability, and land borders. All these factors connect the histories of Argentina and Spain, except for land borders. Seigel, *Uneven Encounters*, 8–11.

13. Milanesio, *Destape*, 5–6.

14. On the political culture of franquismo, see Box, *España, año cero*; and Sanz Hoya, *España en camisa azul*.

15. For an overview of this period, see chapters 4, 5, and 6 of Romero, *History of Argentina*. On the cultural and racialized facets of Peronism, see Karush and Chamosa, introduction to *New Cultural History*, 1–20; and Milanesio, "Peronists and Cabecitas," 53–84.

16. On transnational histories of sex, see Canaday, "Thinking Sex," 1250–57.

17. Hartman, "Venus in Two Acts," 1–14.

18. Halberstam, *Queer Art of Failure.*

19. My main model in pursuing this desire is Green's *Beyond Carnival.* There are excellent, both classical and recent, works on the role of gender and sexuality in nation-building, including Cowan, *Securing Sex*; Salessi, *Médicos maleantes y maricas*; Vázquez García and Cleminson, *Los invisibles: Una historia*; Frazier, *Desired States*; Milanesio, *Destape*; Macías-González and Rubenstein, *Masculinity and Sexuality*; Guy, *Sex and Danger*; Milanich, *Children of Fate*; Rodríguez, *Civilizing Argentina*; and Ruggiero, *Modernity in the Flesh.*

20. I borrow the concept of "rebel archive" from Carpio, "Tales."

21. Tortorici, *Sins against Nature*, 3.

22. Lambe, *Madhouse*, 265.

23. Lorenzo Benadusi emphasizes that, in Mussolini's Italy, fascist and Catholic ideals of masculinity were in tension with each other; the former centering on aggressive prowess and the latter on self-restrain and obedience to the church's moral teachings. Benadusi, *Enemy of the New Man*, 6.

24. Gil-Albert, *Heraclés*, 11. Similarly, in her study of identification photos of Black diasporic subjects, Tina Campt invites us to listen to images that register "state management" and engage with them "as conduits of an unlikely interplay between the vernacular and the state." The resulting method "reckons with the fissures, gaps, and interstices that emerge when we refuse to accept the 'truth' of images and archives the state seeks to proffer through its production of subjects." Campt, *Listening to Images*, 1–8.

25. Lambe, *Madhouse*, 263.

26. Mejía, *Transgenerismos*; Platero, *Por un chato*; Rizki, "Familiar Grammars"; Rizki, "'No State Apparatus'"; Solà and Urko, *Transfeminismos*; Fernández-Galeano, "Running Mascara."

27. Mérida Jiménez, *Transbarcelonas*; Simonetto, *Body of One's Own.*

28. Amin, "Taxonomically Queer?," 93. Ethnographer David Valentine cautions against the assumption that the analytical distinction between gender and sexuality reflects a natural fact or ontology. According to Valentine, this distinction itself must be historicized and critically examined to avoid perpetuating the exclusion of people whose self-identification does not fit into that ontology. Valentine, *Imagining Transgender*, 4–6.

29. Rizki, "Latin/x American Trans Studies," 149.

30. Chauncey, *Gay New York*, xxiii.

31. On the problems of exoticization in the study of (homo)sexualities in Latin America, see Lancaster, "Sexual Positions," 1–16. The debate between "presentism" and "antiquarinism" is as pressing as ever as I finish writing these pages. The most recent episode, and a particularly animated one for that matter, has been the controversy around the position taken in this debate by the president of the American Historical Association. Sweet, "Is History History?" From the vantage point of "trans*

historicities," Leah DeVun and Zeb Tortorici have traced multiple radical alternatives to linear normative notions of historical time. DeVun and Tortorici, "Trans, Time, and History," 518–39.

32. Puto, which literally means "male whore," has a unique history. It was brought to the Americas by Spaniards in the early modern period, but then it fell out of use in Spain over the course of the modern period, while remaining widely used in Latin America until today. Corominas, *Breve diccionario*, 266–67; Sigal, "Introduction," 8.

33. Sívori, *Locas, chongos y gays*, chap. 4.

34. This includes local, vernacular, and situated labels that constitute a "nonce taxonomy" in Eve Kosofsky Sedgwick's terms. Sedgwick, *Epistemology of the Closet*, 23.

35. Authorities and activists disputed each other's "labeling power" to legitimate their views on maricas. I borrow this concept from Prieur, who emphasizes that "power and domination imply mastering the categorizations and evaluations, the possibility of enforcing one's judgments as valid. It is the masculine men who define what homosexuality is and who the homosexual is. . . . They have the labeling power and may thereby affirm their own masculinity. Their categorizations let them themselves go free of stigma." Prieur, *Mema's House*, 232.

36. Amin, "Taxonomically Queer?," 102.

37. These concepts are elaborated by Michel Foucault. Foucault, *History of Sexuality*.

38. I am relying on historical research by Pablo Ben, Máximo Javier Fernández, and Santiago Joaquín Insausti. In the stereotypical understanding of their roles, machos were expected to penetrate other men to release sexual tension and demonstrate their masculinity, while maricas would perform a provocative femininity to satisfy their own desire to be penetrated by other males. Following Ben, this subculture originated in the gender imbalance present in turn-of-the-century Buenos Aires, by then populated by a majority-male migrant workforce. Ben further suggests that participants in this subculture understood sexual penetration as a sign of shifting power relationships between males and not as evidence of their inner essence. Ben, "Plebeian Masculinity," 443–50, 457–58. Fernández and Insausti trace the continuities of this model into the last decades of the twentieth century, when machos and maricas, performing stereotyped gender roles, could encounter and seduce each other in the streets and bars of Buenos Aires. Fernández, "Sociabilidad homoerótica," 31–35; Insausti, "De maricas," 85–123.

39. Tintilay, "Arde Jujuy."

1. Forensic Sexual Violence

1. On Kretschmer's body typology, see Rydström, "'Sodomitical Sins Are Threefold,'" 262–64; on Tardieu's DRE, see Rosario, "Afterword," 168–70.

2. Beccalossi, "Latin Eugenics," 305–29.

3. Lambe, *Madhouse*, 13–14.

4. Saumench Gimeno, "Cálculo médico legal," 5.

5. Ferri, *Positive School*, 10–53.

6. Beccalossi, "Latin Eugenics," 312–14.

7. Ferri, *Positive School*, 107–9.

8. Ferri, *Positive School*, 44, 119.

9. On the ideological underpinnings of Ingenieros's criminology, see Huertas García-Alejo, *El delincuente*, 38–43. On Jiménez de Asúa's proposals, see Terradillos Basoco, *Peligrosidad social*, 53–60.

10. Huertas García-Alejo, *El delincuente*, 9–10, 196–98.

11. Terradillos Basoco, *Peligrosidad social*, 53–60.

12. Platero, "Lesboerotismo," 22.

13. Molina Artaloytia, "Estigma, diagnosis e interacción," 535–42, 558–73.

14. Lévy Lazcano, *Psicoanálisis y defensa social*.

15. Zubiaurre, *Cultures of the Erotic*, 47–57.

16. In fact, as recalled by Eulàlia Torras Armangué, one of the founders of the Spanish Psychoanalytic Society, the few psychoanalysts trained in Spain during Franco's regime had to confront the negative effects of this training on their professional career. Eulàlia Torras Armangué, interview by the author on February 19, 2018, Barcelona, Spain.

17. See, for instance, file 163/1962, Juzgado Especial de Vagos y Maleantes de Barcelona, Arxiu Central dels Jutjats de la Ciutat de la Justícia (hereafter JEVMB-ACJCJB). The reports elaborated for the vagrancy court of the Canary Islands by a forensic doctor serving in Santa Cruz de Tenerife also incorporated a psychodynamic perspective. See, for instance, file 25/1963, box 27, Juzgado Especial de Vagos y Maleantes del Archipiélago Canario, Archivo Histórico Provincial de Las Palmas (hereafter JEVMAC-AHPLP).

18. Molina Artaloytia, "Estigma, diagnosis e interacción," 511–25.

19. Vázquez García and Cleminson, *Los invisibles: Una historia*, 91–110, 123–26; Aresti, *Masculinidades*, 180–238.

20. Ugarte Pérez, "Entre el pecado y la enfermedad," 8.

21. Mora Gaspar, *Al margen*, 84–85.

22. Etchegoyen, "Ángel Garma," 665–66.

23. Garma, "Paranoia y Homosexualidad," 555–78.

24. Plotkin, *Freud in the Pampas*, 76–80, 126–29, 135–39.

25. Plotkin, *Freud in the Pampas*, 4.

26. Freud, *Three Essays*, xv, 97.

27. Freud, *Three Essays*, 11–12.

28. Freud, *Three Essays*, 36–37.

29. Platero, "Lesboerotismo," 18–25.

30. Jiménez de Asúa, "Ley de Vagos," 635.

31. Mariano Ruíz-Funes García, foreword to the report on the Vagrancy Law presented to the Cortes by the commission of the presidency, in Jiménez de Asúa, "Ley de Vagos," 603–8.

32. Terradillos Basoco, *Peligrosidad social*, 54–60.

33. Terrasa Mateu, "La legislación represiva," 96.

34. Mira Nouselles, *De Sodoma a Chueca*, 320–21.

35. Pérez-Sánchez, *Queer Transitions*, 13.

36. "LEY DE 15 DE JULIO DE 1954," 4862.

37. "LEY DE 15 DE JULIO DE 1954," 4862.

38. Terrasa Mateu, "La legislación represiva," 97–98.

39. "LEY DE 15 DE JULIO DE 1954," 4862.

40. This concept implies "excessive appetite" for something, leading someone to acquire damaging habits. Real Academia Española (2014), *Diccionario de la lengua Española*, 23rd ed., http://dle.rae.es.

41. Cleminson and Vázquez García, *"Los invisibles": A History*, 15–16.

42. Haller, "Homosexuality in Seville," 32.

43. "Deposition on February 25, 1969," file 64, Signatura 10992, Juzgado Especial de Vagos y Maleantes de Sevilla, Archivo Histórico Provincial de Sevilla (hereafter JEVMS-AHPS).

44. File 543/1962, JEVMB-ACJCJB. My analysis departs from the scholarship that posits that maricones were primarily defined by their masculine demeanor. Oscar Guasch argues that during the Francoist period, people distinguished between the innate condition that led some men (maricas) to behave like women—becoming "domestic" and taking on a sexually receptive role—and other men (maricones) who choose to have homosexual relationships despite their otherwise masculine demeanor. According to Guasch, while maricas were visible and could elicit feelings of compassion for their condition, maricones were considered more threatening to heterosexual males and children because they could hide their "perversions" behind an otherwise normative appearance. Guasch, "Social Stereotypes," 527–32. Javier Ugarte Pérez posits that until the 1960s, maricones enjoyed a certain degree of social tolerance, especially among the working classes. Their masculine behavior and appearance distanced them from the maricas and allowed them to characterize their homosexual conduct as circumstantial or occasional; they could blame it on alcohol or the seduction strategies of the maricas. Ugarte Pérez, *Las circunstancias obligaban*, 127–58.

45. File 302/1966, Juzgado Especial de Vagos y Maleantes de Bilbao, Archivo Histórico Provincial de Bizkaia (hereafter JEVMB-AHPB), Bilbao/Bizkaia, Spain.

46. File 127/1962, JEVMB-ACJCJB. Following the same pattern, in 1963, a defendant stole from another man with whom he was sharing a room in a boarding house after the latter allegedly tried to touch him in the middle of the night. The defendant left the complainant a note that said, "If you report me, I will report you as a *maricón*. I noticed everything last night. I know your name is. . . . I am taking your suitcase as a reward. I will give you back everything in due time. This is your chance to not go to prison. Think about it." File 40/1963, box 8876, Juzgado Especial de Vagos y Maleantes de Málaga, AHPS (hereafter JEVMM-AHPS). These two cases left a historical trace because the victims of robbery reported the men who threatened to expose them. However, in both cases the sentences confirmed that "real men" had good reasons to believe that they could victimize gender nonconforming individuals with impunity; the man who robbed a "maricón" in Marbella was acquitted, while the "maricón" who was robbed in Barcelona was sentenced to prison and exile. The

state promoted the vulnerability of gender nonconforming people by guaranteeing the impunity of their victimizers.

47. File 168/1959, box 8875, JEVMM-AHPS.

48. Deposition on May 3, 1962, file 40/1962, box 8879, JEVMM-AHPS.

49. Deposition on May 7, 1962, file 40/1962, box 8879, JEVMM-AHPS.

50. Guardia Civil report on May 3, 1962, file 40/1962.

51. Deposition on May 7, 1962, file 40/1962. In fact, the father had apparently chased the adult defendant with a gun, but mostly because he did not want other people to know about an incident that he saw as potentially tainting his family's name. Guardia Civil report on April 25, 1962, file 40/1962.

52. Ruling issued on June 20, 1962, file 40/1962.

53. Although the closest expression in English would be "to take it up the ass," I opted for the literal translation "give it by the ass" because it better reflects the emphasis in Spanish on the act of "giving" it (penetrating) more than on the act of "taking" it up (being penetrated).

54. File 456/1964, box 10823, JEVMS-AHPS.

55. Deposition on February 24, 1961; ruling issued on February 6, 1962, file 185/1961, JEVMB-ACJCJB.

56. Ruling issued on February 6, 1962, file 185/1961.

57. On the concept of "border area," see Oosterhuis and Loughnan, "Madness and Crime," 2.

58. Saumench Gimeno, "Cálculo médico legal," 5–8.

59. Jumilla, "La Política Social franquista," 6–9.

60. Saumench Gimeno, "Cálculo médico legal," 11–15.

61. Saumench Gimeno, "Cálculo médico legal," 22. On the use of positivism to target the demographic sectors that had supported the Second Republic, see Campos, "La construcción," 12.

62. Saumench Gimeno, "Cálculo médico legal," 22–24.

63. Saumench Gimeno, "Cálculo médico legal," 32–33.

64. Saumench Gimeno, "Cálculo médico legal," 35–36.

65. Martínez, "Archives, Bodies, and Imagination," 159–82.

66. Pedrosa Gil, Weber, and Burgmair, "Ernst Kretschmer," 1111.

67. Mildenberger, "Kraepelin," 327–28; Rydström, "'Sodomitical Sins Are Threefold,'" 262–64.

68. Report by the forensic doctor, July 21, 1964, file 176, box 10705; report by the forensic doctor, July 17, 1964, file 180, box 10705, JEVMS-AHPS.

69. The Spanish General Directorate of Prisons measured prisoners according to Kretschmer's body typology. However, the theory did not match the data, as the 1971 statistics showed a correlation between criminals for "lack of sexual control," the group where homosexuality was more frequent, and the "pyknic" body type, while Kretschmer had argued that the correlation was to be found between homosexuality and the leptosomatic body type. Dirección General de Instituciones Penitenciarias, *Memoria*, 28.

70. On forensic psychiatry following moralistic criteria, see Campos, "La construcción," 9–44.

71. Tardieu's techniques have been applied in very distant countries, from Chile to Egypt. Fernández Lara, "Del delito-Pecado," 15; Rosario, "Afterword," 168–70.

72. Forensic report signed on September 28, 1959, file 67/1959, box 19, JEVMAC-AHPLP.

73. Forensic report signed on March 21, 1960, file 14/1960, box 20, JEVMAC-AHPLP.

74. File 44/1955, box 8. In a similar case, the forensic physician reported that given that the defendant had suffered from hemorrhoids and constipation, no valid diagnosis could be produced. Forensic report signed on March 10, 1955, file 53/1955, box 9. In a third case, a forensic physician pointed out that the digital rectal exam (DRE) might also be less reliable if some time had passed between anal coituses. Forensic report signed on March 8, 1955, file 49/1955, box 9, JEVMAC-AHPLP.

75. Forensic report signed on July 22, 1964, file 172/1964, box 10705, JEVMS-AHPS.

76. Forensic report signed on July 28, 1964, file 172/1964.

77. In a related case, even though the DRE did not produce definitive results, the forensic report supported the accusation of homosexuality by pointing to the defendant's "effeminacy" and small genitals. The defense lawyer argued then that if the defendant had been anally penetrated, as testimonies suggested, the "anal stigma" would not have been uncertain, but the judge ignored this controversy and labeled the defendant a social danger, citing the medical exam as evidence. Ruling issued on August 18, 1964, file 175/1964, box 10705, JEVMS-AHPS.

78. Mannered gestures denoted the defendant's sexual inversion, despite the lack of clinical signs of "passive pederasty," according to one such report produced in 1964 in Las Palmas. Forensic Report signed on December 5, 1964, file 31/1964, box 30, JEVMAC-AHPLP. Similarly, two physicians reported to the Barcelona court that they had noted a certain effeminacy in the defendant's "way of being, in his talking and his gestures." Although the physical examination (likely the DRE) did not show signs of homosexuality, physicians repeated it several times, probably expecting that it would eventually conform to their prejudgment. Forensic report, n.d., file 114/1957, JEVMB-ACJCJB.

79. "Although his gestures are mannered and feminoid we haven't found in the examination of his anal vent signs to demonstrate his sexual inversion, but there might have been contact that did not leave a trace." Forensic report signed on April 16, 1957, file 76/1957, JEVMB-ACJCJB.

80. Forensic report signed on July 21, 1964, file 176, box 10705, JEVMS-AHPS.

81. See file 321/1966, JEVMB-AHPB.

82. For more on this case, see Fernández-Galeano, "Is He a 'Social Danger'?," 25–27.

83. Biography and criminal background, submitted to the court by the Guardia Civil sergeant major on October 7, 1961, file 90, box 8902, JEVMM-AHPS.

84. Plea from the public defender on March 17, 1962, file 90.

85. Arnalte, *Redada de violetas*, 88–104.

86. Ruling on March 21, 1962, file 90.

87. Deposition by the defendant on February 7, 1961, file 8/1961, box 8891, JEVMM-AHPS.

88. Deposition by the defendant on February 24, 1961, file 8/1961.

89. Medical certificates issued on February 28, and March 9, 1961, file 8/1961.

90. Letter from the civilian governor, April 14, 1961, file 8/1961.

91. Police report on January 7, 1967, file 23/1967, JEVMB-ACJCJB.

92. Forensic report on January 18, 1967, file 23/1967.

93. Defense plea on June 5, 1967, file 23/1967.

94. Ruling issued on June 7, 1967, file 23/1967.

95. Affidavit on October 27, 1967, file 23/1967.

96. File 21/1957, box 260, JEVMB-AHPB.

97. Forensic report signed on July 17, 1964, file 180/1964, box 10705, JEVMS-AHPS.

98. "If a defective physiological conformation does not derive into a depraved behavior, we would be dealing with an unfortunate case of biological aberration, totally involuntary, more than with a guilty degeneration, deserving the application of punitive measures." Concluding statement by the defense attorney on August 5, 1964, file 180/1964.

99. Concluding statement.

100. Ruling issued on August 11, 1964, file 180/1964.

101. Plea for mercy submitted by the defendant's mother on January 31, 1961, file 489/1960, box 10902, JEVMS-AHPS.

102. Medical certificate signed on January 30, 1961, file 489/1960.

103. Ruling issued on March 25, 1961, file 489/1960.

104. Forensic report on February 11, 1964, file 65/1964, JEVMB-ACJCJB.

105. Affidavit presented by the defense lawyer on May 25, 1964, file 65/1964.

106. Judge's ruling on September 3, 1964, file 65/1964. The hospital staff filled out neither the admission form nor the clinical history, so the file mostly contains the records of communications with the vagrancy court. This is particularly striking considering that during the trial, considerable attention was paid to the relationship between the patient's homosexuality and a thyroid surgery, and he and his lawyer continuously insisted in his willingness to subject himself to treatment to change his sexual orientation. Clinical file 5256, patient committed on September 10, 1964, Hospital Frenopático, Arxiu Municipal del Districte de les Corts, Barcelona.

107. File 348/1964, JEVMB-ACJCJB.

108. File 155/1965, JEVMB-ACJCJB.

109. When in 1968 one such patient was hospitalized for homosexuality, his family asked the administration for a medical certificate that they could submit to the court. After some exchanges of information requests and reports between the hospital and the court, the latter ruled in early 1969 that the patient could be released given the remission of his "sickness." The admission form only noted that he had committed "acts of the homosexual type" and that he was afraid and distracted. His clinical history does not contain any information at all about his treatment. Either there was no treatment, or it was not registered, which is unlikely

considering that other clinical histories include registers of medication and elec-troshocks. Clinical file 7163, patient committed on December 11, 1968. Hospital Frenopático, Arxiu Municipal del Districte de les Corts, Barcelona; file 837/1968, box 3011, JEVMB-ACJCJB.

110. For instance, in 1971 a defendant was hospitalized in the Hospital Frenopático, but the staff did not even fill out the standard admission form. Yet they certified to the court that the patient's family would pay for his treatment. In October, the patient was participating with a good disposition in group therapy and work therapy. And in November 1971 he was released after serving the minimum penalty of four months' internment. Clinical file 8509, patient committed on July 14, 1971, Hospital Frenopático, Arxiu Municipal del Districte de les Corts, Barcelona; file 726/1961, JEVMB-ACJCJB.

111. Plotkin, *Freud in the Pampas*, 46.

112. Plotkin, *Freud in the Pampas*, 44.

113. Garma, "Paranoia y Homosexualidad," 559–62.

114. Garma, "Paranoia y Homosexualidad," 573.

115. Similarly, Durval Marcondes argued that paranoia was not related to homo-sexuality per se but rather was a self-defense mechanism against a "passive role in sexual relationships." Marcondes, "Relaciones de objeto."

116. Thénon and Villar, "Reacción paranoide," 511–27. In 1952, Fidias R. Cesio also discussed the treatment with electroshock of a patient's homosexuality-related para-noia disorder. Cesio, "Estudio psicoanalítico."

117. Ramacciotti and Valobra, "El campo médico," 493–516.

118. See, for instance, files 41838 and 38283, Instituto de Clasificación, Museo Pen-itenciario Argentino Antonio Ballvé, Buenos Aires, Argentina (hereafter MPAAB).

119. "Antecedentes individuales," file 2531, MPAAB. Since the prisoner commonly identified herself as female in the transcripts of her interview, I will use the pro-nouns she/her/hers.

120. "Antecedentes individuales."

121. Prison report issued on March 11, 1940, file 2531, MPAAB.

122. According to historian Pete Sigal, when Spaniards brought this term to the Americas, they found roughly equivalent terms in Indigenous languages. During the colonial period, puto was used "to refer to a man who was seen as effeminate and who was believed to take the 'passive' role in anal intercourse. The *puto*'s pub-lic effeminacy was what characterized him as a *puto*, so his was more of a gender identity than one based on a sexual role." Sigal, "Introduction," 8. In contrast to the modern "homosexual," the meaning of puto was defined in terms of a feminine gen-der performance that encompassed being penetrated. Hence it became a derogatory term and common-use insult, since "being a *puto* was perceived as a horrendous fate." Sigal, "Gendered Power," 103.

123. Pablo Ben describes how in turn-of-the-century Buenos Aires plebeian men who felt pressured to prove their masculinity by penetrating other individuals (whether male or female) "frequently accused one another of being putos" to reaffirm their masculinity by challenging that of other men. Ben, "Plebeian Masculinity," 457.

124. See, for instance, file 573, MPAAB.

125. "Semblanza," file 5858, MPAAB.

126. "Antecedentes familiares," file 5844, MPAAB.

127. "Antecedentes individuales," file 5844.

128. "Antecedentes individuales," file 5844.

129. "Semblanza," file 5844.

130. Final report by the Classification Institute on October 21, 1951, file 9650, MPAAB.

131. "Investigación del informador social," September 17, 1951, file 9650.

132. "Semblanza/Examen Psíquico," file 9650.

133. "Semblanza," file 11971, MPAAB.

134. In 1958, the Classification Institute recommended the prisoner's release before he had served his sentence. Report by the Classification Institute on July 28, 1958, file 11971.

135. "Sentencia," issued on March 8, 1963, file 38615, MPAAB.

136. The psychiatrists classified the prisoner as an "occasional criminal" (per Ferri) and primitive-reactive criminal (per Seelig). "Clasificación," submitted by psychiatrist-chief of criminological services on May 19, 1969, file 38615.

137. Report on August 21, 1969, file 38615.

138. "Antecedentes individuales," file 38283, MPAAB.

139. "Consideraciones Criminológicas," file 38283.

140. "Interpretación del Test de Apercepción Temática," file 38283.

141. "Consideraciones Criminológicas," file 38283.

142. Terry, *American Obsession*, 1–8.

2. The Tacky and the Sublime

1. Molina, *Botín de guerra*, 198.

2. Sebreli, *Escritos*, 313–14.

3. Molloy, "Of Queens," 106–7.

4. Pierre Bourdieu establishes that "taste" stems from the accumulation of cultural capital in the hands of the dominant classes, and thereby it becomes an exercise of symbolic violence in the disavowal of the "tasteless" worldview of the dominated classes. Bourdieu, *Distinction*.

5. Moreover, as James N. Green has demonstrated for Brazilian cities, using terms in English and references to the Anglo-Saxon world also became part of the entendidos' code of cultural sophistication. Green, *Beyond Carnival*, 178–82.

6. Fuss, "Fashion," 730.

7. Fuss, "Fashion," 732.

8. Dante Bertini, "Miguel de Molina," Facebook post, March 3, 2018, https://perma .cc/l393-57nz.

9. Molina, *Botín de guerra*, 79.

10. Malva and Calzón Flores, *Mi recordatorio*, 74.

11. The archival history of these letters illustrates, in and of itself, the circulation of homoerotic materials between Argentina and Spain. After Molina's death in Buenos

Aires in 1993, these letters were sold to a secondhand bookstore of the city, which in turn sold them to the National Library of Spain, where they have been archived since 1996. Calero Carramolino, "La copla," 75–76. A judicial file from Bilbao suggests that the phenomenon of fans sending homoerotic letters to performers was quite generalized in the 1950s. File 18/1957, JEVMB-AHPB.

12. On opacity as a queer tactic, see De Villiers, *Opacity and the Closet.*

13. folder 12 (Dibujos [18] de desnudos), Miguel de Molina Papers, Biblioteca Nacional de España, Madrid, Spain (hereafter Molina Papers / BNE).

14. Letter dated September 8, 1950, folder 1.2, Molina Papers / BNE.

15. Letter dated December 18, 1951, folder 1.6, Molina Papers / BNE.

16. Letter dated September 16; and letter dated September 18, 1950, folder 1.2, Molina Papers / BNE.

17. Letter dated December 21, 1951, folder 1.5; letter dated January 24, 1952, folder 1.10; letter dated October 27, 1950, folder 1.2, Molina Papers / BNE.

18. Letter dated December 15, 1951, folder 1.5, Molina Papers / BNE.

19. Letter, n.d., folder 1.7, Molina Papers / BNE.

20. Letter dated December 23, 1951, folder 1.5, Molina Papers / BNE.

21. Letter dated July 5, 1952, folder 1.12, Molina Papers / BNE.

22. Letter dated July 1952, folder 1.12, Molina Papers / BNE.

23. Letter dated August 24, 1950, folder 1.4, Molina Papers / BNE.

24. Muñoz, *Cruising Utopia,* 5.

25. Letter dated December 17, 1951, folder 1.5, Molina Papers / BNE.

26. Mira Nouselles, *De Sodoma a Chueca,* 379–80.

27. Letter from Tobeyo / Guillermo Sánchez to Juan Gil-Albert on January 2, 1945. In Moreno and Simón, *Cartas a Juan Gil-Albert,* 211–12.

28. Letter from Tobeyo / Guillermo Sánchez to Juan Gil-Albert on July 2, 1958. In Moreno and Simón, *Cartas a Juan Gil-Albert,* 213–16.

29. Gil-Albert, *Heraclés,* 63.

30. Gil-Albert, *Heraclés,* 47.

31. Gil-Albert, *Heraclés,* 47.

32. Gil-Albert, *Heraclés,* 49.

33. On the historical relationship between gay activists and negative views on pathology, see Kunzel, "Queer History," 315–19.

34. Gil-Albert, *Heraclés,* 69.

35. There, he sheltered the Uruguayan diplomat Alberto Nin Frías until the latter's death in 1937. Nin Frías is widely recognized in the Spanish-speaking world as a pioneering homosexual author. In *Homosexualismo Creador* (Creative Homosexuality), published in Madrid in 1933, he articulated the thesis that homosexuality is associated with creative genius. When his fame became a burden, migrating from Europe to a rural town in South America was a valve of escape for Nin Frías, and transatlantic networks provided him with the means to do so.

36. Badanelli, *El derecho penal,* 121.

37. Badanelli, *El derecho penal,* 123–27.

38. Badanelli, *El derecho penal*, 150–51.

39. "Report on depositions copied from file 1/1955," file 2/1955, box 30, JEVMB-AHPB.

40. Ruling issued on April 28, 1955, file 2/1955.

41. Report from probation officer issued on December 24, 1955, file 2/1955.

42. Diego Trerotola, "El affaire Correas," *Soy*, April 13, 2012.

43. Correas, "La narración," 156.

44. Correas, "La narración," 156.

45. Correas, "La narración," 158.

46. Correas, "La narración," 159–61.

47. Correas, "La narración," 166.

48. Surghi, "En busca," 291–307. For more on Correas's work and its significance for the history of sexuality and literature in Argentina, see Fraguas and Muslip, *Decirlo todo*.

49. In his later works (like *Los reportajes de Félix Chaneton*), Correas also explored his relationships with and desire toward maricas/locas.

50. Peralta, "Ediciones Tirso," 192–95; Peralta, *La ciudad amoral*, 33–34.

51. *Du Vésuve a L'Etna* and *Le Prince des Neiges* were fully authorized; censors recommended suppressions in the cases of *Les ambassades, Les fin des ambassades, L'Oracle,* and *La mort d'une mère*; and *Jeunes proies, Les amitiés particulières, Le spectateur nocturne, L'exile de Capri, Les amours singulières, Mademoiselle de Murville, Les clés de Saint Pierre,* and *Chevaliers de Malte* were censored. File 1680/1963, initiated on March 26, 1963, box 21/14468, Archivo General de la Administración, Alcalá de Henares, Spain.

52. Italics added. Report by a censor (illegible signature) on April 30, 1963, file 1680/1963.

53. Report by Miguel de la Pinta Llorente on May 9, 1963, file 1680/1963.

54. "LEY DE 15 DE JULIO DE 1954."

55. Report by Aguirre on April 19, 1963, file 1680/1963.

56. Ramón Cadenas Cornejo, interview by the author on May 12, 2018, Torremolinos, Spain.

57. Maura Ocampo, *Diccionario*, 374–75; Luciana Sica, "Addio a Cóccioli scrittore omosessuale in cerca di Dio," *la Repubblica*, August 7, 2003; Johnson, "Carlo Cóccioli Collection."

58. Emili Boïls i Coniller, Skype interview by the author on August 4, 2018.

59. Boïls i Coniller, interview by the author.

60. As to the events that led up to his arrest, according to the story that the student told the authorities, feeling tired, he had found that the doors of a house were open and decided to spend the night there. The homeowner declared that when he arrived at home and saw the sleeping student, he decided to let him stay because he did not look "suspicious" (*sospechoso*). But then, in the middle of the night, the student tried to touch his host's genitals. The latter called him a "maricón" and reported him to the authorities. Report by the Guardia Civil signed on November 20, 1968, file 906/1968, box 3284, JEVMB-ACJCJB.

61. Clinical file 7132, Hospital Frenopático, Arxiu Municipal del Districte de les Corts, Barcelona.

62. "Historia clínica," clinical file 7132.

63. Italics added. "Manifiesta que no es a su interpretación del significado invertido, sino que se considera y reconoce ser homosexual." Defendant's deposition in front of the court of first instance on November 28, 1968, file 906/1968.

64. Pellegrini, *Asfalto*, 84–88.

65. Brant, "Homosexual Desire," 120.

66. Peralta, *La ciudad amoral*, 34.

67. Pellegrini, *Asfalto*, 14.

68. Pellegrini, *Asfalto*, 84.

69. Pellegrini, *Asfalto*, 93.

70. Pellegrini, *Asfalto*, 88–89.

71. Pellegrini, *Asfalto*, 130–46.

72. Pellegrini, *Asfalto*, 175–76.

73. May 10, 1967, folios 2–5, Legajo R. (referencia) 14.603, Archivo de la Dirección de Inteligencia de la Policía de la Provincia de Buenos Aires (hereafter DIPBA), La Plata, Argentina.

74. Statement on October 19, 1965, Legajo R. (referencia) 14.603, DIPBA.

75. Martí, *Versos Sencillos*, 105.

76. Molloy, "Politics of Posing," 156.

77. García Lorca, *Ode to Walt Whitman*.

78. Mabrey, "Mapping Homoerotic Feelings," 83–84.

79. Moix, *El cine*, 141.

80. In the case of Moix and many other gay men, bodybuilding magazines complemented identification with erotic projection, as they could rejoice in the contemplation of images of muscular male bodies, which were safely marketed under the guise of athletic training. As Alberto Mira studies, while initially Moix associated his eroticization of bodybuilding models with "the crude burden of desire," he gradually realized that only "sexual surrender" overcomes the boundaries to the total connection that "the spirit demands." Moix, *El beso*, 88, 155. Cited in Mira Nouselles, *De Sodoma a Chueca*, 341–42.

81. Moix, *El beso*, 80.

82. Moix, *El cine*, 154. Moix recalls his sexual awakening to the muscles of Saint Sebastian crossed by arrows in the 1949 film *Fabiola*. For him, this experience was "more exhilarating than laughing. [It] replaced the direct feeling of the flesh and can only be explained by looking at the strangest regions of the mind." Moix, *El cine*, 158.

83. "Alfredo Alaria, una figura polifacética," *La Nación*, August 28, 1999.

84. Molina, *Botín de guerra*, 241.

85. Peralta, "De eso no se hablaba."

86. Mira Nouselles, *De Sodoma a Chueca*, 350.

87. Delgado, *Diferente*.

88. Letter from Juan Gil-Albert to Salvador Moreno on August 15, 1966. In Gil-Albert, *Cartas a un amigo*, 55.

89. Delgado, *Diferente*.

90. Melero, "'El paseo,'" 155.

3. Exotic Lubrications

Epigraph: "Informative note" submitted by the police department, n.d., file 10/1960, box 8937, JEVMM-AHPS.

1. By contrast, Matt Houlbrook argues that postwar economic prosperity facilitated the *heterosexualization* of masculinity in the metropolis of the Global North, as working-class men with disposable income were able to socialize with women in public commercial spaces, aiming for the societal ideal of companionate love and detaching themselves from transactional sex with queers. Houlbrook, *Queer London*, 190–94.

2. Sinfield, *On Sexuality*, 1–2.

3. Romero, *History of Argentina*, 141–62.

4. Romero describes it as calling on workers "to abandon their hostile attitude and to join and share in the benefits of an economic development driven by foreign capital, albeit in an unspecified future." Romero, *History of Argentina*, 140.

5. Guillermo Saccomanno, "6 intentos de escribir sobre Oscar Masotta," *Página/12*, January 10, 2010.

6. Perlongher, *La prostitución masculina*, 9.

7. Perlongher, *La prostitución masculina*, 12.

8. Perlongher, *La prostitución masculina*, 13; Fry, *Para inglês ver*, 87–115.

9. Insausti and Fernández, "De chongos y mayates," 133–56.

10. Insausti, "Ni explotación ni trabajo," 44, 48.

11. Steele, introduction to *Queer History*, 45.

12. Manzano, *Age of Youth*, 89–90.

13. Jamandreu, *La cabeza*, 106.

14. Jamandreu, *La cabeza*, 107.

15. Jamandreu, *La cabeza*, 110.

16. Ernesto Schoo, "Aquellos jóvenes iracundos," *La Nación*, November 22, 2008; Marcos Ordóñez "Jóvenes airados: El vendaval de los cincuenta," *El País*, May 2, 2016; Álvaro Cortina, "El legado de los jóvenes airados," *El Mundo*, December 9, 2008.

17. Bazán, *Historia de la homosexualidad*, 384.

18. On the homosexual cartography of Buenos Aires, see Fernández, "Sociabilidad homoerótica," 35; and Simonetto, "Fronteras del deseo," n.p.

19. Becher, *Tiro de Gracia*.

20. Report on the psychological exam signed on February 18, 1964, file 39023, MPAAB.

21. Report by the Classification Institute in February 1964, file 39023.

22. Report submitted in March 1964, file 39289, MPAAB.

23. Report on August 29, 1967; "Antecedentes individuales," file 39289.

24. "Antecedentes individuales," file 39289.

25. Report submitted in March 1964, file 39289.

26. Report on August 29, 1967, file 39289.

27. Prison report on October 16, 1969, file 39289.

28. Rosón, "'No estoy sola,'" 143–77.

29. Fernández-Galeano and Peralta, "Los papeles de Peter."

30. Sigel, *People's Porn*, 75–78.

31. Waugh, *Hard to Imagine*, 217. James N. Green documents this phenomenon in Brazilian cities as well, where these magazines provided the most accessible images of seminude male bodies between the 1940s and 1960s. Green, *Beyond Carnival*, 159–62.

32. Peralta, "Del efebo al chongo."

33. These jeans were an essential component of chongos' performance of rough masculinity, as philosopher Juan José Sebreli points out. Sebreli, *Escritos*.

34. Houlbrook, "Soldier Heroes," 353.

35. Dyer, *Only Entertainment*, 128–29.

36. Antonio Sabater Tomás sentenced him to a year of "internment" (which he served in the labor camp of Nanclares de la Oca), two years of exile, and two years on parole. Ruling by Antonio Sabater Tomás on May 28, 1965, file 155/1965, JEVMB-ACJCJB.

37. Report submitted on 3 January 1967, file 4/1967, JEVMB-ACJCJB.

38. Waugh, *Hard to Imagine*, 158.

39. Antonio Sabater Tomás sentenced him to a maximum penalty of two years of internment (which he served in the labor camp of Nanclares de la Oca), two years of exile, and two years on parole. Ruling by Antonio Sabater Tomás issued on January 26, 1966, file 800/1965, JEVMB-ACJCJB.

40. Sabater Tomás, *Juventud inadaptada*, 18–19.

41. Sabater Tomás, *Juventud inadaptada*, 64.

42. Cleminson, "Act of 'Emotional Rescue,'" 157.

43. Cleminson, "Act of 'Emotional Rescue,'" 158–59.

44. Cleminson, "Act of 'Emotional Rescue,'" 160, 163.

45. Chamouleau, *Tiran al maricón*, 164–78.

46. According to the defendant, although he had sex with many patrons, he had only charged a fee to a straight couple of "viciosos" who wanted to have a threesome. File 258/1968, JEVMB-ACJCJB.

47. Pack, *Tourism and Dictatorship*, 83–84.

48. Benadusi, *Enemy of the New Man*, 153.

49. Lacaba Gutiérrez, "Sitges," 111–24; Ramón Cadenas Cornejo, interview by the author on May 12, 2018, Torremolinos, Spain.

50. Pack, *Tourism and Dictatorship*, 144–45.

51. Serafín Fernández Rodríguez, email message to the author, June 29, 2015.

52. See Fernández-Galeano, "Is He a 'Social Danger'?," 7–11.

53. Ramón Cadenas Cornejo, interview by the author on May 12, 2018, Torremolinos, Spain.

54. Defendant's deposition in front of the judge on May 2, 1963, file 14/1960, box 8937, JEVMM-AHPS.

55. Police report submitted on January 28, 1960, file 14/1960. There is also evidence of a historic-themed gay aristocratic party in which the agreed-upon dress was a Roman tunic and makeup. See file 126/1965, box 10936, JEVMS-AHPS.

56. Defendant's deposition in front of the Guardia Civil on June 30, 1958, file 347/1958, JEVMB-ACJCJB.

57. Defense plea, file 346/1958, JEVMB-ACJCJB.

58. Ruling issued on December 9, 1958, file 346/1958.

59. File 93/1963, box 8935, JEVMM-AHPS.

60. Defendant's deposition in front of the judge on December 9, 1963, file 93/1963.

61. Defendant's deposition in front of the judge on December 17, 1963, file 94/1963, box 8935, JEVMM-AHPS.

62. Defendant's deposition at the police station on June 21, 1964, file 17/1964, box 30, JEVMAC-AHPLP.

63. Ruling on September 18, 1964, file 17/1964; ruling on October 14, 1964, file 18/1964; ruling on October 14, 1964, file 19/1964, box 30, JEVMAC-AHPLP.

64. Police report submitted on October 7, 1965, file 89/1965, box 8892, JEVMM-AHPS.

65. Defendant's deposition in front of the judge on October 9, 1965, file 89/1965. In fact, Norberto handed the photographs over to the court, and they were shown to Carlos in a face-to-face deposition during which Carlos agreed they were not really pornographic but suggested there might be other photographs. Face-to-face deposition on October 13, 1965, file 89/1965.

66. Defense plea presented on November 11, 1965, file 89/1965.

67. Sabater Tomás, *Peligrosidad social*, n.p.

68. Melero, "Queering Archives."

69. Melero, "Un día más."

70. Serafín Fernández Rodríguez, interview by the author on March 19, 2012.

71. These dynamics occasionally had dramatic consequences for gay men who wanted to seduce masculine men by exhibiting a purchasing power that they did not have. In 1968, for instance, an extended network of homosexual men was exposed in Madrid after a young student committed suicide. Allegedly he had previously robbed one of his friends—in addition to using his tuition money and pawning all his personal belonging—to treat an ex-lover and their common friends to nights of partying in clubs, restaurants, and hotels, cruising Madrid in a Dodge Dart with a chauffeur. However, his ex-lover insisted that their affair was over as he was now in a relationship with a woman. Still, he accepted the generosity of the individual who eventually committed suicide. The latter might have made this decision because he was both unable to recover his beloved and aware that he had gone too far by stealing from his acquaintances. In brief, the role of cars and other high-value consumer goods in mediating relationships between these men created expectations for all participants that could not always be fulfilled. Files 506/1968, 507/1968, and 508/1968, Vagrancy Court of Madrid, Archivo General de la Administración, Alcalá de Henares, Spain.

4. People Don't Know What a Homosexual Is

1. Deposition on July 15, 1966, file 32947, folder 4719, box 233, Departamento Archivo Intermedio, Archivo General de la Nación Argentina, Buenos Aires, Argentina (hereafter DAI).

2. Italics added. Deposition CQ, file 335515.

3. Houlbrook, "Soldier Heroes," 354.

4. Houlbrook, "Soldier Heroes," 354.

5. In other words, representations of sexual desire inverted the passive/active binary insofar as the expectation was for "passive" homosexual males to act on their desires and seduce masculine men who would be responsive to these approaches just to release sexual tension. Pablo Ben and Omar Acha have pointed out the predominance of this paradigm during the first Peronist period. Acha and Ben, "Amorales," 217–60. James N. Green has collected testimonies about the relationships between "bichas" and "real men" in Brazil during the 1950s and about the entreaties of "allegedly 'passive' homosexuals" who actively pursued a sexual encounter with a "real" man, challenging "traditional gender roles." Green, *Beyond Carnival*, 149–68.

6. Insausti and Fernández, "De chongos y mayates," 134.

7. "Ley 14.029 / Código de Justicia Militar."

8. See, for instance, ruling number 1/1976 of the Supreme Court of the Armed Forces, issued on April 13, 1976, book of collected rulings from 1976, vol. 1, DAI.

9. Depositions by defendants on April 18, 1978, file 335124, folder 6002, box 32, DAI.

10. Canaday, *Straight State*, 12.

11. Beattie, "Conflicting Penile Codes," 80.

12. Cantilo, *¡Chau loco!*, 26.

13. For instance, in a case from 1967, a defendant acknowledged homosexual practices during his medical exam, but even so he was declared apt for service, file 33149, folder 4817, box 576, DAI.

14. Anonymized informant interviewed in 2017.

15. Anonymized informant interviewed in 2012.

16. *1978 International Guild Guide*, p. 124, folder Gay Guides, International Guild Guide (65–78), IGIC Ephemera. Gay Guides, box 3, New York Public Library Rare Books and Manuscripts Division.

17. Reports by the Counter-Intelligence Division of the Naval Base of Mar del Plata, October 17, 1979, file 335515, folder 6139, box 69, DAI.

18. Premat, "Popular Culture," 43, 50.

19. Houlbrook, "Soldier Heroes," 359, 361.

20. Canaday, *Straight State*, 58.

21. Report by the auditor issued on September 26, 1977, file 335451, folder 6113, box 60, DAI.

22. Deposition on May 8, 1981, file 335496, folder 6131, box 67, DAI.

23. Deposition by J.J.G., file 334743, folder 5866, box 8, DAI.

24. Deposition by J.J.G., file 334743.

25. Ruling issued on April 13, 1977, file 334743.

26. Deposition on December 3, 1964, file 38185, folder 5058, box 88, DAI.

27. Deposition on June 22, 1967, file 33238, folder 4856, box 345, DAI.

28. Deposition on December 6, 1973, file 33986, folder 5576, box 302, DAI.

29. Italics added. Deposition by J.D., file 334737, folder 5864, box 7, DAI.

30. Modarelli and Rapisardi, *Fiestas, baños y exilios*, 80–83.

31. Deposition by J.D., file 334737.

32. Deposition by J.D., file 334737.

33. Deposition by J.D., file 334737.

34. Insausti, "De maricas," 105–6.

35. Deposition by J.D., file 334737.

36. Houlbrook, "Soldier Heroes," 362.

37. Deposition on November 12, 1970, file 38517, folder 5196, box 14, DAI. For more on this case, see Fernández, "Nadie puede juzgar," 52–74.

38. Transcript of the first recorded conversation, file 38517.

39. Deposition on December 18, 1970, file 38517.

40. Defense plea on December 21, 1970, file 38517.

41. Ruling issued on December 21, 1970, file 38517.

42. Deposition on June 13, 1970, file 38459, folder 5171, box 19, DAI.

43. See, for instance, ruling number 84/1956 of the Supreme Court of the Armed Forces, issued on November 30, 1956, book of collected sentences from 1956; and file 38522, folder 5197, box 14, DAI.

44. Deposition on September 4, 1979, file 335301, folder 6062, box 46, DAI.

45. File 34302, folder 5712, box 501, DAI.

46. Canaday, *Straight State*, 192–97.

47. In this context, this term likely referenced the interlocutor's complexion and his hair color, and *not* a racial category.

48. Deposition on November 19, 1974, file 33986, folder 5576, box 302 (second body), DAI.

49. Depositions on April 21, 1977, file 335451, folder 6113, box 60, DAI.

50. Depositions on April 21, 1977, file 335451.

51. Deposition on June 30, 1978, file 335124, folder 6002, box 32, DAI.

52. Prosecutor plea on October 28, 1970, pp. 78–81, file 38522, folder 5197, box 14, DAI.

53. Prosecutor plea on February 13, 1973, pp. 351–56, file 34023, folder 5595, box 348, DAI.

54. Deposition by O.J.C., file 335317, folder 6068, box 48, DAI.

55. Inquiring deposition on December 6, 1968, file 38249, folder 5080, box 372, DAI.

56. Deposition on October 28, 1969, file 38318, folder 5113, box 324, DAI.

57. Medical report on August 12, 1966, file 32947, folder 4719, box 233, DAI.

58. Ruling on May 23, 1967, file 32947.

59. Deposition by medical lieutenant on April 6, 1970, file 34225, folder 5684, box 225, DAI.

60. Medical report on February 10, 1977, file 334743, folder 5866, box 8, DAI.

61. Medical reports on February 15 and 16, 1977, file 334743.

62. Psychological reports on October 11, 1979, file 335301, folder 6062, box 46. Likewise, in a court-martial in 1978, physicians reported based on a series of psychological tests and their personal observations that the individual who had performed the "passive" role in anal intercourse presented a "psychopathic homosexual personality," while the soldier who had penetrated him presented "a psychological structure within the normal limits." Medical reports issued on May 24, 1978, file 335124, folder 6002, box 32, DAI.

63. Psychological exams, file 334737, folder 5864, box 7, DAI.

64. Medical report issued on March 22, 1977, file 334775, folder 5875, box 10, DAI.

65. Ruling number 6/1978 of the Supreme Court of the Armed Forces, issued on February 23, 1978, book of collected sentences from 1978, vol. 1, DAI.

66. Miller, "Dredging and Projecting," 9–15.

67. Davids, Joelson, and McArthur, "Rorschach and TAT Indices," 161–72.

68. Trull and Prinstein, *Clinical Psychology*, 244.

69. Psychological exam of L.A.G., file 334739, folder 5865, box 7, DAI.

70. Physical exam of J.O.H., file 334739.

71. Psychological exam of J.O.H., file 334739.

72. Psychological exam of J.B.G., file 334737, folder 5864, box 7, DAI.

73. Psychological exam of J.E.D., file 334737.

74. Deposition on August 11, 1967, file 38297, folder 5095, box 344, DAI.

75. Deposition by R.R., file 38565, folder 5213, box 14, DAI.

76. Deposition on July 15, 1966, file 32947, folder 4719, box 233, DAI.

77. Forensic report issued on April 20, 1978, file 335317, folder 6068, box 48, DAI.

78. Deposition on January 13, 1978, file 335317.

79. Defense plea of L.M.F., file 334739, folder 5865, box 7, DAI.

80. Defense plea of J.E.D., file 334737.

81. Defense plea of J.E.D., file 334737.

82. Deposition by J.G., file 334737.

83. Defense plea of J.E.D., file 334737.

84. Foucault, *Vigilar y castigar*, 33–34.

85. Defense plea of J.E.D., file 334737.

86. Defense plea of L.A.G., file 334739.

87. See, for instance, defense plea of J.C.G., pp. 180–82, file 33149, folder 4817, box 576, DAI; and defense plea of N.F.D., file 335301, folder 6062, box 46, DAI.

88. See defense plea presented on May 12, 1981, file 335496, folder 6131, box 67, DAI.

89. Prosecution and defense pleas presented on April 30, 1980, file 335393, folder 6095, box 54, DAI.

90. See, for instance, file 34023, folder 5595, box 348, DAI; and file 38522, folder 5197, box 14, DAI.

91. Defense plea presented on October 28, 1970, file 38522, folder 5197, box 14, DAI.

92. Prosecutor plea on October 28, 1970, pp. 78–81, file 38522, folder 5197, box 14, DAI.

93. Police report issued on August 9, 1967, file 33149, folder 4817, box 576, DAI.

94. Prosecution plea presented on March 11, 1968, file 33149.

95. Deposition on July 17, 1967, file 33149.

96. Insausti, "De maricas," 85–105.

97. Defense plea presented on March 13, 1968, file 33149.

98. Defense plea, pp. 133–34, file 4357, folder 1032, Fuerza Aérea, DAI.

99. Deposition by G.A.R., file 4357.

100. Deposition on April 22, 1980, file 335393, folder 6095, box 54, DAI.

101. Guidotti-Hernández, *Archiving*, 2, 4.

102. Pilar Espitia, "Bodies to Reveal and/or Conceal: Baroque Dynamics of the Obscene (Heresy) and Modesty (Saintliness) in Feminine Bodies of the Peruvian Viceroyalty (17th Century)," accepted and forthcoming in the *Journal of Latin American Cultural Studies*, shared with the author.

5. Travesti and Marica Prisoners

1. Interview conducted in 2008 in Buenos Aires, Argentina, oral archive "Memoria Abierta," Buenos Aires, Argentina, June 14, 2012.

2. Malva and Calzón Flores, *Mi recordatorio*, 129–30.

3. Cleto, "Introduction," 2.

4. La Fountain-Stokes, *Translocas*, 2. La Fountain-Stokes's use of the neologism "translocas" aims at incorporating "the potentially dangerous edge of the word loca in Spanish," while also partaking of "the ser marica (being or becoming faggot) and of the inflexión marica (faggot inflection)" and travesti theory, all radical challenges "to the imperialist reach of the Anglo-American category of 'gay.'" La Fountain-Stokes, *Translocas*, 3–4.

5. La Fountain-Stokes, *Translocas*, 1.

6. "Me iba a cenar a un bar de la calle Escudillers, que era de maricones, cada vez que digo esa palabra me hace daño, antes no existía la palabra gay, ni tampoco transexual." Navarro Amo, *La infancia*, 69.

7. Malva and Calzón Flores, *Mi recordatorio*.

8. See the Library of Congress's catalog entry for *Mi recordatorio: Autobiografía de Malva*, accessed November 29, 2022, https://www.loc.gov/item/2011438794/.

9. "Todo ha cambiado en cuanto a la modalidad homosexual. Tengo que aceptar que mi condición de tal no se adecue al sentir y al actuar de hoy." Malva, *Mi recordatorio*, 146.

10. Malva and Calzón Flores, *Mi recordatorio*, 138.

11. Scott, *Weapons of the Weak*.

12. Malva and Calzón Flores, *Mi recordatorio*, 126.

13. Personal communication with the author on November 21, 2022.

14. Navarro Amo, *La infancia*, 14.

15. Iñaki Estella argues that clothes modified for the sake of feminization are "the basis of a transvestite reading" while "clothes also depended on the gestures that were developed with the artist's body in a public space." Estella, "Collective Scene," 505–7.

16. La Fountain-Stokes, "De sexilio(s)," 138–57.

17. Malva and Calzón Flores, *Mi recordatorio*, 135–36.

18. Simonetto and Butierrez, "Archival Riot," 10.

19. Huard, "La huida a la capital," 49–69.

20. For Iñaki Estella, "cabarets were a safe haven because they suspended the rules that applied outside" but "being hunted from bar to bar without the right clothes could, however, lead to jail." Estella, "Collective Scene," 512.

21. Cutuli and Insausti, "Cabarets, corsos y teatros," 23, 28.

22. Cutuli and Insausti, "Cabarets, corsos y teatros," 26. Simonetto and Butierrez point out continuities with today's memory-building praxis: "By retelling the past, focusing on certain figures and common experiences of joy (like the carnivals) or traumatic (such as State violence), these practices participate in building the emotional experience of the community." Simonetto and Butierrez, "Archival Riot," 8.

23. Personal communication with the author on November 17, 2022.

24. Cutuli and Insausti, "Cabarets, corsos y teatros," 22.

25. Álvarez, "Coccinelle"; Berzosa, "Discursos alternativos," 106–8; Cutuli and Insausti, "Cabarets, corsos y teatros," 29–30; Malva and Calzón Flores, *Mi recordatorio*, 123–24.

26. Tania Navarro relates how the sex workers of Barcelona's red-light district cared for her every time her family of origin expelled her from her home being a child. Navarro Amo, *La infancia*.

27. The most well-known literary portrayal of marica subjectivity in a prison context is Manuel Puig's novel *The Kiss of the Spider Woman* (1976). Molina, the marica protagonist of the novel, identifies with female movie stars who suffer for love in scenes full of glamour and narrates to his cellmate (a political prisoner named Vicente) the plot of made-up films.

28. Jamandreu, *La cabeza*, 20.

29. Jamandreu, *La cabeza*, 26.

30. Jamandreu, *La cabeza*, 43.

31. Jamandreu, *La cabeza*, 58–60.

32. Jamandreu, *La cabeza*, 85, 147–48.

33. Jamandreu, *La cabeza*, 71, 74–76.

34. Jamandreu, *La cabeza*, 87–91.

35. Jamandreu, *La cabeza*, 147.

36. Jamandreu, *La cabeza*, 89.

37. Jamandreu, *La cabeza*, 91–93.

38. Jamandreu, *La cabeza*, 98, 162.

39. Jamandreu, *La cabeza*, 97.

40. Jamandreu, *La cabeza*, 121, 134.

41. Jamandreu, *La cabeza*, 141.

42. Jamandreu, *La cabeza*, 141–42.

43. Jamandreu, *La cabeza*, 87–88, 148.

44. Jamandreu, *La cabeza*, 156–57.

45. Jamandreu, *La cabeza*, 158–59, 163.

46. Jamandreu, *La cabeza*, 110–12, 117, 124–28.

47. Jamandreu, *La cabeza*, 136.

48. Jamandreu, *La cabeza*, 143–46.

49. Jamandreu, *La cabeza*, 148, 195.

50. Jamandreu, *La cabeza*, 190–92, 197–99.

51. Jamandreu, *La cabeza*, 209.

52. Jamandreu, *La cabeza*, 212–13.

53. Steele, introduction to *Queer History*, 45–46.

54. Manzano, *Age of Youth*, 21–22.

55. Manzano, *Age of Youth*, 125.

56. Manzano, *Age of Youth*, 137–38.

57. Steele, introduction to *Queer History*, 45.

58. Opizzo, *Alteraciones sexuales*, 216.

59. "Sentencia"; "Semblanza," file 41838, MPAAB.

60. "Antecedentes familiares," file 41838.

61. "Semblanza," file 41838.

62. "Antecedentes individuales," file 41838.

63. "Semblanza," file 41838.

64. "Semblanza," file 41838.

65. Report issued in March 1966, file 41838.

66. Letter by the prisoner, file 41838.

67. Medical exam on November 4, 1969, file 38318, folder 5113, box 324, DAI.

68. "Relaciones sociales," file 48803, MPAAB.

69. "Sentencia," file 48803.

70. "Entrevista con la prima segunda del acusado," file 48803.

71. "Declaración de empleadores," file 48803.

72. "Síntesis diagnostica," file 48803.

73. "Vida sexual," file 48836, MPAAB.

74. "Información Social," file 48836.

75. "Información Social," file 48836.

76. "Información Social," file 48836.

77. Test administered by the Applied Psychology Department, file 48836.

78. Report by the Applied Psychology Department, file 48836.

79. "Síntesis diagnostica," file 48836.

80. Juan Carlos Romi, interview by the author. Buenos Aires, March 6, 2017.

81. Romi, *Investigación clínica*.

82. Romi, "Las Perturbaciones sexuales."

83. Romi, "La homosexualidad," 253.

84. Romi, "La homosexualidad," 254.

85. Romi, "La homosexualidad," 255.

86. Romi, "Delimitación conceptual," 173.

87. Romi, interview by the author.

88. Chamorro Gundin, *Resultados obtenidos*, 18.

89. Dirección General de Instituciones Penitenciarias, *Memoria*, 5–7.

90. Jesús Conde, "La cárcel de homosexuales de Badajoz: Cuando el franquismo castigaba a los que amaban libres," *eldiario.es*, July 3, 2016.

91. Chamorro Gundin, *Resultados obtenidos*, 18.

92. Chamorro Gundin, *Resultados obtenidos*, 10.

93. Chamorro Gundin, *Resultados obtenidos*, 21.

94. Chamorro Gundin, *Resultados obtenidos*, 12–13.

95. Chamorro Gundin, *Resultados obtenidos*, 14–18.

96. Sabater Tomás, *Peligrosidad social*, n.p.

97. Sabater Tomás, *Peligrosidad social*, n.p.

98. Iñaki Berazaluce, "'Grises' contra 'hippies': Ejercicio de represión simulado de la policía franquista (1969)," *Público*, April 10, 2019.

99. Police report on May 30, 1968, file 384/1968, Legajo 1535, Vagrancy Court of Madrid, Archivo General de la Administración, Alcalá de Henares, Spain.

100. Police report on June 3, 1968, file 384/1968.

101. Deposition by the defendant, May 1, 1968, file 384/1968.

102. Letter dated February 24, 1967, file 384/1968.

103. From prison, he addressed another letter to his lawyer complaining that prison officers treated him as a homosexual and forbade him to write to his fiancée, even though he was a "normal person."

104. Defense plea issued on July 8, 1968, file 384/1968.

105. Ruling issued on July 29, 1968, file 384/1968.

106. Deposition on July 28, 1967, file 447/1967, Legajo 5033, Vagrancy Court of Madrid, Archivo General de la Administración, Alcalá de Henares, Spain.

107. Deposition on October 21, 1967, file 447/1967.

108. Defense plea on October 31, 1967, file 447/1967.

109. Sontag, "Notes on 'Camp,'" 55.

110. Cited in Ramírez Pérez, "Franquismo y disidencia sexual," 158.

111. Ruling on November 3, 1967, file 447/1967.

112. Prosecutor's statement on March 11, 1975, file 164/1975, Juzgado Especial de Peligrosidad y Rehabilitación Social de València, Arxiu Històric de la Comunitat Valenciana, València, Spain (hereafter AHCV).

113. Defense attorney's statement on June 17, 1975, file 164/1975.

114. Ruling on June 20, 1975, file 164/1975.

115. Serafín Fernández Rodríguez, interview by the author on April 17, 2020.

116. File 789/1967, JEVMB-ACJCJB.

117. Halperin, *How to Be Gay*, 407–8.

118. Defense attorney's statement on September 5, 1975, file 610/1975, Juzgado Especial de Peligrosidad y Rehabilitación Social de València, AHCV.

119. File 25/1972, Juzgado Especial de Peligrosidad y Rehabilitación Social de Castellón, AHCV.

120. Report by the treatment commission on August 26, 1972, file 1125/1966, JEVMB-ACJCJB.

121. Second prison report on September 30, 1972; third prison report on October 28, 1972, file 1125/1966.

122. Guardia Civil report, file 556/1968, box 2005, JEVMB-ACJCJB.

123. File 556/1968.

124. File 771/1961, JEVMB-ACJCJB.

125. Halperin, *How to Be Gay*, 205.

126. Deposition, n.d., file 126/1965, Signatura 10936, JEVMS-AHPS.

127. Deposition, n.d., file 126/1965.

128. Police report on March 9, 1968, file 221/1968, JEVMB-ACJCJB.

129. Guardia Civil report on March 14, 1968, file 157/1968, JEVMB-ACJCJB.

130. Italics added. Police report on February 20, 1968, file 157/1968.

131. Other prisoners strategically showed willingness to mend their ways just to be released from prison. One defendant nicknamed Chelo and Juanita Reina (like a famous Spanish actress) was arrested in 1976 in the region of València, accused with no specific evidence of trying to seduce young men. According to official reports, Juanita usually wore women's wigs and spent more money that she made. However, prison wardens informed the court that Juanita seemed "rehabilitated" but qualified this statement by pointing out that this rehabilitation was due to awareness of the penalties rather than to an internalized belief. File 423/1976, Juzgado Especial de Peligrosidad y Rehabilitación Social de València, AHCV.

132. File 846/1965, JEVMB-ACJCJB.

133. Police interrogation on November 29, 1965, file 846/1965; ruling on June 3, 1966, file 912/1965, JEVMB-ACJCJB.

134. Prison report on November 30, 1972, file 912/1965.

135. Prison report on December 3, 1972, file 912/1965.

136. Deposition on July 24, 1972, file 717/1971, Juzgado de Peligrosidad y Rehabilitación Social de Barcelona, ACJCJB.

137. Letter from the defendant on April 27, 1968, file 363/1968, JEVMB-ACJCJB.

138. Letter from the defendant's mother on March 11, 1971, file 363/1968.

139. File 674/1966, legajo 2275, AGA.

140. Elche Police's report on September 25, 1976, file 497/1976, Juzgado Especial de Peligrosidad y Rehabilitación Social de València, AHCV.

141. Deposition in Elche on September 25, 1976, file 497/1976.

142. Preciado, "The Ocaña We Deserve," 3.

143. Deposition in Elche on September 25, 1976, file 497/1976.

144. Elche Police's report on October 11, 1976, file 497/1976.

145. Defense lawyer's statement on January 19, 1977, file 497/1976.

146. Forensic report on February 15, 1977, file 497/1976.

147. Ruling on April 15, 1977; report on September 10, 1977, by the Elche city government, file 497/1976.

148. File 833/1977, Juzgado de Peligrosidad y Rehabilitación Social de Madrid, included in file 497/1976.

149. Declaration on July 4, 1975, file 861/1966, Juzgado de Peligrosidad y Rehabilitación Social de Barcelona, ACJCJB.

150. Defense attorney's statement on July 198, 1975, file 861/1966.

151. Police report on November 12, 1975, file 465/1975, Juzgado de Peligrosidad y Rehabilitación Social de Barcelona, ACJCJB.

152. Declaration on November 12, 1975, file 465/1975.

153. Declaration on December 21, 1977, file 511/1977, Juzgado de Peligrosidad y Rehabilitación Social de Bilbao, included in file 465/1975.

154. Declaration on June 18, 1976, file 465/1975.

155. On this subculture, see Fernández-Galeano, "'El Todo Poderoso,'" 334–35.

156. On the importance of clothing for Argentine travesti activism, see Álvarez, "'Ahora empezamos.'"

157. At the same time, La Fountain-Stokes points out that Puerto Rican translocas are "political except when [they] are not," providing a cautionary note against over-generalizing models that flatten subjects' varied perceptions of the political implications of their performance. La Fountain-Stokes, *Translocas*, 1.

158. Estella, "Collective Scene," 508.

159. La Fountain-Stokes, *Translocas*, 3.

6. From Inverse to Converging Paths

1. Luis Troitiño interview with Juan Queiroz, selections published with the title "La historia de nuestra historia," *Moléculas Malucas*, April 2020, https://www.moleculasmalucas.com/post/la-historia-de-nuestra-historia.

2. Fernández-Galeano and Queiroz, "Agosto de 1971."

3. Héctor Anabitarte Rivas, interview by the author on June 25, 2012, Madrid, Spain; Anabitarte Rivas, *Nadie olvida nada*, 30–34.

4. Emili Boïls i Coniller, Skype interview by the author on August 4, 2018.

5. Cosse, "Everyday Life," n.p.

6. Romero, *History of Argentina*, 180–91.

7. Cosse, "Everyday Life," n.p.

8. Romero, *History of Argentina*, 173–80.

9. Anabitarte Rivas, interview by the author.

10. Ben and Insausti, "Dictatorial Rule," 300–309.

11. Fernández-Galeano and Queiroz, "Agosto de 1971."

12. Marlene Wayar, "Escribir la propia historia," *Revista Cabal*, accessed on April 25, 2023, https://www.revistacabal.coop/actualidad/marlene-wayar-escribir-la-propia-historia.

13. Letter to the Mattachine Society of Washington DC, August 12, 1963, folder 7, box 82, Kameny Papers, Library of Congress, Washington DC.

14. Letter from Franklin E. Kameny, September 11, 1963, folder 7, box 82, Kameny Papers.

15. Santiago proposed, as he had already done in 1963, to take on the role of the Mattachine Society's international representative in Argentina, emphasizing that given his professional position and responsibilities, his discretion would be guaranteed. This letter had a more institutional tone than his 1963 letter, but Santiago's views still manage to come through: "Here as always, 'our' point of view is wrong; however, things begin to change and I hope someday, perhaps soon, we can have the same freedom you have to be ourselves, with our particular sentimental point of view." Letter to the Mattachine Society of Washington DC, October 1968, folder 7, box 82, Kameny Papers. This condescending view on Argentine society—as well as Santiago's adoption of an English-sounding pseudonym—fits with the entendidos' veneration of the Anglo-Saxon world. John W. Baldwin's response as the Mattachine secretary was discouraging. He explained to Santiago that his organization intended to maintain its independent approach to homophile politics, and for this reason they could not appoint him as their representative. Baldwin acknowledged that they maintained only a limited communication with the organizations of other countries, which did not seem to be among their priorities. Letter from John W. Baldwin, November 13, 1968, folder 7, box 82, Kameny Papers.

16. Romero, *History of Argentina*, 180–91.

17. Simonetto, *Entre la injuria y la revolución*, 30.

18. "Informe sobre Homosexuales," *Confirmado*, March 10, 1971.

19. Anabitarte Rivas, interview by the author.

20. Fernández-Galeano and Queiroz, "Agosto de 1971."

21. Juan José Sebreli, interview by the author on June 2, 2012, Buenos Aires, Argentina.

22. Sebreli, *El tiempo*, 241.

23. Blas Matamoro, interview by the author on June 24, 2012, Madrid, Spain.

24. Anabitarte Rivas, interview by the author.

25. Anabitarte Rivas, interview by the author.

26. Sara Torres, interview by the author on June 7, 2012, Buenos Aires, Argentina.

27. Matamoro, interview by the author; Sebreli, interview by the author.

28. Rapisardi, "Escritura y lucha," 982.

29. "Homosexualidad masculina y machismo," *Homosexuales* (July 1973), n.p., box 7, folder 3, Robert Roth Papers, Division of Rare and Manuscript Collections, Cornell University Library, Ithaca, NY (hereafter Roth Papers).

30. "Homosexualidad masculina y machismo."

31. Rapisardi, "Escritura y lucha," 983; Theumer, "Políticas homosexuales," 109–26; Vespucci, "Explorando," 187–90; Marcelo Benítez, interview by the author on June 13, 2012, Buenos Aires, Argentina.

32. Perlongher, *Prosa plebeya*, 81–82.

33. Benítez, interview by the author.

34. Matamoro, interview by the author.

35. Sebreli, interview by the author.

36. Benítez, interview by the author.

37. Sebreli, interview by the author.

38. Benítez, interview by the author.

39. Carlos Oller, email communication with the author on January 4, 2018.

40. Sebreli, interview by the author.

41. Fernández-Galeano and Queiroz, "Agosto de 1971."

42. Romero, *History of Argentina*, 196–97.

43. Simonetto, *Entre la injuria y la revolución*, 46–48.

44. Matamoro, interview by the author; Sebreli, interview by the author.

45. For more on the Latin American left's take on homosexuality in these decades, see Green, "'Who Is the Macho?,'" 450.

46. Rubén Tosoni, interview by the author on July 6, 2016, Barcelona, Spain.

47. Duberman, *Cures*, 100.

48. Rafael Freda, for instance, was a member of a Trotskyist party. The party's leaders tried to set him up with a female comrade in the mid-1970s to counteract his homosexual tendencies. Around the same time, a psychotherapist diagnosed him as suffering from "anxious neurosis." Over the course of two and a half years, Rafael would eventually convince his psychotherapist that there was nothing pathologically the matter with him. Rafael Freda, interview by the author on March 12, 2017, Buenos Aires, Argentina.

49. Daniel Molina, email communication with the author on May 9, 2017; Daniel Molina, "Empecé a morir en las cárceles de la dictadura," *Clarín*, March 3, 2012, https://perma.cc/B6GQ-4CE4.

50. Molina, "Empecé a morir."

51. Romero, *History of Argentina*, 203–14.

52. "Acabar con los homosexuales," *El Caudillo*, February 12, 1975, box 6, folder 16, Roth Papers.

53. Manzano, *Age of Youth*, 223.

54. Malva and Calzón Flores, *Mi recordatorio*, 130. The press also associated the "growing, serious" issue of homosexuality with "unisex clothing," as in a 1977 article that argued that homosexuality was a cultural phenomenon with severe implications for public health because gay men's "incredible promiscuity" was related to the increasing rate of sexually transmitted diseases. "No se nace homosexual," press clipping from January 1977, Marcelo Manuel Benítez Papers, folder 7, Centro de Documentación e Investigación de la Cultura de Izquierdas (CeDInCI), Buenos Aires, Argentina.

55. For more on the functioning of international advocacy networks, see Keck and Sikkink, *Activists beyond Borders*, 2.

56. Letter from the FLH to Robert Roth, Buenos Aires, March 18, 1974, box 6, folder 16, Roth Papers.

57. Letter from the FLH to Robert Roth, Buenos Aires, May 6, 1974, box 6, folder 17, Roth Papers; letter from the FLH to Robert Roth, Buenos Aires, June 6, 1974, box 6, folder 16, Roth Papers.

58. Letter from Héctor Anabitarte to Robert Roth, Buenos Aires, February 23, 1976, box 6, folder 16, Roth Papers.

59. Keck and Sikkink, *Activists beyond Borders*, 6–7.

60. Letter from Carlos Oller to the Mattachine Society. Buenos Aires, September 29, 1975, box 6, folder 16, Roth Papers.

61. Carlos Oller, interview by the author on March 4, 2017. Buenos Aires, Argentina.

62. Insausti, "De maricas," 165–70; Green, *Beyond Carnival*, 268–70.

63. Oller, email communication with the author.

64. Oller, email communication with the author.

65. Letter from Carlos Oller to the Mattachine Society. Buenos Aires, September 29, 1975, box 6, folder 16, Roth Papers; letter from Robert Roth to Carlos Oller, November 23, 1975, box 6, folder 16, Roth Papers.

66. Oller, interview by the author; Oller, email communication with the author.

67. Romero, *History of Argentina*, 215–20.

68. Letter from the FLH to Robert Roth, Buenos Aires, March 24, 1976, box 6, folder 16, Roth Papers.

69. Letter from the FLH to Robert Roth, Buenos Aires, April 15, 1976, box 6, folder 16, Roth Papers.

70. FLH de la Argentina, "Boletín de emergencia" (March 1976), box 6, folder 16, Roth Papers.

71. Vespucci, "Explorando," 174–97.

72. Insausti, "Los cuatrocientos homosexuales desaparecidos," 63–82; Benítez, interview by the author.

73. Casanova and Gil Andrés, *Twentieth-Century Spain*, 265–66.

74. Boïls i Coniller, interview by the author.

75. Boïls i Coniller, interview by the author.

76. López Clavel, "El rosa," 119.

77. Boïls i Coniller, interview by the author.

78. Letter from the Fraternidad Cristiana de la Amistad to Robert Roth, September 1979, València, box 5, folder 20, Roth Papers.

79. Letter from the Fraternidad Cristiana de la Amistad to Robert Roth, September 1979, València.

80. Cowan, "'Passive Homosexual Element,'" 198.

81. Monferrer Tomás, "La construcción de la protesta," 171–204.

82. Casanova and Gil Andrés, *Twentieth-Century Spain*, 246–47.

83. Martínez, *Lo nuestro*, 88–89.

84. Armand de Fluvià, interview by the author on July 4, 2016, Barcelona, Spain.

85. Huard, *Los antisociales*, 313; Jackson, *Living in Arcadia*, 287n52.

86. Martínez, *Lo nuestro*, 89–94.

87. Huard, *Los antisociales*, 314–19.

88. Fluvià, interview by the author.

89. Monferrer Tomás, "La construcción de la protesta," 194.

90. Fluvià, interview by the author.

91. Fernández-Galeano, "'El Todo Poderoso.'"

92. Letter to the bishops signed on February 20, 1970, folder 31, Armand de Fluvià Papers (415), Arxiu Nacional de Catalunya (hereafter ANC).

93. Letter to the bishops signed on February 20, 1970.

94. Fernando Herrero Tejedor "Enmienda Numero 8 al Proyecto de Ley de Peligrosidad Social," 1–2, presented on January 24, 1970, to the Justice Committee, Archivo del Congreso de los Diputados, Madrid, Spain.

95. "Ley 16/1970 sobre peligrosidad y rehabilitación social," 12551–57.

96. "Decreto 1144/1971," 8895–903.

97. File 733/1969, box 2915, JEVMB-ACJCJB.

98. File 778/1972, box 4134, Juzgado de Peligrosidad y Rehabilitación Social de Barcelona, ACJCJB.

99. Monferrer Tomás, "La construcción de la protesta," 185.

100. Note by Armand de Fluvià published in *Arcadie* in 1972, folder 53, Armand de Fluvià Papers (415), ANC.

101. Huard, *Los antisociales*, 319–20.

102. Mira Nouselles, De *Sodoma a Chueca*, 476–78.

103. Armand de Fluvià, "Los movimientos de liberación homosexual en el estado español" (1977), folder 4, Armand de Fluvià Papers (415), ANC.

104. Martínez, *Lo nuestro*, 91–92.

105. Huard, *Los antisociales*, 321–22.

106. Interview between Armand de Fluvià and Amanda Klein, in Fluvià, *El moviment gai*, 104–5.

107. Fluvià, interview by the author.

108. Folder 42, Armand de Fluvià Papers (415), ANC; Fluvià, interview by the author.

109. Letter from Armand de Fluvià to Robert Roth on November 16, 1973, Barcelona, folder 20, box 5, Robert Roth Papers.

110. Fluvià, interview by the author.

111. "Gay liberation front manifesto" (London, 1971), English version and translation into Spanish, folder 33, Armand de Fluvià Papers (415), ANC.

112. Italics added. Gorria, "Las mariconas se rebelan," AGHOIS 17 (September–October 1973): 8, folder 26, box 9, Robert Roth Papers.

113. Gorria, "Las mariconas se rebelan."

114. "Mesa redonda sobre una tipología del homófilo español," roundtable on the typology of the Spanish homophile, held in January 1974, p. 2, folder 37, Armand de Fluvià Papers (415), ANC.

115. "Mesa redonda," 1.

116. "Mesa redonda," 4.

117. "Mesa redonda," 2.

118. Kunzel, "Queer History," 315–19.

119. "Mesa redonda," 4.

120. "Mesa redonda," 4.

121. "Mesa redonda," 5.

122. Ricardo Lorenzo Sanz and Héctor Anabitarte Rivas, "Homosexualidad y machismo: Análisis desde una perspectiva liberacionista," *Ajoblanco*, May 1979, 40–41.

123. On mariquitas' roles in entertainment shows, see Haller, "Homosexuality in Seville," 27–35.

124. Eduardo Haro Ibars, "Los mariquitas," *Triunfo*, December 22, 1979, 54.

125. Chamouleau, *Tiran al maricón*, 15–21.

126. Anabitarte Rivas, *Nadie olvida nada*, 39–40.

127. Anabitarte Rivas, interview by the author.

128. Anabitarte Rivas, *Nadie olvida nada*, 33–44.

129. This chapter is based on the methodologies of queer oral history, insofar as it pays particular attention to the texture of subjective accounts and historical actors' reinterpretations of the meaning of facts, instead of focusing exclusively on the factual basis of their testimonies. See Portelli, "Peculiarities," 96–107; Murphy, Pierce, and Ruiz, "What Makes," 1–24; and Boyd and Roque Ramírez, *Bodies of Evidence*.

130. On exile becoming an interruption in the normal flow of life, see Green, *Exile within Exiles*, 161.

131. Rubén Mettini, interview by the author on April 16, 2021.

132. This gap also explains the success that Oscar Masotta had in disseminating Lacan's work during his exile in Barcelona. Silvina Friera, "Oscar Masotta, el marxista de los happenings," *Página/12*, September 11, 2004.

133. Dante Bertini, interview by the author on May 23, 2018, Barcelona, Spain.

134. Albin Krebs, "Jacobo Timerman, 76, the Torture Victim Who Documented Argentina's Shame, Dies," *New York Times*, November 12, 1999.

135. Gabriela Cabezón Cámara, "La Pluma Alzada," *Página/12*, October 23, 2015.

136. Avellaneda, *Censura, autoritarismo y cultura*, 141.

137. Alejandro Modarelli, "Adiós al represor Menéndez: El cuchillo y la sangre," *Página/12*, March 2, 2018.

138. Matamoro, interview by the author.

139. Matamoro, interview by the author.

140. Sergio Pérez Álvarez, interview by the author in Buenos Aires, Argentina, on June 6, 2012.

141. Bertini, interview by the author.

142. Mettini, interview by the author.

143. Mettini Vilas, "Interiores gais," 163–70. Rubén's account aligns with Soledad Cutuli and Joaquín Insausti's work on historical spaces and practices of marica transgression. Cutuli and Insausti, "Cabarets, corsos y teatros," 19–39.

144. Mettini Vilas, "Interiores gais," 171–76.

145. Mettini Vilas, "Interiores gais," 176.

146. Mettini, interview by the author.

147. Pablo Stajnsznajder, interview by the author on April 22, 2021.

148. Stajnsznajder, interview by the author.

149. Stajnsznajder, interview by the author.

150. Tosoni, interview by the author.

151. Radcliff, *Modern Spain*, 191–94.

152. Radcliff, *Modern Spain*, 205–6.

153. Tosoni, interview by the author.

154. Fluvià, interview by the author.

155. Mérida Jiménez, *Transbarcelonas*, 112–14.

156. Bertini, interview by the author.

157. According to Mérida Jiménez, Ocaña's street performances related to an anarchist-inspired "critique of religious condemnations" and "bourgeois heteronormative institutions." See Mérida Jiménez, *Transbarcelonas*, 128–29, 148–51.

158. Martínez, *Lo nuestro*, 134–37.

159. Subrat, *Invertidos y rompepatrias*, 473–76.

160. Cited in Subrat, *Invertidos y rompepatrias*, 476.

161. Navarro Amo, interviews in May 2022.

162. Cited in Subrat, *Invertidos y rompepatrias*, 477–78.

163. Subrat, *Invertidos y rompepatrias*, 478.

164. Subrat, *Invertidos y rompepatrias*, 488.

165. Mérida Jiménez, *Transbarcelonas*, 149–50.

166. Chamouleau, *Tiran al maricón*, 141–62, 178–236.

167. Skype interview by the author (anonymous informant), July 21, 2017.

168. Pepe Ribas, "Julio de 1977: Jornadas Libertarias," *Kaosenlared*, July 31, 2017.

169. On rehabilitation therapies, see Huard, *Los invertidos*, 89–96.

170. Héctor Anabitarte Rivas and Ricardo Lorenzo Sanz, "Conversatorio con Gema Pérez-Sánchez," Modern Languages and Literature Department at the University of Miami, September 17, 2020.

171. Stajnsznajder, interview by the author.

172. Stajnsznajder, interview by the author.

173. Mettini, interview by the author.

174. Anabitarte Rivas, *Nadie olvida nada*, 37–38.

175. Fernández-Galeano and Insausti, "Archivos Digitales Queer."

176. Héctor Anabitarte Rivas, letter to Armand de Fluvià and Pablo Stajnsznajder, February 4, 1977, fondo Moviment Gai, Arxiu Nacional de Catalunya. On the correspondence between Anabitarte and Fluvià, see Fernández-Galeano and Pérez-Sánchez, "Pioneros de la fraternidad homosexual."

177. Fernández-Galeano and Insausti, "Archivos Digitales Queer."

178. Héctor Anabitarte Rivas, letter to Robert Roth, January 7, 1978, box 6, folder 16, Robert Roth Papers.

179. Héctor Anabitarte Rivas, letter to Robert Roth, May 18, 1978, box 6, folder 16, Robert Roth Papers.

180. Personal communication with Juan Queiroz on March 24, 2021.

181. "Gay in Argentina," *GaysWeek* 62 (May 1, 1978), consulted at Archivos Desviados.

182. This trope traverses, for instance, Edward Carpenter's *Maurice*; Christopher Isherwood's fascination with working-class young men; and Daniel Guérin's commitment to antifascist activism. Tamagne, *History of Homosexuality*, 85–88, 262–69.

183. This mentality is akin to Germán Garrido's notion of cosmopolitics: "The queer cosmopolitics that inform the works of Moreno, Copi and Perlongher are not set in motion by 'citizens of the world' or members of a select elite but, rather, by subjects who do not enjoy full citizenship in their own countries of origin and who develop transnational affective ties and political alliances." Garrido, "La Internacional Argentina," 3–4.

184. Armand de Fluvià, letter to Héctor Anabitarte Rivas, February 8, 1976, fondo Moviment Gai, Arxiu Nacional de Catalunya.

185. Fernández de Alba, *Sex, Drugs, and Fashion*, 42–68.

186. Anabitarte Rivas and Lorenzo Sanz, *Homosexualidad*, 15.

187. File 05399, May 19 1980, Signatura 73/07251, AGA.

188. "EHGAM ante la ofensiva de UCD," folder 33, box 4, Robert Roth Papers.

189. Ricardo Lorenzo Sanz and Héctor Anabitarte Rivas, "La tolerancia no incluye la homosexualidad," May 16, 1980, fondo Moviment Gai, Arxiu Nacional de Catalunya.

190. Anabitarte Rivas, *Nadie olvida nada*, 43–44.

191. Héctor Anabitarte Rivas and Ricardo Lorenzo Sanz, letter to Armand de Fluvià, June 10, 1980, fondo Moviment Gai, Arxiu Nacional de Catalunya.

192. Santos, *333 historias*, 306–7.

193. Green, *Exile within Exiles*, 163.

194. Green, *Exile within Exiles*, 165–67.

195. Since the 1980s, Argentine and Spanish LGBT organizations followed a parallel trajectory in the formulation and realization of their demands. Both adopted a human rights frame that associated legal and social homophobia with each country's historical experience living under dictatorial rule. Majoritarian LGBT groups considered that, to be able to affect public opinion and policies, the first step was to be legalized. On July 16, 1980, the Front d'Alliberament Gai de Catalunya was the first LGBT organization to be granted legal status by the Spanish government, after a lobbying campaign supported by left-wing parties, feminists, and civil society organizations. Vicent Canet, "Treinta años de la legalización de la primera asociación LGTB," *Diagonal*, January 13, 2011. The Comunidad Homosexual Argentina (CHA) initiated in 1987 the process to receive its legal status (*personería jurídica*), but the Argentine Supreme Court backed the government in its decision to deny the CHA's request. Then the CHA mobilized its international support network during president Memen's visit to the United States, pressuring and moving him to grant the *personería* request in 1992. During the legal campaign to pass egalitarian marriage in Argentina in 2010, Spanish activists shared the resources and strategies that they had used to lobby and work with the public and legislators to pass Spain's egalitarian marriage law in 2005. Friedman, "Constructing," 29–59.

196. On "incompatibility," see Lancaster, "Comment on Arguelles," 190; and Murray, "Family," 33–48. On "diffusion," see Fernández-Galeano, "Cartas desde Buenos Aires," 608–22; Brown, "'Con discriminación y represión,'" 119–38; and Murray and Arboleda, "Stigma, Transformation, and Relexification," 138–44.

197. See Chamouleau, *Tiran al maricón*; Insausti, "De maricas"; and Modarelli and Rapisardi, *Fiestas, baños y exilios*, among others.

198. For instance, Bazán's *Historia de la homosexualidad*; and Ugarte Pérez, *Una discriminación universal*.

199. See Encarnación, *Out in the Periphery*; and Martínez, *Lo nuestro*.

Conclusion

1. Following Chauncey, my intention is "to convey both the extent of antigay policing and the resiliency of so many people in the face of that policing." Chauncey, *Gay New York*, 17.

2. File 44/1966, Signatura 11793, Juzgado Especial de Vagos y Maleantes de Granada, Archivo Histórico Provincial de Málaga, Málaga, Spain.

3. On objectification, see Lancaster, *Life Is Hard*, 278. Ethnographic research in Latin America and the Mediterranean has challenged Western narratives about the emergence of homosexuality as an identity by focusing on the positionality of male power. It has traced the origins of a sexual system structured by the passive/active binary (feminine insertee and masculine inserter) to machismo, a Mediterranean-wide pattern of semicoerced intergenerational sex between males, and the traumatic experiences of the European conquest of the Americas. On Mediterranean sexual cultures, see Chauncey, *Gay New York*, 74–75; and Cleminson and Vázquez García, *"Los invisibles": A History*, 275–76. For different theories on machismo in Latin America, see Prieur, *Mema's House*, 214–21. The "Latino-Mediterranean sexual system" theory has been subject to much scrutiny and criticism on the grounds that it puts too much emphasis on cultural representations, assuming that these are broadly homogenous across distant regions, and does not reflect the malleability of sexual practices. In this line, James N. Green has studied the historical experiences of Brazilian feminized "bichas," who actively pursued their desires whether or not these conformed to discursive binaries. Green, *Beyond Carnival*, 89–92. Similarly, Pablo Ben has argued that in nineteenth-century Buenos Aires, most men adopted both sexual roles at different moments of their lives and did not think of these acts as defining their "essence." Ben, "'Maricas,'" 39–56. Despite these criticisms, the active/passive paradigm continues to inform research on same-sex desires in Latin America and the Mediterranean.

4. Lancaster, *Life Is Hard*, 237–45.

5. Lancaster, "Comment on Arguelles," 190.

6. O'Higgins and Foucault, "Sexual Choice," 22.

7. Ian Hacking explains why expert categories and subjects' social behaviors tend to fit each other, as if "our classifications and our classes conspire to emerge hand in hand, each egging the other on." Hacking, "Making Up People," 228. Hacking's theory is indebted to Michel Foucault's insights into the role of nineteenth-century experts in shaping the human kind of the homosexual, defined as a "species" with a distinct way of being inscribed in their bodies and minds. This was a departure from the premodern judicial concept of sodomy, centered on aberrant acts that did not mark the person committing them as an *essentially* different being. Foucault, *History of Sexuality*, 43. For a critique of this theory, see Norton, *Mother Clap's*

Molly House. Hacking posits that labels, along with the people that fit in them, come to be through the interplay between different actors, including medical doctors and patients. While the study of this historical process has been refined over time by expanding the range of actors to include homosexual patients and activists as well as political authorities, its origins remain implicitly located in the metropolises of Northern Europe and America. However, an emerging body of scholarship is focusing on knowledge production in the Global South and colonized societies. See Fuechtner, Haynes, and Jones, *Global History*. Beyond the chronological scope of this book lies the question of whether hegemonic views on the nature versus nurture question had developed within vernacular sexual cultures before authorities intervened in them. However, from the archival sources produced as a result of those interventions, it is clear that those hegemonic views were mobilized to confront state policies between the 1940s and 1980s.

8. Mariquitas mobilized a widespread naturalistic view on sexuality, which is characteristic of nonurban societies according to the specialized scholarship. See, for instance, Healey, *Homosexual Desire*; Reid, *How to Be a Real Gay*; Rydström, *Sinners and Citizens*; and Cáceres-Feria and Valcuende del Río, "Globalización y Diversidad Sexual," n.p.

9. Beachy, *Gay Berlin*; Mancini, *Magnus Hirschfeld*.

10. Anabitarte Rivas, "La situación," 225–46.

11. In Spain, Geoffroy Huard attributes this phenomenon to the Francoist "class justice." Huard, *Los antisociales*, 33–34. In Argentina, Alejandro Modarelli and Flavio Rapisardi describe the informal class-biased mechanisms through which the police predominantly targeted working-class maricas. Modarelli and Rapisardi, *Fiestas, baños y exilios*, 29–31.

BIBLIOGRAPHY

Manuscripts and Archives
Argentina

Archivos Desviados
Biblioteca del Congreso de la Nación, Hemeroteca, Buenos Aires
Centro de Documentación e Investigación de la Cultura de Izquierdas, Buenos
    Aires (CEDINCI)
Comisión Provincial por la Memoria, La Plata
        Dirección de Inteligencia de la Policía de la Provincia de Buenos Aires
        (DIPBA)
Departamento Archivo Intermedio, Archivo General de la Nación, Buenos
    Aires (DAI)
    Armada
    Sentencias
    Fuerza Aérea
Museo Penitenciario Argentino Antonio Ballvé, Buenos Aires (MPAAB)
    Instituto de Clasificación
Oral Archive "Memoria Abierta," Buenos Aires

Spain

Archivo General de la Administración, Alcalá de Henares (AGA)
Arxiu Nacional de Catalunya, Sant Cugat del Vallès (ANC)
Archivo del Congreso de los Diputados, Madrid
Arxiu Municipal del Districte de les Corts, Barcelona
Archivo Histórico Provincial de Bizkaia, Bilbao/Bizkaia (AHPB)
    Juzgado Especial de Vagos y Maleantes de Bilbao
Arxiu Central dels Jutjats de la Ciutat de la Justícia, Hospitalet de Llobregat (ACJCJ)
    Juzgado Especial de Vagos y Maleantes de Barcelona
    Juzgado de Peligrosidad y Rehabilitación Social de Barcelona

Archivo Histórico Provincial de Las Palmas, Las Palmas de Gran Canaria (AHPLP)
    Juzgado Especial de Vagos y Maleantes del Archipiélago Canario
Archivo Histórico Provincial de Sevilla, Sevilla (AHPS)
    Juzgado Especial de Vagos y Maleantes de Málaga
    Juzgado Especial de Vagos y Maleantes de Sevilla
Arxiu Històric de la Comunitat Valenciana, València (AHCV)
    Juzgado Especial de Peligrosidad y Rehabilitación Social de València
Archivo Histórico Provincial de Málaga, Málaga
    Juzgado Especial de Vagos y Maleantes de Granada
Biblioteca Nacional de España, Madrid
    Molina Papers
Biblioteca de la Secretaría General de Instituciones Penitenciarias, Madrid

United States

Cornell University Library, Ithaca NY
    Robert Roth Papers
Library of Congress, Washington DC
    Kameny Papers
New York Public Library, New York City NY
    Rare Books and Manuscripts Division

Published Works

Acha, Omar, and Pablo Ben. "Amorales, patoteros, chongos y pitucos: La homosex-
    ualidad masculina durante el primer peronismo (Buenos Aires, 1943–1955)."
    Trabajos y Comunicaciones 30–31 (2004–5): 217–60.
Alberto, Paulina L., and Eduardo Elena. "Introduction: The Shades of the Nation."
    In *Rethinking Race in Modern Argentina*, edited by Paulina L. Alberto and Edu-
    ardo Elena, 1–22. Cambridge: Cambridge University Press, 2018.
Álvarez, Ana. "'Ahora empezamos con el quilombo': Resistencia travesti en la razia
    del 23 de noviembre de 1996." *Moléculas Malucas*, October 11, 2022. https://www
    .moleculasmalucas.com/post/ahora-empezamos-con-el-quilombo.
———. "Coccinelle: Entre el cabaret y la pantalla grande." *Moléculas Malucas*, June 16,
    2021. https://www.moleculasmalucas.com/post/coccinelle-entre-el-cabaret-y
    -la-pantalla.
Amin, Kadji. "Taxonomically Queer? Sexology and New Queer, Trans, and Asexual
    Identities." GLQ: *A Journal of Lesbian and Gay Studies* 29, no. 1 (2023): 91–107.
Anabitarte Rivas, Héctor. "La situación de las dictaduras argentinas y España." In
    Ugarte Pérez, *Una discriminación universal*, 225–46.
———. *Nadie olvida nada*. Aranjuez, Spain: Ediciones Impublicables, 2005.
Anabitarte Rivas, Héctor, and Ricardo Lorenzo Sanz. *Homosexualidad: El asunto
    está caliente*. Madrid: Quiemada, 1979.

Aresti, Nerea. *Masculinidades en tela de juicio: Hombres y género en el primer tercio del siglo XX*. Madrid: Ediciones Cátedra, 2010.

Arnalte, Arturo. *Redada de violetas: La represión de los homosexuales durante el franquismo*. Madrid: Esfera de los Libros, 2003.

Avellaneda, Andrés. *Censura, autoritarismo y cultura: Argentina 1960–1983*. Buenos Aires: Centro Editor de América Latina, 1986.

Badanelli, Pedro. *El derecho penal en la Biblia: Los grandes delitos sexuales*. Buenos Aires: Tartessos, 1959.

Bazán, Osvaldo. *Historia de la homosexualidad en la Argentina: De la conquista de América al siglo XXI*. Buenos Aires: Marea, 2004.

Beachy, Robert. *Gay Berlin: Birthplace of a Modern Identity*. New York: Knopf, 2014.

Beattie, Peter. "Conflicting Penile Codes: Modern Masculinity and Sodomy in the Brazilian Military, 1860–1916." In *Sex and Sexuality in Latin America*, edited by Donna Guy and Daniel Balderston, 65–85. New York: New York University Press, 1997.

Beccalossi, Chiara. "Latin Eugenics and Sexual Knowledge in Italy, Spain and Argentina: International Networks across the Atlantic." In *A Global History of Sexual Science, 1880–1960*, edited by Veronika Fuechtner, Douglas E. Haynes, and Ryan M. Jones, 305–29. Oakland: University of California Press, 2018.

Becher, Ricardo, dir. *Tiro de Gracia*. Buenos Aires: Contracuadro, 1968.

Ben, Pablo. "'Maricas' and 'Lunfardos' in Buenos Aires: A Critique of the Latino-Mediterranean Model of Sexuality." In *Modern Argentine Masculinities*, edited by Carolina Rocha, 39–56. Chicago: Intellect, 2013.

———. "Plebeian Masculinity and Sexual Comedy in Buenos Aires, 1880–1930." *Journal of the History of Sexuality* 16, no. 3 (2007): 436–58.

Ben, Pablo, and Santiago Joaquín Insausti. "Dictatorial Rule and Sexual Politics in Argentina: The Case of the Frente de Liberación Homosexual, 1967–1976." *Hispanic American Historical Review* 97, no. 2 (2017): 297–325.

Benadusi, Lorenzo. *The Enemy of the New Man: Homosexuality in Fascist Italy*. Madison: University of Wisconsin Press, 2012.

Berzosa, Alberto. "Discursos alternativos de modernidad y sexualidad en el cine rodado en Torremolinos." In *Cruising Torremolinos: Cuerpos, territorio y memoria*, edited by Javier Cuevas del Barrio and Ángelo Néstore, 95–116. València: Tirant Humanidades, 2022.

Bourdieu, Pierre. *Distinction: A Social Critique of the Judgement of Taste*. Cambridge MA: Harvard University Press, 1984.

Box, Zira. *España, año cero: La construcción simbólica del franquismo*. Madrid: Alianza, 2010.

Boyd, Nan Alamilla, and Horacio N. Roque Ramírez, eds. *Bodies of Evidence: The Practice of Queer Oral History*. New York: Oxford University Press, 2012.

Brant, Herbert J. "Homosexual Desire and Existential Alienation in Renato Pellegrini's Asfalto." *Confluencia: Revista Hispánica de Cultura y Literatura* 20, no. 1 (2004): 120–33.

Brown, Stephen. "'Con discriminación y represión no hay democracia:' The Lesbian and Gay Movement in Argentina." *Latin American Perspectives* 29, no. 2 (2002): 119–38.

Cáceres-Feria, Rafael, and José María Valcuende del Río. "Globalización y Diversidad Sexual, Gays y Mariquitas en Andalucía." *Gazeta de Antropología* 30, no. 3 (2014).

Calero Carramolino, Elsa. "La copla y el exilio de Miguel de Molina (1942–1960)." PhD diss., Universidad Autónoma de Madrid, 2014.

Campos, Ricardo. "La construcción psiquiátrica del sujeto peligroso y la Ley de Vagos y Maleantes en la España franquista (1939–1970)." *Revista Culturas Psi* 7 (2016): 9–44.

Campt, Tina. *Listening to Images.* Durham NC: Duke University Press, 2017.

Canaday, Margot. *The Straight State: Sexuality and Citizenship in Twentieth-Century America.* Princeton NJ: Princeton University Press, 2009.

———. "Thinking Sex in the Transnational Turn: An Introduction." *American Historical Review* 114, no. 12 (2009): 1250–57.

Cantilo, Miguel. *¡Chau loco!: Los hippies en la Argentina de los setenta.* Buenos Aires: Galerna, 2006.

Carpio, Genevieve. "Tales from the Rebel Archive: History as Subversive Practice at California's Margins." *Southern California Quarterly* 102, no. 1 (2020): 57–79.

Casanova, Julián, and Carlos Gil Andrés. *Twentieth-Century Spain: A History.* Cambridge: Cambridge University Press, 2014.

Cesio, Fidias R. "Estudio psicoanalítico de un caso de depresión hipocondríaca a través de su tratamiento por electroshocks y psicoterapia." *Revista de Psicoanálisis* 9, no. 2 (1952): 172–83.

Chamorro Gundin, Fernando. *Resultados obtenidos con técnicas proyectivas en una muestra de 200 delincuentes homosexuales españoles.* Madrid: Dirección General de Instituciones Penitenciarias, Departamento de Homosexuales de la Central de Observación, 1971.

Chamouleau, Brice. *Tiran al maricón: Los fantasmas "queer" de la democracia (1970–1988), una interpretación de las subjetividades gais ante el Estado español.* Madrid: Ediciones Akal, 2017.

Chauncey, George. *Gay New York: Gender, Urban Culture, and the Making of the Gay Male World, 1890–1940.* New York: Basic Books, 2019.

Cleminson, Richard. "An Act of 'Emotional Rescue': Homosexuality and Resistance in Lagos, Portugal (1965)." *International Journal of Iberian Studies* 35, no. 2 (2022): 155–73.

Cleminson, Richard, and Francisco Vázquez García. *"Los invisibles": A History of Male Homosexuality in Spain, 1850–1939.* Cardiff: University of Wales Press, 2007.

Cleto, Fabio. "Introduction: Queering the Camp." In *Camp: Queer Aesthetics and the Performing Subject; a Reader,* edited by Fabio Cleto, 1–42. Edinburgh: Edinburgh University Press, 2008.

Corominas, Joan. *Breve diccionario etimológico de la lengua castellana.* Madrid: Gredos, 1983.

Correas, Carlos. "La narración de la historia." In *Las fieras,* edited by Ricardo Piglia, 151–69. Buenos Aires: Alfaguara, 1999.

Cosse, Isabella. "Everyday Life in Argentina in the 1960s." In *Oxford Research Encyclopedia of Latin American History*, edited by Susan Kellogg. Oxford University Press, 2016; online ed., July 27, 2017. https://oxfordre.com/latinamericanhistory/display/10.1093/acrefore/9780199366439.001.0001/acrefore-9780199366439-e-316.

Cowan, Benjamin. "'A Passive Homosexual Element': Digitized Archives and the Policing of Homosex in Cold War Brazil." *Radical History Review* 120 (2014): 183–203.

———. *Securing Sex: Morality and Repression in the Making of Cold War Brazil*. Chapel Hill: University of North Carolina Press, 2016.

Cutuli, María Soledad, and Santiago Joaquín Insausti. "Cabarets, corsos y teatros de revista: Espacios de transgresión y celebración en la memoria marica." In *Memorias, identidades y experiencias trans: (In)visibilidades entre Argentina y España*, edited by Jorge Luís Peralta y Rafael Mérida, 19–39. Buenos Aires: Editorial Biblios, 2014.

Davids, Anthony, Mark Joelson, and Charles McArthur. "Rorschach and TAT Indices of Homosexuality in Overt Homosexuals, Neurotics, and Normal Males." *Journal of Abnormal and Social Psychology* 54, no. 3 (May 1957): 161–72.

"Decreto 1144/1971, de 13 de mayo, por el que se aprueba el Reglamento para la aplicación de la Ley 16/1970, de 4 de agosto, sobre peligrosidad y rehabilitación social." *Boletín oficial del estado* 132 (June 3, 1971): 8895–903.

Delgado, Luis María, dir. *Diferente*. Madrid: Aguila Films, 1961.

D'Emilio, John. "Capitalism and Gay Identity." In *The Lesbian and Gay Studies Reader*, edited by Henry Abelove, Michèle Aina Barale, and David M. Halperin, 467–78. New York: Routledge, 1993.

De Villiers, Nicholas. *Opacity and the Closet: Queer Tactics in Foucault, Barthes, and Warhol*. Minneapolis: University of Minnesota Press, 2012.

DeVun, Leah, and Zeb Tortorici. "Trans, Time, and History." *TSQ: Transgender Studies Quarterly* 5, no. 4 (2018): 518–39.

Dirección General de Instituciones Penitenciarias. *Memoria de la Dirección General de Instituciones Penitenciarias 1971*. Alcalá de Henares, Spain: Talleres Penitenciarios, 1972.

Duberman, Martin. *Cures: A Gay Man's Odyssey*. Boulder CO: Westview, 2002.

Dyer, Richard. *Only Entertainment*. London: Routledge, 1992.

Encarnación, Omar G. *Out in the Periphery: Latin America's Gay Rights Revolution*. New York: Oxford University Press, 2016.

Estella, Iñaki. "The Collective Scene: Transvestite Cabaret during the End of Francoist Spain." *TSQ: Transgender Studies Quarterly* 8, no. 4 (2021): 498–515.

Etchegoyen, R. Horacio. "Ángel Garma." In *International Dictionary of Psychoanalysis*, edited by Alain del Mijolla, 665–66. Detroit: Thomson Gale, 2005.

Fernández, Máximo Javier. "Nadie puede juzgar qué es bueno y qué es malo: Sexualidad masculina y sexo entre varones en los delitos contra el honor militar en la Armada Argentina, 1960–1980." *Sexualidad, Salud y Sociedad*, no. 29 (2018): 52–74.

——. "Sociabilidad homoerótica en la ciudad de Buenos Aires: Maricas y marine-ros durante los sesenta y los setenta." In *Deseo y represión: Sexualidad, género y estado en la historia argentina reciente*, edited by Débora D'Antonio, 21–41. Buenos Aires: Imago Mundi, 2015.

Fernández de Alba, Francisco. *Sex, Drugs, and Fashion in 1970s Madrid*. Toronto: University of Toronto Press, 2020.

Fernández-Galeano, Javier. "Cartas desde Buenos Aires: El movimiento homosex-ual argentino desde una perspectiva transnacional." *Latin American Research Review* 54, no. 3 (2019): 608–22.

——. "'El Todo Poderoso nos ayude, para llegar a lo que deseamos': Homosexu-ality and Catholicism in Franco's Spain (1954–1970)." *Journal of Spanish Cul-tural Studies* 22, no. 3 (2021): 331–50.

——. "Is He a 'Social Danger'? The Franco Regime's Judicial Prosecution of Homo-sexuality in Málaga under the Ley de Vagos y Maleantes." *Journal of the His-tory of Sexuality* 25, no. 1 (2016): 1–31.

——. "Running Mascara: The Hermeneutics of Trans Visual Archives in Late Franco-Era Spain." *Radical History Review*, 142 (2022): 72–92.

Fernández-Galeano, Javier, and Santiago Joaquín Insausti. "Archivos Digitales Queer: Cartografías Digitales de las Redes Transnacionales LGBTQ en Latinoamérica a través del Archivo de Robert Roth." *Moléculas Malucas*, April 29, 2020. https://www.moleculasmalucas.com/post/archivos-digitales-queer.

Fernández-Galeano, Javier, and Jorge Luís Peralta. "Los papeles de Peter: Un archivo inédito de escritura y pornografía maricas." *Moléculas Malucas*, May 2022. https://www.moleculasmalucas.com/post/los-papeles-de-peter.

Fernández-Galeano, Javier, and Juan Queiroz. "Agosto de 1971. Nace el Frente de Lib-eración Homosexual de Argentina." *Moléculas Malucas*, August 2021. https://www.moleculasmalucas.com/post/agosto-de-1971.

Fernández-Galeano, Javier, and Gema Pérez-Sánchez. "Pioneros de la fraternidad homosexual: La correspondencia entre Héctor Anabitarte y Armand de Fluvià (1974–1980)." *Moléculas Malucas*, July 31, 2020. https://www.moleculasmalucas.com/post/pioneros-de-la-fraternidad-homosexual.

Fernández-Galeano, Javier, and Mir Yarfitz. "Serious Maricas and Their Male Con-cubines: Seeking Trans History and Intimacy in Argentine Police and Prison Records, 1921–1945." *Hispanic American Historical Review* 103, no. 4 (2023): 651–78.

Fernández Lara, Leonardo. "Del delito-Pecado al delito-enfermedad: Construcción de la homosexualidad en Chile." *Liminales: Escritos sobre psicología y sociedad* 1, no. 7 (2015): 13–26.

Ferri, Enrico. *The Positive School of Criminology: Three Lectures*. Translated by Ernest Untermann. Chicago: C. H. Kerr, 1913.

Finchelstein, Federico. *Transatlantic Fascism: Ideology, Violence, and the Sacred in Argentina and Italy, 1919–1945*. Durham NC: Duke University Press, 2010.

Fluvià, Armand de, ed. *El moviment gai a la clandestinitat del franquismo*. Barcelona: Laertes, 2003.

Foucault, Michel. *The History of Sexuality*. New York: Pantheon, 1978.

———. *Vigilar y castigar: Nacimiento de la prisión*. Buenos Aires: Siglo XXI Editores Argentina, 2002.

Fraguas, José, and Eduardo Muslip, eds. *Decirlo todo: Escritura y negatividad en Carlos Correas*. Los Polvorines, Argentina: Universidad Nacional de General Sarmiento, 2011.

Frazier, Lessie Jo. *Desired States: Sex, Gender, and Political Culture in Chile*. New Brunswick NJ: Rutgers University Press, 2020.

Freud, Sigmund. *Three Essays on the Theory of Sexuality*. Translated by James Strachey. New York: Basic Books, 1975.

Friedman, Elisabeth Jay. "Constructing 'The Same Rights with the Same Names': The Impact of Spanish Norm Diffusion on Marriage Equality in Argentina." *Latin American Politics and Society* 54, no. 4 (Winter 2012): 29–59.

Fry, Peter. *Para inglês ver*. Rio de Janeiro: Zahar, 1982.

Fuechtner, Veronika, Douglas E. Haynes, and Ryan M. Jones, eds. *A Global History of Sexual Science, 1880–1960*. Oakland: University of California Press, 2018.

Fuss, Diana. "Fashion and the Homospectatorial Look." *Critical Inquiry* 18, no. 4 (1992): 713–37.

García Lorca, Federico. *Ode to Walt Whitman and Other Poems*. Translated by Carlos Bauer. San Francisco: City Lights, 1988.

Garma, Ángel. "Paranoia y Homosexualidad." *Revista de Psicoanálisis* 4, no. 1 (1944): 555–78.

Garrido, Germán. "La Internacional Argentina: Las cosmopolíticas queer de Copi, María Moreno y Néstor Perlongher (1971–1992)." PhD diss., New York University, 2017.

Gil-Albert, Juan. *Cartas a un amigo*. València: Pre-Textos, 1987.

———. *Heraclés: Sobre una manera de ser*. Madrid: Josefina Betancor, 1975.

Gill-Peterson, Jules. *Histories of the Transgender Child*. Minneapolis: University of Minnesota Press, 2018.

Giorgi, Gabriel. *Sueños de exterminio: Homosexualidad y representación en la literatura argentina contemporánea*. Rosario, Argentina: Beatriz Viterbo, 2004.

Green, James Naylor. *Beyond Carnival: Male Homosexuality in Twentieth-Century Brazil*. Chicago: University of Chicago Press, 1999.

———. *Exile within Exiles: Herbert Daniel, Gay Brazilian Revolutionary*. Durham NC: Duke University Press, 2018.

———. "'Who Is the Macho Who Wants to Kill Me?' Male Homosexuality, Revolutionary Masculinity, and the Brazilian Armed Struggle of the 1960s and 1970s." *Hispanic American Historical Review* 92, no. 3 (2012): 437–69.

Guasch, Oscar. "Social Stereotypes and Masculine Homosexualities: The Spanish Case." *Sexualities* 14, no. 5 (2011): 526–43.

Guidotti-Hernández, Nicole Marie. *Archiving Mexican Masculinities in Diaspora.* Durham NC: Duke University Press, 2021.

Guy, Donna J. *Sex and Danger in Buenos Aires: Prostitution, Family, and Nation in Argentina.* Lincoln: University of Nebraska Press, 1991.

Hacking, Ian. "Making Up People." In *Reconstructing Individualism: Autonomy, Individuality, and the Self in Western Thought,* edited by Thomas C. Heller, Morton Sosna, David E. Wellbery, 222–36. Stanford CA: Stanford University Press, 1988.

Halberstam, Jack. *The Queer Art of Failure.* Durham NC: Duke University Press, 2011.

Haller, Dieter. "Homosexuality in Seville." *SOLGAN* 14, no. 3 (1992): 27–35.

Halperin, David M. *How to Be Gay.* Cambridge MA: Harvard University Press, 2012.

Hartman, Saidiya V. "Venus in Two Acts." *Small Axe* 12, no. 2 (2008): 1–14.

Healey, Dan. *Homosexual Desire in Revolutionary Russia: The Regulation of Sexual and Gender Dissent.* Chicago: University of Chicago Press, 2001.

Houlbrook, Matt. *Queer London: Perils and Pleasures in the Sexual Metropolis, 1918–1957.* Chicago: University of Chicago Press, 2005.

——. "Soldier Heroes and Rent Boys: Homosex, Masculinities, and Britishness in the Brigade of Guards, Circa 1900–1960." *Journal of British Studies* 42, no. 3 (2003): 351–88.

Huard, Geoffroy. "La huida a la capital: La emigración homosexual durante la dictadura franquista." In *Cruising Torremolinos: Cuerpos, territorio y memoria,* edited by Javier Cuevas del Barrio and Ángelo Néstore, 49–69. València: Tirant Humanidades, 2022.

——. *Los antisociales: Historia de la homosexualidad en Barcelona y París, 1945–1975.* Madrid: Marcial Pons Historia, 2014.

——. *Los invertidos: Verdad, justicia y reparación para gais y transexuales bajo la dictadura franquista.* Barcelona: Icaria, 2021.

Huertas García-Alejo, Rafael. *El delincuente y su patología: Medicina, crimen y sociedad en el positivismo argentino.* Madrid: Consejo Superior de Investigaciones Científicas, 1991.

Insausti, Santiago Joaquín. "De maricas, travestis y gays: Derivas identitarias en Buenos Aires (1966–1989)." PhD diss., Universidad de Buenos Aires, 2016.

——. "Los cuatrocientos homosexuales desaparecidos: Memorias de la represión estatal a las sexualidades disidentes en Argentina." In *Deseo y represión: Sexualidad, género y estado en la historia argentina,* edited by Débora D'Antonio and Máximo Javier Fernández, 63–82. Buenos Aires: Imago Mundi, 2015.

——. "Ni explotación ni trabajo: Repensando el estatus de la prostitución a la luz de la historia del sexo compensado entre varones en Argentina." *Confluenze: Rivista di studi iberoamericani* 14, no. 2 (2022): 35–54.

Insausti, Santiago Joaquín, and Máximo Javier Fernández. "De chongos y mayates: Masculinidades y sexo heterosexual entre hombres en Argentina y México (1950–1990)." *Historia crítica,* no. 77 (2020): 133–56.

Jackson, Julian. *Living in Arcadia: Homosexuality, Politics, and Morality in France from the Liberation to Aids*. Chicago: University of Chicago Press, 2009.

Jamandreu, Paco. *La cabeza contra el suelo*. Buenos Aires: Ediciones de la Flor, 1976.

Jiménez de Asúa, Luis. "Ley de Vagos y Maleantes: Un ensayo legislativo sobre peligrosidad sin delito." *Revista General de Legislación y Jurisprudencia* 58 (1933): 577–635.

Johnson, Michael A. "Carlo Cóccioli Collection." *E3W Review of Books* 9 (2009).

Jumilla, J. A. "La Política Social franquista: Del organicismo social al Estado autoritario del Bienestar (1939–1977)." *La Razón Histórica* 1 (2007): 3–11.

Karush, Matthew B., and Oscar Chamosa. Introduction to *The New Cultural History of Peronism: Power and Identity in Mid-Twentieth-Century Argentina*, edited by Matthew B. Karush and Oscar Chamosa, 1–20. Durham NC: Duke University Press, 2010.

Keck, Margaret E., and Kathryn Sikkink. *Activists beyond Borders: Advocacy Networks in International Politics*. Ithaca NY: Cornell University Press, 1998.

Kunzel, Regina. "Queer History, Mad History, and the Politics of Health." *American Quarterly* 69, no. 2 (2017): 315–19.

Lacaba Gutiérrez, José Juan. "Sitges (Catalunya) y el carnaval gay: El turismo y sus nuevos peregrinajes." *PASOS: Revista de Turismo y Patrimonio Cultural* 2, no. 1 (2004): 111–24.

La Fountain-Stokes, Lawrence M. "De sexilio(s) y diáspora(s) homosexual(es) latina(s): Cultura puertorriqueña y lo nuyorican queer." *Debate feminista* 29 (2004): 138–57.

———. *Translocas: The Politics of Puerto Rican Drag and Trans Performance*. Ann Arbor: University of Michigan Press, 2021.

Lambe, Jennifer L. *Madhouse: Psychiatry and Politics in Cuban History*. Chapel Hill: University of North Carolina Press, 2017.

Lancaster, Roger N. "Comment on Arguelles and Rich's 'Homosexuality, Homophobia, and Revolution.'" *Signs* 12, no. 1 (1986): 188–92.

———. *Life Is Hard: Machismo, Danger, and the Intimacy of Power in Nicaragua*. Berkeley: University of California Press, 1992.

———. "Sexual Positions: Caveats and Second Thoughts on 'Categories.'" *The Americas* 54, no. 1 (1997): 1–16.

Lévy Lazcano, Silvia. *Psicoanálisis y defensa social en España, 1923–1959*. Madrid: Los Libros de la Catarata, 2019.

"LEY DE 15 DE JULIO DE 1954 por la que se modifican los artículos 2º y 6º de la Ley de Vagos y Maleantes, de 4 de agosto de 1933." *Boletín oficial del estado* 198 (July 17, 1954): 4862.

"Ley 14.029 / Código de Justicia Militar." Enacted on July 4, 1951. *Boletín oficial del estado*. Biblioteca del Congreso de la Nación / Hemeroteca, Buenos Aires, Argentina, August 6, 1951.

"Ley 16/1970 sobre peligrosidad y rehabilitación social de 4 de agosto." *Boletín oficial del estado* 187 (August 6, 1970): 12551–57.

Llamas, Ricardo. *Teoría Torcida: Prejuicios y discursos en torno a la "homosexualidad."* Madrid: Siglo XXI, 1998.

López Clavel, Pau. "El rosa en la senyera: El movimiento gay, lesbiano y trans valenciano en su perigeo (1976–1997)." PhD diss., Universitat de València, 2018.

Mabrey, María Cristina C. "Mapping Homoerotic Feelings and Contested Modernity: Whitman, Lorca, Gingsberg, and Hispanic Modernist Poets." *South Atlantic Review* 75, no. 1 (2010): 83–98.

Macías-González, Víctor, and Anne Rubenstein, eds. *Masculinity and Sexuality in Modern Mexico.* Albuquerque: University of New Mexico Press, 2012.

Malva, and Natalia Calzón Flores. *Mi recordatorio: Autobiografía de Malva.* Buenos Aires: Libros del Rojas, Universidad de Buenos Aires, 2011.

Manalansan, Martin F., IV. "Diasporic Deviants/Divas: How Filipino Gay Transmigrants 'Play with the World.'" In *Queer Diasporas*, edited by Cindy Patton and Benigno Sánchez-Eppler, 183–203. Durham NC: Duke University Press, 2000.

Mancini, Elena. *Magnus Hirschfeld and the Quest for Sexual Freedom: A History of the First International Sexual Freedom Movement.* New York: Palgrave Macmillan, 2010.

Manzano, Valeria. *The Age of Youth in Argentina: Culture, Politics, and Sexuality from Perón to Videla.* Chapel Hill: University of North Carolina Press, 2014.

Marcondes, Durval. "Relaciones de objeto en la paranoia masculina y femenina." *Revista de Psicoanálisis* 4, no. 3 (1947): 492–507.

Marshall, Daniel, and Zeb Tortorici. "Introduction: (Re)turning to the Queer Archives." In *Turning Archival: The Life of the Historical in Queer Studies*, edited by Daniel Marshall and Zeb Tortorici, 1–31. Durham NC: Duke University Press, 2022.

Martí, José. *Versos Sencillos: Simple Verses.* Translated by Manuel A. Tellechea. Houston TX: Arte Público, 1997.

Martínez, María Elena. "Archives, Bodies, and Imagination: The Case of Juana Aguilar and Queer Approaches to History, Sexuality, and Politics." *Radical History Review* 120 (2014): 159–82.

Martínez, Ramón. *Lo nuestro sí que es mundial: Una introducción a la historia del movimiento LGTB en España.* Barcelona: Editorial Egales, 2018.

Maura Ocampo, Aurora. *Diccionario de escritores mexicanos, siglo XX: A–CH.* Ciudad de México: Universidad Nacional Autónoma de México, 1988.

Mejía, Norma. *Transgenerismos: Una experiencia transexual desde la perspectiva antropológica.* Barcelona: Bellaterra, 2006.

Melero, Alejandro. "'El paseo de los tristes': Homosexuality as Tragedy in the Spanish Films of the 1960s." *International Journal of Iberian Studies* 23, no. 3 (2010): 141–57.

———. "Queering Archives: Censorship, Sexuality and Gender Representation in Pedro Balañá's Films." Conference presentation. II Congreso internacional tránsitos: Identidades y culturas en movimiento. Corporalidades: Diálogos en torno a sujeto y género. Cádiz, Spain, September 30, 2022.

———. "Un día más: Pere Balañá y el rastro del cine gay español." *Filmoteca española*, accessed December 1, 2022. https://www.culturaydeporte.gob.es/dam/jcr:

f7645095-6524-4fe0-8173-2067f84dfdc3/un-d-a-m-s--de-pere-bala-----flores
-en-la-sombra.pdf.

Mérida Jiménez, Rafael Manuel. *Transbarcelonas: Cultura, género y sexualidad en la
España del siglo XX*. Barcelona: Bellaterra, 2016.

Mettini Vilas, Rubén. "Interiores gais: Recuerdos de un argentino en las décadas de
los 50, 60 y 70 del siglo XX." In *Antes del orgullo: Recuperando la memoria gay*,
edited by Jorge Luís Peralta, 161–84. Barcelona: Editorial Egales, 2019.

Milanesio, Natalia. *Destape: Sex, Democracy, and Freedom in Postdictatorial Argentina*. Pittsburgh PA: University of Pittsburgh Press, 2019.

———. "Peronists and Cabecitas: Stereotypes and Anxieties at the Peak of Social
Change." In *The New Cultural History of Peronism: Power and Identity in
Mid-Twentieth-Century Argentina*, edited by Matthew B. Karush and Oscar
Chamosa, 53–84. Durham NC: Duke University Press, 2010.

Milanich, Nara B. *Children of Fate: Childhood, Class, and the State in Chile, 1850–1930*.
Durham NC: Duke University Press, 2009.

Mildenberger, Florian. "Kraepelin and the 'Urnings': Male Homosexuality in Psychiatric Discourse." *History of Psychiatry* 18, no. 3 (2007): 321–35.

Miller, Jason. "Dredging and Projecting the Depths of Personality: The Thematic
Apperception Test and the Narratives of the Unconscious." *Science in Context*
28, no. 1 (March 2015): 9–30.

Mira Nouselles, Alberto. *De Sodoma a Chueca: Una historia cultural de la homosexualidad en España en el siglo XX*. Barcelona: Editorial Egales, 2007.

Modarelli, Alejandro, and Flavio Rapisardi. *Fiestas, baños y exilios: Los gays porte-
ños en la última dictadura*. Buenos Aires: Sudamericana, 2001.

Moix, Terenci. *El beso de Peter Pan*. Barcelona: Plaza & Janés, 1993.

———. *El cine de los sábados*. Barcelona: Plaza & Janés, 1990.

Molina, Miguel de. *Botín de guerra: Autobiografía*. Edited by Salvador Valverde and
Alejandro Salade. Córdoba: Editorial Almuzara, 2012.

Molina Artaloytia, Francisco. "Estigma, diagnosis e interacción: Un análisis episte-
mológico y axiológico de los discursos biomédicos sobre la homosexualidad
en los regímenes autoritarios ibéricos del siglo XX." PhD diss., Universidad
Nacional de Educación a Distancia, 2016.

Molloy, Sylvia. "Of Queens and Castanets: Hispanidad, Orientalism, and Sexual Difference." In *Queer Diasporas*, edited by Cindy Patton and Benigno Sánchez-
Eppler, 105–21. Durham NC: Duke University Press, 2000.

———. "The Politics of Posing." In *Hispanisms and Homosexualities*, edited by Sylvia
Molloy and Robert McKee Irwin, 141–60. Durham NC: Duke University Press, 1998.

Monferrer Tomás, Jordi M. "La construcción de la protesta en el movimiento gay
español: La Ley de Peligrosidad Social (1970) como factor precipitante de la
acción colectiva." *Revista Española de Investigaciones Sociológicas* 102 (2003):
171–204.

Mora Gaspar, Víctor. *Al margen de la naturaleza: La persecución de la homosexualidad durante el franquismo, leyes, terapias y condenas*. Barcelona: Debate, 2016.

Moreno, María Paz, and Claudia Simón Aura, eds. *Cartas a Juan Gil-Albert: Epistolario selecto.* Alicante: Instituto Alicantino de Cultura, 2016.

Moya, José C. *Cousins and Strangers: Spanish Immigrants in Buenos Aires, 1850–1930.* Berkeley: University of California Press, 1998.

Muñoz, José Esteban. *Cruising Utopia: The Then and There of Queer Futurity.* New York: New York University Press, 2019.

Murphy, Kevin P., Jennifer L. Pierce, and Jason Ruiz. "What Makes Queer Oral History Different." *Oral History Review* 43, no. 1 (2016): 1–24.

Murray, Stephen O. "Family, Social Insecurity, and the Underdevelopment of Gay Institutions in Latin America." In *Latin American Male Homosexualities*, edited by Stephen O. Murray, 33–48. Albuquerque: University of New Mexico Press, 1995.

Murray, Stephen O., and Manuel Arboleda G. "Stigma, Transformation, and Relexification: Gay in Latin America." In *Latin American Male Homosexualities*, edited by Stephen O. Murray, 138–44. Albuquerque: University of New Mexico Press, 1995.

Navarro Amo, Tania. *La infancia de una transexual en la dictadura.* Barcelona: Planeta, 2021.

Norton, Rictor. *Mother Clap's Molly House: The Gay Subculture in England 1700–1830.* London: Gay Men's Press, 1992.

O'Higgins, James, and Michel Foucault. "Sexual Choice, Sexual Act: An Interview with Michel Foucault." *Salmagundi* 58–59 (Fall 1982–Winter 1983): 10–24.

Olmeda, Fernando. *El Látigo y la Pluma: Homosexuales en la España de Franco.* Madrid: Oberon, 2004.

Oosterhuis, Harry, and Arlie Loughnan. "Madness and Crime: Historical Perspectives on Forensic Psychiatry." *International Journal of Law and Psychiatry* 37, no. 1 (2014): 1–16.

Opizzo, José A. *Alteraciones sexuales: Diagnóstico y orientación del enfermo sexual.* Buenos Aires: printed by the author, 1963.

Pack, Sasha D. *Tourism and Dictatorship: Europe's Peaceful Invasion of Franco's Spain.* New York: Palgrave Macmillan, 2006.

Pedrosa Gil, Francisco, Matthias M. Weber, and Wolfgang Burgmair. "Ernst Kretschmer (1888–1964)." *American Journal of Psychiatry* 159, no. 7 (2002): 1111.

Pellegrini, Renato. *Asfalto.* Buenos Aires: Ediciones Tirso, 1964.

Peralta, Jorge Luís. "De eso no se hablaba: Gustavo Juan Pueyrredón, una biografía desobediente." *Moléculas Malucas*, September 2022. https://www.moleculasmalucas.com/post/de-eso-no-se-hablaba.

———. "Del efebo al chongo: Representaciones corporales en Manuel Mujica Lainez y Oscar Hermes Villordo." In *(Re)leer literatura argentina y latinoamericana: Perspectiva de cultura, sociedad y género*, edited by Carmen Toriano, 161–89. Mendoza, Argentina: EDIUNC: Editorial de la Universidad Nacional de Cuyo, 2018.

———. "Ediciones Tirso y la difusión de literatura homoerótica en Hispanoamérica." In *Lengua, cultura y política en la historia de la traducción en Hispanoamérica,* edited by Francisco Lafarga and Luis Pegenaute, 191–99. Vigo, Spain: Academia del Hispanismo, 2012.

———. *La ciudad amoral: Espacio urbano y disidencia sexual en Renato Pellegrini y Carlos Correas*. Villa María, Argentina: Eduvim, 2021.

Pérez-Sánchez, Gema. *Queer Transitions in Contemporary Spanish Culture: From Franco to la Movida*. New York: SUNY Press, 2007.

Perlongher, Nestor. *La prostitución masculina*. Buenos Aires: Ediciones de la Urraca, 1993.

———. *Prosa plebeya: Ensayos, 1980–1992*. Edited by Christian Ferrer and Osvaldo Baigorria. Buenos Aires: Colihue, 1997.

Platero, Lucas. "Lesboerotismo y la masculinidad de las mujeres en la España franquista." *Bagoas* 3 (2009): 15–38.

———. *Por un chato de vino: Historias de travestismo y masculinidad femenina*. Barcelona: Bellaterra, 2015.

Plotkin, Mariano Ben. *Freud in the Pampas: The Emergence and Development of a Psychoanalytic Culture in Argentina*. Stanford CA: Stanford University Press, 2001.

Portelli, Alessandro. "The Peculiarities of Oral History." *History Workshop* 12 (1981): 96–107.

Preciado, Paul B. "The Ocaña We Deserve." *Stedelijk Studies Journal* 3 (2015): 1–41.

Premat, Adriana. "Popular Culture, Politics, and Alternative Gender Imaginaries in 1960s and 1970s Argentina." *Studies in Latin American Popular Culture* 33 (2015): 41–56.

Prieur, Annick. *Mema's House, Mexico City: On Transvestites, Queens, and Machos*. Chicago: University of Chicago Press, 1998.

Puig, Manuel. *Kiss of the Spider Woman*. New York: Vintage, 1991.

Queiroz, Juan. "La historia de nuestra historia." *Moléculas Malucas*, April 2020. https://www.moleculasmalucas.com/post/la-historia-de-nuestra-historia.

———. "Memorias del desvío: Entrevista a Hugo." *Moléculas Malucas*, February 2021. https://www.moleculasmalucas.com/post/memorias-del-desvío.

Radcliff, Pamela Beth. *Modern Spain: 1808 to the Present*. Hoboken NJ: John Wiley, 2017.

Ramacciotti, Karina Inés, and Adriana María Valobra. "El campo médico argentino y su mirada al tribadismo, 1936–1955." *Estudios Feministas* 16, no. 2 (2008): 493–516.

Ramírez Pérez, Víctor M. "Franquismo y disidencia sexual: La visión del Ministerio Fiscal de la época." *Aposta: Revista de Ciencias Sociales* 77 (2018): 132–76.

Rapisardi, Flavio. "Escritura y lucha política en la cultura argentina: Identidades y hegemonía en el movimiento de diversidades sexuales entre 1970 y 2000." *Revista iberoamericana* 74, no. 225 (2008): 973–95.

Reid, Graeme. *How to Be a Real Gay: Gay Identities in Small-Town South Africa*. Scottsville, South Africa: University of KwaZulu-Natal Press, 2013.

Rein, Raanan. *Entre el abismo y la salvación: El pacto Franco-Perón*. Buenos Aires: Ediciones Lumiere, 2003.

Rizki, Cole. "Familiar Grammars of Loss and Belonging: Curating Trans Kinship in Post-dictatorship Argentina." *Journal of Visual Culture* 19, no. 2 (2020): 197–211.

——. "Latin/x American Trans Studies: Toward a Travesti-Trans Analytic." *TSQ: Transgender Studies Quarterly* 6, no. 2 (2019): 145–55.

——. "'No State Apparatus Goes to Bed Genocidal Then Wakes Up Democratic': Fascist Ideology and Transgender Politics in Post-dictatorship Argentina." *Radical History Review* 138 (2020): 82–107.

Rodriguez, Julia. *Civilizing Argentina: Science, Medicine, and the Modern State.* Chapel Hill: University of North Carolina Press, 2006.

Romero, Alberto. *A History of Argentina in the Twentieth Century.* University Park: Pennsylvania State University Press, 2013.

Romi, Juan C. "Delimitación conceptual de las perturbaciones sexuales." PhD diss., Universidad de Buenos Aires, 1980.

——. *Investigación clínica del Lorazepam en pacientes con perturbaciones sexuales.* Buenos Aires: Universidad de Buenos Aires, 1980.

——. "La homosexualidad: Un enfoque general." *Neuropsiquiatría* 6, no. 4 (1975): 243–56.

——. "Las Perturbaciones sexuales: Críticas a su inclusión como trastornos mentales en el DSM IV TR." *Psiquiatría Forense, Sexología y Praxis* 6, no. 1 (2008): 24–49.

Rosario, Vernon A. "Afterword: Sex and Heredity at the Fin de Siècle." In *Sexuality at the Fin de Siècle: The Makings of a "Central Problem,"* edited by Peter Cryle and Christopher E. Forth, 168–90. Newark: University of Delaware Press, 2008.

Rosón, María. "'No estoy sola': Álbum fotográfico, memoria, género y subjetividad (1900–1980)." *Journal of Spanish Cultural Studies* 16, no. 2 (2015): 143–77.

Ruggiero, Kristin. *Modernity in the Flesh: Medicine, Law, and Society in Turn-of-the-Century Argentina.* Stanford CA: Stanford University Press, 2004.

Rydström, Jens. *Sinners and Citizens: Bestiality and Homosexuality in Sweden, 1880–1950.* Chicago: University of Chicago Press, 2003.

——. "'Sodomitical Sins Are Threefold': Typologies of Bestiality, Masturbation, and Homosexuality in Sweden, 1880–1950." *Journal of the History of Sexuality* 9, no. 3 (2000): 240–76.

Sabater Tomás, Antonio. *Juventud inadaptada y delincuente.* Barcelona: Editorial Hispano-Europea, 1965.

——. *Peligrosidad social y delincuencia.* Barcelona: Nauta, 1972.

Salessi, Jorge. *Médicos maleantes y maricas: Higiene, criminología y homosexualidad en la construcción de la nación argentina (Buenos Aires: 1871–1914).* Rosario, Argentina: Beatriz Viterbo, 1995.

Santos, Carlos. *333 historias de la Transición: Chaquetas de pana, tetas al aire, ruido de sables, suspiros, algaradas y consenso.* Madrid: La esfera de los libros, 2015.

Sanz Hoya, Julián. *España en camisa azul: Falange, cultura política y poderes locales.* Granada: Editorial Comares, 2022.

Saumench Gimeno, Domingo. "Cálculo médico legal de un índice de peligrosidad." PhD diss., Universidad de Barcelona, 1960.

Scott, James C. *Weapons of the Weak: Everyday Forms of Peasant Resistance.* New Haven CT: Yale University Press, 2008.

Sebreli, Juan José. *El tiempo de una vida*. Buenos Aires: Editorial Sudamericana, 2005.

———. *Escritos sobre escritos, ciudades bajo ciudades, 1950–1997*. Buenos Aires: Editorial Sudamericana, 1997.

Sedgwick, Eve Kosofsky. *Epistemology of the Closet*. Berkeley: University of California Press, 1990.

Seigel, Micol. *Uneven Encounters: Making Race and Nation in Brazil and the United States*. Durham NC: Duke University Press, 2009.

Sigal, Pete. "Gendered Power, the Hybrid Self, and Homosexual Desire in Late Colonial Yucatan." In *Infamous Desire: Male Homosexuality in Colonial Latin America*, edited by Pete Sigal, 102–33. Chicago: University of Chicago Press, 2003.

———. "Introduction: (Homo)Sexual Desire and Masculine Power in Colonial Latin America: Notes toward an Integrated Analysis." In *Infamous Desire: Male Homosexuality in Colonial Latin America*, edited by Pete Sigal, 1–24. Chicago: University of Chicago Press, 2003.

Sigal, Lisa Z. *The People's Porn: A History of Handmade Pornography in America*. London: Reaktion, 2020.

Simonetto, Patricio. *A Body of One's Own: A Trans History of Argentina*. Austin: University of Texas Press, 2024.

———. *Entre la injuria y la revolución: El Frente de Liberación Homosexual. Argentina, 1967–1976*. Bernal: Universidad Nacional de Quilmes, 2017.

———. "Fronteras del deseo: Homosexualidad, sociabilidad y afecto en la ciudad de Buenos Aires (1950–1983)." *Cadernos Pagu* 49 (2017).

Simonetto, Patricio, and Marce Butierrez. "The Archival Riot: Travesti/Trans* Audiovisual Memory Politics in Twenty-First-Century Argentina." *Memory Studies* 16, no. 2 (2022): 280–95.

Sinfield, Alan. *On Sexuality and Power*. New York: Columbia University Press, 2004.

Sívori, Horacio Federico. *Locas, chongos y gays*. Buenos Aires: Editorial Antropofagia, 2004.

Solà, Miriam, and Elena Urko, eds. *Transfeminismos: Epistemes, fricciones y flujos*. Tafalla, Spain: Txalaparta, 2013.

Sontag, Susan. "Notes on 'Camp.'" In *Camp: Queer Aesthetics and the Performing Subject; a Reader*, edited by Fabio Cleto, 53–65. Edinburgh: Edinburgh University Press, 2008.

Steele, Valerie, ed. *A Queer History of Fashion: From the Closet to the Catwalk*. New Haven CT: Yale University Press, 2013.

Subrat, Piro. *Invertidos y rompepatrias: Marxismo, anarquismo y desobediencia sexual y de género en el estado español (1868–1982)*. Madrid: Imperdible, 2019.

Surghi, Carlos. "En busca de la experiencia perdida: Carlos Correas y la narrativa autoficcional." *Lingüística y Literatura* 62 (2012): 291–307.

Sweet, James H. "Is History History? Identity Politics and Teleologies of the Present." *Perspectives on History*, American Historical Association, August 17, 2022.

Tamagne, Florence. *A History of Homosexuality: Europe between the Wars*. New York: Algora, 2003.

Terradillos Basoco, Juan. *Peligrosidad social y estado de derecho*. Madrid: Akal, 1981.

Terrasa Mateu, Jordi. "La legislación represiva." In *Una discriminación universal: La homosexualidad bajo el franquismo y la transición*, edited by Javier Ugarte Pérez, 79–107. Madrid: Editorial Egales, 2008.

Terry, Jennifer. *An American Obsession: Science, Medicine, and Homosexuality in Modern Society*. Chicago: University of Chicago Press, 1999.

Thénon, Jorge, and Héctor Villar. "Reacción paranoide y homosexualidad." In *Temas actuales de psicología normal y patológica*, edited by Enrique Mouchet, 511–28. Buenos Aires: Médico Quirúrgica, 1945.

Theumer, Emmanuel. "Políticas homosexuales en la Argentina reciente (1970–1990s)." *INTERdisciplina* 5, no. 11 (2017): 109–26.

Tortorici, Zeb. *Sins against Nature: Sex and Archives in Colonial New Spain*. Durham NC: Duke University Press, 2018.

Trull, Timothy J., and Mitchell J. Prinstein. *Clinical Psychology*. Belmont, CA: Wadsworth / Cengage Learning, 2013.

Ugarte Pérez, Francisco Javier. "Entre el pecado y la enfermedad." *Orientaciones: Revista de homosexualidades* 7 (2004): 7–26.

———. *Las circunstancias obligaban: Homoerotismo, identidad y resistencia*. Barcelona: Editorial Egales, 2011.

———, ed. *Una discriminación universal: La homosexualidad bajo el franquismo y la transición*. Madrid: Editorial Egales, 2008.

Valentine, David. *Imagining Transgender: An Ethnography of a Category*. Durham NC: Duke University Press, 2007.

Vázquez García, Francisco, and Richard Cleminson. *Los invisibles: Una historia de la homosexualidad masculina en España, 1850–1939*. Granada: Editorial Comares, 2011.

Vespucci, Guido. "Explorando un intrincado triángulo conceptual: Homosexualidad, familia y liberación en los discursos del Frente de Liberación Homosexual de Argentina (FLH, 1971–1976)." *Historia crítica* 43 (2011): 174–97.

Waugh, Thomas. *Hard to Imagine: Gay Male Eroticism in Photography and Film from the Beginnings to Stonewall*. New York: Columbia University Press, 1996.

Wilcox, Melissa M. *Queer Nuns: Religion, Activism, and Serious Parody*. New York: New York University Press, 2018.

Zubiaurre, Maite. *Cultures of the Erotic in Spain, 1898–1939*. Nashville TN: Vanderbilt University Press, 2012.

INDEX

Page numbers in *italics* refer to figures.

abuse, sexual, xv, xxiii, 14, 35–37, 108, 198, 241. *See also* assault, sexual; rape

active/passive binary, 12, 51–52, 101, 124–25, 159, 189–90, 231, 262n5, 278n3. *See also* anal sex; penetration; sexual roles

adolescents, 43, 51–52, 55, 59, 62, 148, 151, 154, 157, 170, 196–97; and military, 104, 117, 123, 130, 133. *See also* youngsters

aesthetic, 40, 45–46, 54, 70, 79–80, 88–90, 148–49, 152, 192, 238, 239; and criminology, xx, 147, 151, 154–55, 157, 165; and *maricas*, xviii, 142–43, 159, 172–73, 176, 243; and masculinity, 49, 65; and transactional sex, 69, 74, 93. *See also* fashion

affection, between males, 52, 100, 111–16, 243. *See also* intimacy: between males

agency, xxv, 11–13, 32, 37–38, 40, 42, 66, 190

Agrupamiento Homófilo para la Integración Social (AGHOIS), 205, 208

Alaria, Alfredo, xix, 41–42, 63–65, 149

Amin, Kadji, xxix

Anabitarte, Héctor, xvii, 177, 182, 187–89, 196–97, 213–14, 215, 219, 226–34, 235, 236

anal sex, xxiv, xxiv, 3, 83, 100, 108, 113, 121, 126. *See also* penetration

antisocial behaviors. *See* behaviors, antisocial

anuses, 91, 108–9, 118, 121, 126; medical examination of, 17–19, 104, 121, 126

Arcadie, 183, 184, 188, 201–2, 205. *See also* transnational networks

archives, xv, xvii, xxix, 87, 121, 138, 196; ethics in research with, xxiii–xxvii; images in, 71, 96, 247n24; and *maricas*, xxiii, xxv, 23, 78, 176, 238; and voyeurism, xx, xxiv, 99, 104, 119. *See also* clinical history; forensic reports; military records; police records; prison records

Argentina, xviii–xix, xxi, 34, 55, 74, 147, 242; activism in, 179–80, 188, 227, 237, 277n195; censorship in, 51, 185; coups in, xxii, xxiii, 103, 156, 180, 181, 194, 197–99, 211–12, 219; criminology in, 4–5, 6–7, 29, 33, 37–38, 76; economic and political situation in, 103, 151–52, 180–81, 185–86, 192, 194, 197–99, 215, 246n12; European migration to, 6, 49, 215, 217, 246n12; homophile canon in, 53, 187, 255n11; military in, xxiv–xxv, 70, 103, 105, *106*, 137; psychoanalysis in, xxiii, 6–7, 27; public debates in, 39, 58, 71; sexual culture in, 80, 103, 137, 151–52, 180–81; and Spain, xxi–xxiii, 225, 246n12, 255n11

Argentine Armed Forces. *See* military: in Argentina

Arias, Abelardo, 53, 59

Asfalto (Pellegrini), 41, 58–60. *See also* Pellegrini, Renato

assault, sexual, xxiv, 6, 12, 13–14, 28, 108, 115, *145*. *See also* abuse, sexual; rape

Badanelli, Pedro, 41, 46, 47–49
Balañá i Bonvehí, Pere, 94
Barcelona (Spain), 58, 59, 62, 83, 95, *145*,
    200, 226, 238, 250n46; activism in, 201,
    205, 207–8, 209, 210, 212, 214, 220–21,
    224–25; courts of, 12, 15, 16, 17, 22, 24–25,
    57, 85, 88–89, 171, 252n78; exiles in, 217,
    219–20, 226–27, 230, *235*; homosexual
    social life in, 63, *64*, 86; sex work in, 86,
    147, 166, 168, 266n26; *travestis* in, 147, 174
Bartolomé, Martín, 216–17
bathrooms, xv–xvi, 13–14, 26, 59–60, 70,
    108, 112–14, 118, 120, 130, 195, 211, 237
Baudry, André, 183, 202, 205
beatniks, 75, 77, 96, 162, 164–65
beauty, 44, 54, 63, 80, 166
behaviors, antisocial, 15, 93, 128, 162
behaviors, sexual, 30–32, 103, 134–35, 158;
    and danger, 6, 29, 38, 176
Ben, Pablo, 182, 248n38, 254n123, 262n5,
    278n3
Benadusi, Lorenzo, 87, 247n23
Benítez, Marcelo, 190–91, 192
Berón, Andrés, xxix, xxx
Bertini, Dante, 42, 215, 221
Bilbao (Spain), 12, 23, 49–50, 51, 175
bishops, 201, 202–3, 206. *See also* Catholic
    Church
Bloch, Ernst, 45–46
bodies, xxi, 38, 49, 54, 66, 113, 149, 265n15,
    278n7; and defendants' liability, 8, 11,
    20–22; eroticization of, xxvii, 100, 212;
    forensic legibility of, 17–20, 153, 155, 243,
    251n69; images of, 41, 43–44, 57, 62–65,
    79–85, 94, 258n80, 260n31; self-control
    over, 6, 14, 132; and sex work, 72, 93, 147;
    transformation of, xxix–xxx, 142, 147, 176
bodybuilding. *See* magazines: about
    bodybuilding
Boïls i Coniller, Emili, 55–57, 177–78,
    199–200
Brando, Marlon, xix, 69, 72, 74, 75
Brazil, *48*, 72, 144, 255n5, 260n31, 262n5
Buenos Aires (Argentina), 6, 26, 49, 53, 105,
    134, 157, 181, 186, 195, 217, 224, 226–27, 229;
    carnivals in, 143–44; migration of *maricas*
    to, 30, 43, 46, 59, 143, 144, 148; sexual

subcultures in, xvi, 39, 41, 60, 112, 114–15,
    134–35, 183, 248n38, 254n123, 278n3
Butierrez, Marce, 144, 266n22

cabarets, 42–43, 144, 147, 148, 174, 220,
    266n20
camp (style), xvi, xvii, 43, 45–46, 60, 142,
    164, 172–73, 222, 238–39, 243
Canaday, Margot, 107, 119
carnivals, 266n22; cross-dressing in, xvi,
    xxix–xxx, 143, 144, 170, 218
Catholic Church, 54, 206, 239; stance on
    homosexuality, 49, 57, 199, 202
Catholicism, xxv, 3, 5–6, 34, 74, 179, 199,
    238, 247n23; homosexuals within, xvii,
    49, 55–57, 199–200, 203, 242; popular
    expression of, 45–46, 221, 241; and
    sublimation, 46–47, 199, 203
censorship, xxv; in Argentina, 51, 53–54,
    75, 181, 185; in Spain, 46, 51, 54–55, *56*, 58,
    63, 94, 199, 225, 231–33, 257n51. *See also*
    Franco regime
Chamorro, Fernando, 159–61
Chamouleau, Brice, 213, 224
chastity, 47, 49, 241
chongos, xvi, 53, 65, 73–75, 80, 158, 186, 218,
    260n33. *See also* machos
cinemas, 62, 63, 218; as cruising spots, xv, 75,
    76, 211, 238, 245n3
Classification Institute, xix, 5, 6–7, 28, 29, 36,
    76, 96, 152, 154–55, 255n134
Cleto, Fabio, 142
clinical history, 25, 253n106, 253n109. *See*
    also archives
Cóccioli, Carlo, 55–57
collages, 78–83, *82*, 96, 238–39. *See also*
    bodies: images of; fantasies
Col·lectiu de Maricons Autònoms, *146*
Comité Anti-Sida de Madrid, 214
compensated sex. *See* transactional sex
Comunidad Homosexual Argentina (CHA),
    277n195
conscripts, 100, 103, 122–23, 134; and
    masculinity, 98–99, 102; superiors
    having sex with, 33, 109, 117–18, 126; and
    transactional sex, 105–7. *See also* military
    service; soldiers

consumer culture, xix, 71–72, 180; and
transactional sex, 69–70, 74, 93, 107,
164–65
conversion therapy, 34, 193, 226
Coordinadora de Col·lectius per
l'Alliberament Gai (ccag), 207–8, 222
Correas, Carlos, 41, 51–53, 72, 257n48, 257n49
courts, vagrancy. See vagrancy courts
courts-martial, xix–xx, 98, 100–101, 103–4,
136–37; humiliation in, 102, 123
crime, 16, 17; and homosexuality, 29, 33, 34,
76, 98–99; inclination to, 8
criminology, xx, xxv, 4–5, 15, 29–38, 76–78,
96, 168; and fashion, 142, 147–48, 152–57;
and psychoanalysis, 7, 28, 29, 35–37, 133
cruising, xv–xvi, xvii, 94–95, 164, 182, 186,
261n71
Cutuli, Soledad, 147, 275n143

danger, xxv, 37–38, 49, 161, 172, 176, 186, 239,
252n77; as major or minor, 28, 29, 32, 153,
157; to society, xviii–xix, 13, 14, 15, 17, 19,
22, 24, 25, 29, 34, 54, 76, 88, 89, 90, 91, 155,
163, 168, 170, 203–4, 243
dangerousness, 5, 8–10, 16, 29, 37–38, 77–78,
242
Daniel, Herbert, 234
Dean, James, xix, 41, 42, 63, 69, 72, 74, 80,
94, 96
de Fluvià, Armand, 201–3, 205, 206–7, 207,
208, 219, 220, 227, 231, 233
desire, sexual, xxvi, 13, 39, 44–45, 60, 65, 70,
74, 79, 80, 84, 138, 157, 187, 257n49, 258n80;
and active/passive binary, 11–12, 32–33,
126, 131, 262n5, 278n3; of being penetrated,
12, 27–28, 32–33, 117, 134–35, 248n38; and
Catholicism, 6, 46, 53–54, 55–57, 177–78,
199–200, 203, 204; and identification, xix,
41–42; of maricas, 83, 96, 134–35, 143, 147,
167, 168, 179, 241–42; and masculinity, 28,
69, 71, 72, 83, 96, 99–100, 210; as same-sex
oriented, 8, 20, 22, 40, 58, 102, 209, 243; of
soldiers, 104, 107, 111, 113, 136; sublimation
of, 6, 28, 46, 53–54, 57, 153–54, 179, 203,
204, 241–42
Diagnostic and Statistical Manual (dsm),
157–58

dictatorship, xvii, 16, 208–9, 226–27; and
cultural life, 214, 215, 232; and exile, 217,
219–20; resistance to, 103, 180, 185, 228, 230;
and state violence, 141–42, 197–99, 216, 230
Diferente (Delgado), 63–65, 149
disease, 214, 238, 272n54; fear of, 121;
homosexuality as, 6, 131, 195
drag shows, 42–43, 60, 144, 148, 166–67,
169–70
drive, sexual, 7, 36, 157, 198; and sexual role,
126, 132–33
Duberman, Martin, 193
Dyer, Richard, 83

ejaculation, 30, 52, 59, 134; and military
officers, xxiv, 98, 118, 119–22, 130–31
electroshock, 28, 57, 58, 177, 253n109,
254n116. See also homosexuality: medical
treatments of
endocrinology, 6, 22, 25, 160, 173, 243
entendidos, 38, 40–41, 49, 54, 59, 65–66,
148–49, 179, 183, 185, 187, 197, 202, 218, 271n15;
and cultural sophistication, 40, 64–65, 218,
255n5; and love models, 52–53, 60–62; and
maricas, xix, 40, 60, 62, 65, 148–49
Eros (group). See Frente de Liberación
Homosexual (flh): and Eros
Escuela Oficial de Cinematografía (Spain),
94. See also censorship: in Spain
essentialism, xxvii–xviii, 20, 242; and
homosexuality, 6, 22, 129, 135–36, 205
Estella, Iñaki, 176, 265n15, 266n20
ethos, 150, 173, 221; of homosexuality, 47,
205, 210
exile, xx, xxiii, 5, 55, 226, 234, 242, 275n132;
of homosexual activists, 180, 199, 211–12,
214–30, 233; as sentence, 13, 58, 163,
250n46, 260n36, 260n39. See also sexilio

Fabrizio Lupo (Cóccioli), 55–57
family, xvii, 36, 37, 63, 77, 164, 166, 192,
198, 203, 232, 233, 266n26; as cause of
homosexuality, 152–53, 154; as chosen,
xxix, 168–69; and dangerousness, 16–17,
24, 167; and hospitalization, 57–58,
253n109, 254n110; and reputation, 14, 26,
127, 251n51. See also parents

fantasies, 34, 70, 96, 132, 153–54, 189–90, 212, 234; and masculinity, 69, 75, 79–83, 96, 99–100, 149. *See also* desire, sexual

fashion, xix, xxix, 42, 43, 65, 72, 80, 88–89, 93, 96, 147, 148–50, 157, 181; and criminologists, 147–48, 152–58, 161–62, 164; and Jamandreu, 147, 148–50; and *maricas*, 142, 147–48, 151, 153–55, 164, 165–67, 176, 238–39; policing of, 136, 142, 148, 151–52, 162–64, 165–67; and transactional sex, 74–76, 93, 164–65. *See also* aesthetic

FCA. *See* Fraternidades Cristianas de la Amistad (FCA)

femininity, 12, 14, 15, 33, 43, 137, 220, 221, 222; and criminologists, 29, 32, 35, 38, 127–28, 152, 155, 161, 243; and *maricas*, 30–32, 35, 38, 40, 110, 112–15, 134–35, 143, 144, *146*, 148, 165, 168, 174, 179, 189–91, 208–13, 243, 245n1, 248n38; and *mariquitas*, 11, 15, 17, 208–13, 242. *See also* masculinity

Fernández, Máximo Javier, 100, 248n38

Fernández, Serafín, 95, 166

Ferri, Enrico, 4, 255n136

films, xxv, 40, 41, 44, 62–65, 75–76, 94–95, 147, 175, 195, 231, 238, 266n27

flamenco, xvi, 39, 42–43, 221, 238. *See also* Spanish folk culture

FLH. *See* Frente de Liberación Homosexual (FLH)

forensic reports, 18–20, 23, 29, 30, 32, 96, 124, 155, 242–43. *See also* archives

forensic techniques, 5, 17–20, 252n71; digital rectal examination (DRE), 3, 18–19, 104, 252n74, 252n77; Rorschach test, 17, 128; thematic apperception test (TAT), 127–28; threefold body typology, 3, 251n69

Foucault, Michel, 132, 241, 248n37, 278n7

Francino, Francesc, 201–2, 205

Franco, Francisco, xxii, 180, 207, 211–12, 213, 214, 217, 226–27

Franco regime, xxii, 5–6, 95, 178, 205, 209, 220, 241–42, 245n3, 246n12; censorship in, 46, 51, 54–55, *56*, 58, 63, 94, 199, 225–26, 231–33, 257n51; confrontations with, 201, 202, 206; criminalization under, 9, 63, 201, 204; economic framework of, 85, 86–87;

escaping from, 6, 26, 215, 228–29; last years of, 199, 200, 209; marginal lifestyles under, 9, 16, 148, 180, 213, 220, 225; and psychoanalysis, xxiii, 5–6, 209, 249n16

Fraternidades Cristianas de la Amistad (FCA), 178, 199, 200–201

freedom, sexual, 42, 63, 86, 234

Frente de Liberación Homosexual (FLH), xvi–xvii, 180, 186–93, 194, 195, 211–12, 215, 216; dissolution of, 197–99; and Eros, xvi–xvii, 179, 186–87, 188, 190–91, 192, 208, 217–18, 222; and exile, 211–12, 214–15, 216, 217, 219, 224–25, 227, 228–29; and *marica* femininity, xvii, 179, 186–87, 189–91, 207; and Profesionales, xvii, 186–87, 189, 192; and *Somos*, xvii, *xviii*, 195, 196, 197, 215; and transnational networks, 187, 196

Frente Homosexual de Acción Revolucionaria, 228

Freud, Sigmund, 5, 7, 41

frivolity, 148, 176, 182, 222

Front d'Alliberament Gai de Catalunya (FAGC), 208, 221–22, 233–34, 277n195

Fronte Unitario Omosessuale Rivoluzionario Italiano (FUORI), 219

Fry, Peter, 73–74

Fuss, Diana, 41

García Lorca, Federico, 62, 149

Garma, Ángel, 6–7, 26–28

gay identity, xvii, xviii, xxvii, xxx, 179, 196–97, 224, 246n9

Gay Liberation Front (GLF; U.S.), 188

gay movements, 77–89, 182, 187–88, 200, 201, 210–11, 214, 221, 233–34

gender, xxiii, 12, 237, 247n19; concept of, xx–xxi, xxvii, 247n28; erotization of, xxvii, 65–66, 83; norms of, 29, 30, 33–34, 46, 76, 152. *See also* femininity; masculinity

gender-affirmation surgeries. *See* surgeries: gender-affirmation

gender expression, 40, 144, 151, 170, 179

gender performance, 59, 136, 175, 242, 254n122; and forensic evaluation, 13, 18–19, 32, 33–34, 35, 38, 101–3, 153, 155, 160; of *maricas* and *chongos*, 7, 30, 40, 65, 99, 101–3, 144, 151, 169, 176, 191, 210,

248n38; and military, 101–3, 118, 136–38; as nonconforming, 30, 33–34, 40, 65–66, 167, 169, 195, 250n46; and sex work, 74, 96, 174; and Spanish folk culture, 44, 46, 60, 246n11

gender roles, 7, 12, 28, 29, 52, 53, 59, 99, 100, 102, 103, 137, 142, 174, 181, 196, 206, 231, 262n5. *See also* sexual roles

gender transgression. *See* gender performance: as nonconforming

genitals, 30, 76, 110, 113, 118, 121, 127–28, 216, 257n60; exhibition of, 28, 221; images of, 79, 80, 81–83, 84, 90, 91, 96, 212; physical exams of, 18–19, 160, 173, 252n77

Gide, André, 64–65, 149, 192

Gil-Albert, Juan, xxv, 40–41, *48*, 49, 64–65; *Heraclés*, 46–47

goods, consumer, 70, 71–72, 95, 107, 180–81. *See also* consumer culture

Green, James N., 234, 247n19, 255n5, 260n31, 262n5, 278n3

Guardia Civil, 10, 11, 13, 14, 168, 170

guerrillas, 162, 185, 192–93, 194, 197, 215, 234

Halberstam, Jack, xxiii

Haller, Dieter, 11

Halperin, David, 166

harassment, 12, 13, 28, 32, 108; by the police, xv, xvi, 144, 170, 175, 186, 222, 243

Haro Ibars, Eduardo, 212–13

Hartman, Saidiya, xxiii

hedonism, 57, 69–70, 76, 150, 151, 152

Hermandad Obrera de Acción Católica (HOAC), 200

Hernández, Juan José, 182, 187–88

Herrero Tejedor, Fernando, 204

hierarchy, 38, 62, 96, 107, 115, 170, 173; and desire, 70, 73–74; within the military, 117–18

hippies, 103, 181, 195; and aesthetic, 136, 141–42, 147, 151–52, 162–63, 164–65, 166–67

HIV, xxi, xxvii, 196, 213–14

homophile canon, 40, 46, 50, 53–57, 64–65, 179, 187, 191

homophobia, 144, 152, 186, 194, 206–7, 211, 277n195; response to, 57, 61, 190, 228

Homosexuales de Buenos Aires, 177, *178*, 182, 184–85

homosexual/heterosexual binary, xx, 99, 101–2, 206

homosexuality: causes of, 6–7, 15, 20–21, 22, 23–24, 25, 29–30, 33, 34–35, 47, 69, 125, 129–31, 135, 153, 154, 160, 170, 171–72, 173, 177, 193, 203–5, 243; criminalization of, 6, 9, 63, 201, 204; and death, 245n8; decriminalization of, 5, 8, 203, 221, 224, *224*; definition of, 14, 49, 99, 101, 102, 122–24, 203, 248n35, 254n122, 278n7; demonization of, 130–31; as a disorder, 6, 15, 21, 25, 27, 28, 157–58; as friendship between men, 46–47, 60–61, 200; medical treatments of, 20, 24–26, 157, 159, 161, 172, 173, 209, 226, 242–43, 253n106, 254n110, 254n116; as a sin, 6, 47. *See also* behaviors, antisocial; Catholicism: homosexuals within; crime: and homosexuality; danger; disease: homosexuality as; essentialism; homophobia; hospitalization; paranoia; pathologization; psychoanalysis: and homosexuality; *puto*: and the term "homosexuality"

honor: defense of, 13, 14, 36, 110; and masculinity, 29, 110

hospitalization, 15, 20, 24–26, 57–58, 168, 177, 199, 253n109, 254n110

Houlbrook, Matt, 99–100, 107, 115, 259n1

Huard, Geoffroy, 144, 202, 279n11

humiliation, 85, 110; during interrogations, 102, 119, 123

hustlers, 72, 210, 211

identification, xxvii, 65, 127–28, 173, 204, 239; and desire, 41–42, 258n80

identity, 57, 65, 80, 137, 142, 158, 196–97, 226, 237; and *entendidos*, xix, 40; and history, xxvii–xxix; and homosexuality, 37, 42, 59, 189, 191, 210, 232, 278n3; and *maricas*, xxviii–xxix, 40, 42, 137, 147. *See also* gay identity

immigration, xxii, 85–86, 137, 144, 217, 246n12, 248n38. *See also* exile; *sexilio*

inmates. *See* prisoners

Insausti, Santiago Joaquín, 74, 100–101, 147, 182, 248n38, 275n143

instincts, 17, 36, 59–60, 125, 200; and
     femininity, 58, 153
Institute of Criminology. *See* Classification
     Institute
insults, xvi, 32, 123, 254n122. *See also* stigma
intimacy, xx, xxiv, xxix, 32, 83, 136–37, 156;
     between males, 52, 100–102, 111–16, 118–19,
     123, 243
Italy, 87, 246n12, 247n23

Jamandreu, Paco, 74–75, 147, 148–51, 155
Jiménez de Asúa, Luis, 4–5, 8–9
Jones, Cleve, 222
judges, 3, 6, 10–11, 19–20, 22, 36, 88, 93,
     100, 122, 171, 239. *See also* courts-martial;
     vagrancy courts

Kameny, Franklin E., 183
knowledge, scientific and medical, xviii,
     3–4, 27, 35, 37, 103, 119, 159–60, 192, 203
Kretschmer, Ernst, 3, 18, 153, 251n69
Kunzel, Regina, 210–11

Lacan, Jacques, 41, 192, 275n132
La Fountain-Stokes, Lawrence, 142, 176,
     246n10, 265n4, 270n157
Lambe, Jennifer L., xxiv
"La narración de la historia" (Correas),
     51–53
Lancaster, Roger N., 239–41
leftism, xvii, 16, 61, 181, 188, 194–95, 217–18,
     219, 230, 277n195; and homophile
     organizations, 179, 180, 182–83, 186,
     191–94, 199
legal defense, 7, 12, 15, 19, 20, 89, 99, 103,
     116, 123, 129, 130–36, 163, 165, 173; strategic
     pathologization as, 15, 22, 23–24
Les amitiés particulières (Peyrefitte), 53–55,
     57, 257n51
letters, xxv, 105, 132, 152, 177, 202–3, 227–28,
     231, 238–39, *240*; as evidence in court, 163,
     171–72; of lovers, 32, 46–47, 171; to Miguel
     de Molina, 40–41, 42, 43–45, 256n11;
     and prison, 32, 153–54, 171, 268n103;
     and transnational homophile networks,
     183–83, *184*, 196–97, 198, 202, 206–7,
     228–29, 233–34, 271n15

L'exile de Capri (Peyrefitte), 54, 257n51. *See
     also* Peyrefitte, Roger
liability, personal, xviii–xix, 4–5, 6, 8, 15, 24,
     32–33, 135–36, 171, 242; and *vicio*, 11–12
liberation movements, sexual, xx, 179–80,
     186, 189, 205, 208, 211, 214, 228, 230–31, 243
libido, xxiii, 70, 113, 117, 153–54, 198, 231, 243;
     heterosexual/homosexual orientation of,
     7, 27–29, 35, 100, 102–3, 129–31, 136, 193.
     See also criminology: and psychoanalysis
locas. See maricas
López Clavel, Pau, 200
López Ibor, Juan José, 172
Lorenzo, Ricardo, 226–29, 231–34, *235*, *236*
love, 60, 87, 116, 150, 225, 232, 259n1; virile
     models of, 46–47, 49, 53, 62, 149
Luque Vera, Nazario, 221, 223, 225

machismo, 206, 239–41, 278n3; and *maricas*,
     189–90, 212, 222. *See also* masculinity
machos, xvi, 62, 73, 75, 80–81, *82*, 103, 150,
     208–9; and aggressiveness, 35, 80; and
     relationships with *maricas*, xxix, 66, 73,
     100, 110–15, 131–32, 168; sexual culture
     of, xix–xx, 7, 35, 51–52, 97, 99, 101–2, 124,
     137–38, 248n38. See also *chongos*
Madrid (Spain), 94, 95, 172, 177–78, 202,
     205, 212, 213–14, 217, 227, 230, 232, 245n3,
     256n35, 261n71; nightlife of, 41–42, 174, 226
magazines, 51, 152, 186, 196–97, 212, 228–29,
     231, 233, 234; about bodybuilding, 63, 79,
     258n80, 260n31; about porn, 90, 117–18
Malva, 43, 142, 143–44, 195
Manzano, Valeria, 74, 151–52
Marañón, Gregorio, 6, 22, 24, 25, 160, 243,
     246n11
marica politics, xx–xxi, 187, 239, 243
maricas, xviii, 31, 64, 240; and *chongos*, xvi,
     xxix, 65, 73–74, 80; as a critical lens, xxvii;
     definition of, xv, xxix, 158, 179; disdain of,
     xvii, xix, 34, 40, 41, 42, 60, 62, 66, 134–35,
     187, 209–10, 211–12; and labels with the
     same root, xxviii, 11, 239; lived experiences
     of, xxiii, xxiv, 40, 108, 147, 176, 241; and
     masculinity, xix–xx, xxix, 70–71, 78, 83,
     96, 101–2, 110; as revolutionary subject,
     179, 190–91; and sexual culture, xix–xx,

xxiii, xxix, 7, 34, 35, 41, 60, 70, 78, 97, 99, 100, 124, 137–38, 179, 237, 241; and use of female clothes and/or makeup, xv, xvi, 29–30, 33, 142, 144, 152, 155, 165–66, 169–70, 171, 173, 174, 218, 221; vocal attitudes of, xvii, 8, 157–59, 167, 170, 176, 190, 221–22, 241

mariconas, 144, 148, 168, 176, 208–10, 241

maricones, xviii, xxv, 6, 11–15, 142, 143, 148–49, 168–69, 195, 208–9, 215, 222, 239, 250n44, 250n46, 257n60, 265n6

mariquitas, xvii, xix, xxviii, 11, 17, 62, 166, 179, 180, 199, 203, 204, 208–10, 212–13, 218, 225, 241–42, 279n8. See also *maricas*: and labels with the same root

marriage, 23, 156, 175; homosexual disdain for, 127–28, 162; between *maricas* and *machos*, 112; as same-sex, 161–62, 237, 277n195

Martí, José, 61–62

masculinity: erotic cult of, 60, 63, 149; and fascism, 17, 247n23; formation of, 107; and heterosexuality, xxvi, 29, 94–95, 99, 100–101, 259n1; models of, xxv, 27, 73, 82, 151–52, 155, 189, 246n11; performance of, 18, 28, 29, 33, 35, 41–42, 70–71, 72–73, 75, 115, 137, 210, 260n33; questioning of, 12–13, 27, 32, 77, 98, 117, 136, 142, 161

Masotta, Oscar, 72, 275n132

Massera, Rubén, 187–88

masturbation, 23, 26, 32, 52, 59, 98, 118, 132, 134, 136, 153

Matamoro, Blas, 186–89, 191, 216–17

Mattachine Society, 183–84, *184*, 188–89, 196–97, 271n15. See also transnational networks

Melero, Alejandro, 65, 94

Mérida Jiménez, Rafael Manuel, 221, 276n157

Mettini, Rubén, 214–15, 217–19, 226, 275n143

Mexico, 46, 55, 234

middle class, 7, 69–70, 74, 75, 78, 132–33, 179, 181, 211, 213, 242–43; lifestyle of, 71–72, 76–77, 80, 107

Milanesio, Natalia, xxii

military, 33, 100, 107–10, 239; in Argentina, xxiv, 70, 72, 97, 103, 185, 197–98, 225; and crimes against humanity, xxiv, 141–42,

193–94, 197–98, 215, 216, 225; discipline in, 100, 102, 116–17, 137; and masculinity, 80, *82*, 99, 102, 107–15, 118–19, 132, 134–36, 137; sexual violence in, 107–10; and transactional sex, 70, 75, 105, *106*, 110

Military Code of Justice, Argentine, 98, 101–2, 123. See also courts-martial

military courts. See courts-martial

military officials: and sex descriptions, xx, xxiv, xxv, 102, 118–19, 121; and sex with soldiers, 33, 102, 108–10, 116–17, 118, 121, 122, 126; and soldiers' socialization, 99, 102, 117–19, 120, 121–23, 137

military records, 99, 100, 103, 115, 125; access to, xxiv–xxv; descriptions of sexual acts in, 102, 118–19. See also archives

military service, 108, 137, 200; and homosexuality, 103–4

Mira, Alberto, 9, 64, 258n80

Modarelli, Alejandro, 216, 279n11

Moix, Terenci, 41, 62–63, 258nn80–82

Molina, Daniel, 193–94

Molina, Francisco, 6

Molina, Miguel de, xix, 39–46, 63, 149, 195, 255n11

Molloy, Sylvia, 39, 61–62

Monroe, Marilyn, 150, 234

Montiel, Sara, xvii, 165–66, 173

morality, 5, 37, 51, 62, 69, 86, 116, 181, 201, 232; challenging of, 78, 199, 233, 239; lack of, 21–22, 36, 69, 131; offense against, 10, 172, 232; of prisoners, 20, 21–22, 131

Mora y Mora, Antonio José, 177–78, 200

Morgan, Christina, 127

movies. See films

movie stars, 42, 62, 166, 218, 266n27. See also films

Movimiento Democrático de los Homosexuales, 228

Movimiento Español de Liberación Homosexual (MELH), 180, 205, *207*

Muñoz, José E., 45–46

Murray, Henry A., 127

National Gay Task Force, 196

Navarro Amo, Tania, 143–44, *145*, 222, 266n26

Nazario. *See* Luque Vera, Nazario
neurosis, 17, 133–35, 158, 209, 212–13, 272n48. *See also* psychoanalysis
New York City, 186, 188, 195–96, *207*, 228–29

Ocaña. *See* Pérez Ocaña, José
Oedipal complex, 17, 35, 128. *See also* psychoanalysis
Onganía, Juan Carlos, 103, 151, 180, 181
Opizzo, José A., 152
oppression, 190, 192, 193, 208, 230, 231
oral sex, xxiv, 13–14, 21, 22, 59–60, 153–54; images of, 79, 80, 81–83, 85, 90, 91; and military, 95, 100, 102, 107, 108–9, 115, 121–22, 131, 133; and sexual role, 100
orgies, 39, 91, 170. *See also* parties
Ortega y Gasset, José, 5, 246n11

Pack, Sasha D., 86, 87
paranoia, 6, 8, 27–28, 92, 103–4, 165, 254nn115–16. *See also* homosexuality; sexual roles
parents, xxix, 8, 14, 24, 34–35, 45–46, 57, 115, 154, 157, 171–73, 239, 241, 251n51; and gender roles, 7, 29. *See also* family
Paris (France), 50, 202, 219–20, 229
parody, 221, 222, 245n5; and gender, 60
parole requests, 29, 33, 35, 37, 76, 260n36, 260n39. *See also* forensic reports
parties, xxix–xxx, 39, 49–50, 60, 65, 89, 165–67, 169–70, 218, 237, 245n1, 261n55, 261n71
passive/active binary. *See* active/passive binary
pathologization, xxiii, xxvi, 8, 16–17, 36, 37, 155, 157–58, 172, 192, 209, 210–11; as a strategy, 20–21, 24–25
Pavlovsky, Ángel, 220–21
Paz, Teddy, 187
Pellegrini, Renato, 41, 53, 58–60
penetration, 28, 64, 91, 102, 116–17, 121–22, 125–26, 127, 130, 132–33, 134, 136, 152–53, 170, 173, 243, 254n122, 264n62; forensic evidence of, 3, 18–20, 125–26, 252n77; images of, 79, 81, 83, 90, 96; and masculinity, 12–13, 17, 29, 30, 36, 100, 109–10, 111–12, 130–31, 189–90, 239,

248n38, 254n123; and pleasure, 33, 98, 109–10; semiotics of, 65–66, 100–101, 124; and sexual agency, 11–13, 32, 134–35. *See also* anal sex
penises, 121; and criminology, 14, 18, 19; images of, 79, 80, 81–83, 84, 91, 96; and masculinity, 110, 113. *See also* genitals
Peralta, Jorge Luís, 40, 53–54, 59, 63, 78, 80
Pérez Álvarez, Sergio, 214, 217
Pérez Argiles, Valentín, 6, 21
Pérez Ocaña, José, 221, 223, 225, 276n157
Pérez-Sánchez, Gema, 9
Perlongher, Néstor, xvi–xvii, 72–74, 186–87, 188, 190–91, 192, 198, 217–18, 277n183. *See also* Frente de Liberación Homosexual (FLH)
Perón, Eva, xv, 42, 149, 150
Perón, Juan Domingo, xvi, xxii, 7, 180, 185–86, 192, 194, 246n12
Peronism, xxii, 71–72, 74, 181, 185–86, 191, 192, 194–95
personality disorder, psychopathic, 21, 57, 125–29, 155, 172, 264n62
perversion, 5–6, 12, 24, 29, 30, 124–25, 153, 195, 209, 241, 242, 250n44
Petit, Jordi, 233
Peyrefitte, Roger, xvi, 53–59, 56, 149
photographs, xxiv, 57, 63, 212, 222, 229, 247n24; in archives, xxv, 78–79, 96; and fashion, 93, 161–62, 238–39; and *marica* desires, 79–83, *81*, *82*; and Miguel de Molina's fans, 42, 44–45; of sex acts, 83–85, 90, 91, 92, 96, 261n65. *See also* collages; pornography
Pitana, Jorge, 182–83
pleasure, xx, xxii, 23, 32, 80–81, 101, 113, 243; of being penetrated, 33, 98, 109–10, 131, 173; and interrogations, xxv, 104, 119; of *maricas*, xviii, xix, xxv, xxvii, xxix, 81, 100, 173, 190; and violence, xxix, 70, 81, 238–39. *See also* desire, sexual
Plotkin, Mariano Ben, 26–27
police, xvi, xvii, 8, 10, 26, 50, 134, 154, 168–69, 172–74, 177, 182, 185, 196–97; confrontations with, 89, 186, 221–22, 223–24; harassment by, xv–xvi, xxi, 43, 85, 141–42, 144–47, 148, 159–60, 162–63,

164, 165–66, 174–75, 186, 195, 223, 227, 239, 242, 243, 245n1, 279n11; and pornography, 83–84, 90; and tourism, 86, 87–88

police records, xxiii, xxiv, xxv, 20, 61, 69, 163, 176

policies, state, xxiv, 53, 87–88, 123, 148, 159, 180–81, 195, 197, 204, 241, 242, 243, 277n195; confrontations with, 148, 181, 201–2, 205–6, 233, 278n7; and economy, xix, 70, 86

pornography, 54–55, 70, 83, 90–91, 92, 117–18, 162, 215, 231, 233–34, 261n65. *See also* collages; desire, sexual; photographs; transactional sex

Portugal, 85, 230, 234

positivism, xviii–xix, 4–5, 7–8, 16, 17–18, 37, 192, 242. *See also* criminology

power, xviii, xxvi, xxix, 9, 51, 78, 90, 107, 118, 142, 166, 172, 209–10, 225, 239, 248n35; and masculinity, xxvi–xxvii, 32, 70–71, 80, 83, 95, 96, 101, 110, 115, 132, 136–37, 239, 248n38, 278n3

Preciado, Paul, 172–73

predators, sexual, 6, 13, 59, 60, 116, 131–32, 178, 200, 241–42

priests, xv, 89, 92, 166, 185; and attitudes towards homosexuality, 47, 199–200, 209, 241

prisoners, xx, xxix, 7, 8, 37, *145*, 148–49, 151, 155, 160, 170, 171, 221, 269n131; forensic evaluation of, 4, 5, 29, 76, 159, 251n69; gender performance of, 32, 35, 160–61; research on, 17, 160–61; solidarity between, 168, 175–76

prison records, xxviii, 8, 147

prisons, 10, 22, 36, 159–60, 175, 251n69; hospitals as an alternative to, 20, 25, 26; *maricas* in, 32, 144–47, *145*, 148, 150, 167–68, 176, 266n27

promiscuity, 60, 65, 116, 148, 272n54; and *maricas*, xxix, 41, 158, 211, 241, 243

prostitutes, 5, 29–30, 175, 203; as *macho* or *chongo*, 73, 158

Proust, Marcel, 60, 64–65, 192

pseudonyms, xxv, 192, 202, 205–6, 207, 210, 238, 271n15

psychiatrists, 18, 28, 36, 104, 124, 157–59, 172, 177, 209, 255n136

psychiatry, 5–6, 15

psychoanalysis, xviii, 127, 209, 215, 224–25; in Argentina, xxiii, 6–7, 26–27; and criminology, 28, 29, 35–37, 133; and homosexuality, 7, 27–28, 125, 243; in Spain, xxiii, 5–6, 226, 249n16

public spaces, 51, 227, 237, 259n1, 265n15; and (in)visibility, 38, 211; sex in, 59, 94–95, 237

Pueyrredón, Gustavo Juan, 63, *64*

Puig, Manuel, 187–88, 266n27

puto, xix, xxviii, 41, 42, 59, 60, 99, 100, 102, 110, 113–15, 131–32, 143–44, 218, 248n32, 254nn122–23; as insult, 32, 43, 141, 193, 215, 239; self-labeling as, 41, 53, 239; and the term "homosexuality," 122–24. See also *maricas*

Queiroz, Juan, 78, 182, 245n1

Raab, Enrique, 216

rape, 13, 36–37, 108–9, 125–27, 130, 241. *See also* abuse, sexual; assault, sexual

respectability, 11, 69, 71, 91, 148, 149–50, 185, 189, 203, 205; and masculinity, 40, 49, 59, 65, 149

restrooms, public. *See* bathrooms

Rizki, Cole, xxvii

Roma (ethnicity), xxi, 16, 178, 225

Romi, Juan Carlos, 157–59

Rosillo y Herrero, Rafael, 202, 205

Rosón, María, 78

Roth, Robert A., 195–97, 198, 200, 206–7, *224*, 228–29

Rucci, José Ignacio, 220

Sabater Tomás, Antonio, 22, 24–26, 85, 88, 89, 93–94, 96, 161–62, 164, 260n36, 260n39

Saumench Gimeno, Domingo, 16–17

scandal, 48–49, 55, 63, 89, 166; and *marica* femininity, xvii, xxviii, 40, 41, 182, 187, 209

schizophrenia, 18, 125, 154, 155

Sebreli, Juan José, 39, 72, 186–88, 189, 191–92, 260n33

Second Republic, 5, 8. *See also* Spain

seduction, xxvii, 33, 40, 50, 51, 65–66, 73, 85, 96, 105, 110–15, 117, 131–32, 137, 186, 250n44; and sexual role, 100, 102–3, 118, 121, 124–26, 130, 248n38, 262n5

self-control, 15, 38, 102, 243–44, 246n11, 247n23; lack of, 11, 148–49, 153–54
self-labeling, 53, 58, 168
Serenata del amor triunfante (Badanelli), 47–49
Sevilla (Spain), 18, 23–24, 88, 200
sexilio, 144, 148, 172. *See also* exile
sexology, xxii, 152, 157, 192
sexual inversion, 22–23, 29, 34, 52, 53, 69, 85, 165–66, 168, 169, 170, 204, 242, 252nn78–79; and the term "homosexuality," 58–59, 60
sexuality, 5, 40, 119, 179, 208, 209, 231, 232–33, 237, 248n38, 279n8; as contingent, 123, 131, 136; distinction between gender and, xxi, xxvii, 247n28; as essence, 129; in nation-building, xxiii, 247n19; policing of, 142, 201; and power, 78, 96
sexual roles, 33, 80, 101, 102, 108, 117, 119, 124–25, 159, 161–62, 189, 239, 248n38, 278n3; as insertive or "active," 20, 98, 100, 103, 109, 110, 121–22, 126–27, 132–34, 158, 161; as receptive or "passive," 3, 7, 83, 100, 103, 104, 121–22, 123–24, 126, 133–34, 161, 190, 250n44, 254n115, 254n122, 264n62. *See also* active/passive binary; penetration
sexual subculture, 34, 85, 90, 96, 208, 248n38, 278n7; and cross-class relationships, 49–51, 53; of *machos* and *maricas*, xix–xx, xxiii–xxiv, xxix, 7, 34, 35, 41, 60, 70, 78, 99, 124, 137, 179; and masculinity, 29, 36–37, 102, 131–32, 137; and military, 99–100, 102, 103, 104, 122, 131–32, 137–38
sex work, xxvii, 34, 71, 72–74, 85–86, 144, 147–48, 174–75, 176, 222. *See also* transactional sex
Sigel, Liza, 79
Simonetto, Patricio, 144, 266n22
Sinfield, Alan, 70
Sitges (Spain), 87, 89
Sívori, Horacio F., xxviii
sociability, xxvii, 14–15, 51, 60, 65, 175, 183, 187, 234; of *maricas*, xvi, xx, 64, 101, 103, 147
Social Danger Law, 124–29, 131, 166, 180, 201–5, 206, 221, 224, 224, 242

soldiers, xxix, 96, 102, 103, 104, 105–7, 108–9, 129, 132; defense strategies of, 103, 123, 129, 131, 133, 135; as objects of desire, 80–81, 96; and sex narrations, xxiii, 98, 99–100, 104, 118–22, 137; sexual culture of, 99–100, 104, 122, 137; socialization of, 99, 118–19; from United States, 70, 95. *See also* conscripts
Sontag, Susan, 164
Spain, xxii–xxiii, xxv, xxiv, 9, 11, 20, 26, 37–38, 63, 70, 71, 86–87, 95, 164, 173, 201–2, 208, 222, 227–28, 231–32; activism in, xxi, 179, 211–12, 214–15, 222, 228, 237, 242, 277n195; and Argentina, xxi–xxiii, 225, 246n12, 255n11; and Catholic values, xxv, 5, 8, 199; and colonialism, 90, 91, 92–93, 246n12, 248n32; criminology in, xix, xxv, 5–6, 37, 71; democratic transition in, 199, 207–8, 211–12, 213, 214–15, 217, 225, 230–31; and the expulsion of gay tourists, 88, 89–90; homophile canon in, 53–54, 55, 57, 255n11; migration to, xx, 180, 199, 211–12, 214–20. *See also* censorship: in Spain
Spanish folk culture, 39–40, 42–44, 60, 144, 148, 225, 241–42. *See also* flamenco
Stajnsznajder, Pablo, 219–20, 226–27
Steele, Valerie, 93, 151
stigma, xxvi, 3, 15, 18, 27, 33–34, 47, 59, 101, 108, 119, 167, 213, 239, 248n35; *maricón* as, 6, 14; *puto* as, 122, 123. *See also* insults
Stonewall, 186, 187, 188–89, 201–2, 243
subjectivity, 41, 53, 65–66, 143, 147, 157, 179, 210, 213, 237; of *maricas*, xvii, xx, xxi, xxvii, 115, 148, 186, 266n27; of *travestis*, 174
sublimation, 29, 41, 64, 76, 152–54, 179, 212–13, 242, 243; and Catholic religiosity, 6, 46–49, 199, 203, 204; in passive homosexuals, 6, 27–28. *See also* desire, sexual
Subrat, Piro, 221, 222
surgeries: endocrine, 25, 253n106; gender-affirmation, xxi, 142, 147, 174
Surghi, Carlos, 53

tackiness, 39; and the sublime, 41, 62–63. *See also* aesthetic; taste
Tardieu, Auguste Ambroise, 3, 18, 252n70
taste, 39–40, 149–50, 158, 172–73, 255n4. *See also* aesthetic; tackiness

taxonomy, xxi, xxvii–xxix, 17–18, 125, 143, 158, 204, 241–43, 248n34; and prison, 159–60

terrorism, state, xxii–xxiii, 197–99

Terry, Jennifer, 37

Thénon, Jorge, 28

Timerman, Jacobo, 216

Tintilay, Ivana, xxix

Tiro de Gracia (Becher), 75–76

Tirso, 53–54, 58–60

Torremolinos (Spain), 55, 69, 87, 88–89, 238

Torres, Sara, 188

Tortorici, Zeb, xxiv, 247n31

torture, 193–94, 198, 216–18, 230; by police officers, xvi, 141–42

Tosoni, Rubén, 193

tourism, 55, 85–90; and transactional sex, 88, 144, 164, 238

transactional sex, xix, xxvi–xxvii, 30, 96, 107, 110, 259n1; embodied language of, 69–70, 74–75, 93–95; masculinity in, 75, 86, 96, 107, 169; and military, 105, 132, 136; policing of, 71, 76, 85; and tourism, 88, 144, 164, 238. *See also* consumer culture; sex work

transnational networks, 3, 55, 196–97, 215, 228–29, 256n35, 277n183

travestis, xxviii, 143, 148, 167, 174–75, 176, 208, 220–22, 223, 237; as a critical mode, xxvii; and *maricas*, xxix–xxx, 147; migration of, 144

Troitiño, Luis, 177, *178*, 182–83

Trotskyism, 181, 185, 190–91, 193–94, 216, 272n48; and Frente de Liberación Homosexual (FLH), 179, 191. *See also* leftism

unions, 72, 177, 182–83, 185–86, 187, 201, 215

United States, 70, 79, 95, 150–51, 179, 186, 188–89, 210–11, 229, 243, 277n195

upper classes, 183–85, 231, 242–43; lifestyle of, 80, 107; and sexual freedom, 86

vagrancy courts, xix, 58, 89–91, 210; criminology in, 6, 7–8, 18; research on, xxiii–xxiv, 88

Vagrancy Law, 5, 8–11, 15, 95, 201, 208, 242. *See also* homosexuality: criminalization of

València (Spain), 46, 164–66, 172, 178, 200, 269n131

viciosos, 8, 11–15, 47, 93, 238, 239, 241–42, 260n46. See also *maricones*

Villar, Héctor, 28

violence, xix, xxi, xxiii, xxv, xxvii, 100, 102, 107–9, 144, 194, 222, 239, 241, 255n4; and forensic evaluation, 3, 17, 37; and masculinity, xxix, 7, 27, 32, 36, 70–71, 83; and pleasure, xxix, 32, 70, 83, 238; and police, xxi, 141, 144, 222; and politics, xxii, 103, 180, 192–93; and state, xxiii, xxiv, xxvii, 3, 13, 176, 197–99, 215, 237

visibility, xix, xxi, 38, 144–48, 166, 176, 192–93, 197, 211, 215, 222, 223, 239, 250n44

voyeurism, 80, 83, 137; and archives, xx, xxiv, 99, 104, 119

Warner, Michael, 176

Waugh, Thomas, 79, 84

Wayar, Marlene, 183

Whitman, Walt, 47, 57, 61–62, 149

Wilde, Oscar, 47, 64–65, 165

work camps, 10, 26, 88, 260n36, 260n39

working classes, xxii, 16, 40, 64, 75, 88, 143, 181, 182, 250n44, 279n11; and cross-class relationships, 40, 41, 50, 51–53; and masculinity, xix, 74, 169, 259n1; and sexual subculture, 35, 114, 131, 132–33

Yarfitz, Mir, xv

Yé-yé, 164–65, 238–39

youngsters, 77–78, 103, 152, 162, 164, 173, 199, 201; and fashion, 71, 74, 80, 85, 96, 162, 181, 195, 227; and transactional sex, 69–70, 73–76, 85–86, 94–95, 96, 151, 164–65

In the Engendering Latin America series

Sex and Danger in Buenos Aires: Prostitution, Family, and Nation in Argentina
Donna J. Guy

Between Civilization and Barbarism: Women, Nation, and Literary Culture in Modern Argentina
Francine Masiello

Women, Feminism, and Social Change in Argentina, Chile, and Uruguay, 1890–1940
Asunción Lavrin

I'm Going to Have a Little House: The Second Diary of Carolina Maria de Jesus
Carolina Maria de Jesus
Translated by Melvin S. Arrington Jr. and Robert M. Levine

White Slavery and Mothers Alive and Dead: The Troubled Meeting of Sex, Gender, Public Health, and Progress in Latin America
Donna J. Guy

Class Mates: Male Student Culture and the Making of a Political Class in Nineteenth-Century Brazil
Andrew J. Kirkendall

Female Citizens, Patriarchs, and the Law in Venezuela, 1786–1904
Arlene J. Díaz

False Mystics: Deviant Orthodoxy in Colonial Mexico
Nora E. Jaffary

Mexican Karismata: The Baroque Vocation of Francisca de los Ángeles, 1674–1744
Ellen Gunnarsdóttir

The Case of the Ugly Suitor and Other Histories of Love, Gender, and Nation in Buenos Aires, 1776–1870
Jeffrey M. Shumway

A Culture of Everyday Credit: Housekeeping, Pawnbroking, and Governance in Mexico City, 1750–1920
Marie Eileen Francois

From Colony to Nation: Women Activists and Gendering of Politics in Belize, 1912–1982
Anne S. Macpherson

Domestic Economies: Family, Work, and Welfare in Mexico City, 1884–1943
Ann S. Blum

Maricas: Queer Cultures and State Violence in Argentina and Spain, 1942–1982
Javier Fernández-Galeano

To order or obtain more information on these or other University of Nebraska Press titles, visit nebraskapress.unl.edu.

www.ingramcontent.com/pod-product-compliance
Lightning Source LLC
Chambersburg PA
CBHW020455270326
41926CB00008B/617